A DAY IN OLD ROME

INTERIOR OF GREAT PUBLIC BATHS IN IMPERIAL ROME.
Restoration according to Von Falke.

A DAY IN OLD ROME

A PICTURE OF ROMAN LIFE

BY

WILLIAM STEARNS DAVIS

PROFESSOR OF HISTORY IN THE
UNIVERSITY OF MINNESOTA

BIBLO and TANNEN
NEW YORK
1967

BIBLO and TANNEN

BOOKSELLERS and PUBLISHERS, INC.

63 Fourth Avenue   New York 3, N. Y.

Library of Congress Card #61-24993

Printed in U.S.A. by
NOBLE OFFSET PRINTERS, INC.
NEW YORK 3, N. Y.

PREFACE

This book tries to describe what an intelligent person would have witnessed in Ancient Rome if by some legerdemain he had been translated to the Second Christian Century, and conducted about the imperial city under competent guidance. Rare and untypical happenings have been omitted, and sometimes to avoid long explanations *probable* matters have been stated as if they were ascertained facts: but these instances it is hoped are so few that no reader can be led into serious error.

The year 134 after Christ has been chosen as the hypothetical time of this visit, not from any special virtue in that date, but because Rome was then architecturally nearly completed, the Empire seemed in its most prosperous state, although many of the old usages and traditions of the Republic still survived, and the evil days of decadence were as yet hardly visible in the background. The time of the absence of Hadrian from his capital was selected particularly, in order that interest could be concentrated upon the life and doings of the great city itself, and upon its vast populace of slaves, plebeians, and nobles, not upon the splendid despot and his court, matters too often the center for attention by students of the Roman past.

To acknowledge all the modern books upon which the writer has drawn heavily would be to present a list of almost all the important handbooks or discussions of Roman life and antiquities. It is proper to say, however,

that such secondary sources have been mainly useful so
far as they reënforced a fairly exhaustive study of the
Latin writers themselves, especially of Horace, Seneca,
Petronius, Juvenal, Martial, and, last but nowise least,
of Pliny the Younger. Inevitably this volume follows the
lines of its companion "A Day in Old Athens," published
several years ago, a book which has enjoyed such public
favor as to prove the usefulness of this method of presentation; but life in the Roman Imperial Age has seemed so
much more complex than that in the Athens of Demos-
thenes, and our fund of information is so much greater,
that the present volume is perforce considerably longer
than its companion. The "day" devoted to Rome will
probably seem therefore a somewhat lengthy one.

To my colleague and friend Dr. Richard C. Cram, Professor of Latin in the University of Minnesota, I am deeply
grateful for a careful reading of the manuscript and for
many helpful and incisive suggestions; and for a careful
checking over of every feature of the work I must once
again gladly acknowledge the gracious and untiring services of my wife.

The illustrations, which, it is hoped, add considerably
to the interest of the book, have been collected from many
sources. Many of the highly informational "resto-
rations" included are from the monumental work of Jakob
von Falke, *Hellas und Rom*, the English version whereof
has long ceased to be available to American readers.

W. S. D.

THE UNIVERSITY OF MINNESOTA
    MINNEAPOLIS

CONTENTS

Contents

Chapter III. The Homes of the Lowly and of the Mighty

Chapter IV. Roman Women and Roman Marriages

Contents

Chapter VII.   The Social Orders: The Slaves

Chapter VIII.   The Social Orders: Freedmen, Provincials, Plebeians, and Nobles

Contents

Chapter X. Children and Schooling

Contents

Chapter XIV.   The Fora, Their Life and Buildings.
The Daily Journal

Contents   xiii

Contents

Chapter XVII. The Senate: A Session and a Debate

Contents

Chapter XVIII. The Courts and the Orators. The Great Baths. The Public Parks and Environs of Rome

Contents

Chapter XIX. The Public Games: the Theater, the Circus, and the Amphitheater

Contents

ILLUSTRATIONS

A DAY IN OLD ROME

A DAY IN OLD ROME

CHAPTER I

THE GENERAL ASPECT OF THE CITY

1. The Prosperity of Rome in the Reign of Hadrian (117–138 A.D.). — In the year 134 A.D. the great Emperor Hadrian was turning his steps back to Rome after three long journeys of inspection over his enormous dominions. Never before had that Empire seemed so prosperous. No serious war was upon the horizon. The Parthian king and the Germanic chiefs were only too happy to keep beyond the Euphrates or the Rhine and the Danube, highly respectful before the disciplined power of the guardian legions.

In the provinces there was generally loyalty and contentment, save only in unhappy Judæa where the Roman generals were stamping out the last embers of a desperate rebellion, undertaken by those Jews allowed to remain in Palestine after Titus's capture of Jerusalem (70 A.D.). The imperial government created by Augustus and strengthened by later emperors appeared an unqualified success, while the tyrannies of Nero and Domitian were becoming things merely of frightened memory.

All over this vast Empire with a population and area nearly equal to that of the United States there reigned the blessed *Pax Romana*. Robbers had been cleared from the roads and pirates from the seas. Commerce went to and fro with surprisingly little interference from customs barriers or provincial boundaries. The same coin was current from the

1

cataracts of the Nile to the Caledonian Wall across Britain. A scientific system of law, on the whole administered with remarkable firmness and justice, prevailed between the same wide boundaries.

The central government was, indeed, in essence a despotism, but it was a despotism infused with an extreme intelligence, and it left many of the forms of liberty, especially of local liberty, in the municipal matters which touch men nearest home. The Emperor Hadrian, himself, although sometimes guilty of eccentricities and even harshness, was, in the main, a ruler singularly intent upon benefiting his subjects. In all his constant travels he had showered favors upon the communities which he visited. It was as if he (and his great predecessor Trajan) had set out to justify monarchy as an ideal government by showing how much good monarchs could do to the governed.

2. Increasing Glory of the Imperial City. — All this prosperity had inevitably reacted upon the city of Rome itself. In a most literal sense of the word " all roads led to Rome," not merely the vast network of government highways and the paths of maritime commerce, but those of intellectual, artistic, and moral influence. Rome was incomparably the best market for the merchant, it provided the largest audiences for the philosopher or rhetorician, the wealthiest patrons for the sculptor. It had, in fact, become the common center and crucible for everything good and bad in the huge, teeming Mediterranean World.

Outwardly the city was near the summit of its architectural perfection. In Cicero's day it could not compare in the elegance of its squares and avenues, and the magnificence of its buildings with Alexandria, Antioch, or several lesser cities which lay at the mercy of the legions; but with the coming of the Empire there has been an incessant process of demolishing, rebuilding, and extending. " I found Rome built of brick; I leave it built of marble," Augustus had boasted when near his end (14 A.D.). However, even after him, there had been only a gradual transformation until the great fire of Nero in 64 A.D. Terrible as has then been the devastation, the calamity has at least required a general rebuilding of almost half of the city usually upon a much handsomer and more artistic scale. Since then each succeeding Emperor has tried to leave some great architectural memorial behind him. Vespasian and Titus have built the Flavian Amphitheater (Colosseum), Trajan a noble Forum, and Hadrian is now completing a magnificent "Temple of Venus and Rome."

After this time there will perhaps be a few more remarkable structures erected, *e.g.* the Baths of Caracalla and of Diocletian and the Basilica (Court House) of Constantine, but for practical purposes imperial Rome has now been created. In 134 A.D. it is already architecturally what it will be in 410 A.D. (except then for a certain decadence) when Alaric's Goths knocked at the gates. There is, therefore, hardly a better time than this year, 134 A.D., to visit the "Eternal City," if we would discuss the best and the worst, the strength and the weakness of that Roman society which is to hold men fascinated across the ages. Let it be assumed, therefore, that on a warm spring morning we are being guided about the enormous capital of which bronze-skinned Arabs and blond-haired Frisians alike speak in awestruck whispers; the city apparently ordained by the gods to be the center and ruler of the conquered world.

3. **Population and Crowded Condition of Rome.** — Before entering such a metropolis it is a fair question to present: "How large is Rome, at this time of our supposed visit?" Unfortunately the imperial government will fail to transmit to later ages its census statistics, and the conjectures of learned men will vary most seriously. By taking into ac-

count some data as to the number of citizens receiving grain doles, by adding to these the known size of the garrison, by establishing the extent of a great colony of resident foreigners and the still greater hordes of slaves, assertions can be made that the population exceeds 2,000,000, and again that it is barely 800,000. Both reckonings may be quite wrong. It seems reasonable to suppose that in Julius Cæsar's day the city lacked considerably of 1,000,000 inhabitants, but these probably increased with the rising prosperity of the Empire. Hadrian's " City Praefect " perhaps has to administer the peace for some 1,500,000 people. In later generations, however, the population will again slowly dwindle with the wave of the imperial system.

However, this million and a half produces a sense of immensity greater perhaps than that in a later New York or London. Rome is, roughly speaking, some three miles long and nearly the same in breadth, no remarkable area as American cities will go ; [1] but, as duly explained, population within these limits is extraordinarily congested. The streets overflow with pedestrians to the exclusion of most wheeled traffic. There are no " rapid transit " cars, no taxicabs, no telephones, and even no public postal service.

If, therefore, you have the slightest business across the city, you must walk the entire distance, or be borne in a litter or send a messenger — methods taking about equally long. As will be seen, even the use of horses and carriages is largely prohibited. Besides, the mild climate and method of building the houses compel people to spend a great fraction of their day in the streets, or in the public plazas and buildings. Human life teems everywhere. One is overwhelmed by the jostling multitudes even in the remoter

---

[1] Outside of these limits were, of course, wide and populous suburbs whose inhabitants might be included in the estimated total of 1,500,000.

quarters. Everything (including many personal acts which other ages keep in strict privacy) seems going on in public. There is, in fact, no city where it is easier to be "lost in a crowd" than in Rome; no city where the good and the bad, the divine and the bestial in humanity are so incessantly in evidence and in such abrupt contact.

4. The Country around Rome. — Rome is some thirteen miles from the nearest seacoast, but the distance down the twisting "yellow" Tiber to Ostia ("River Mouth") is nearly twice as great. The city itself lies near the northerly end of that broad plain later called the Campagna which stretches southeasterly for nearly seventy miles but whereof the width betwixt ocean and Apennines seldom exceeds twenty-five. Looking off from any of the heights of Rome towards the east, the whole horizon from north to south seems traced by a continuous chain of mountains about ten to twenty miles distant. Very beautiful they are when seen through a soft blue or golden haze beneath the Italian sky; and by facing straight north one can discover the round isolated peak of Mount Soracte (2420 feet high), made famous by the poets, near whose southeastern base the Tiber winds on its tortuous progress towards the sea.

Then following the line of mountains southward one can notice the chain of the Sabine hills, some with peaked and lofty summits, and next is discovered the spot where the Tiber rests embosomed in its gray olive groves. More southward still are the hills on whose slopes rests "Cool Præneste," and then, running over a horizon of four or five miles and ending in the plain, is beheld the noble form of Mount Albinus, the isolated volcanic peak sacred to the Latin Jupiter and at whose base by tradition lay Alba Longa, the parent town of Rome; after that the view takes in nothing but the undulating plain, which at length sinks off into the sea.

5. The Tiber and Its Valley. — Near at hand, of course,
is the Campagna itself, a series of gentle ridges, covered at
this epoch with one long series of delightful suburban villas
and thrifty produce farms, sometimes grouped into rich little
villages.[1] In a general direction of north to south the Tiber
flows along the western skirts of Rome, with only a minor

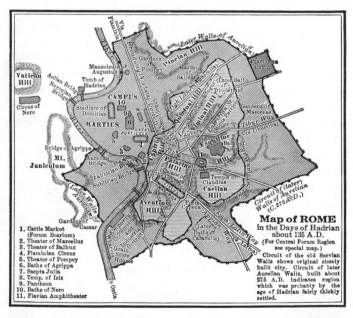

1. Cattle Market
   (Forum Boarium)
2. Theater of Marcellus
3. Theater of Balbus
4. Flaminian Circus
5. Theater of Pompey
6. Baths of Agrippa
7. Saepta Julia
8. Temp. of Isis
9. Pantheon
10. Baths of Nero
11. Flavian Amphitheater

Map of ROME
in the Days of Hadrian
about 135 A.D.
(For Central Forum Region
see special map.)
Circuit of the old Servian
Walls shows original closely
built city. Circuit of later
Aurelian Walls, built about
275 A.D. indicates region
which was probably by the
age of Hadrian fairly thickly
settled.

settlement on the western banks.   If it ran by a less famous
city, the Tiber would pass for a rather ordinary stream.   Its
yellow, turbid waters come with such force from the Apennines that there can be little navigation for part of the year
beyond the point where the Anio flows into it from the east,
about three miles above Rome.   Grain and timber can, how-

[1] At present, of course, largely a treeless waste, very sparsely popu-
lated and afflicted with malaria.

ever, be floated down on barges, and when the mountain snows are melting the river swells to a truly dangerous size, flooding all the lowlands near the city and sometimes, despite a careful system of dykes, causing freshets which are simply ruinous to large sections of the metropolis inhabited by the very poor. The Emperors Augustus and Tiberius set up a regular board of " Tiber Commissioners " to keep the rebellious river in bounds, but their efforts are still often vain.

Between Rome and Ostia the Tiber is indeed navigable at most seasons for the smaller kind of vessels, but, as will be seen, Rome is scarcely a first-class seaport; however, special river craft easily bring up heavy freight from Ostia— an enormous economic advantage for the great city.

6. A View over Rome from the Campus Martius. — Before descending into the city it is well to ascend some height or lofty building well to the western verge of the *Campus Martius* (" Field of Mars ") at the great bend of the Tiber as it sweeps by its levees. Before the onlooker there spreads what seems at first an indescribable confusion of enormous buildings, gilded roofs, stately domes, serried phalanxes of marble columns and far-stretching porticoes, some on level ground, others upon the summits or clinging to the slopes of several hills. Mixed with these are an incalculable number of red-tiled roofs obviously covering more humble private structures. Here and there, mostly on the outskirts, are also broad patches of greenery, public parks, and private gardens.

After more study, however, the first confusion begins to adjust itself into a kind of order. It is possible, for example, to recognize directly in the foreground a small and comparatively abrupt hill crowned at either end by temples of peculiar magnificence. This is the *Capitol*, particularly the seat of the fane of *Jupiter Optimus Maximus* (" Jupiter Best and Greatest "), officially the chief temple of Rome. Beyond it at a certain distance rises a gray cylinder of enormous

bulk.   That, of course, is the *Flavian Amphitheater*, and in
the hollow between it and the capitol but nigh concealed by
many structures stretches the *Old Forum* of the Republic
— the most famous spot in Rome.   To the south of the
Forum, and in no wise concealed, lifts another hill covered
with a vast complex of buildings, which, even when seen in
the distance, is of extraordinary splendor.   This is the *Palatine*, the present residence of the Cæsars and the seat of the
government.

CAPITOLINE HILL AND TEMPLES AS SEEN FROM PALATINE: restored according to Von Falke.

Just to the south and right of the Palatine there runs a long
hollow, the edges of which flash with settings of marble;
it is the *Circus Maximus*, the chief race course.   These are
the structures or localities that stand out clearly at first
glance.   Close at hand, in the Campus Martius itself, is a
perfect labyrinth of covered promenades, dome-capped public baths, theaters, and circuses, as well as the remarkable
Pantheon and other far-famed structures, the details whereof
can wait.   Behind the onlooker is winding the Tiber, spanned
by at least eight bridges; and across the river, before the

view wanders off into the hills of Etruria, are seen numerous suburban settlements and heights whereof the most conspicuous is that around *Mount Janiculum* crested with verdant gardens. But our attention must be centered upon Rome itself. Before descending from the coign of vantage it is needful to distinguish her Seven Hills.

7. The Seven Hills of Rome. — The two most famous of these hills (the *Capitoline* and the *Palatine*) have been named already, but they have five distinguished rivals. Probably in prehistoric days all these " mountains " rose like separate islands from a treacherous marsh or even from a lake connected with the Tiber; but long since they have silted down, and presently man came to add his drains and channels. They are now, therefore, connected by valleys which are crammed with habitations, although in any case the most desirable residences are near the summits of the hills and the humble folk are compelled to live in the gulleys. Each of these hills has a history : for example, the Aventine is alleged to have remained apart from the others for long after the founding of the city, merely as a fortified outpost for the protection of shepherds; but we cannot stop to recite pleasant legends.

The " Seven Hills " of Rome have really become eight, as the city has extended. Not one of these is lofty, but they give a diversity to the city that prevents the great masses of blank walls and of ungainly tenement houses lining most of the streets from becoming too ugly, and they secure light and air to many quarters that are grievously congested.

These hills can be thus catalogued:

1. *Capitoline*, about 150 feet above sea level.[1]
2. *Palatine* (S. E. of Capitoline), about 166 feet high.

---

[1] These are modern heights; since the days of the Empire there has been much leveling down. All the hills were then somewhat higher.

3. *Aventine* (South of Palatine), about 146 feet high.
4. *Cælian* (East of Palatine), about 158 feet high.
5. *Esquiline* (North of Cælian), about 204 feet high.
6. *Viminal* (North of Esquiline), about 160 feet high.
7. *Quirinal* (N. E. of Capitoline), about 170 feet high.

To the familiar " seven " ought to be added the hill of the great northern suburb.

8. *Pincian*, or " Hill of the Gardens " (North of Quirinal), about 204 feet high.

Highest of all rises the *Janiculum* beyond the Tiber, 297 feet high; commanding a noble prospect over the city and the whole Campagna beyond. It formed, therefore, in the olden days, a very proper place for the fort with its watch-tower and its sentinel, when Rome dreaded an Etruscan raid from the north, and when the citizens dropped their tools to seize their weapons the minute the " flag on Janiculum " was struck as signal that the foe was at hand.

8. Building Materials Used in Rome. — The most cursory view of the city gives an overwhelming impression of the *enormous quantities of building material*, as well as of the expenditure of human labor which has gone into the creation of Rome. Strabo the geographer [1] has wisely observed that it is lucky that the city can get a constant supply of stone, timber, etc., on account of " the ceaseless building which is rendered needful by the pulling down of houses and on account of the great fires and constant sales of [house] property," everybody being incessantly scrapping old buildings, erecting new ones, and speculating generally in real estate.

Of course, the great public buildings are erected with extremely durable materials which will defy the assaults of time, but the vast districts of ugly tenement houses are often

---

[1] He wrote his great " Geography " not long after 1 A.D.

thrown together in as flimsy a manner as those in the least elegant quarters of American cities of another age. However, there are almost no wooden houses in Rome; and for the better structures there is provided most excellent building stone. The standard masonry is of *tufa*, a soft red or black stone needing a stucco to protect it from the weather; for superior work there is dark brown *peperino*, golden *travertine*, and last but not least, for the finest buildings, white and many colored *marble*. The marble trade, as will be explained, is, in fact, one of the greatest commercial activities of the city.

9. The Great Use of Concrete. — Going about Rome one is led to imagine, however, that many very pretentious structures are of solid brick. This is seldom the case. Bricks and tiles are often in evidence because they can be worked into the face of naturally ugly concrete to disguise the nakedness of its surfaces. *Concrete* has really made it comparatively easy to create Rome as an enormous city. If concrete has not been invented by the Romans, they are at least the first great people to put it to a very general use. In their neighborhood can be found huge quantities of *pozzolana*,[1] a volcanic deposit which can be readily worked up into admirable cement. It is this very practical material which makes the vast domes, cupolas, and other architectural triumphs possible. Many a pretentious temple or residence flaunts a marble exterior; this, however, is a mere shell and covering; strip it away, and within is an enormous mass of concrete.

This material can be handled by comparatively small labor gangs, rendering it feasible to erect huge structures without mobilizing such wholesale man-power as was needed for the great monuments of Egypt. It is very durable,

---

[1] This and many other terms for Roman building materials are from the modern Italian.

almost nothing can destroy it. Indeed it will be written later that " This *pozzolana* [for concrete] more than any other material contributed to make Rome the proverbial ' Eternal City.' " [Middleton.]

10. Greek Architectural Forms Plus the Arch and Vault. — Every building by the Tiber apparently bears the impress of

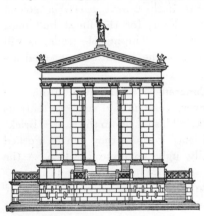

TYPICAL TEMPLE FRONT.

Greece. Greek architects are said to have designed many of the finest public edifices, while Greek artists have chiseled the statues or painted the pictures which all the Roman world admires. The " orders " of the columns everywhere in evidence are the Doric, Ionic, or Corinthian that one might find at Athens, although it can be complained that the Romans are over-fond of the most ornate form — the florid Corinthian.

In general, lovers of the purer architectural types of Hellas may allege that Roman architecture and ornamentation is too elaborate and extravagant. There are too many scrolls and floriated designs. Every possible surface is covered with statuary or bas-reliefs, often in decidedly inferior taste. There is too garish a display, also, of blue, green, white, and orange-colored marble. The whole effect of most Roman buildings is, therefore, *grand rather than beautiful.* It is the architecture of a civilization apparently growing a little weary and striving to startle itself by remarkable effects.

Nevertheless, this borrowing from Greece has not been slavish. Romans, if not great artists, are master adapters. Perhaps they have not invented the *arch* and the *vault,* [1] but in any case they have utilized them in connection with the Greek system of columns to produce magnificent effects whereof Argos and Ephesus never dreamed. By concrete

ARCH OF CONSTANTINE: typical of many triumphal arches: date about 315 A.D.

vaulting can be made those enormous substructures which sustain the great palaces, and again, the lofty domes of such splendid creations as the Pantheon. By the arches can be upheld the tiers of the Flavian Amphitheater, the pretentious company of theaters and circuses, and last but not least the long arrays of stately aqueducts which bring the great water

[1] Very possibly the Etruscans were the actual inventors, although the principle of the arch was known in the Old Orient.

supply so many miles to Rome.   Underground also the arch system is upbearing the vast network of sewers which has redeemed the city from a quagmire.   In the *fora* and across many avenues are thrown in their turn the imposing *triumphal arches*, crowned with heroic statues or with prancing chariots which are unmatched by anything in Greece.

Having taken in the generalities, it is now proper to go down from our viewpoint and plunge boldly into the vast city.   The wise man should not, however, visit at first the Fora, the Palatine, and the other " show places " which officious guides here as everywhere are always glad to display to visitors.   More helpful it is to examine at the outset certain typical streets first in a poor and next in a more aristocratic quarter, to enter the houses, and to penetrate the daily lives of the masses of the people.   Then with better understanding can one approach the famous " Heart of Rome."

CHAPTER II

STREETS AND STREET LIFE

11. The Regions of Rome: Fashionable and Plebeian Quarters. — The great Augustus divided the capital into 14 *regiones* or "wards" and these in turn into 265 *vici* or precincts. Obviously some of these districts are more select than others. No citizen of decent tastes will, unless compelled by dire poverty, live in the network of hovels beyond the bridges and under the brow of the Janiculum, where a great colony of Jews and other Orientals exist in what is alleged to be extreme squalor. If you go south also from the Forum and Palatine, you are likely to run into a wide complex of unlovely industrial districts and laborers' quarters, especially along the Tiber, although there are still some very good residential streets upon the Aventine.

In general the northern end of the city is the fashionable section, although the Subura, the street running out between the Esquiline and the Viminal, is notorious for containing some of the vilest tenements in all Rome. To live in a " Subura garret " is about the greatest possible degradation socially. Right above this ill-favored avenue, however, slopes the Esquiline itself, lined with the palaces of many of the most exclusive Senators. Pliny the Younger resided there in his lifetime,[1] and a rich ex-consul has his house at present. Rome is, in fact, decidedly like many later cities; walk only a few blocks, and one can pass from the bottom to the top of the social ladder. Further north, in the regions of the parks and public gardens, the fine residences are prob-

---

[1] He died about 110 A.D.

ably more continuous, but one can never know Rome by merely visiting its ultra-genteel quarters. There is, consequently, no better place to begin an investigation than near the Esquiline, let us say where the disreputable Subura runs northeast towards the somewhat more select " Patrician Street " (*Vicus Patricius*).

STREET IN POMPEII: present state. Note the pavement, the stepping stones, the wayside fountain, and the numerous subdivisions into small houses or shops.

12. A Typical Short Street, "Mercury Street." — We may wisely take our stand facing somewhat southward, with our backs to the Viminal and with the domes of the huge Baths of Trajan partially in sight upon the heights ahead. It is a little after dawn on a warm spring morning; but all Rome, we shall discover, rises very early, and normally goes to bed correspondingly early. Even the sedate " Conscript Fathers " of the Senate are supposed to convene at *prima luce,* — gray morn. What can be seen?

To any later judgment this " Mercury Street " (so named from a local temple) [1] is very narrow, not over fifteen feet from housewall to housewall. Although the sun has now risen the way is still uncomfortably dark, because the houses pressing on either side rise to at least thirty or forty feet. The roadway, one discovers, is skillfully and durably paved with heavy lava blocks, and since it forms a regular thoroughfare it has been swept reasonably clean; although to right and left in the semi-darkness can be descried impossible alleys barely ten feet wide winding off between the tall buildings, and these side passages are more than dirty. This street, like the great majority in Rome, is comparatively short. You come to an

STEPPING STONES ACROSS A SIDE STREET : a gentleman followed by personal slave with umbrella. *After Von Falke.*

abrupt turn, or perhaps to an ascending flight of stone steps worn slippery by innumerable sandals, and immediately enter into a quite different quarter.

There is a very narrow stone sidewalk but it differs slightly before each house, every owner being required to make his own repairs. In the pavement broad ruts have been worn

---

[1] A well-known avenue in Pompeii was called "Mercury Street."

by the wagons, despite the restrictions (presently stated) upon wheeled traffic. Very few streets of Rome are wide enough for two carts to pass freely; and every driver has to look ahead and frequently to wait at corners to let other teams get by. Upon the pavement and especially at intersecting crossways are set groups of four or five large oblong stepping stones; these seem needless at present but can be a veritable godsend in the rainy season when every " Via " and " Vicus " in Rome seems converted into a raging torrent.

13. The House and Shop Fronts. — Looking upward now, one is instantly confronted by a long expanse of stuccoed walls — some pink, yellow, or bluish, but mostly an ugly brown. The lower story, quite on the street level, is broken either by the petty shops which open their shutters and thrust their counters clear out upon the pavement, or else it is merely a solid blank space with only here and there a doorway, or a few small windows, mere peep-holes for fear of burglars. The second and upper stories, however, are less solid. There are many larger windows set with window-boxes displaying bright flowers, or even with projecting balconies which reach out so far that neighbors in opposite houses can sometimes clasp hands above the hurrying life below.

Shops abound almost everywhere. In the great commercial quarters by the fora, the Tiber and the Campus Martius, will be found the splendid establishments which cater to wealth, but no quarter of Rome is too mean for its bakeries, vegetable stands, wine shops, and cheap restaurants. In fact, the absence of a speedy means of interurban communication makes a multiplication of small shops absolutely necessary. Most of these retailers do business on the pettiest scale, and a glance reveals that nearly the whole stock in trade is spread on the counter facing the street. As for the shopkeeper, ordinarily he lives and sleeps either in a dark cell just in the rear or in an equally narrow chamber directly

STREET SCENE BEFORE A COOK-SHOP. *After Von Falke.*

above his business. "Born over a shop," snobbish people say when they wish to brand some person as a nobody.

14. **Street Shrines and Fountains.** — Nevertheless, commonplace and darksome as this street may seem, there are clear tokens both of an active religious, also of an artistic

SHRINE AT THE CROSSWAYS.

life. On the flat wall, beside a grocer's stand, two serpents are crudely painted in yellow — emblems of the guardian genii of the place. Opposite, by a money-changer, is painted a fairly presentable Mercury, the god of Gain. As one goes about the city the painted snakes appear almost everywhere, and also pictures of Jupiter, Minerva, and Hercules.

At the nearby crossroads, however, is something more important. Set against the side of a building is a little niche let into the wall in lieu

of an altar. Upon this pious neighbors can deposit small articles of food for the "Gods of the Street Crossings" (*Lares Compitales*), and above is a low relief of two youthful deities, male and female. Early as it now is, an old woman has already stolen up to deposit a small crust — for the little neighborhood Lares are good and trusty friends; they will never be forgotten.

Opposite this shrine, however, a group of laughing, chattering girls is mustering around a gushing fountain. Romans are justly proud of their excellent water supply. Every house of any pretentions has its separate faucets, perhaps in great number; but the poor tenement dwellers must depend upon the street fountains. Pure, clear water is shooting from a metal pipe into a broad separate stone basin. The stream is issuing from the sculptured head of a Medusa executed with admirable detail and vigor, although this is only one of thousands of similar fountains all over the city. At the next corner the water is spouting from an eagle's beak; at another from the mouth of a calf, or the head of a Mercury.

The surplus water overflowing the basin trickles away in a streamlet down to the middle of the street, and although this adds to the inconvenience of pedestrians the pitch of the ground makes the flow carry away much of the rubbish (often very filthy) which is thrown out recklessly from the shops and even from the upper windows. It is thanks partly to this admirable water system that Rome is not even more scourged by epidemics, than is unhappily the case.[1]

15. Typical Street Crowds. — So much for the inanimate objects in Mercury Street; what now of its surging humanity? A wise law of Julius Cæsar has indeed forbidden the ordinary use of wheeled vehicles in the city streets between sunrise and the "tenth hour" (4 P.M.). This is a blessed regulation considering the narrow width of even the finest avenues, but, nevertheless, the wagons that were allowed to enter by night bringing heavy building materials to the Senator Rullianus's new mansion have now to be suffered to depart, and also the wain that had rattled up in the

[1] In describing Roman street life and its scenes let it be said once and for all that many very obvious things were so disgusting and revolting to modern notions that any description thereof is perforce omitted. Ancient life contained a great deal of social dross and filthy wickedness. There is no need to dwell on such matters, but their existence should not be forgotten.

darkness with flour for the nearby public bakery. Also one
may possibly see a Vestal Virgin or one of the superior priests
exercising their special privileges and driving in a chariot.

The street, however, is crowding with life, even if not a
horse is in sight. The most conspicuous are literally dozens
of men, each with a heavy toga wrapped carelessly around
him, hurrying frantically in every direction. In other cities
and other ages they might be " making a train." Here they
are in fact " clients," duty bound to be at the doors of their
patrons early every morning to pay their respects and seek
their bounty (see p. 149) — but almost every other type of
humanity is represented. Great numbers of boys and girls
are trudging reluctantly along to their schools, the poorer
bearing their own packages of writing tablets, the better
dressed each followed by a sedate male attendant, a pedagogue, bearing the weapons of learning.

In and out there also go youths in humble attire, often
running at breakneck speed, thrusting and jostling to make
their way; they are the slave messengers from the great
houses flying on early errands for their masters. One of
them elbows aside a tall and venerable man with a prodigi-
ously long beard and wrapped in a trailing but none too spot-
less mantle — he is a Greek philosopher on his way to some
mansion where he will perhaps expound the theories of Epicurus to a pleasure-loving nobleman. A few steps further
and there is seen a fair-haired German clad in his outlandish
costume of undressed wolf skins; hardly behind him is a red-
headed Gaul in a short tartan cloak; one can speedily recognize also a hawk-eyed, white-robed Arab from the edge of the
deserts and presently appears a grinning negro, black as
ebony and in a splendid gilt and scarlet livery — the foot-
boy probably of some rich lady.

16. Frequent Use of Greek in Rome. — The bulk of the
crowd, to be sure, is Italian, with keen, olive faces, dark

hair, and rather short stature, graceful and incessantly gesturing. But the Latin chattered on every hand is full of uncouth idioms, the *sermo plebis* calculated to make Cicero turn in his grave, and there is a great co-mingling of foreign words; above all, about one person out of every four seems to be *speaking Greek*, now abominably corrupt, now in the purest Attic, and upon penetrating the great houses one would discover Greek to be even more truly a familiar language.

All educated Romans write and speak Greek as Englishmen and Americans will never learn to use French. Learned books arc being written by the Tiber in the incomparable tongue of Hellas, and only the most ignorant Romans fail to understand simple Greek sentences. In short Rome seems close to becoming a bi-lingual city. The reigning emperor is so enthusiastic for things Hellenic that his foes brand Hadrian as " the Graecule." Athens and Corinth seem almost to have conquered their conquerors.

17. Clamor and Thronging in the Streets. — As the sun rises, every instant the street becomes more crowded. A great din is rising from a forge just inside an alley; a second noise from a carpenter shop. As if determined to be heard above everything else, from a second story comes a voice bawling out some kind of a declamation — it is a rhetoric school getting into action, and an ambitious youth is denouncing the dead tyrant Phalaris at the top of his lungs. By yonder wall, almost completely blocking the sidewalk, a nondescript barber has set down a stool and is clipping a victim with huge scissors. Close by him stands a cook's boy guarding two braziers, on one of which are boiled peas, on the other small sausages that are kept smoking hot. Early as the hour may be, workmen and others who have an active day before them are standing around and laying in a hearty breakfast. Almost upsetting this throng comes a countryman flogging a donkey whose huge paniers laden with garden truck project dangerously to either side.

The noise increases continually.   From another lane there comes more shouting.   An auctioneer is knocking down the furniture of a poor bankrupt, and the bidding is growing violent.   All the shopkeepers are bawling their wares to each prospective purchaser.   Now there is a clang and jangling; pushing the crowd aside march ten soldiers, five abreast, with insolent strides, their *optio* (sub-centurion) stalking before them.   Their gilded armor and helmets and the scarlet kilts peeping under their cuirasses, proclaim them to be " Praetorians," proud members of the imperial guard. Gilded shields clatter on their backs; they warn the slaves and hucksters away with their spear butts while their officer's red plume nods arrogantly.

Hardly are they gone before there comes the crash of some barbaric music; one hears castinets, trumpets, drums, and sistra (a kind of glorified bronze rattle), and unmelodious singing.   Tossing their arms, waving blunted swords or pounding them on light shields, along comes a troupe of the priests and priestesses of Cybele, the uncouth Asiatic goddess; the women, dark-skinned Syrians, whirling in wild dances with hair aflying, the priests puff-cheeked, smooth-faced creatures, busily pounding with their noise-making instruments.   They are headed for their temple to spend a day of orgy.

18. The Processions Attending Great Nobles. — Suddenly there is a partial silence.   Youths in livery are moving down the street flourishing white wands : " Way, way for his Excellency ," they are shouting.   Instantly the word flies around, " The Praetor Fundinus ! "   Hucksters cease shouting.   Everybody stands still and all who wear hoods or hats hastily bare their heads, [1] for the praetor represents " The Majesty of the Roman People."   Behind his *viatores*

---

[1] If a magistrate had met any persons on horseback, they also would have been bound to dismount on meeting him.

("Way Clearers") a full score of toga-clad clients swing into
sight marching ahead of the great man.   He rides in a blue
tasseled litter borne by eight tall Cappadocians of equal
height and pace.   Just in front of them march two haughty
lictors, attendants of honor, with bundles of rods, the official
"fasces," conspicuously resting upon their shoulders.[1]
Close beside the litter walks a well-groomed man with a
marked Greek profile — the confidential freedman and man
of business of the magistrate.   Behind trail more clients and
a greater retinue of slaves.   Fundinus himself heeds little
the incessant greetings cast at him.   He can be seen lolling
on his cushions, with the little curtains thrown back just
enough to show the purple embroidery on his official toga.
A book, half unrolled, is in his hand — for it is the best of form
to affect a certain bookishness in scenes of great distraction.

As the praetor's train advances, however, it is met by
another headed in the opposite direction.   A great concourse
appears of handsome slaves, all wearing brown coats and
each bearing a box or package upon his shoulder; then follows a group of pretty Levantine slave-girls gaudily clad,
then a brown Egyptian boy carrying a pet monkey; then
a simpering Celtic maid with a large basket from which peers
a small and very uneasy lap-dog; next a perfect hedge of
upper slaves and freedmen, some carrying musical instruments, some small caskets obviously crammed with valu-
ables, and some conveying ostentatiously costly garments,
and then borne high by her eight slaves in light red livery
comes a great lady herself — an ex-consul's wife, the multi-
millionaire Faustina.

19. A Great Lady Traveling. — "Her Magnificence"
(*Clarissima*) also leans back on her cushions with a studied
attitude of indifference and boredom, letting the whole

---

[1] If a praetor had been acting as governor, he would probably have had
six lictors instead of merely two while he was a judge in Rome.

street take in the silky sheen of her embroidered mantle, the gem-set handle of her ostrich fan, the gold dust that her maids have sprinkled on her tall pile of brown hair, and the great pearls that shed luster from her ears, neck, and every finger. She is merely making one of her incessant pilgrimages between her Viminal palace and some one of her ten country villas. She would feel disgraced to travel with less than about two hundred slaves and freedmen. Very likely her grandfather was a freedman himself; what matter? — official rank yields to the conquering flash of gold.

Fundinus's lictors lower their fasces; his litter is set down hastily. As the trains meet the great man hastens to the side of the greater *matrona*. Faustina is evidently in a gracious mood. She is seen to flip the praetor's face daintily with her fan. The magistrate climbs back to his own litter smilingly — perhaps he has been bidden to an ultra-select house party at Tusculum. The two trains of attendants elbow past each other, and the street resumes its plebeian bustle.

20. Public Salutations: the Kissing Habit. — As the crowds thin a little, so that the types and faces are more easily seen, several things become noticeable. First the salutations — there are surely advantages in being borne high in a litter. No person in good clothes can proceed far without being incessantly beset with greetings. Everybody seems to know everybody else. It is polite to cry *Ave!* (" Hail ") or *Salve!* (" I hope you're well ") to persons of the scantiest acquaintance, and then, when they return your salute, if there is nothing more to add, *Vale!* (" Good luck ").

More serious, however, is the incessant kissing. A sedate old gentleman with a narrow purple stripe on his tunic (the token of the " equestrian " rank) appears followed by two spruce slave boys. A nondescript fellow immediately pushes up to him, seizes his hand, then smacks him roundly on the cheek. Doubtless the rascal's lips are foul and his breath charged with garlic; it is nevertheless most discourteous for the older man to resent it. There is no escaping the incessant attacks, unless you can have a litter, and the poet Martial has vainly complained of acquaintances who insisted on kissing him in December " when round his nose hangs a veritable icicle." Even the Emperor has to submit to the usage, although the privilege is confined to that envied and exalted circle known as " Cæsar's friends."

21. The Swarms of Idlers and Parasites. — Another thing becomes obvious after a short scrutiny — *the vast number of idlers.* People are incessantly lounging up and down the street manifestly with nothing important to do. Hard work and common trade are, as later explained (see p. 146), by no means genteel; and many a Roman who possesses merely a threadbare toga and has his name on the list for corn doles prefers living by his wits in busy idleness, fawning on the great, and hunting dinner invitations to doing a stroke of honest labor.

Most of the idlers nevertheless are slaves. In the vast *familia* of the palaces the tasks are all so subdivided that the average slave has far too much time on his hands. He puts in many hours, therefore, wandering about the sights of the city, gaming, following coarse love affairs, and seeking tips on the circus and amphitheater contests. The amount of worthless chatter is infinite. Even at this early hour from the tables of a wine-shop comes the rattle of dice boxes. Another dirty group is actually throwing dice on the pavement under pedestrian's heels. The law nominally forbids open gaming, but the police are very busy men. Rome, one discovers thus promptly, is all too much a city of " parasites." By exploiting the world, she is able to maintain a horde of human bipeds, bond or free, who minister nothing to her prosperity.

The gamesters on the pavement halt, however, instantly, when a tumult arises from a neighboring vintner's stall. A Spanish boy has tried to steal a jar of fine old Massic, but the vessel has been wisely fastened to a pillar with a chain. While he tugs to break this the dealer spots him : " Stop thief ! " rises the cry. Instantly appear two broad-shouldered men, in half armor with small steel caps. They carry stout poles tipped with strong hooks useful in fires.

MONUMENT OF A WINE SELLER.

These are *vigiles* (police-firemen) of the city watch. The thief is seized and hustled off howling and protesting, to tell his troubles at the court of the City Praefect. Before the players can resume, they have to stand aside also for a funeral procession — flute players, professional mourners screaming and gesticulating, manumitted slaves of the deceased wearing liberty caps, mourning relatives around the bier ; all headed for the cremation-pyre outside the gates.

22. Public Placards and Notices. — Just as the dice are about to rattle again a shrewd-looking fellow with a piece of red chalk is seen stepping up to a space of blank wall. " Celer, the notice writer," whispers everybody. A large crowd elbows and gathers around him, as to general delight, with quick strokes he letters the following announcement of a gladiator fight :

IN THE AMPHITHEATER OF TAURUS
THE GAMES OF THE AEDILE BALBUS

From the 12th to the 15th of May

THE 'THRACIAN' PUGNAX

OF THE

NERONIAN GLADIATORIAL SCHOOL

Who Has Fought Three Times Will Meet

THE 'MURMILLO' MURANUS

OF THE

SAME SCHOOL

And The Same Number of Fights

THE 'HEAVY ARMOUR FIGHTER' CYCNUS

FROM THE

SCHOOL OF JULIUS CAESAR

Who Has Fought Eight Times

WILL MEET

THE 'THRACIAN' ATTICUS

OF THE

SAME SCHOOL

And of Fourteen Fights

Awnings will be provided against the sun

" *Euge! Euge!* Bravo, Balbus ! " cry the expectant idlers as they go back to their game, and Celer hurries off to repeat his notice on some wall in the next street.

The dice contest can be omitted. Not so with the wall inscriptions which we now discover are scattered over almost

every space of available stucco along the thoroughfare.
Some are formal notices of games, articles for sale, auctions,
tenements to let, etc., written with some skill, although with
many puzzling abbreviations, by professional sign-writers
like Celer.   Thus on one building can be read in tall red
letters: " *To rent, from the first of July, shops with the
floors above them and a house in the Arrius Pollio block, owned
by Nigidius Maius.   Prospective lessees may apply to Primus
his slave,*" and another sign advertises the " *Venus baths,
fitted up for the best people, shops, rooms over shops and second
story apartments, in the property owned by Julia Felix.*" [1]

23. Wall Scribblings. — More interesting really are the
wall scribblings of the humble.   " The walls were the writing
paper of the poor," will be declared later by students of
Rome.   All kinds of sentiments are scratched upon the
stucco; sometimes with considerable care with a stylus;
sometimes with merely a finger nail; sometimes drawn with
charcoal or a red crayon.   There are indeed so many writings,
especially in frequented places, that we notice a wag has actually added a word of protest :

> I wonder O wall,
> That your stones do not fall
> All scribbled thus o'er
> By the nonsense of all!

Every kind of opinion is to be found along a limited
stretch of wall.   Coarse insults abound where your enemy
can promptly see them: " Vile wretch," " Bold rascal,"
" Old focl," " I hope you'll die ! " " May you be crucified ! "
— these are merely the mildest.   Then other sentiments are
more friendly: " Luck to you ! " " Good health to you
everywhere ! "   " A Happy New Year and a lot of them,"

---

[1] The wall placards and inscriptions quoted in this and the following
section are all substantially as found at Pompeii.

and " What wouldn't I do for *you*, dear eyes of Luscus" (the names of the enemy or friend involved being often added).

Lovers also take up their tale. A girl records her frank opinion: " Virgula to her dear Tertius — You are mighty mean."   A penitent swain spreads forth this " personal " to his mistress: " *Do* have pity on me and let me come back." A young lady announces tartly: " Where Verus is there's nothing *veracious*" (a pun on words).   A gay philanderer explains, " A blonde girl taught me to hate brunettes, and I *will* hate them if I can — but loving them would come so much easier ! "   And another youth demands passionately: " My dear Sava, please do love me ! "   While finally a jealous suitor has broken into verse:

> If any man shall seek
> My girl from me to turn,
> On far-off mountains bleak,
> May Love the scoundrel burn!

The prosing moralist must likewise have his say. Somebody has sagely scribbled, " A trifling ailment if neglected can grow to be very serious."   There are in addition conundrums and children's sketches — pictures of playmates, friends, foes, and especially of popular gladiators, marked with red ochre or charcoal, and sometimes limned with considerable vigor, but usually in the manner of the childish drawings in all ages, with forehead and nose marked by a line and with two dots serving for eyes. School boys have scratched down some of the verses in Vergil and Ovid that have just been flogged into them by their masters.

The only thing we can miss in Rome are the election notices which would abound on the walls of all chartered provincial or free Italian cities, entreating us to vote for so-

and-so for *duumvir* " he's a good man " ; or declaring that
" all the fullers' guild are out for —— as aedile." [1]   Rome,
alas! has lost her liberty; the city is paternally governed
by the Emperor aided by the Senate, and popular elections
are a thing of the past.

24. The Streets Dark and Dangerous at Night. — One is
warned, however, not to tax the patience of the adjacent
shopkeepers and linger too long in this street.   Written above
a drug seller's stand appears clearly, " *No idlers here!   Move
on you loungers!* " and a little distance along upon a wall,
" *Here you!   What are you loitering for?* "   Indeed the passing throngs are becoming somewhat monotonous.   The hurly-
burly abates.   About noon almost everybody will take first
a fairly hearty luncheon, and then a siesta.   Nearly every
shop will be closed.   Then the bustle will be resumed while
the more genteel element will be seen headed in great
numbers towards the public baths.

By four o'clock, however, the shops will be closing behind
heavy shutters, the clamor from the work rooms will cease,
and even the humble will begin to prepare for the crowning
event of a Roman's day — dinner, often begun still earlier.
After sundown the silence almost of the grave shuts down
upon avenues which a few hours earlier were simply swarming
with life.   There are no street lights.   Nobody stirs outdoors if possible, unless accompanied by friends or slaves with
lanterns or torches ; and it is no harm to carry heavy bludge-
ons, for despite the watch there are all too many sneak thieves,
cutpurses, and even open bandits, " dagger men " (*siccarii*),
with their " your money or your life."   Also lawless young
nobles sometimes get an evil pleasure (as did Nero and his
companions) by ranging the streets and beating up harmless
and poorly guarded citizens.

---

[1] For quotations of election notices at Pompeii see the author's "Readings in Ancient History," Vol. II, "Rome," pp. 261–262.

25. Discomforts of Life in Rome. — People also tell you that at night there is no small peril of being brained by loose tiles which rattle down from the lofty house-tops, or less dangerous but most disgusting, of being drenched by buckets of filthy slops flung recklessly from upper windows into the streets. Then toward dawn your sleep is ruined by the incessant rumbling of the wagons with timber, brick, building stone, cement, and all kinds of food supplies which have to be excluded from the city in the day hours. These are all part of the general discomforts of life in Rome, along with the squalid flat-buildings, the peril from the collapse of rickety houses, the occasional great floods of the Tiber, the fearful conflagrations, the ubiquitous throngs of people, and the grievous absence of privacy.

The complaints are incessant. " School masters in the morning; corn grinders at night; and braziers' hammers day and night " are subjects for standard diatribes of poets like Martial and Juvenal. And they, like everybody, first praise the quiet simple life possible in the Italian country towns — and then they remain in Rome. The great city with its multitudes, its ceaseless variety of all things good and bad, its appeal to every kind of human interest holds them with so many other mortals fascinated. They are unhappy while in Rome; but still more unhappy until they can return to her.

So much for the merely outward side of a typical street on the slopes of the Esquiline. We can now penetrate the homes of the people, first visiting an *insula*, a great tenement block of the lowly, and then investigating a more elegant *domus*, the residence of a magnate.

CHAPTER III

THE HOMES OF THE LOWLY AND OF THE MIGHTY

26. The Great _Insulæ_ — Tenement Blocks. — Perhaps another age will imagine that most Romans have lived in vast marble palaces, moving through spacious halls amid stately pillars and spraying fountains. Nothing like this is the case for the great majority. A census report declares "there are some 44,000 tenement blocks (_insulæ_) in the city and only about 1750 separate 'mansions' (_domus_)."[1] Such figures can merely imply that an overwhelming proportion of "the toga-wearing race, the Lords of the world" (to quote Virgil's threadbare line) are flat-dwellers.

Considering the extreme congestion of population, no other solution than this is possible if Rome is to remain Rome. There is a great profit in building these huge, ungainly "islands," the tenement blocks. Everywhere around the city we meet the gangs of laborers mixing the concrete whereof the structures are mostly constructed, or setting the wooden molds to shape the material as it solidifies; or else tearing down and carting away the wreckage of insulæ that have begun to decay. Such property employs a great amount of capital. Nearly every senator has his men of business caring for his housing investments and rentals, and the "realtor" is a very familiar personage.

Rightly is it complained also that many insulæ are put up in a cheap and absolutely dangerous manner, and at

---

[1] These figures seem to come from the fourth century, but there is no reason to think that housing conditions in Rome had changed very much since the second century.

best are dark, dirty, and unsanitary. The very name implies that they should be built with a free space all around them. The old law of Twelve Tables (450 B.C.) required a passage way (*ambitus*) of at least two and a half feet on either side, but this law was recklessly disregarded until the great fire of Nero enabled the government to enforce a fairly scientific building code. Even now, however, the tenement houses are often hemmed in on all sides by miserable black alleys hardly accessible to the public scavengers.

This struggle to use every scrap of ground is completely matched by the effort to build as high as possible. " The immense size of Rome," wrote Vitruvius, about 1 A.D., " makes it needful to have a vast number of habitations, and as the area is not sufficient to contain them all on the ground floor, the nature of the case compels us to raise them in the air."

There are no passenger elevators in Rome; furthermore, the concrete construction does not permit the safe erection of extremely high buildings without unusual precautions, and with such narrow streets tall structures obstruct both light and air; nevertheless, the real estate interests grumbled loudly when Augustus limited the height of dwellings to seventy feet. Hadrian has just vexed them still more by a decree that if an owner allows his insula to fall into dangerous repair, he must either sell it, or rebuild it thoroughly. For all that, many insulæ seem to be towering rookeries, ready to collapse at any flood or earthquake.

27. A Typical Insula. — Upon Mercury Street, which we have just examined, stands a very average insula, built about forty years ago, and, therefore, loyally named the *Flavia Victoria* for the then reigning dynasty. It belongs to the widow of the rich eques Gaius Macer, and is managed by the lynx-eyed procurator, or bailiff, who superintends her estate. Despite the fact that it is safer than some of its neighbors, the tenants complain on rent days that the upper stories are built so largely of wood as to be in peril of fire, and that one of the outer walls is so cracked that it has to be propped up with heavy timbers.

The *Flavia Victoria* is just under the legal building height, and contains five stories.   On the street there are several shops of the usual kind, also several separate entrances whereof the doorways, flanked with pillars, give access to certain extra-select flats above ; but most of the tenants have to go in through the central portal under the eyes of a porter.

Upon entering they find themselves in a fairly ample square court, upon which open many windows of the tiers of rooms in the upper stories.   There is a fountain in the court, but the pavement below is decidedly slimy and dirty.   Quantities of half-naked small children are scampering about in noisy play.   The windows, however, like those facing upon the streets, often have balconies on which simple boxes of flowers are blooming.   The blue Italian sky above and the bars of intense sunlight upon the flag-stones make the filthiness of the court and the dinginess of the yellow stuccoed walls less obnoxious.   Dirt and even the numerous fleas lose part of their terrors amid picturesque surroundings in a mild climate.

28. The Flats in an Insula. — From the courtyard several staircases, often dark and dank, rise to the tenements above. The *Flavia Victoria* is a fair-sized insula, and just as in European flat buildings later, can contain many social strata under one ample roof.   In the apartments on the first floor, there are really comfortable suites, each with a series of rooms — living room (*atrium*), dining room, kitchen, bedrooms, and the like, chambers not large indeed, but sufficient for a modest household keeping perhaps ten slaves.   The walls are covered with bright frescoes, and the floors with very fair mosaics.   Such a superior apartment can bring some 10,000 sesterces ($400) per year, and a good many flats rent for even more.[1]

The rentals fall rapidly as the tenants scale higher. In the second floor the apartments are much smaller; there is merely a living room and a few smaller chambers. The appointments are correspondingly mean and dingy, while the annual rent is only 2000 sesterces ($80); and between the prosperous grain factor on the third floor and the hardworking brickyard superintendent on the fourth there is never the least sociability.

29. The Cheap Attic Tenements and Their Poor Occupants. — Both unite, however, in despising the wretched creatures who plod wearily up to the dirty, vermin-infested sleeping pockets upon the fifth or sixth stages, where, under the roof tiles, the hot sun beats pitilessly. If we care to thrust ourselves into the tiny chambers of the unfortunate Codrus, the bath attendant, we will find, perhaps " a bed too small for the dwarf Procula, a marble slab whereon are set six small food jars and a small drinking cup, a statue of Chiron [some decaying heirloom], and an old chest of Greek books gnawed by the unlettered mice."[2]

Vainly do Codrus and his wife complain to the bailiff that the roof is collapsing over them. He merely laughs and bids them " sleep at ease," although a deadly crash is threatened any night. They have another peril, because fire may at any time break out in Ucalegon's flat below and leave them cut off, possibly while in their beds, and with no chance of escape after the alarm spreads.

Such poor tenants never stay in one place long. Rome is a city of inveterate flat-hunters. The first of July (the

---

[1] Rentals in Rome, for all classes of lodgings, were unreasonably high, as compared with the relative cost of other necessities: just as is now complained to be the case in New York, Paris, and other great cities.

[2] A familiar description of such a place by Juvenal.

Calends) is the regular moving day.   Every tenant who cannot or will not pay his rent, has to go forth seeking even
cheaper and more squalid quarters.   There are endless family
processions bearing off the few poor chattels.   The satirists
make ungenerous fun of their plight, telling how a wretched
man has to march away followed by " his carroty-headed
wife, his white-haired mother and his giantess of a sister."
Between them they carry off " a three-legged bed, a two-
footed table, a lamp, a horn-cup, a rusty brazier, some cracked
dishes, some jars of very stale pickled fish," also a supply of

TENANTS PAYING RENT TO A LANDLORD'S AGENT.

cheese and onions, and " a pot of resin belonging to the poor
fellow's mother and used by the beldame for anointing herself."

Such luckless plebeians, of course, may delude some house
agent in a distant part of the city into giving them a dark
garret in the vain hope that they can pay their rent; " but
really," — says the bailiff with a shrug, " they belong at the
Aricine bridge — the haunt of the beggars."

Unfortunately a large fraction of Rome is little better off
than this. Poverty stalks everywhere. There are plenty
of fetid insulæ which do not contain a single family that
can be sure of next week's dinners. Nevertheless there are

mitigations; as will be seen, the government takes great pains that in Rome nobody will actually starve; and again, there are so many free circuses and gladiatorial shows that a man has abundant diversion from his troubles. There is a magnificent water supply, and the kind Italian sun prevents heavy fuel bills. Poverty, therefore, does not imply the acute misery which it does in the North.

Nevertheless, the most fortunate insula dweller probably dreams of the day when he can crown his inevitable ambition. " When can I cease to live in a *cenucula* (flat) and live in a *domus?* " [1]

30. A Senatorial " Mansion " (*Domus*). — Publius Junius Calvus is a senator of ancient lineage, whose domus lifts itself arrogantly near the summit of the Esquiline, at the head of Mercury Street, looking down upon the tiles of the humble insula *Flavia Victoria.*

Calvus, although a member of the upper aristocracy, is not extraordinarily wealthy. He does not, like some of his friends, possess simultaneously three large city houses, often moving from one to another according to season and mood. He has only four country villas, one far in the North by the Italian lakes, one in the Etruscan hills, one fairly close to Rome, and a fourth on the delightful Bay of Naples. His city residence is inferior in magnificence not merely to those of many senators but even of many equites (second-class nobles) and of a whole cohort of rich, upstart freedmen. Nevertheless, it is a fine mansion, which has been in the Calvian family for many generations, and it is crammed with treasured heirlooms. Calvus, unlike certain noble col-

---

[1] In small provincial cities like Pompeii the proportion of the people who could live in separate houses was much greater than in Rome; in fact separate residences were somewhat the rule. The Pompeiian houses were usually of two stories and nearly all were decidedly small. In Rome itself real estate was far too valuable to permit separate houses except for the wealthy.

leagues, is happily married and rejoices in two half-grown sons
and a daughter.   For them a *familia* of only one hundred
and fifty slaves suffices, although the noble Gratia sometimes
complains to her husband :   " Our staff is disgracefully small."

The Calvi are really an extremely old family in what is
now becoming a city of upstarts.   Publius's forebears have
lived for centuries on the Esquiline and their domus has been
rebuilt many times.   In Punic War days it probably consisted
only of a central atrium, with an opening in the ceiling to
admit light and emit smoke, and a few dark cell-like chambers
radiating from the great living room.   This hall rightly received its name of the " black place " (*ater*) from the soot
from the open hearth which was perpetually caked around
the rafters.   The walls were of rubble, the floor of simple
tiles or even merely of pounded earth, and the roof was of
thatch.   Such a house could stow away the many children
and the relatively few servants of a senator who helped to
humiliate Carthage.

31. The Plan of a Large Residence. — Very different is
the domus now as we approach the lofty Ionic pillars before
its portal, nevertheless, the plan of the old house has not quite
vanished in the stately mansion.   The Roman house is
always (like the Greek) essentially the typical *southern* dwelling built around *courts*, and getting its light thence, and with
little dependence upon exterior windows.   What has happened now is that the old living room has expanded into a
magnificent light-bathed hall, with the sun streaming not
through a smoke-hole but an ample opening.   The rooms
leading from this court have multiplied in number and vastly
increased in size.   Then through a series of passages one
enters a second court even larger and handsomer, and
with another array of dependent chambers.

In such a house the main apartments are on the first floor,
but there is a second story for the lodging of the retinues of

slaves. In the rear of all there is usually a garden. Every domus has its own particular plan and pretentions but all conform to the general scheme of two main courts, just as almost every house of another civilization will demand its parlor and its dining room.

Calvus's mansion is priced by the real estate experts at about 3,500,000 sesterces (say $140,000);[1] but there are

Atrium of House in Pompeii looking towards the Peristylium: present condition.

not a few houses of richer senators worth four times as much. The structure faces a street which is reasonably clear of shops and where all the neighbors are at least equites or else very wealthy freedmen. The building does not rise as high as an insula; in fact it possesses only two stories: the first

[1] That was the price that Cicero paid for his town house, at a time when Roman real estate was worth probably much less than in the days of Hadrian.

broken by mere peepholes in the solid stuccoed walls, the
second by larger windows all heavily grated. One can guess
part of the reason for these bars from a placard hanging in
the entrance:

NO SLAVE IS TO QUIT THE HOUSE WITHOUT
THE MASTER'S ORDERS. PENALTY 100 LASHES

---

32. Entrance to the Residence. — The entrance itself, however, is handsome. The columns on either side are of fine
Luna marble. Pass between these, and you enter a vestibule,
a considerable outer chamber with fine pilasters let into the
walls, where at this moment a swarm of the Senator's clients
are mustering. Then you approach the actual doors of the
ostium. These stand open but every passer is being scrutinized, and if questionable, is stopped by a janitor, a highly
responsible slave, who has a seat just inside. Many a janitor
is supported in his duty by a surly dog, but here there is
merely a life-like mosaic creature, wrought in the tiles of the
pavement, with CAVE CANEM (" Beware the dog ") written
beneath him. Overhead in a gilt cage however is swinging
a tame magpie, and the creature croaks out his " *Salve!
Salve!* " as the guests press into the atrium.

33. The Atrium and the View across It. — The moment
we are inside the transformation of scene from the dusty,
dingy street is startling. If other persons do not obstruct
the view, you can see clear down the long vistas of the house
from the entrance to the greenery of the garden. Before
us is the atrium, a magnificent court, paved with elaborate
mosaics, and with four elegant Corinthian columns in pink
marble upholding the roof around a wide light-well. Under
this light-well is a complicated fountain, where bronze tritons

and dancing nymphs are shooting great jets into a white
marble basin in which grow luxurious water plants. On
the inner sides of the atrium, and on either of the numerous
doors opening into the
same, stand statues,
bronze or marble, upon
carved stone pedestals.

Many of the door-
ways around this ele-
gant hall are closed by
heavy curtains, of rich
saffron, purple, olivine,
or blue, the hues being
selected to blend mar-
velously with the tints
of the columns. Where
the walls are not a
sheen of marble, they
are spread with elab-
orate and wonderfully
decorative frescos — of
which more hereafter.
On special pedestals of
honor are fine art ob-
jects, valuable bric-a-
brac, tripods, vases,
silver cups, war tro-
phies. The mosaics on
the floor (could we stop
to gaze) are more beau-

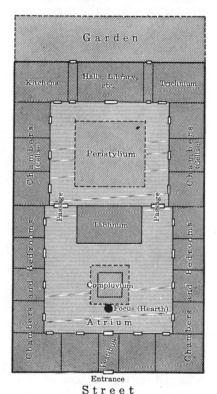

Entrance
S t r e e t
PLAN OF A ROMAN MANSION (*Domus*).
strictly conventionalized.

tiful than any carpet. In brilliant jewel work, for it is little
else, has been wrought out a series of pictures showing the
campaigns of Alexander. There is another series giving the
legend of Perseus. The sunlight, the spray from the foun-

tain, the sheen of the marbles, the brilliance of the frescos, all combine in an effect that is dazzling.

34. The Rooms in the Rear and the *Peristylium*. — But this hall is merely the beginning, not the end of the domus. In the rear of the atrium there is the master's office, the *tablinum*, a very large alcove, a handsome apartment where he

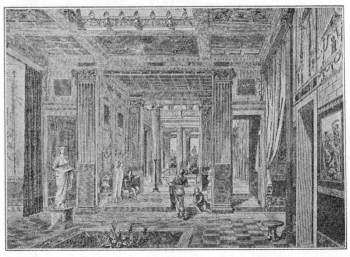

INTERIOR OF A ROMAN MANSION, LOOKING FROM THE ATRIUM INTO THE PERISTYLIUM : restored.

will receive those guests who are come strictly on business. This and the atrium, however, are merely the public rooms of the house; the real living rooms are beyond, although, by a survival of old custom, the symbolic marriage couch of the master and mistress stands on a back wall by the tablinum. The heavy curtains have been swept aside from the broad passageways (*fauces*) which lead into the second court — the *peristylium*.

Here the atrium is duplicated — but on a much more elaborate scale. There is another column-girdled court; but the pillars are taller and of an exquisite blue-veined marble. A huge curtain swings on its cords ready for expansion as the sun grows hot. Beneath the light-opening, there is not merely a second fountain, but a real plat of greensward, a *viridarium*, with a bright bed of rare flowers and even a few tropical plants. There is another phalanx of statues. Under

SCENE IN A PERISTYLIUM.

the long quadrangular colonnades around the court are spread out deeply upholstered couches, easy chairs, small tables, and other appurtenances for luxurious existence. The ceilings of the colonnades and of the rooms leading thence are covered with metallic fretwork gilded in a soft sheen, while the intense light filters down gratefully between the columns, and sinks to a pleasant twilight in the niches and nooks in the walls of the peristylium.

35. The Dining Room (*Triclinium*) and the Chapel. — From this second court to left and to right open doors which lead to the master's and mistress's sleeping chambers, and those of their children, their guests, and their upper servants. The rooms are small, but are always daintily frescoed.

Far more important than these chambers is the great dining room (*triclinium*). Calvus's friends tell him he really ought to rebuild his residence and provide a special " summer dining room " on the north side of the house, and a warmer

ROMAN TYPE OF HOUSE AT POMPEII, LOOKING ACROSS THE ATRIUM:
present condition.

" winter dining room " on the south side as in all the newer mansions.[1] However, his triclinium is very handsome; with good pilasters of Hymettus marble, fine statuary, sideboards loaded with rare old plate, and a ceiling fretted with ivory and arranged so that it can be partly opened at the climax of a feast to drop garlands and to spray down unguents upon the guests.

[1] Petronius represents his rich upstart Trimalchio as having four ordinary dining rooms and also a special second story dining room.

In the rear of the house there are also a smaller breakfast room, and a special hall (*oecus*) for the display of even additional art objects, likewise a library, and a private bathroom, both to be described later; while in the rear of the peristylium is one of the most important rooms assuredly in the entire mansion — the kitchen (*culina*), where Gratia's proudest possession, a truly superior cook, prepares dinners that atone for the sorrowful fact that "we have only one dining room."

Off the peristylium, too, one notes what amounts to a miniature chapel. Before a temple front composed of short columns mounted on a kind of table are set several little images of beautiful fairy-like creatures of both sexes. These are the family *lares*, the honored guardians of the old house of the Calvi. Once they stood in the atrium, but in later days although withdrawn to the more private peristylium, they have not ceased to be dear. Calvus discusses with his philosopher friends, "Are there really any gods?"; but he never fails to cast his incense night and morning upon the small gilt brazier which smokes before his family lares. In the kitchen, also, there is a second little niche and still other images of the lares, where they receive bits of food and innocent prayers from all the servants — even more devotedly than from the lordly folk in the peristylium.

36. The Garden and the Slaves' Quarters. — Another passage beside the kitchen leads us into what can be just glimpsed as one enters the atrium — the rear garden set in by high walls. Land is too valuable in Rome for Calvus to permit himself much more than a short graveled walk under a few fine old box trees, but by an intensive gardening that another age might style "Japanese" there is laid out a miniature brooklet, a cascade plunging into a little pool containing tame lampreys, and some small pines, which have been forced into the semblance of a tiny forest. A broad marble seat now strewn with cushions, a good statue of a dancing Pan, the rushing music of the water, and the breeze rustling the foliage—all these make the tumultuous, squalid street and the dirty garrets of the *Flavia Victoria* seem very far away. — In reality they are barely a stone's throw down the hill.

Where do Calvus's slaves keep themselves? Undoubtedly in the very cramped barracks of the second story, a section of which looks down from an upper tier of columns above the court of the peristylium. Even lordly Romans spend little time in their chambers and need only small bedrooms. For the slaves there is extremely little accommodation; any kind of a sleeping pocket, very truly called a "cell" (*cella*) will answer, where a stool, a blanket,

CORNER IN A GARDEN IN REAR OF A ROMAN HOUSE.

and a thin mat on the floor suffice for all save the upper servants.

Under the house there are ordinary cellars for the storage of provisions. Somewhere, too, is a strong room, with barred windows, and heavy door, and inside, fastened upon the floor, a set of stocks and manacles. Lucky is the day when, in a slave-familia of this size, this lockup has not at least one backsliding occupant.

37. The Floors and Windows. — Inquiring about certain details of such a mansion we discover that like most other Roman houses, it is built of concrete, faced with brick or coarse stone and stucco, and then with as many interior surfaces as possible, covered with slabs of marble or decorative frescos. The roof is of brick tiles; the floors in the humbler chambers, where mosaic is unnecessary, are partly of concrete and partly of small pieces of stone and tile roughly fitted together and then pounded down by a rammer (*pavimentum*). Two or three rooms most used in winter have a special and very luxurious device — part of their floors are made of hollow tile pipes, and through these hot air from a furnace can be forced to warm them precisely as is done at the baths.[1]

Little thus far has been said about the windows. These open mainly upon the courts, and they are so few that very many rooms, especially those used by the slaves, seem disagreeably dark, although in the long, hot season this drawback somewhat vanishes. Most of the windows are closed merely by board shutters swinging in leaves, and rather handsomely paneled; but shutting them results in a state of artificial night.

For certain rooms used by the master and mistress there is a much better arrangement. Numbers of small pieces of glass are set in bronze lattices and inserted in the windows. Glass cannot be made that is strictly transparent, but it is highly translucent. Such rooms are delightfully illuminated all day long. Certain other wealthy houses use windows set with translucent talc (soft magnesium silicate), but these openings are hardly as satisfactory. Glass is slowly coming

---

[1] This heating by *hypocausts* was used much more in Roman villas in Gaul, the Rhinelands, and Britain, where winters were severe, than in Italy. In Rome itself people ordinarily managed to shiver through the relatively short cold spells by means of portable *charcoal braziers*, placed in the more important rooms, and by piling upon themselves extra tunics.

into general use, and the window panes will improve as glass-makers learn how to blow larger sheets and to make their product more transparent.

38. Frescos, Beautiful and Innumerable. — From the house itself we can turn to its ornamentation and furniture. The use of marble columns and of great slabs of marble veneer has been repeatedly mentioned. Africa, Egypt, and Greece as well as Italy have been ransacked by Roman contractors for their treasures of stone.[1] Even this private mansion of the Calvi boasts its green and black monolithic pillars, as well as its ceiling of gilded fretwork.

Where the sheen of polished marble does not meet the eye almost invariably there are bright *frescos*. These are the *Roman wall paper*. Even in the poorest insulæ we have met them, cheap hackneyed things, garish in color, the work not of artists but of common craftsmen. Yet most of even these are not without a certain decorative beauty and their number is enormous.[2] In the humble tenements the pictures often consist of pillars painted upon the walls, with gardens and landscapes represented as if seen between the portico, so the lodgers may have the pretence of looking upon the greenery reserved for the mighty.

In a fine domus, however, the frescos, infinite in number, often approximate real works of art. There is no time to discuss their types and history; it is sufficient to say the decorative effect is amazingly effective. Some rooms have their walls covered with a variety of bright conceits and patterns,

---

[1] One can make a long list of the marbles constantly used at Rome : *e.g.* white marbles from Carrara, Paros, and Pentelicos ; crimson-streaked from Phrygia ; orange-golden from Numidia ; white and pale green from Carystos ; serpentine from Laconia ; porphyry from Egypt, etc.

[2] At this writing the number of wall paintings rescued from the excavations of Pompeii runs well up to 4000 ; and Pompeii was a city perhaps only a fortieth the size of Rome.

— balconies, perches, tapestries of fruit and flowers, garlanded columns and flying sprites and maidens. Another room has pictures of all the possible handicrafts and trades; but with cupids working the forges and wine presses, or chaffering as merchants. Gratia's boudoir is full of amorous scenes of brides adorning themselves and of lovers' meetings. In the triclinium there are elegant pictures of still life — fishes, fruit, birds; and in the peristylium and atrium are elaborate landscapes, scenes from Greek mythology, and a series of pictures depicting the voyages and adventures of Æneas.[1] There are no picture frames, but a skilful use of colored lines and sometimes of a painted setting of columns and architectural pediments makes each scene stand out to great advantage.

The colors of all these frescos are very brilliant but they are never painfully crude. Where the walls are not covered by painting or marble they are tinted a soft brown or gray; and where the columns are not of naturally shaded marble they also are gently tinted to a neutral tone, although the lower third is usually painted a bright red or yellow.

The numerous statues about the house are all in their turn given a kind of flesh color, with some other hue laid upon their drapery. Perhaps in the open, under the light of a northern summer these features would appear barbaric and offensive; under the gentle radiance diffused from the apertures of the atrium and the peristylium they create a scene of marvelous beauty, fascinating, and generally restful to the eye.

39. The Profusion of Statues and Art Objects. — So much for the wall decorations, and we must turn to the statues. The mansion seems to swarm with slaves, yet they are hardly more numerous than the sculptures in bronze and marble.

---

[1] Most of the finer scenes in Roman frescos seem to have been pretty good copies of famous paintings from Greek mythology originally produced by the masters of the Hellenistic age.

Many of these are good copies of the best masterpieces of Greece. The splendid athlete in the atrium is from an original by Praxiteles; the Penelope in the peristylium follows precisely the noble work of Scopas. Many others are simply graceful and ornamental but less pretentious works by lesser geniuses, often adapted in detail by the clever copyists.

PORTRAIT BUST — POMPEY THE GREAT.

The whole quantity of art objects in such a house is enormous. The legs and arms of the chairs and every knob and handle upon the furniture are chased or carved with an amazing skill. The veriest knick-nacks and articles for every-day life have been trans-formed into things of beauty. In the triclinium is a long series of statuettes present-ing the myths of Bacchus — the god himself, the drunken Silenus, the satyrs, bac-chants, and all the other revelers. It would be easy, indeed, to reconstruct a good part of the standard Græco-Roman mythology from the statues, statuettes, and reliefs, no less than from the frescos scattered about the mansion and garden.

40. Family Portrait Busts. — However, there is one lengthy array of sculptures in the atrium that does not bear the hand of Greece. These are the portrait busts of the Junii Calvi. There they stand, a full score of them; all the more distinguished members of the great house since sculpture became a facile art in Rome.

It is an array of cold, hard, yet withal terribly efficient faces. Slightly battered is the broad homely countenance of that tough old Calvus who was Scipio's legate at Zama. Here also is the sharp shrewd face of his great-grandson who was prætor under Sulla; here the more refined and intellectual lines of the grandson of the last named worthy who won Octavius's thanks at Actium for gallantry with his bireme, and afterward was a famous governor of Syria; here the high forehead of that courageous Stoic, the present master's grandfather, who bade Nero do his worst, and who calmly " opened his veins " when the centurion arrived with the tyrant's order to commit suicide. There are also displayed the busts of several distinguished women of the family including that Junia who was the bosom friend of the Empress Livia.

TYPICAL ROMAN PORTRAIT — MARC ANTONY.

In addition to these, there are the portrait busts of the present Publius Calvus, of his wife Gratia, and of his three children. They are all executed with remarkable verisimilitude and without the least flattery. Customs with the hair often change, and the headdress of Gratia is made detachable so that if her style of headdress alters, the portrait may he promptly brought up to date. Young Sextus the second boy had a birthday yesterday; his statue is still hung with wreaths; flowers too hang around the likeness of Gnæus Calvus, Publius's brother, who lately died while proprætor of Bætica (South Spain).

41. Death Masks (*Imagines*). — The sight of these busts is a constant incentive to both the young Calvi to remember their lordly lineage; but they have a still prouder treasure. The enormously rich freedman Vedius just down the street would give twenty million sesterces for the social preëminence implied by the possession of the great cupboard all bound with gilt and bronze bands which stands in the tablinum. Here, carefully labeled, are kept several scores of waxen death masks, blackened, marred, and ugly enough now, but all taken when the successive heads of the family lay in their last slumber.

Many of these date from before the production in Rome of sculptured portrait statues. Here, for example, is the mask of the Calvus who helped win the consulship for the plebeians; and here of him who seconded Appius Claudius in the Senate when he turned away the glozing envoys of Pyrrhus. When alien upstarts complain of "noble pride," it is easy for a Calvus to toss his head : "Have we not something to be proud of !" — and later, it will be duly explained how these waxen *imagines* appear very conspicuously at public funerals (p. 175).

42. Couches, Their General Use. — One cannot, however, sit or lie down upon statues or portrait busts, and the domus is well provided with conventional furniture. In general the Romans prefer to *recline* when men of a later age may prefer to *sit*. Visitors sprawl down on couches for a little conversation, and the regular method of writing is not at a desk but lying on a couch with the right leg doubled and the tablet held on the knee. Long habit makes this attitude quite comfortable.

There are many special kinds of beds for reading, dining, and for sleeping. Of course the latter are the most elaborate, and in Calvus's and Gratia's chamber the wooden bed is so high that it has to be reached by a footstool. The legs are of bronze, elaborately turned and carved, the frame is ve-

neered with tortoise shell and the supports at the sides of the
sloping pillow-rest are set with plates of silver. As for the
thick mattresses they are of the finest down and the ample
blankets are dyed purple and embroidered with gold thread.
The couches in the triclinium are lighter and lower although
of very fine cabinet work,[1] but they have to be made larger

ROMAN LAMPS : collection in Naples Museum.

for they must accommodate three diners. The reading
couches (*lectuli* — " little beds ") are still lighter and simpler,
although of elegant design, and those scattered under the
peristylium are overlaid with plates of gold leaf.

43. Elegant Chairs and Costly Tables. — Excluding the
couches the furnishings of a Roman domus seem much simpler

---

[1] It may be noted that the Romans seldom had built-in upholstery
upon their couches and chairs. They depended upon removable cushions and apparently they had no metal springs.

than those used in a later age. There are few carpets, no
great loss in view of the beautiful mosaic floors, although
there are rich, heavy portières across many passages. The
chairs, frequently of light and elegant workmanship, are as
a rule simple and often backless. Some, however, are splendidly inlaid with silver, and there are a few great *cathedræ*,
ponderous arm chairs with lofty
backs.

ALTAR WITH DESIGN OF A CU-
RULE CHAIR.

In the atrium, moreover, there
stands an object surveyed with
great pride by Calvus's children
— their father's *sella curulis*, the
folding, backless arm chair with a
seat of leather straps which the
senator had occupied while prætor. Presently (they hope) he
will sit again thereon before the
admiring Senate house, this time
presiding as the veritable consul.
The " curule chair," despite its
gold and ivory arms and cushions
covered with purple Alexandrian
fabrics, is anything but a comfortable seat through a tedious
official ceremony ; but who
thinks of personal comfort when reckoning the glories of its
public occupancy !

Besides the chairs there are everywhere the tables.   These
are numerous but low and small.   In the dining room they are
round and barely two feet in diameter ; but what a wealth
of art and taste has gone into their making ! All are of
extremely fine wood, but the three reserved for the regular
couches of the dinner guests have their legs overlaid with
plates of magnificently embossed gold, and the material

upon the tops is composed of single thin slabs cross-sawn
from the trunks of the great citrus trees (a form of cypress)
on Mount Atlas.

This wood can be finished to show an exquisite wavy pattern or curly veins — "tiger citrus," "panther citrus," or
"peacock-tail citrus" — the experts call the varieties.
Over really fine specimens true connoisseurs go into ecstasies,
and fortunes can be wasted. A table somewhat larger than
Calvus's has been known to sell for 500,000 sesterces ($20,000),
and there is a record price of twice that figure. The tables
in the present mansion are nowhere nearly so valuable; yet
they are among the most precious objects in the house. If
there is a fire, they will be rescued almost before anything
else, always barring the waxen *imagines*.

44. Chests, Cabinets, Water Clocks, and Curios. — Of
course there are many other articles of furniture like the
great *arca*, the master's strong box in the tablinum; heavily
locked and riveted down upon the stone beneath. There
are the elegant tall candelabra, of bronze or even of silver,
elaborately ornamented and swinging at night with such bat-
teries of olive-oil lamps as to make the marbles, frescos, and
mosaics give back an alluring glitter. There is the water
clock in the peristylium, a kind of glorified hour-glass, so
adjusted as to record small fractions of time, and beside
which a special slave usually stands all day long to call off
the passage of each hour to the family. There are great
cabinets, chests, and cupboards full of plate, fine blankets, and
extremely elaborate wardrobes.

In addition to all these upon a kind of sideboard there
stand forth real or alleged objects of value or antiquity, a
silver cup taken at the capture of Syracuse; a tall black and
red vase signed by the master potter Callisthenes; and a
statuette of a dancing girl which is probably a true work of
Lysippus. Conspicuous, too, is a silver bowl, battered and

discolored, and of extreme simplicity.   Mock it not, however, it is "the ancestral salt cellar" (as remarks Horace), the one silver dish possessed by the good old Calvi, when in all the Roman Senate there was only a single complete silver dinner service to be exchanged from house to house when high officials entertained ambassadors.

45. Spurious Antiques. — Publius Calvus is happy in possessing undeniably genuine antiques.   He can afford to laugh at the collection of the rich freedman across the way. That poor fellow, anxious to "keep in style" and to display an art collection, has fallen into the clutches of unscrupulous dealers.   He has filled his atrium with absurd specimens such as "cups from the table of Laomedon, a double vase that belonged to Nestor and a tankard used by Achilles." His citrus tables are of very thin veneer, and in his atrium his impossible wife has actually on display a ponderous golden box in which her husband's first beard is deposited. It is also gossiped about that this crude fellow actually pretended sickness lately, merely that he might receive condoling friends in bed and display to them the gold chasings on the bedstead, the magnificent scarlet coverlets, and proclaim his riches by having the mattress steeped in expensive perfumes.

46. Pet Animals. — One thing more must be stated about the house of the Calvi before passing to its human denizens. There are a great many tame animals in evidence.   Over the doorway one already notes the caged magpie.   From a dark corner within a large cage blinks a morose-looking owl. The master's fine greyhound has a litter of puppies which are now scrambling around the peristylium with a special slave to look after them.   Behind a column is seen gliding a slinky civet.   The children delight in a small monkey tethered now in the garden.   Gratia especially has her own be-

loved lap dog and its personal slave-boy custodian. She
does not, however, imitate a certain female friend who
dotes upon snakes, and who has a whole cage of the creatures which she often twines about her neck to scare her
companions.

So much for the material aspects of a Roman insula and a
Roman domus. It is time to examine their inhabitants.

CHAPTER IV

ROMAN WOMEN AND ROMAN MARRIAGES

47. Honorable Status of Roman Women. — Calvus is the lordly senator when his litter swings him down to the Curia by the Old Forum to participate in what is still the most venerable council in the world, but in his own house his authority is divided. He is not even sure that one-half the power is really his. In all private matters his sway is shared by his spouse Gratia.

Many are the evils inflicting Imperial Rome, but oppression of women is not one of them. By the age of Hadrian it has long since come to pass what Cato the Elder sadly predicted three centuries earlier, when Roman women were learning the way to freedom: " On the day that women are our equals, they will be our masters."

Roman women are, indeed, excluded from seats in the Senate and from the long-defunct right to vote in the public assemblies.[1] They cannot command armies nor receive governorships, although every now and then an angry senator vainly proposes a resolution that governors shall not take their wives along with them to their provinces, lest the latter constitute themselves the real rulers of the district. Women do not act as judges or jurors. Nay more: legally they are under legal disabilities calculated to stir the rage of their " equal suffrage " sisters of a later day. They have always the status of minors, and are subject to the legal control of either father, guardian, or husband to their dying hour.

---

[1] It had been suppressed for all practical purposes soon after 14 A.D.

All this is true, yet, what of it? The jurists have long ago devised fictions of the law whereby the women have practically as complete control of their property as have their brothers; and the government of the Empire is peculiarly a government of backstairs intrigues and of secret influence. What chance have mere men against women in such warfare? Custom also assigns to women an amount of freedom in most social matters which makes Imperial Rome a feminine paradise that can only be matched by Twentieth Century America.

48. Men Reluctant to Marry. — Long since leaders of the bolder sex have had to reason with their fellow citizens on the necessity of marriage as a patriotic duty. The pragmatic old censor Quintus Metellus in 102 B.C. delivered a kind of a lay sermon: " If we could get along without wives, fellow citizens (*Quirites*) we should all spare ourselves the *tedium* of marriage, but nature has ordained that we can neither live pleasantly with wives, nor exist at all without them — therefore let us sacrifice our personal interests to those of society." After him Emperor Augustus enacted stiff laws to decrease the alarming number of bachelors, and to give special privileges to the parents of three children. This does not prevent many prominent Romans from looking upon a wife as a kind of expensive bondage often to be shunned altogether.

49. Rights and Privileges of Married Women. — The great majority of all Romans are married. Even the slaves are allowed to join in a kind of unofficial wedlock known as *contubernium*, which only a very harsh master will dissolve. As for the free married women they go everywhere and do almost everything. No husband's permission is needed when they visit the Forum or theater. They can sue and be sued or give testimony in the courts without his intervention. They manage their own property. Gratia, for example, is well off in her own right. Her estates are in charge of a dapper young freedman Ephorus, who is incessantly visiting her, and who never dreams of taking orders from her husband. So long as Gratia is barely faithful to Calvus he has no right to complain. He thanks his " Good Genius," therefore, that things are not as in his friend Probus's house, where the mistress's factotum is suspected of being on altogether too familiar terms with his fair employer.

Nevertheless, this freedom is supposed to carry with it corresponding responsibilities. Every Roman woman theoretically is responsible for her husband's good name and for the wise ordering of his family. No right-minded woman dismisses the hope that at the end they will put the great words on her tombstone : " *She counselled well. She managed well. She spun wool.*"

The control of the vast *familia* of slaves is usually in a matron's hands, a duty calculated to bring out every executive quality within her. She largely conducts the education of her sons, no less than of her daughters. No Roman is ashamed to admit (as an Athenian in Pericles's day might have been ashamed) that in the great crises of life he took the authoritative advice of his mother.[1]

A ROMAN MATRON.

[1] Witness, as most famous example, the case of Cornelia, mother of Tiberius and Gaius Gracchus. Very many other instances could be cited.

Roman civilization is, therefore, for better or worse, a civilization to which women no less than men have been suffered to apply the full powers of their genius. *It is a " hundred per cent civilization "*; whereas, that of Athens, considering the manner in which Athenian women were confined and ignored, was hardly more than a " fifty per cent civilization."

50. Selection of Husbands for Young Girls. — It is a fact, however, that in one great and vital matter Roman women are not free agents. They usually have their husbands, at least their first husbands, chosen for them by their parents. This comes to pass largely because usage requires that girls should be married so young that no rational romance on their part is really possible.

Custom amounting to law requires that a girl shall be at least twelve, and a boy fourteen before marriage. In the case of girls this minimum is often adhered to pretty closely, but betrothals can be arranged still earlier. Cicero's daughter Tullia was betrothed at ten and married at thirteen — a very common arrangement. Nobody imagined she had the least right to complain. Marriage involves a great shift in family relations, and the control of the family pertains strictly to the *pater familias* and to his *matrona*. They will ordinarily exercise loving pains in selecting a suitable spouse for a daughter, but the decision must be very largely theirs.

Boys as a rule marry much later, often not until well into manhood. They can demand inevitably a certain right of choice, although the parents still exercise a marked authority. As for bachelors, if they indulge in various coarse " affairs " with dancing girls, only very peevish persons are critical. After marriage, however, they must treat their wives with reasonable outward respect, if by no means always with austere faithfulness. In any case a girl is likely to be married off too young either to resist her parents' choice or to pick out intelligently any proper husband for herself.[1]

51. A Marriage Treaty among Noble-Folk. When Gratia's parents decided she was old enough to " become settled " they applied to a distinguished kinsman, an ex-consul, to help them to find a suitable bridegroom. This noble gentleman looked over a list of his younger friends, selected Calvus, and wrote a careful letter commending him, praising his lineage, and his firm hopes of official distinction, and telling how " he had a frank, open countenance, fresh colored and blooming and a handsome well-knit figure "; in short " he was quite the fellow to deserve so fine a girl." The great man went on to add that the favored candidate had a respectable fortune, for " though I dislike to speak of the financial aspects of the matter, still one must consider the tendencies of the day." Not one word was said as to how Gratia herself might want to be consulted; her consent was taken for granted.[2]

Gratia's parents, therefore, approached Calvus's guardian, his uncle. He being satisfied as to dowry and social adjust-ments, both young people were informed of what had been determined for them. Gratia and Calvus alike had always expected some such arrangement and capitulated with reason-able grace. The ensuing marriage, founded not on any ro-

---

[1] Readers of Plutarch will recall the story of how Appius Claudius, then "Princeps Senatus," proposed to Tiberius Gracchus at an evening banquet of the College of Augurs that he should marry Claudius's daughter. Young Gracchus promptly accepted and the older nobleman rushed home in delight (Tiberius being a great "catch"). On entering his house Claudius called out with loud voice to his wife "Antistia, I've got a husband for Claudia!" "What's all the hurry about," answered she, "unless he's Tiberius Gracchus?" Antistia evidently had to be informed first; the glad news could be broken to her daughter later.

[2] This anecdote and the quotations are all from the letter of Pliny the Younger to his friend Mauricius advising the latter (as per request for counsel) to seek the hand of Minucius Ancilianus for his niece.

mance, but on a cold-blooded study of what supposedly made for domestic happiness, in this case at least has been fortunate and fruitful. The wedded pair have come truly to love one another, and they dwell in great harmony. In this general manner marriages are arranged every day in Rome.

Of course these are first marriages. Let Gratia become a widow, or let her imitate so many of her friends and divorce her husband, and her second spouse will ordinarily be of quite her own choosing; and Calvus, of course, in selecting again, would be completely his own master.

52. A Betrothal in Wealthy Circles. — Gratia's daughter Junia is only ten, yet her parents are already beginning to think about betrothals; but only a block up the street there has just been the excitement of an actual wedding. Aulus Statilius Pomponius is only an eques, but the gods have blessed him with a hundred million sesterces ($4,000,000). He and his wife have a daughter who will inherit vast possessions, and wealth is a splendid substitute for lineage. They have found a young Gaius Ulpius Pollio, already in the Senate, who claims a distant cousinship to the Emperor himself. Pollio is none too wealthy and is already a widower, but Statilia and her mother are infinitely delighted at an alliance with the edges of an imperial house. Nothing has lacked, therefore, for an ultra-fashionable wedding, the talk of the entire capital.

First came the betrothal, a great social concourse in Pomponius's atrium, a throng of equites and senators with their wives, jewels flashing, countless tongues gossiping, with Statilia led in by her father to the center of the circle to meet the bridegroom-to-be. Statilia said not a word through the entire proceedings. All Pollio's dealings were with her father, and in clear voice the two men exchanged the legal formulas: "Do you promise to give your daughter, Statilia to me, to be my wedded wife?" said the younger man.

" The gods bring luck!   I betroth her."

" The gods bring luck!"

After that technically Statilia became a bride-elect; she was a *sponsa*. Either side had legally the right still to break the agreement, but it was socially ruinous to do so. Pollio presented Statilia with various valuable toilet articles, and especially with a ring to be worn on the third finger of the left hand, because everybody said that " a nerve ran directly from this particular finger to the heart."   It was the engagement ring of a later age almost precisely.

53. Adjusting the Dowry. — Then followed weeks of frantic preparation: the women busy with the things which always have made women busy over weddings long before the days of Romulus and Remus; Pomponius and Pollio with wrestling over the very nice legal adjustments of Statilia's dowry. How much would the old eques give in all, in cash, land, and banker's securities? How much for his daughter's special use? How much as *dos*, the funds which the new son-in-law could touch? How could the property be arranged so that if the marriage ended presently in a divorce (as spiteful wagers were already being laid that it might) the *dos* could be given back to Statilia without grievous loss of principal?

At one time the betrothal almost had to be cancelled, such extreme shrewdness was shown on both sides. But finally the matter was adjusted. Three noble friends for either side pressed their seal rings in witness to the contracts. The day came for the wedding.

54. Dressing the Bride. — Family exigencies required a springtime wedding, when there were a great many unlucky days to be avoided; but an expert Etruscan haruspex at length found a day that satisfied Statilia and her parents' scruples. On the night before the great event she laid all her playthings, her childish amulet (*bulla*), and her childish garments on the altar of the paternal Lares whose protection she was quitting forever. Then she went to bed in a *tunica recta*, a fine, yellow garment woven in one piece, supposedly an article of extremely good omen.

The next day the bride was dressed personally by her mother with unusual care. However expensive her ornaments she had to wear this same one-piece tunic next to her skin, the gown being held around the waist by a band of wool tied with a complicated "knot of Hercules." She wore, of course, all the jewels loaded upon neck, ears, arms, and fingers which by the contract she was to bring Pollio in her trousseau. Her long hair had been parted according to ancient custom by a spear into six locks, braided now with ribbons weighted down with pearls. Her shoes were of finest white leather covered with more pearls. Over her head streamed a long, gauzy flame-colored veil of silk — worth very literally more than its weight in gold.[1] Pressing down this bridal veil was a garland of flowers picked, as custom required, by the bride's own hand, and interspersed with sprigs of the sacred " verbena " herbs. Pollio, when he presented himself, was in the best gala costume of a senator, but there were no special " wedding garments " for the bridegroom, corresponding to the bridal veil.

55. The Marriage Ceremonies. — The afternoon was at hand, and the insulæ in neighboring quarters emptied their plebeian throngs to gaze at the gilded litters which went swinging up to the house of Pomponius, the armies of scarlet-clad running footmen, the pompous freedmen marching beside their patron's sedans, the bravery of purple robes, the flash of gold and of jewels. Of course, the atrium had

---

[1] All silk was imported by extremely long caravan routes from China. If this veil was actually of pure silk and not mixed with cotton, it was of enormous value.

been hung with garlands. The air inside was heavy with the perfumes of flowers, of costly unguents, and of the finest Arabian incense, while the noble guests elbowed and pushed one another to get near the altar near the tablinum and win the best sight of the happy pair.

Roman marriages are pretty strictly civil ceremonies. There is no legal requirement for any religious rites. Hardly anybody now is married according to the stale old formula of the *confarreatio*, when the betrothed couple became wedded by eating a cake which had just been consecrated by the Pontifex Maximus. A much simpler form is now used, but before the ceremony there always has to be the sacrifice.

Amid a decently pious hush a sheep is led to the side of the water tank (*impluvium*) in the atrium; the shrewd-eyed old haruspex, trailing his long robe and muttering jargon that passes for Etruscan, is aided by two skillful assistants in killing the creature promptly and avoiding disgusting gore; then in ripping open its belly and examining with expert eye the still quivering entrails. (See p. 429.) It is proper now for Statilia to turn pale and clutch the arm of her mother. What if the signs were unfavorable? " Whoever heard of bad omens being discovered at a great wedding?" cynically whispers a senator. " *Bene* — good !" announces the haruspex with a leer. " *Bene! Bene!*" echo all the guests. The soothsayer retires. The wedding can proceed.

The final ceremony is very simple. First the tablets of the marriage contract and the transfer of the dowry are produced, read, and, if not already witnessed, are signed by the proper attestors. Then a young matron-of-honor, Statilia's *pronuba*, leads the bride up to Pollio. She thrusts out her hand from under her great veil and takes the hand of her husband-elect. Everybody listens while he, and not any priest or official for him, puts the direct question : " Will you be my *mater familias?*" " Yes," answers Statilia, perhaps a little too readily; and then she asks him openly: " And will you be my *pater familias?*" " Yes," and immediately there is a general shout of congratulation.

These decisive words once spoken, Pollio, his bride, and her parents unite in placing a cake of coarse bread upon the altar, uttering brief dedications of the food to Jupiter and Juno, and also to the quaint rural gods Tellus, Picumnus, and Pilumnus who will bless the estates of the new couple. The cakes are presented in a basket held by a young boy, Statilia's cousin, her *camillus*, both of whose parents are required to be living. The company now redoubles its cry of " Good luck! Good luck! *felicitas!*" — and everybody is assuredly in excellent appetite for the ensuing wedding feast.

56. The Wedding Procession. — This is not the place for describing a great banquet (see p. 113); it is enough here to state that Pomponius is obliged to justify his wealth by a prodigal hospitality. Vain has proved Augustus's law limiting the cost of wedding feasts to one thousand sesterces ($40). Such regulations win only laughter!

As the climax after the dainties comes the distribution of pieces of the huge wedding-cake (*mustaceum*), made of fine meal steeped in new wine and served upon bay leaves. By this time everybody has drunk enough good Massic and Falernian to be excited and talkative, it has become twilight in the street, and Pomponius's chief freedman (the master of ceremonies) gives the signal: " The procession!"

In the vestibule musters a squad of flute players and torch bearers. As the music strikes up, good form requires Statilia to cast herself into her mother's arms and weep and scream violently. Good form equally requires Pollio to tear her thence with playful violence — " a remembrance," people say, "of the Romans' rape of the Sabines." Statilia promptly ceases struggling and submits cheerfully to being led through the door.

The wedding procession is an indispensable part of the ceremony. Probably if Pollio lives in another city, some family friend will now loan his residence for " leading home the bride." As it is, the bridegroom fortunately possesses a handsome house about a mile distant on the Quirinal. For all her wealth Statilia has to walk the entire way.

First go the flute players bringing the crowds out of all the insulæ when they cross the Subura; then long files of the younger guests of both sexes, talking vivaciously, and flourishing white-thorn torches; then the camillus and a youthful assistant bearing ostentatiously the bride's spindle and distaff, token of the household labors presumably ahead of her; then the bride herself, led on either hand by a boy both of whose parents are living, while a third of like good fortune carries a special torch of honor. Pollio himself walks just behind the bride, and is kept busy tossing walnuts to all the children in the crowd in token of the fact that he has now (for the second time) put away childish things. After them, with more flambeaux and in merry disorder, taking pains to exhibit their fine robes and jewels, follow all the older relatives and friends of both parties. The torchlight, the music, the brave colors, and gems gleaming out of the darkness make the scene bewitching. No wonder all the gaping crowds join in the marriage shouts " Io Talasse!"[1] or in the oft-repeated "Felicitas!"

57. At the Bridegroom's House. — The guests and many of the spectators fail not also to raise the " Fescinne songs " proper for marriage processions; old folk songs very coarse, and interspersed with extremely broad quips and personalities. At last the house of Pollio is reached. It is a blaze of light from vestibule to garden, and all the

---

[1] Possibly meaning "Hurrah for Talassus, the marriage god!" but the exact significance of this time-honored shout had probably been long since lost.

decuriæ (squads of ten) of slaves are mustered to greet their new *domina*.

At the entrance Statilia stops to wind the door pillars with bits of wool, and to touch the door itself with oil and fat, the emblems of plenty. She is then promptly *lifted* over the threshold to avoid an ill-omened stumble, and is immediately confronted by her husband who has slipped in before her and who now presents her with a cup of water and a glowing fire brand, token that she is entitled to the protection of his family Lares. Statilia accepts these and in clear voice repeats the very ancient and famous marriage formula, " Where thou art Gaius, I am Gaia " (*Ubi tu Gaius, ego Gaia*).

The invited guests now sweep inside and there is more elbowing while Statilia produces three silver coins ; one of these she gives to her husband as emblem of her dowry ; one she lays on the altar for the Lares of her new home ; one she casts back into the street, a gift to the " Lares of the Highway " who guarded the door. Then her marriage torch is blown out, and tossed away to be scrambled for as emblem of supreme good luck by all the younger guests. The matron of honor has already arranged the luxurious marriage chamber, and the happy pair are led inside and the door shut upon them, while all their friends join in the rollicking " nuptial song " just outside the portal. There is nothing left now for the guests to do but to go home ; all being invited, however, to return to Pollio's house the next day to join in a second great feast, with Statilia this time presiding as mistress of the establishment.

58. Honors and Liberties of a Matron. — Before her marriage Statilia had been a mere girl, completely controlled by her parents, unable to appear in public save under severe restrictions, and apparently with hardly a will of her own. The day after entering Pollio's house she finds herself become by one act a noble *matrona*, with the destinies of a huge retinue of slaves and freedmen at her disposal, enjoying a great property, meeting her husband's friends as their equal, going where she pleases, saying what she pleases, almost (within wide limits) doing what she pleases.

Abroad in crowds, her dress, the *stola matronalis*, secures the young married woman extreme respect. Every March, she, with all the other honorable wives in Rome, enjoys the honors of the *matronalia*, an official festival, kind of "Mother's day" devoted to celebrating the virtues of the gracious heads of each household. On this day no less than on her birthday, she receives presents from her husband, her family, and all her dependents. Finally, being a Senator's wife, when she comes to die, she probably will be entitled to a great state funeral, with a formal eulogy in the Forum as if she were a public personage. No wonder that Roman girls yearn eagerly for marriage! It is their astonishing emancipation.

59. Unhappy Marriages and Frivolous Women. — Will a fashionable alliance like that of Statilia and Pollio turn out happily? There are scoffers even among the friends who bore the torches. Nobody expects Pollio (a gay young aristocrat) to prove an example of austere faithfulness, although he must never do anything to insult his wife publicly. As for Statilia the cynics about the fair sex are very many. Long ago Ovid has written, "Every woman may be won if only she's rightly tempted." If a young wife is light-minded, she has plenty of opportunities to acquire lovers, and at the great festivals and banquets, at the theaters, gladiator fights, and circuses women have every chance to meet intriguing men without interference by their husbands.

The very fact that as unmarried girls Roman matrons were denied all chance for lawful romances, now makes devious love affairs seem all the more racy. Any number of fine ladies have indulged in unwise "friendships" with dissolute actors, public dancers, or even gladiators. In many a mansion there is a handsome freedman or even a slave who can become extraordinarily familiar with his mistress. There are said to be coarse-grained mothers who actually teach their married daughters how to push intrigues and to smuggle in or out love-letters under the very noses of their husbands; and there are plenty of young men, rich, "noble," and very idle, who spend their time philandering with married ladies.

With every deduction and allowance for scandal the number of such unsteady women is very great. "What snakes are driving you mad," cried Juvenal, "that you think of taking a wife? Why not leap from a high window or from the Æmilian bridge rather than submit to a she-tyrant?"

However, even if women lead lives that are outwardly respectable, there are plenty of minor charges against Roman ladies. Some are utterly extravagant; haunting the fine shops along the Via Lata and running up ruinous bills. Some are laughed at for taking up music, poetry, or Greek antiquities as shallow fads and "chattering in a mixture of Latin and Greek, and making their tongues go incessantly like a gong." Some are said to take fencing lessons and to waste their days practicing on a dummy antagonist with a foil, and learning to handle a shield as if intending to join the army. Others are never happy unless they know all the latest news : "What the Thracians and the Seres (Chinese) are doing "; "Who has just married a notorious widow "; "Whether a comet threatens the King of Parthia." Others are utterly selfish and heartless ; they will weep at the loss of a pet sparrow, but treat their slave girls with hideous brutality, and "let a husband die to save a lap-dog's life." Worst of all are certain women actually suspected of giving their unloved husbands a dose of poison when various reasons make a divorce inconvenient.

60. Divorces, Easy and Frequent. — However, divorce is the regular outcome of very many unlucky marriages. Every Roman girl, when her parents tell her " We have chosen for you "; knows in the back of her mind : " Marriage will give me freedom. If this wedlock isn't a success, my next husband will probably be my own choosing."

The first divorce mentioned in Roman history was in 231 B.C. when a certain Ruga put away a truly beloved wife, out of a high sense of public duty — because she bore him no children. The public was shocked at such action then, but soon it was shocked no longer. Under the later Republic lucky was the nobleman or noblewoman who was not divorced at least once. Cicero divorced Terentia after a long wedded life seemingly because he wanted a new marriage portion ; Cato the Younger (immaculate Stoic) repudiated his wife to please a friend, then calmly took her back again at the friend's death.

Under the Empire things hardly seem to have become any better. " Trial marriages " are not a recognized institution ; but surely they exist. It is direfully easy for either a man or woman to take the initiative. No court proceedings are necessary. " Take away your property !" spoken formally and before witnesses is sufficient to break up the household, although the more usual method is to " *send a messenger* "; *i.e.* dispatch a delegation of friends to the other party to break the news. Vainly did Augustus try by legislation to make divorces less prompt and convenient. The whole proceeding is still grievously popular and simple.

Of course, divorced persons are under no stigma in the fashionable set. Many a time a couple has separated, married elsewhere, separated again, and then resumed the old wedlock. Women are charged with " flitting from one home to another, wearing out the bridal veil "; and indeed, spicy instances are cited of ladies who boasted " eight husbands in five autumns, a fact worthy of commemoration on their tombs "; or of reckoning the years not by the annual consuls but by their annual husbands.

61. Celibacy Common: Old Families Dying Out. — Under such conditions what wonder many a rich Roman prefers celibacy! They often proclaim the " advantages of child-lessness." Old men of property without children are fawned upon with offers of every kind of service. Social and even public honors are thrust upon them. Their atria are crowded every morning with genteel visitors; their least wishes anticipated — all in the desperate hopes that " when their tablets are opened " they will have remembered the swarm of lackeys in their wills. Indeed, adventurers have been known to go far in Rome by making a false show of wealth, concealing the fact they actually have children, and " seeming bilious and complaining of indigestion." Every-body apparently will give them favor or credit. It is a familiar scandal.

Under such circumstances what wonder most of the old Republican families have died out by the age of Hadrian, that the Calvi feel very isolated; and that of the strictly patrician families only the famous Cornelii appear now to survive.

62. Nobler Types of Women. — But do the above stories represent the true moral condition of most women in Rome? Certainly not, or society could not exist. In the first place such women represent the rotten crust of the nobility; the ordinary equestrian and middle-class women are still rela-tively modest and moral, efficient managers, good mothers, and, if they are poor, hard workers. In the second place, even among the upper Senatorial nobility, there are plenty of matronæ of the very best type; true props to their hus-bands, wise mothers to their children, kindly mistresses to their slaves.   Gratia has many friends whose households are schools of virtue, and many a Roman, from the Imperial Augustus down, has confessed that his wife has been his tower of strength.

63. Famous and Devoted Wives. — People still talk of the famous Arria, wife of Cæcina Pætus, who, when the Emperor Claudius ordered him to commit suicide, and he could hardly pluck up courage for a manly exit from life,

WEDDED PAIR WITH CAMILLUS   (Boy Attendant).

as an example plunged the dagger in her own breast, then held it out to her husband, saying, " Pætus, it doesn't hurt me."   Her own daughter, the younger Arria, and Fannia, the wife of the philosopher Helvidius Priscus, grossly murdered by Nero, won hardly less reputations for fortitude.   Pliny the Younger has recorded a more humbly born Italian dame, who, when her husband was suffering from incurable ulcers, but lacking the hardihood to kill himself alone, tied herself to him and with him jumped into the lake at Larium so that both were drowned.

Fortunately the days of tyrannous emperors seem long since over.   Wives usually can show their virtue by living for their husbands and not by dying with them.   Rather lately there passed away an old man, Domitius Tullus.   Vast was his wealth but it brought him no pleasure ; he was so crippled and racked in every limb " that he could only enjoy his great riches by looking at them. He was so helpless that he had to get others to clean and wash his teeth." He had a young and a very pretty wife; but so far from neglecting him or trying to hasten his end, she kept him alive for years by extraordinarily faithful personal care. Lately, too, the venerable Senator Macrinus has lost his wife, " who if she had lived in the good old days would have been counted an exemplary woman. They lived together for thirty-nine years, with never a single quarrel or disagreement." [1]

These are simply random cases. Of course, many people know the tribute Pliny the Younger paid to his own wife Calpurnia, much younger than himself but absolutely devoted to her husband: " She has a keen intelligence, she is wonderfully economical, and she loves me." He went on to add that she read all his literary effusions most carefully, sat behind a curtain to listen when he gave public recitations before a male audience, and that when he had to argue in court had relays of runners to keep her informed as to how well he was impressing the judges. When the twain were separated she " would embrace his letters as though they were himself," while he (if he got no new letters from her) " would read over her old letters and take them up again and again as though they were new ones."

SEATED NOBLEWOMAN.

---

[1] Both of these instances are from Pliny the Younger.

64. The Story of Turia. — One day when Gratia had caught young Junia overhearing a very uncanny story of a rich old lady who kept a whole troupe of profligate actors for her own private amusement, she took her out upon the magnificent avenue of stately tombs along the Appian Way to visit the memorial to a venerated ancestress, a certain Turia who had lived in the troubled days of the Second Triumvirate, and who by her rare courage, fortitude, and intelligence had saved her husband the noble Vespillo from disgrace and death.

Turia's husband in a long inscription recited how she had saved his life in the Civil Wars at sore peril to her own, and how she had lived with him afterward in perfect affection and harmony, although, being childless, such was her devotion to him that she actually offered to let Vespillo divorce her that he might have children by a second marriage, promising very literally " to be a sister " to his new wife. But her husband repudiated the strange idea with anger : " That you should have ever thought it possible we could be separated save by death was most horrible to me. The one sorrow that was in store for me was that I was destined to survive you."

And thus the tablet concluded : " You were a faithful and obedient wife; you were kind and gracious, sociable and friendly; you were assiduous in your spinning; you followed our family and national religious rites and admitted no foreign superstitions; you did not dress conspicuously, nor make any kind of household display. Your management of our house was exemplary; you tended my mother as carefully as if she had been your own. You had innumerable other excellencies, common to the best type of matrons, but these I mention are peculiarly your own."[1]

---

[1] For a complete quotation of this highly interesting tablet, see Fowler's "Social Life at Rome," pp. 159–167.

Turia has been dead over a hundred years, but there are still high-born women in Rome who are her equals. One of them, Calvilla, has a fine young son now about thirteen, who owes an infinite debt to his mother, and whom the Emperor will presently select as the heir presumptive to the throne. History will call him Marcus Aurelius.

CHAPTER V

COSTUME AND PERSONAL ADORNMENT

65. The Type of Roman Garments. — How is it possible
to mention Roman women and Roman weddings without
thoughts also of Roman costume and personal adornment?
Seldom, indeed, has there been or will there be an age in which
fine wearing apparel, and jewelry, and elaborate hair dressing
can occupy so great a place in the thoughts of both sexes as
it does in this era of the Roman Empire.

Good clothes and fine rings are in fact so important that
if you do not possess them, on many social occasions you must
hire them. There were several guests at Statilia's wedding
who appeared in gala robes with handsome jewels to match.
With them went attendants who passed for confidential freedmen; yet it was whispered they were actually the agents of
costume purveyors charged to see that every hired banqueting gown and topaz-set ring was promptly returned.

Roman garments are like the Greek: they **are usually**
wrapped on, they are not like those of a later age which must
be *put on*. Pins, buckles, and brooches usually take the place
of buttons. Sometimes, however, costumes of a different
type can be met with in the cosmopolitan crowds in the fora.
Occasionally are seen Persians and Parthians wearing tight-
fitting leathern casings around their lower limbs, like the
articles that another day will style " trousers "; and more
frequently are met blond or red-headed Gauls wearing *cara-
callæ*, close-fitting garments with long sleeves, slit down in
front and reaching to the knee.[1] Such dresses are, however,

[1] The use of this garment gave his familiar nickname to the Emperor
Bassianus, "Caracalla," who reigned 212–217 A.D. The Gauls also had

exceptional.   Loose shawl-like apparel prevails in Rome just
as with nearly all the classical Mediterranean peoples.

66. The Toga, the National Latin Garment. — But
Roman tailors have never been servile imitators of Sparta
or Athens.   Long before Greek costumers became familiar
visitors by the Tiber, the Latin folk had found their own na-

ROMANS WEARING THE TOGA.

tional garment — the *toga*.   Every true Roman is proud of
the right to wear this distinctive garment, and its use is prohibited to non-Romans, however princely or wealthy.   A
group of ex-slaves has just come from the prætor, where their
master has emancipated them — thereby making them
Roman citizens.   In a body they are flocking to the clothiers'

---

a kind of trousers.   This was counted against them as a token of sheer
barbarism : *bracatæ nationes* ("trouser-wearing peoples") was a term of
extreme contempt in Italy.

stalls whence they can emerge as arrogant *togati* — lawful
members of the imperial race.   An unfortunate senator has
lately been condemned for malfeasance in office and sentenced
to banishment.   It is not the least of his penalty that he
must also divest himself of his toga : it can never be worn by
a degraded exile.   Clients have to wear this gown *de riqueur*
when they visit their patrons in the morning — he would
feel insulted if they omitted it.

Anybody also having the least official business at the palace
must wear the toga ; and the reigning Hadrian has just
issued an edict commanding all senators and equites to wear
the garment on the city streets at all times except when returning from dinner parties ; while the distinguished rhetorician Titus Castricius has lately delivered a public lecture,
— probably by imperial request, on " the proper costume for
senators walking about Rome, " urging obedience to the law.
The toga in short occupies a place in Roman manners hardly
equaled by any other garment in any other nation.

Nevertheless, many a client or nobleman, as he dons this
mantle, inwardly curses the folly of the men of " the good old
times " in selecting the toga as the national garment.   It is
very hot, very clumsy, very hard to drape around one's self
without expert assistance.

Everybody knows the story of old Cincinnatus, how when
he was out plowing and the committee of Senators suddenly
appeared to say, " You are named dictator ; make haste to
save the imperilled army " ; would not receive them until his
wife had run and fetched his toga and he was suitably clad.
In his day, however, the toga was almost the only garment
worn and was hardly more than a small-sized woolen shawl.
Now one always wears a *tunica* as a house and undergarment,
and the toga has been growing ever larger and more elaborate.
Dandies still wear togas so huge as to justify Cicero's sneer :
" They wrap themselves in *sails* not in togas."   But even for

decent citizens the garment is disagreeably complicated. The use thereof is one of the penalties for the splendid right to boast, " Civis Romanus sum ! "

67. Varieties of Togas. — The normal toga is always of wool and is usually of a dull white, the natural color of the wool; but in the Republican days seekers for election to public office would have their togas bleached to a conspicuous snowy whiteness, and hence their name, *Candidati* — " extra-white " men. Boys wear the *toga prætexta*, a toga with an elaborately embroidered purple hem. When they put this off on reaching manhood (fourteen to sixteen) they proudly assume the pure white toga, inwardly hoping, however, that they can some day reappear in the *prætexta* — for it is also the official robe of the high " curule " magistrates.

More glorious still is the *toga picta* entirely of purple and with gold embroidery, which can be worn by great officials while they are presiding over public games, and which is used by the Emperors on all state occasions. Quite different, of course, is the gloomy *toga pulla*, dyed to some dark color, and worn as mourning or to excite sympathy in some threatened calamity; *e.g.* if one is the defendant in a dangerous lawsuit.

68. Draping the Toga. — The plain white toga, however, suffices in most cases for most Romans. Of course, there is a vast difference between the dirty shawls not without moth holes, which some of Calvus's clients have thrown around them the morning we visit his mansion, and the garment which his special valet, Parmenio, drapes about him when presently the Senator announces, " I must visit the Forum."

Parmenio has to be assisted by no less than three other slaves while he literally winds the soft white mass of fine Milesian wool around his master. When skillfully draped, the toga appears to be an easy and elegant garment, leaving

the right arm at liberty, and flowing around the person in
noble lines implying dignity and deliberation. Well can it
be called " one of the handsomest dresses ever worn by man";
but who can tell the pains required to get the huge semi-
circular fabric into shape.[1]

Every fold has to settle with precision; every corner has
to trail to exactly the right length; and the whole has to be
so adjusted that Calvus can walk easily without fear of dis-
locating his toga, although it is without brooches or other
fastenings. When at last, however, all is ready, the results
justify the effort. Its wearer appears every inch a Senator:
one of the leaders of the arrogant imperial race.

69. The *Tunica*. — The toga has to be worn everywhere
in public, but the instant he is back from the hot Forum, Calvus is more than glad to fling it off. Indoors he, with all other
Romans, wears the *tunica*. The tunic is a comparatively
new garment in Italy. In early Rome probably the toga was
the only clothing worn at all except a simple undershirt or
loin cloth. The tunic in fact resembles closely the Greek
chiton,[2] and is made much the same for men and for women.
It is a kind of long shirt fashioned by sewing two pieces of
cloth together, with holes for the arms or with short sleeves,
and secured around the waist by a girdle. Long sleeves
(Gallic style) are not unknown but they are accounted very
effeminate. Without the belt the tunic falls well down to the
ankles, but it is easily shortened by drawing the cloth up

---

[1] Probably there were simpler and more complicated forms of togas.
The first were apparently shaped like an irregular semicircle. We hear
of extremely large togas (in bad taste) whereof the total length was four
yards before draping. Experiments in certain American universities at
making and then draping a toga corresponding in effect to many well-
known statues have amply illustrated the great difficulty of putting on
the garment gracefully, and the real art required of a Roman nobleman's
valet.

[2] See "A Day in Old Athens," p. 44.

through the girdle and letting it tumble around the waist in a loose fold.

In warm weather the tunic is often the only garment that a Roman wears indoors. In cold weather he will put a second tunic (or two or three extra, as did Augustus) under his outer one. Like the toga the tunic is ordinarily made of white wool, the finer the better, but, unlike the toga, if the wearer is of the nobility, the tunic is never plain. When the owner is an eques a narrow strip of purple (*angusticlavia*), if a senator a broad strip (*laticlavia*), runs down the entire length of the garment both behind and in front. This is the official token of his rank, that all men may reverence his nobility, and one of the chief tasks of a great man's valets is to hang the toga so that the purple strips on the tunic will always peep out conspicuously from the undergarment.

70. Capes, Cloaks, and Gala Garments. - - The toga and the tunic are the two standard male garments in peace times, but they do not meet every requirement. On festival days, unless the imperial edict is very strictly enforced, most of the younger citizens will be seen streaming to the theater or circus in the *lacerna*. This, at first, was merely a short sleeveless mantle of light stuff thrown over the toga to protect against dust or rain. Presently it was made into a more festive garment, usually of brilliantly dyed wool, and was substituted for the toga outright. There is a hood usually attached and it is convenient, therefore, to wear the lacerna if one is not anxious to be recognized on the streets; it is so very easy to conceal one's face.

In bad weather, and with poor country people in general, however, the *pænula* is more useful. This is much like the lacerna, a sleeveless ("Shaker") cloak or cape, also provided with a hood, but always made of coarse heavy material. Most travelers wear the pænula, and it is a common garment for the slaves.

Like the pænula in turn is a third type of swinging cloak, but usually cut shorter, — the *sagum*, issued to soldiers. Sometimes it is of rough material for the severest purposes, sometimes it is a truly elegant garment for officers, floating in bright colors over flashing armor. The generals wear a special sagum of conspicuous red, the *paludamentum*. The sagum is, in fact, so decidedly the military cloak that the phrase " changing the toga for the sagum " has become a regular way of saying " being suddenly called to arms."

One can see many Oriental and Greek-style garments in Rome, but native gentlemen have only one other article of apparel that must be mentioned. Everybody ought to keep a gauzy and brilliantly dyed *synthesis* for indoor wear at formal dinner parties, to wear over the tunic. It can never be worn outdoors except during the jolly riot of the Saturnalia, but indoors it is light, comfortable, and a fine contrast to the heavy togas. Saffron, amethystine, and azure are the favorite colors, and at ultra-fashionable parties it is good form for a male guest to rise between courses and put on a new synthesis of a different hue, held ready by his slaves.

71. Garments of Women : the *Stola* and the *Palla*. — Calvus, of course, keeps many specimens of all these garments in his wardrobe. The average poor citizen gets along with a toga, a tunic or two, and probably a pænula. Gratia's clothes chests and presses are inevitably more ample than her husband's, but the garments of a Roman lady resemble those of a Greek — they are far more like the masculine garments than are those of women of a later age. Gratia really seldom wears any save three kinds of garments : her tunics, her stolæ, and her pallæ.

Roman ladies anxious about their figures cannot squeeze themselves with corsets, but sometimes they do wear bands of soft leather pressed tightly around their bodies. Then comes the tunic, extremely like the inner tunic worn by the

men, but it fits the body rather more closely; sometimes it
has no sleeves, and it falls only to the knee and it needs no
belt. Over this single garment is the essential dress of the
Roman matrona, her *stola*. It is decidedly more elaborate
than the outer tunic of the men. In the main it is not sewn,

but is held together by a
whole series of clasps and
pins — giving an admirable
opportunity for the display
of gem-set buckles. There is
a girdle, passing high, above
the waist; the many folds
tumble to the feet, but at the
very bottom there is an embroidered flounce or hem, and
with noble women at least
this flounce is always of
purple as is the border around
the neck.

Like the toga, the stola is
an extremely ample garment,
giving its owner a chance to
display innumerable graceful
folds; and like the toga, good
taste requires that it should
usually be of clear white.
To wear the stola is the
proud privilege of Roman

A Roman Matron: showing the
stola and *palla*.

matrons, and in it no woman of light character is permitted to flaunt herself.[1] Girls put on the stola immedi-

---

[1] There were various simpler garments, similar to the stola, permitted
to common women and to young girls. The distinctive feature of the
stola, forbidden to all save honorable matrons, seems to have been the
lower flounce, reaching to the feet.

ately after their marriage, and even more than the toga it is a garment of grace, permitting beautiful poses of statuesque dignity.

Outdoors a Roman lady will wrap herself in her *palla*. This is merely a large shawl, although often with elaborate arrangement. Gratia's maids usually throw one third of its length over her left shoulder, letting the end trail almost to her feet, while the remainder is carried behind the back and wound skilfully around the wearer, although if a head covering is needed, one can draw up some of the cloth and form a loose and convenient hood.

Every woman in Rome possesses a palla; and the wealthy, of course, own whole arsenals of them in every possible size, weight, material, color, and embroidery, suitable for all purposes from winter travel to snaring susceptible youths beside one in the theater.

72. Materials for Garments. Wool and Silk. — So much for the types of garments. Needless to say that their fabrics and details are infinite. *Wool* is still the standard material. Even now " in these degenerate days " the best Roman matrons keep the spindles and distaffs working with their maids in the peristylia, and make up a large part of all the coarser garments needed by the household. Calvus takes pride in wearing and exhibiting a really handsome toga and in telling his friends " my Gratia made that "; but various other senators can utter like boasts, their wives merely imitating such empresses as Livia, who wove all Augustus's everyday garments.

On the great villa estates the slaves are kept from busy idleness in winter by weaving cloth, not merely for themselves, but for their masters' families in the city. But such fabrics, ordinarily, are decidedly coarse. There are really fine woolens made in southern Italy, but the very best comes from the East. " Milesian wool " is a trade name in every market, though very likely much of it actually is from Tyre, Sidon, or Alexandria. A good deal of linen is woven up into comfortable house dresses. Enough cotton comes in from the Orient to make it no rarity for superior garments, but it is too scarce for any common use. What every Roman of fashion dotes upon, however, is *silk*.

Far away in the East is a half-mythical land, *Serica* or *Seres*. Hardly any European has ever penetrated there,[1] but caravan traders pass along small parcels of a wonderful material alleged to grow on trees. Garments made thereof are incomparably lovely; but the material is worth its full weight in gold or even more. As a result the stuff is spun up into the flimsiest and gauziest gala dresses imaginable, and these are often partly made of cotton. Seneca has written in disgust " We see silken garments, if indeed, they can be called ' garments ' which neither afford protection to the body, nor concealment to modesty." For all that women like Statilia and her mother will be miserable if they have not plenty of " Serician tissues " wherewith to float into the Amphitheater or Circus and dazzle their rivals in a city where, as complains Juvenal: " Everybody always dresses above his means."

73. Styles of Arranging Garments. Fullers and Cleaners. — With garments so simple in their sewing as togas and stolas there is little call in Rome for exclusive tailoring establishments or for fashionable makers of " gowns." Practically all purchased clothing, however costly, is " ready-made," although the shifting styles in girding, arranging the folds, buckles, etc., are infinite. For example, there is a special arrangement of the toga in peculiarly ample folds known as

---

[1] About twenty years after the reign of Hadrian, Chinese annals record that certain "Roman" (Græco-Levantine?) traders actually reached China, and gave themselves out as envoys to the "Son of Heaven" from "Antun" (Antoninus Pius).

the " Gabinian cincture," and this form is practically required
every time a man joins in an important sacrifice.

If, nevertheless, the dressmaker's skill is simple, there is
constant demand for that of the *cleaner's*, whose art is
brought to great perfection. The huge squares of fine woolen
seem continually going to or coming from the fullers' establishments. The fullers pass for peculiarly jovial, friendly
people, and the " jolly fuller " is a stock character in
comedy.

Soap is a Gallic invention and it is just coming into fairly
common use. Garments are still cleansed, however, with
"fuller's meal," a kind of alkaline earth. Wherever you go
around the humbler parts of Rome you hear a monotonous
song being trolled over and over, and coming usually from a
pungently smelling establishment. It is the fullers' *tripu-
dium* ("three step "), sung as they tread out the clothes in
the great vats all day long. After the direct cleaning, a fine
garment has to be recarded to bring up the soft nap, then it is
carefully smoothed in a large wooden press with powerful
screws.[1] Every household can do its own laundry work, but
in no later age will the " cleaner " reign with the supremacy
which he enjoys in Rome. His justification comes when, at
great public assemblies, thousands of togas and stolas veri-
tably shine under the Italian sun like newly fallen snow.

74. Barber Shops. The Revived Wearing of Beards.
— Rome, too, is a city of barbers. Their shops abound
everywhere and are great places for lounging and gossip.
Most men have their hair clipped quite short, although a
good many dandies delight in wearing fringes or rows of short
crisped curls (as did Nero) often reeking with pomatum.
People who dislike appearing old sometimes use black hair
dye; and not a few elderly senators are said to wear wigs.

---

[1] Very like a modern copying press.

The barber shops, however, have recently received a terrific blow; and loud is the lament of the entire profession shared in by all those private " house barbers " who care for the wealthy.   Since not long after 300 B.C. Romans have been smooth shaven, beards ordinarily being counted the sign of rusticity or of poverty; although teachers of philosophy wore long whiskers as a kind of professional badge.   The day when

SCENE BEFORE A BARBER SHOP.

a youth shaved off his first beard was celebrated almost as elaborately as the day he assumed the pure white " manly " toga.   But to general consternation the reigning Emperor Hadrian, in his passionate admiration for Periclean Athens, has astonished all Rome by appearing with a full beard.   Of course, every courtier and government official has loyally imitated him.   Of course, every senator and eques has with equal loyalty done likewise.   Feminine protests have been

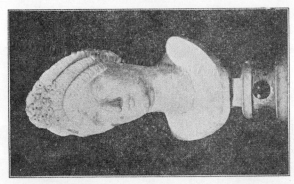

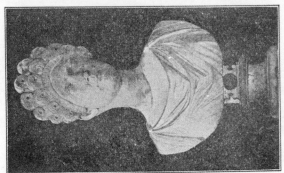

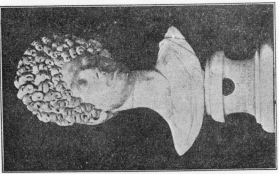

Roman Female Heads : showing elaborate arrangement of the hair.

utterly vain.   Beards, sometimes closely trimmed, sometimes long and venerable, have blossomed on almost every manly chin across the entire Empire.   Imperial Rome will henceforth continue bearded until the era of Constantine, nearly two hundred years, when the razor will suddenly resume its sway.   Such is the power of Cæsarian example!

75. Fashions in Women's Hairdressing.   Hair Ornaments. — If the barbers are unhappy, their gentler rivals, the *ornatrices*, who dress the hair of ladies, still reign in full glory.   No Roman girl dreams of cutting off her hair, but the modes of arranging it are, as says Ovid, " More numerous than the leaves on the oak or the bees on Mount Hybla."   Fashions come and go with astonishing rapidity, and we have seen how Gratia's statue was devised so that a new coiffure could be substituted for the old (see p. 53).

As a rule young girls bind back their hair in simple coils or clusters of curls, but some of the styles permitted to them from the moment they become matrons defy easy description. The prevailing mode rather favors building up the hair in an elaborate semicircular mound in front with ringlets and plaits behind ; but many a lady appears with a perfect towerlike structure that would collapse instantly were it not an affair compacted with extreme art.   Of course, such edifices put a premium on false hair, preferably blonde from Germany, or even on wigs.   Auburn hair, however, is extremely fashionable, and many a lady buys the expensive " Batavian caustic " supposed to bleach to the proper shade.   Even very modest women can rejoice in great treasure chests of hair ornaments, elaborate hair pins, and combs made of precious metal or fine boxwood, ivory, and tortoise shell ; besides all kinds of snoods and wimples usually of scarlet, amethystine, or ivory.   Noble dames will keep at least one *diadem*, a long band of golden chains set with as many pearls and jewels as possible.   On simple social occasions they will wear

their hair in a net of gold thread.   As for the very wealthy,
they have one simple and favorite method of displaying their
riches — that of bidding their maids, almost every day, to
sprinkle the whole coiffure liberally with pure gold dust.

76. Elaborate Toilets. — Needless to say, the toilet is, to
ladies of fashion, a slow and serious business, consuming most
of the morning.[1]   Statilia's mother, for example, who is now
old enough to have to guard her complexion, has as her first
duty that of suffering her maidens to peel off the thick layer
of cosmetic paste smeared upon her face ere retiring.   She
complains that her husband is stingy because he will not let
her imitate Poppæa (Nero's Empress), who took a bath in
asses' milk every morning to improve her looks.

Such a lady, of course, requires two maids to dress her and
to pile the masses of hair upon her head; the pair being supported and directed by an old freedwoman who " assists at the
council," skilfully improves and flatters, and who perhaps
can do something to assuage the domina's fury if the latter's
silver mirror reveals a misplaced curl, and she stabs the
clumsy maid's arm with a sharp hairpin, or even shrieks out
in wrath " Bring in the whipper!"

Blessed with such " tiers and storys" upon their heads,
Roman women seldom need anything else out-of-doors except
a veil or hood in extreme heat or bad weather.   There are no
milliners' shops along the Via Lata or Vicus Tuscus.   The
men likewise seldom bother about hats, and everybody on
normal days goes about town bareheaded, although travelers
have the hoods upon their pænulas.   Workingmen, however,
who are continually exposed to the weather, wear small
conical felt hats — the pilei; and travelers who find hoods

---

[1] Apuleius, writing probably a little later than this time, asserts that
a lady, with no matter how fine clothes or jewels, cannot be considered
really handsome unless an equal amount of attention has been bestowed
upon her hair.

irksome can keep off the sun by a comfortable broad-brimmed hat, the *petasus*.

77. Sandals and Shoes. — Shoes, however, are more necessary and nobody but a slave goes barefooted around the streets. In the house nevertheless it is sufficient to wear very light and simple sandals, mere leather soles fastened to the foot with thongs; and even these are laid aside when you stretch out on the couch for meals. To " call for your sandals " is the same thing as " leaving the table."

Outdoors one often puts on the *calceus*, which is practically like the shoe of other ages, although fastened not so much by

SANDALS.

lacings as by a complicated system of straps. Women's shoes are much like men's, although inevitably lighter and more often made of brightly colored leathers. High magistrates are proud to wear red " Patrician shoes " with an extra elaborate scheme of bands and an ivory ornament " C " conspicuous upon the outside of the ankle.[1] Ordinary senators wear red shoes without the " C "; and equites a kind of tall boot recalling the days when to be an eques really implied being a horseman. Soldiers naturally clatter about in hobnailed *caligæ*, ponderous sandals with such heavy straps and

---

[1] Called the "luna" (crescent); but the origin is really unknown, although attempts were made to trace it back to some institution of Romulus.

thongs that they become practically marching boots.   As for stockings, they are all but unknown in Rome.

78. The Mania for Jewels and Rings. — But what dandy and what fashionable woman is content to appear merely with the standard quantity of clothing?   The mania for jewelry is inordinate.   Teachers of oratory have to warn their pupils as did the great Quintilian that " the hand [of a good public speaker] should not be covered with rings, and especially these should not be set below the middle joint."   Exquisites of both sexes, in fact, often wear half a dozen rings at once; all with as fine jewels as possible, and with a separate " light " set of rings for summer, and a " heavy " set for winter.

The jewelry work is, of course, exquisite.

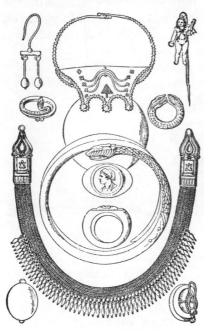

ROMAN JEWELRY AND ORNAMENTS.

In the best shops by the Campus Martius can be seen rings of magnificent chasing and carving, set with onyx, sard, banded agate, amethyst, ruby, and sapphire,[1] — some plain,

[1] Diamonds were not unknown, but they were so hard to cut and so scarce that they figured rather seldom in Roman jewelry.   They do not appear in the list of the twelve precious stones given in Revelation, **XXI**: 19–20.

some engraved, and all of a beauty which any later age can envy. Inevitably there are pendants, coronets, and innumerable brooches, and buckles every whit as fine.

In addition, every Roman of equestrian or senatorial rank will wear with pride one perfectly *plain* gold ring (like a later wedding ring) as the token of his own nobility, and as the memorial of a time when a simple gold ring was the sign of real wealth. Every person of consequence also will wear a special signet ring, often an intaglio cut with some mythological character. The impression of this frequently takes the place of a personal signature, and the illicit use of such a ring constitutes the gravest kind of forgery.

79. Pearls in Enormous Favor. — Time fails to speak of the beautiful cameos, intaglios, engraved medals, and huge engraved gems which are the triumphs of the lapidaries, and which many rich connoisseurs put in their collections; but one must not omit certain precious objects which Romans seem to prize above all others: *pearls*. The more pearls apparently that the fashionable can spangle upon shoes, dress, fingers, and (for women) upon the hair, the better. The great jewelers will say that they sell more pearls than all the ordinary gems put together.

The imperial councilors protest in vain at the ceaseless export of gold to India to pay for the unprofitable imports of pearls from Taprobane (Ceylon), but the mania for such gems continues. People still tell how Julius Cæsar gave to Servilia, the mother of Marcus Brutus, a single weight pearl worth six million sesterces ($240,000); or how the inordinately rich Lollia Paulina, one of Caligula's overnumerous wives, appeared at a dinner party, with great pearls spangled over her unlovely person worth all together every whit of forty million sesterces ($1,600,000).[1] There are no such

[1] Stories about pearls are easily multiplied: *e.g.* how the son of Asopus, a famous actor, on coming into a vast patrimony, deliberately dissolved

tantalizing collections as hers now in Rome, but many a lady of modest means has in her coffers a few pearls large and beautiful; and the cynics declare that in a crowd " the sight of a big pearl in a woman's ear is better than a lictor to clear the way for her."

80. Perfumes: Their Constant Use. — Nevertheless, something else is needful for a fine toilet beyond clothes, rings, and pearls, namely, perfumes. The old-line Italians were a coarse and hardy folk; and later the Orientals, whom slavery or self-interest has brought into Italy, have a truly barbaric love for powerful odors. Even modest women, therefore, of reputed good taste like Gratia, will appear in public charged with scents which another generation would find highly unwelcome.

There is no alcohol in which to carry perfumery. The odorous substances have to be dissolved in olive oil, making them at best greasy and liable to grow flat and obnoxious after a little exposure. But perfumery is practically indispensable. Men use it hardly less than do women. At fine banquets vials of perfumery are passed among the guests to pour over their heads and hands. The foppish youths who wave the hair on their heads, and render the rest of their bodies sleek and shiny with depilatories, simply reek with strong perfumery.

On almost every important street you can find the little shops, usually kept by women, where are sold scented powders, fragrant oils for bathers, and the precious bottles of gold, silver, glass, and alabaster for the unguents, as well as the standard perfumes themselves. Profitless it is to catalogue these last; Pliny the Elder has listed twenty-one standard varieties mostly named after favorite flowers (*e.g.* narcissus)

a large pearl in vinegar, then drank it down, in order to boast that he had "tossed off a million sesterces ($40,000) at one gulp!"

or Oriental spices (cinnamon, etc.).[1]   Every funeral demands
its supply of myrrh; every sacrifice a quantity of Arabian
frankincense.   The perfume trade with the East is an important factor in Roman commerce, but very many of the popular unguents are compounded in Italy.   The great city of
Capua in Campania grows rich by the industry;[2] and the
" perfumery interest " is one of the prime business elements
in the economic life of the Empire.   So much for the garments
and ornaments which typical Romans put upon their persons.
It is now right to ask concerning a more important matter
still — what do they have for dinner?

---

[1] Even less profitable, it would seem, is to try to list the cosmetics
wherewith many Roman ladies, like their sisters of all times, covered
their faces.   Rouge was used in great quantities, and effeminate young
men were known to have employed it.   Eyebrows were blackened with
antimony; lips were reddened, and of course hair dye was a familiar
article.   Propertius suggests that some women went so far as to trace
over the veins in their temples with blue.   Other women indulged in
small black patches somewhat as did English ladies in the days of Queen
Anne: — "There is nothing new under the sun."

[2] In Capua there was a whole great square of the city, the Seplasia,
given over to perfumery shops and their wholesale trade.

CHAPTER VI

FOOD AND DRINK. HOW THE DAY IS SPENT.
THE DINNER

81. Romans Fond of the Table. Gourmandizing. The Famous Apicius. — Seldom can there be another age when the importance of good eating and drinking occupies the place that it does in Rome. Vast numbers of coarse-grained people devoid of the least ability to criticize fine bronzes or to comprehend Homer or Virgil can go into ecstasies over superior oysters. Epicurean philosophers can argue that " the true, the beautiful and the good " are to be as genuinely apprehended by the enjoyment of ravishing tastes as by ravishing music. Gastronomy has become a kind of supreme science and art, and no slaves sell for better prices than truly expert cooks.

Repeatedly huge fortunes have been ruined merely because their possessors wished to surpass all rivals with the extravagant refinements of gluttony. Since 69 A.D. and the coming to power of the simpler Flavian Cæsars there has been a fortunate decline in many absurdities, but there are still plenty of people who admire and envy the fame of Apicius, the true example for the gourmand.

Marcus Apicius flourished in Tiberius's age; and he developed a positive genius for inventing new sources of culinary delight. Every quarter of the Roman world was ransacked to find strange objects whereon to whet his appetite. In Hadrian's day people continue to eat Apician cakes and Apician sauces, such as are described in his encyclopædic cook books. But although he inherited a hundred million ses-

ROMAN BANQUET SCENE. *After Von Falke.*

terces ($4,000,000), at last his steward reported glumly,
" You have only ten million ($400,000) left." How was it
possible for a true gourmand to exist in such poverty? —
Apicius, therefore, committed suicide rather than live on
commonplace fare! Many will tell you that he showed the
right spirit and that his busts stand as a kind of inspiration
for dozens of rich epicures in their marble triclinia.

82. Vitellius, the Imperial Glutton. — One of Apicius's
disciples, Vitellius, rose to Empire. In his brief reign (April
— December 69 A.D.) before Vespasian's troops killed him,
he taught his subjects how truly a man can live to eat. He
had trained himself by the constant use of emetics to devour
four heavy meals per day.[1] His senatorial friends, obliged
to invite him to their houses, never dared to offer him a dinner
costing less than 400,000 sesterces ($16,000). His brother
gave him a banquet at which were served " 2000 choice
fishes and 7000 birds "; but he returned the favor by giving
a feast at the imperial palace in which he served his favorites
with " The Shield of Minerva " — a kind of salad-supreme
made of " the livers of charfish, the brains of pheasants and
peacocks, the tongues of flamingoes, and the entrails of lampreys." Warships had been sent as far as the Ægean or
Spain to round up some of these viands. It was lucky for
the treasury that his reign was a very short one.

83. Simple Diet of the Early Romans. — And yet these
worthies gorged and guzzled in a city whose founders had
been famous for their abstemiousness. For many a generation even prosperous Romans had lived very largely on coarse
bread or even on a coarser wheat porridge (*puls*). Wheat
porridge was what supplied the brawn and courage to the
legionaries who brought to ruin Pyrrhus, Hannibal, Philip

---

[1] Vitellius was by no means alone in this disgusting practice. Seneca
denounced the numerous gluttons who "Vomit that they may eat, and
eat that they may vomit."

of Macedon, and Antiochus. They were fortunate if their meal was not made of barley, later counted as being barely fit for inferior slaves.

Even senators, we are told, were glad to pick a few green vegetables in their gardens to help out the porridge. On feast days there would be a little pork or bacon from the hanging rack, and if there was a public sacrifice the worshipers might each take home a lump of beef. Such was the

dietary of the men who originally made possible the fortunes of an Apicius, and as late as 174 B.C. there were no professional cooks in Rome. Now, however, there are plenty of purple-fringed exquisites who "can tell at first bite whether an oyster comes from Circeii, or the Lucerine rocks or clear from Britain; or at one glance discover the native shore of a sea-urchin."

GRIST MILL TURNED BY HORSE AND FILLED AND EMPTIED BY A SLAVE.

84. Bread and Vegetables. — However, there are still multitudes who have to be content with very simple fare, and for them bread in some form is (as with all the Mediterranean peoples) very literally "the staff of life." In the great mansions there is, of course, a bakehouse for the huge familia, but the bulk of people frequent the numerous public bakeries, near which the mills driven by patient donkeys or by less patient slaves are incessantly grinding flour.

The standard loaves are made very flat, of moderate size, and about two inches thick, their backs often marked with six or eight notches. There is a cheap bread of coarse grain (*panis sordidus*) for the humblest; a second quality (*panis secundus*) for better class purchasers, and also the very white and sweet *siligineus*. You ask for " Picenian bread " if you want fine biscuit, and for *libæ* if you desire smaller rolls. At feasts there will be wonderful structures of pastry, and by use of honey and chopped fruits sweet " cake " truly delectable comes out of many ovens.

Vegetables and fruits can hardly play the part that they will in later gastronomy : potatoes, tomatoes, oranges, lemons — all these are grievously wanting. But there are admirable cabbages, " the finest vegetable in the world," declared Cato the Elder, and turnips, the favorite dish of tough old Manius Curius, conqueror of the Samnites. Around Rome, for many miles, are long stretches of profitable truck gardens, which send an incessant supply of artichokes, asparagus, beans, beets, cucumbers, lentils, melons, onions, peas, and pumpkins into the city. A visitor to Rome should promptly accustom himself to garlic; and there is a certain fashionable rusticity about garlic eaters, as if they were trying to bring back the flavor and odor of " the good old times."

85. Fruits, Olives, Grapes, and Spices. — Italy, of course, is an excellent fruit country. In the markets are apples, pears, plums, and quinces, besides an abundance of very fine nuts, such as walnuts, filberts, and almonds. Peaches, apricots, cherries, and pomegranates are familiar, although some of these are rather late introductions to the peninsula from the East. Of course, in season there never fail magnificent olives and grapes which have abounded in Italy since time immemorial.

A great demand exists, too, for all kinds of salad greens; cresses and fine lettuce, also edible mallows. Poppy-seed mixed with honey is a standard dish for desserts, and such seasonings as anise, fennel, mint, and mustard can be bought in all the innumerable little grocery shops scattered over Rome. In the larger foodshops can be had likewise those Oriental spices in heavy demand by the epicures; and also very costly imported fruits, often preserved with great ingenuity in an age that knows not the use of canning processes, refrigerating plants, or sugar.

86. Meat and Poultry. — The demand for meat has been steadily increasing with the growth of luxury and economic prosperity. Butchers' shops abound. Poor people buy goats' flesh, which, however, is completely disdained by the finical. Many citizens nevertheless never taste beef or mutton except when it is distributed in the form of a sacrifice at some of the great public festivals; and even for the rich beef is not in extraordinary favor.

Pork, however, is always popular. The despised Jews never seem to the Romans to show their national folly more clearly than in refusing to eat thereof. Pork in all forms, especially bacon and pork sausages figure in every important banquet; and up in the Apennines in the vast acorn forests, uncounted herds of swine are always fattening to satisfy the incessant demands of the great capital. Poultry is on the whole in greater demand than meat.[1] Squawking coops of common fowl, ducks, and geese are on sale at almost every street corner. There is also good money in raising upon country preserves quantities of partridges, thrushes, and grouse, and even of cranes. In Cicero's day peacocks made a very fashionable dish, and they are still in request, although losing their old popularity. Hares, rabbits, venison are comparatively cheap, and everybody with a price can buy wild boar at the better purveyors' shops.

---

[1] The difficulty of preserving fresh meat, once butchered, would militate against its use as compared with poultry easily killed for each customer.

87. Fish in Great Demand. — Rome, however, somewhat resembles Athens in one particular; the butcher shops are less important than the fish dealers' stalls.[1] Poor people eat salt fish or pickled fish, from little sardines to slices of the big *cybium*, as forming frequently the only break in an otherwise vegetarian diet. They also make up salt fish with various vegetables and cheese into a kind of fishballs. A man of income, however, is unhappy without his fresh fish daily. This creates a serious and expensive problem for Rome. There are a few eels and pike of good flavor caught right in the Tiber between the bridges, but the great fish supply must be brought from a distance — often in warm weather without aid of refrigerating plants. Frequently along the road from Ostia, and very often down the Via Appia clear from Puteoli can be seen large wagons tearing in hot haste. They bring not government dispatches but fresh fish that will frequently command absurd prices in the city.

Often all kinds of sea-food are transported still alive in small tanks; and sometimes the distance whence they can be imported is astonishing. The best turbots (large flat fish) come from Ravenna on the Adriatic. Eels can be brought in good flavor from Sicily and even from Spain. Gourmands go into ecstasies over oysters from Circeii or Baiæ, but of late people wishing to astonish their fashionable friends have actually claimed to import such shellfish from Britain. The real fish for the epicure, notwithstanding, is by common confession the noble mullet. The flavor of the best specimens is ravishing, and, for a truly large and perfect mullet, the prices paid are astonishing. It is a common story that a certain Crispinus, a satellite of Domitian's, once gave 6000 sesterces ($240) for a single six-pound mullet; "More than the cost of the slave-fisherman!" indignantly exclaimed the outraged Juvenal.

[1] See "A Day in Old Athens," p. 20.

Many great nobles, however, disdain having to depend on the public markets. At their seaside villas they have huge salt-water tanks and artificial fishponds; therein mullet, turbot, carp, and eels can be bred, fattened, and brought to perfection, and on the day of a feast a slave will hurry them up to Rome still gasping.

88. Olive Oil and Wine: Their Universal Use. — Supplementing the salt fish and bread, the poor of the capital, like all genuine Mediterranean folk, seldom fail to get their oil and wine. Olives are gladly eaten green, ripened, or preserved in great quantities with salt or pickle, but their greatest value comes from their oil. To Rome as to Athens olive oil is not merely food; it largely takes the place of toilet soap, and it supplies also the most common illuminant (see " A Day in Old Athens," p. 177). It is a complete substitute for butter in the average dietary, often making dry or moldy bread palatable, and as earlier stated (p. 98), it is the basis for most of the ointments and perfumery wherein the average citizen delights.

As for drink, practically every Roman has his wine. There are, indeed, beverages made from wheat and barley, and also from fermented quince juice, but for daily purposes beer and distilled liquors never appear at Italian banquets. Cider is sometimes drunk, and a little so-called " wine " made from mulberries; but the enormous vineyards existing in every part of the country testify to the importance of ordinary grape wine.

Vintners' stalls are almost as common along the streets as bakeries. The drink they sell in jars, skins, or small flagons is sometimes decidedly resinous after the Greek fashion, and in any case is extremely sour, so that a large admixture of honey is often required to make the favorite sweet *mulsum*. In any case only sheer barbarians will drink their wine undiluted, and really good wine can stand as much as eight parts of water to one of itself without losing too much flavor.

89. Vintages and Varieties of Wine. — There are as many varieties of wine as there are regions around the Mediterranean.   Each produces a vintage that is tolerable, and some are highly select.   Your average poor plebeian can get a large jug of palatable stuff for a sesterce (4 cents).   The wealthy will think nothing of paying heavily for *amphoræ* (tall jars) of choice old Setinian (the best wine in Italy), or for Falernian, Albanian, or Massic which count next among the native vintages.   If, however, you are giving a formal dinner party, etiquette dictates that at least one imported drink should be served.   It makes an excellent impression to bring in Chian, Thasian, or Lesbian from the Ægean, or even Mareotian from Egypt and the splendid Chalybonium from Damascus, the delight of Oriental kings.

In summer time wines, of course, are drunk cold, and at luxurious banquets they are even chilled with snow water. In winter, however, you will often see a kind of bronze samovar, heated by charcoal, used for preparing *calda*, warm water and wine, heavily charged with spices; and at the cheap eating houses the calda counter is often thronged, especially on chilly afternoons.   Common soldiers, slaves, and plebeians of the lowest class have a special beverage all their own, namely *posca*, which is simply vinegar mixed with enough water to make it palatable.   It probably forms a really refreshing drink, if one can acquire the taste for it.[1]

Time fails to tell of various rare vintages which are treasured by the epicures as if worth their weight in gold.   In 121 B.C. there was a wonderful yield of wine called Vina Opimia from the then Consul Opimius.   By Hadrian's day

---

[1] *Posca* was probably the drink in which the sponge was steeped, that was extended to Jesus as He hung on the cross.

the last drops of this precious liquor have long since disappeared, but men still discuss the traditions of its nectarous flavor. In every great house the wine cellar retains a number of web-covered and dirty glass jars carefully sealed with gypsum, and with labels showing that they were laid away perhaps a hundred years ago. As for the undesirability of wine-drinking, that idea has hardly crossed any man's head; and Horace in Augustus's day voiced a universal thought when he sang that good wine, " Made the wise confess their secret lore; brought hope to anxious souls, and gave the poor strength to lift up his horn."

90. Kitchens and the Niceties of Cookery. — With such attention to good eating and drinking a Roman kitchen necessarily requires an elaborate equipment. Cook stoves there are none; but there are extensive masonry or brick hearths. The charcoal fire heats the stones until a broad surface is glowing and ready for remarkable culinary achievements. The head cook in Calvus's house rejoices in a great battery of copper utensils often of truly elegant shape; and copper ware (more expensive than tin, but far more durable) appears in every Roman kitchen. There are pastry molds, dippers, ladles, great spoons, little spoons, baking pans for small cakes, in short, everything to delight the heart of the housewife of another age.

Nobody expects us to investigate rudely the peculiar dishes evolved in the kitchen of a genuine gourmand. Cookery, the disciples of Apicius aver, is not a common handicraft, but the noblest of sciences. Only a thrice-initiated epicure, a man who has carefully trained his tongue to discriminate the least shades of taste, and his fingers to endure hot viands so that he may pluck out the morsels at precisely the proper temperature, can appreciate many of the refinements.

Calvus laughs, indeed, at a friend of his who lately insisted on serving " a wild boar from Lucania caught when the South wind was blowing," with "honey apples picked under a waning moon," and "lampreys caught just before spawning." Such people will also explain dogmatically that "eggs of oblong shape have better flavor than round ones;" and that "after drinking wine the appetite is better stimulated by dried ham than by boiled sausage," or that "it spoils the flavor of Massic wine to strain it through linen; but you can clear it by mixing with the lees of Falernian and then adding the yolk of a pigeon's egg."[1] A new dish coming loyally into favor is that to which Hadrian is personally so partial — a huge meat pie wherein pheasant, peacock, sow's udder, and wild-boar flesh are all baked up together.

Needless to say many coarse fellows who boast themselves "epicures" really are merely gluttons. Their appetites have become simply animal. Rome has plenty of twin-brothers to that Santra derided by Martial, who at a banquet "asked three times for boar's neck, four times for the loin, then for hare, thrushes, and oysters." After that he bolted sweet cakes, and finally devoid of all decency hid some fruit and a cooked dove in the folds of his gown and sneaked home with a small jar of wine!

91. A Roman Gentleman's Morning: Breakfast (*jentaculum*) and the Visit to the Forum. — However, even gluttons like Santra spend all the earlier part of the day under conditions of relative abstemiousness. Romans never eat three hearty meals a day; they merely stay their stomachs until dinner, the event they ordinarily look forward to from early morning. In Calvus's house everybody is supposed to rise at gray dawn. Just as the first bars of light are making darkness visible a *decuria* (squad of ten) of slaves under a chamberlain (*atriensis*) brushes down the atrium and peristylium before the master and mistress rise and are dressed by

---

[1] A long and curious list of gourmand's precepts are enumerated ironically by Horace in a familiar Satire (*Sat.*, bk. II. 4).

their body servants. As promptly as possible these noble folk are served, often in their chambers, with their breakfast, the *jentaculum* — merely a few pieces of fine bread, sprinkled with salt or dipped in wine, and with a few raisins and olives, and a little cheese added. If Calvus is now expecting to go on a journey or to put in a hard day debating in the Senate, he may however call for some eggs and a cup of heartening mulsum.

After that, the clients are let into the atrium, greet their patron with their *aves,* receive his counter greetings, and get their money doles for service (see p. 150). Next, upon an ordinary day, Calvus calls for one of his second-best togas, and issues forth. If the Senate is convening, he, of course, seeks the Curia. If not, he will often visit his banker upon the Via Sacra to talk over investments, will call at the mansion of a sick friend, will go to witness a will for another friend (a very familiar ceremony), or will go to one of the Basilicas, where still another friend is arguing a case, and expects all his best acquaintance — the more distinguished the better — to sit near him and applaud as he makes his points. During all these rounds Calvus is, of course, followed by some two dozen clients and freedmen as well as by at least as many slaves.

92. The Afternoon and Dinner-Time. Importance of the Dinner (*cena*). — After that it is near the sixth hour (12 m.). All over Rome work ceases almost automatically; the poorer classes make for the cook shops or itinerant food venders; while people of rank either go home or accept the hospitality of friends for the mid-day lunch, the *prandium.* This is a real meal, although taken as informally as possible. The food is mostly cold, — bread, salads, olives, cheeses, and meats remaining from last night's dinner; although sometimes there are hot dishes, such as hams and pigs' heads, and a good deal of common wine is drunk.

During the next hour everybody who can possibly spare the time takes a short siesta. Rome, in fact, in summer seems to have gone to sleep under the glaring sun. Then for the humbler folk toil resumes; while the fortunate classes make for the great baths where, indeed, under the guise of sociability a great deal of real business can be transacted. By the ninth hour (3. P.M.) Calvus and Gratia alike have usually finished all the formal duties for the day and are being escorted homeward preparatory to the standard climax of every four-and-twenty hours — the dinner.

The dinner (*cena*) is always eaten at home or at the house of some friend. It is so strictly personal an affair that there are almost no first-class, handsomely appointed, public restaurants in Rome, although there is a superabundance of cheaper eating houses, yet many of these close up during the afternoon. There are almost no other evening entertainments — no receptions, no balls, no theaters, no concerts.[1] But Italians in every age have been a sociable, talk-loving, gregarious people, and the dinner seems to many of them apparently the " be all and end all " of existence.

93. Dinner Hunters and Parasites (" Shadows "). — Wealthy and popular personages never have to bother about the dinner problem; every night they can invite whom they desire, or be sure of a summons to a congenial board. Plenty of substantial citizens are willing and happy to join in a simple family meal in the good old style, the master reclining on a couch, with his wife in a somewhat more conventional attitude beside him, the younger children sitting on a lower couch, the freedmen and more important slaves arranged on benches at a respectful distance.

---

[1] The very imperfect means of illumination alone available with olive-oil lamps, would make many modern evening entertainments out of the question. The ancient lamps were beautiful in shape but utterly ineffective for lighting large halls, indoor theaters, etc.

The city nevertheless abounds in shabby-genteel individuals or social climbers who are miserable every afternoon because some senator or an eques does not tell them, " Come home to dinner ! " For example, there is a certain ubiquitous Selius. He hangs about the law courts, and if a pleader is rich and noble, is always interrupting with a loud " Excellent ! " or " How clever ! " Some afternoons, however, he is seen dragging about, " the picture of misery." Has his wife just died or his steward embezzled? Not so. He " must dine alone at home." Thus there develops a type of high-class parasites, " *shadows*," men of thick hide and nimble wit who snap at every possible excuse for thrusting into a dinner party, and who are willing to pay for the least honored place on the couches by becoming the butts of the jests, or by bringing laughter on themselves by such feats as swallowing whole cheese cakes at a mouthful.

94. **The Standard Dinner Party — Nine Guests.** — In Athens in other days a delightful informality prevailed at banquets. The number of guests was seldom fixed, and it was quite proper to intrude two or three more at the last minute. Romans are more grave, methodical, and, be it said, more commonplace. The standard size for a dinner party is determined by an almost inflexible custom — nine. Three couches, three guests to a couch ; — that number can concentrate around a single set of serving tables, and let everybody mingle easily in the conversation.

Of course, you can get along with fewer guests, but it is the height of meanness to have more than three to a couch. For a larger affair one must therefore have two or three or more triclinia, — eighteen or twenty-seven guests, etc. Unlike Athens, however, it is perfectly proper to invite high-born ladies to mixed dinner parties, although not to the free and easy drinking bouts that sometimes follow ; and the women apparently recline on the couches with perfect decorum and modesty. Nevertheless, "stag" parties are extremely common, and one such, of a very conventional nature, Calvus gave recently in honor of a friend, Manlius, who was just departing as *proquæstor* (assistant governor) of Africa.

95. Preparing the Dinner and Mustering the Guests. — The guests were invited by personal greetings at the Forum or Baths of Trajan except one who had to be summoned by slave messenger at his home. However two places on the couches have been left vacant deliberately to let Manlius invite any two acquaintances he desired — a frequent prerogative of the guest of honor. The dinner was to be a strictly decorous affair, and, therefore, it did not begin before the tenth hour (4 P.M.). If Calvus had desired a carouse, he might have begun at 3 P.M. in order to get plenty of leeway for a long riotous evening; but "early dinners" are ordinarily as great a reproach in Rome as "late dinners" will be later.

During the morning while the master-cook was tyrannizing over his scullions in the kitchen, and evolving various triumphs in pastry, the chamberlain, an upper-slave, was standing whip in hand over a whole platoon of lower slaves, giving orders like a centurion: "Sweep and scrub the pavement!" "Polish up those pillars!"   "Down with all those spider webs!"   "One of you clean the plain silver ware, and another the embossed dishes!" The whole mansion, therefore, was furbished up thoroughly, for a few signs of dirt before dinner guests is the most disgraceful of shortcomings.

By the tenth hour the triclinium was in perfect order. The three elegant sofas with purple cushions embroidered with gold thread were arranged around the finest citrus-wood table. Small pillows were laid upon the cushions to mark the positions of the feasters and for them to thrust under their elbows as they lay and ate. Presently the street before the vestibule became jammed with the retinues of the eight guests as each swung up in his litter. Calvus greeted each of the invited friends in the atrium, while the bulk of their escorts turned back home to return again with torches when the party should be over; but each guest was followed into the house by his own special valet, who took off his shoes as soon as he stretched himself out upon the couch, and then stood by to help Calvus's servants serve his own master. The triclinium was thus a decidedly crowded place, with eight strange slaves present, besides a mobilization of all the handsomest and most efficient of the house servants.

96. **Arrangement of the Couches : Placing the Guests.** — The guests were each in the gay *synthesis* or other gala costume, and quite in the mood to obey the grave *nomenclater*, a handsome and experienced slave of the host who pointed out to each his place on the couches. This location of feasters, however, was an extremely solemn business. How many social feuds have been created by blunders concerning it! Nay, if the guest chances to be a public character, a certain position is really a matter of legal right to many dignitaries and its refusal possibly can give matter for a lawsuit.[1] The three couches were set around three sides of the table, the fourth being left open for the service. Approaching from the open side that couch to the right was reckoned the first (*summus*), then the middle one opposite (*medius*), then the one on the left (*imus*).

The best place of all was reckoned to be the third position on the middle couch " The Consul's Post,"[2] and here, or course, Manlius was consigned. Calvus by custom took the host's place, on the third couch, but nearest the guest of

---

[1] The love of "first-seats" at feasts, denounced in the New Testament, was anything but a strictly Jewish vice ; Greeks and Romans were every whit as bad as Orientals.

[2] So given because here dispatches, etc., could be most readily handed to a consul or other great officer if he were among the guests.

honor. The distribution of the other places was a matter for great discrimination, but peace was kept by placing the two African gentlemen whom Manlius brought, upon the middle couch beside him, and setting the young eques Nepos (the junior of the company) at the outer end of the third couch. All nine, therefore, spread themselves out unconventionally and chattered about the newest jockeys in the circus, while a troupe of slave-boys, half-stripped but pomaded and curled, passed around silver bowls of water and fine towels for washing and wiping the hands.[1] This ceremony happily accom-

NINE GUESTS IN A TRICLINIUM.

plished, a tall upper slave magnificently arrayed nodded from the doorway to Calvus that the cook had declared himself ready, and Calvus nodded back his approval. The dinner could begin.

97. Serving the Dinner. — The giver of this feast only desired a grave and conventional dinner for sedate people, and a strictly normal order was followed without epicurean niceties or a low revel as a climax. No tablecloths ; the serv-

---

[1] Sometimes a guest's personal valet brought a special towel for his own master. Diners of an objectionable variety were occasionally charged with stealing the towels or napkins if the host supplied them.

ing boys running to and from the kitchen set on the beautiful polished surface of the table before the guests first a preliminary course, the *gustatio*, supposed to stimulate the appetite. On silver dishes were served some choice crabs, salads, mushrooms, and also eggs. The guests ate these without forks, dexterously picking up the food in their fingers. The handsomely embossed silver cups were handed about filled with sweet mulsum properly diluted in order not to befuddle the intellect; after that followed the formal dinner itself.

At really elaborate feasts there would be six or even seven courses, but Calvus had merely ordered the orthodox number of three — a succession of daintily cooked meats and fish tastily garnished with vegetables, but with no rarities such as heathcock from Phrygia or sturgeon from Rhodes. The honor of the house, however, required that every viand should be arranged carefully on its

ROMAN SERVING FORKS.

dish, and every dish upon its tray by a special slave, the *structor*, a true artist, who also acted as master carver, cutting up a roast of boar with his knife keeping time to a flute-player. The mere fact, however, that one man was allowed both to arrange the dishes and then to do the carving was a sign that Calvus was among the less ostentatious senators.

Between each course water and towels were again passed about, and the guests washed their hands. Finally for dessert there was brought on a great quantity of curious pastry — artificial oysters and thrushes filled with dried grapes and almonds; and a great dish whereon stood an image, made of baked dough, of the orchard god Vertumnus, holding a pastry apron full of fruits, while heaped around his feet were sweet quinces stuck full of almonds, and melons cut into fantastic shapes.[1]

98. The Drinking Bout (*Comissatio*) after the Dinner. — This concluded the regular dinner, but Calvus had invited his friends (since Manlius had much to talk about) to stay to a *comissatio*, a social drinking spell afterwards. The nine guests rose and adjourned to the host's private baths, whence, after they had refreshed themselves and taken a turn around the colonnades in the peristylium, they returned to the tri- clinium to find that the slaves had changed all the couch

DRINKING CUP.

covers and pillows, had swept the floor, and had actually brought in new tables. It was now quite dark, beautiful silver lamps gleamed on high against the fretwork of the ceiling and on the tall inlaid sideboard stood two great silver tankards ; one was filled with snow ;[2] the other had a charcoal brazier beneath it and steamed with hot water.

If Calvus's party had now been composed of younger merrymakers, some one would have called out, " Let's drink in the ' Greek style ' and elect a king" ; and everybody would have joined in throwing dice to select the *rex*, or lord of the revels. That potentate would have been obligated to decide how much water was to be mixed with the wine, and how

---

[1] This, of course, was a very simple private dinner.   For the menu of a really extensive banquet, see the citation from Macrobius, in the writer's "Readings in Ancient History," Vol. II (Rome), p. 253.

[2] Brought, of course, from the summits of the Apennines with infinite labor.

many cups must be drunk to the health of each feaster's lady love, and to arrange the forfeits, riddles, and practical jokes inseparable from a jolly evening.   If the party had been still more uproarious, Spanish dancing girls might have been provided by the host, or a corps of pantomimes, acrobats, or farce players, and the whole scene could have ended in a very coarse orgy.

In the present case Calvus had decided to let his friends merely drink enough to loosen their tongues and to exchange their best wit and wisdom.   The slaves, therefore, brought in with decent solemnity the little images of the family lares, and a small smoking brazier, and Calvus cast a trifle of meal and salt and a few drops of wine upon the fire.   " The gods are propitious ! " announced a slave in loud voice, after which the guests preserved a reverent silence for an instant, to be followed by vigorous conversation the moment the divine images were carried out.

99. Distribution of Garlands and Perfumes.   Social Conversation. — While one corps of slaves was passing about the wine, asking each guest whether " Hot ? " or " Cold ? " others were distributing wreaths of fragrant flowers, to put on the forehead and even around the neck (by their odor supposedly preventing drunkenness) and also little alabaster vials of choice perfumes which the guests immediately broke and poured upon their hands and hair.   Then followed long conversations, grave or gay according to the mood.   Calvus had not provided any professional entertainers, but all through the drinking a good flute-player and a good harpist hid behind a curtain kept up a soft pleasing melody.

While Manlius and the older guests discussed the control of the Moorish tribes of Numidia, young Nepos and one or two others found much to say about a new " Thracian " who had just fought at the Flavian Amphitheater, and presently all the others pressed the host (knowing him to be a little vain

on the subject) to show some new moves in "robbers"
(*latrunculi*, a board game with men extremely like checkers)
which he had evolved with peculiar pride. It would have
been good form also to have played at making impromptu
verses, or at matching riddles, but for a Roman gentleman to
indulge in anything like singing a song, even before a group
of friends, would have been undignified; Nero possibly
shocked public opinion even more by appearing openly as a
common theater performer than he did by killing his mother!

At last the evening ended. It was only 8 o'clock by later
reckoning; but everybody had to be up again by gray dawn.
The streets were already dark and deserted save by prowlers
and the police-watch. "My shoes, boy," called Manlius
to his valet. All the other guests imitated him, and already
their retinues with slaves and torches were crowding in the
vestibule. The eight diners departed after thanking Calvus.
The slaves cleared out the triclinium, and quenched the lights.
Soon the whole domus was asleep.

**100. Elaborate and Vulgar Banquets. Simple Home
Dinners**. — Such was a very decorous and ordinary dinner.
It could easily have run off to greater follies and vastly greater
magnificence, useless to describe. Space lacks, also, to describe the magnificent imperial banquets at the palace when all
the gold, glitter, and luxury of the capital is on display. Calvus is no great philosopher, or he might have followed the
mode and insisted upon his guests conversing solely about
the "Stoic Conception of Duty"; or the "Immortality of
the Soul."

A host of another type might have imitated certain very
mean patrons who would invite poor clients to fill up the triclinium and then deliberately serve them with cheap wine
and coarse scrappy food, while the best was being set before
himself and the guests of honor. Such great men were also
equal to pettiness of stationing special slaves behind each

less-favored guest to watch lest the latter should with his finger nails pick out the gems set in the drinking cups. Pliny the Younger has already recorded his emphatic opinion of noblemen who will not serve dependents with as good fare as they get themselves, — declaring that if the host *must* economize, he should eat and drink nothing better that night than what he gives his clients and freedmen.

Of course, many an evening meal is far simpler than the one just described. If the triclinium is not full, Calvus and Gratia may sometimes offer their near acquaintances merely " some lettuce, three snails, two eggs, spelt mixed with honey and snow, olives from Spain, cucumbers, onions, and a few like delicacies." Old Roman simplicity still — but every dish will be perfect of its kind, and the cookery excellent; and even the modest Calvi are none too fond of this diet praised by the philosophers. Rome is not merely the mistress of the world, she is the citadel of the gourmands.

CHAPTER VII

THE SOCIAL ORDERS: THE SLAVES

101. Enormous Alien Population in Rome. The " Græcules." — Rome, as already discovered, is a city with an enormous cosmopolitan population, and in that population is a sadly large proportion of drones, parasites, and selfish purveyors to the vices or luxuries of the rich. The influx of aliens, of course, impresses one at every turn, be the visit to obscure Mercury Street or to the famous Old Forum. " The Syrian Orontes (quoting lines of Juvenal hackneyed already) has long since poured into the Tiber, bringing its lingo and its manners, its flutes and its timbals, and its coarse girls who hang around the Circus."

A large fraction of these invaders, however, are not confessed Orientals, but olivine-featured, nimble creatures of very Levantine morality who like to be called " Greeks." The poet, just cited, has other familiar lines deriding their suppleness, servility, and willingness for any shift promising favor or reward. The self-same adventurer is ready to be " grammarian, orator, geometrician, painter, trainer, ropedancer, augur, doctor, or astrologer," or if you bid " ' Græculus ' to mount to heaven — why, to heaven he'll go ! ' " They squeeze out tears or split with laughter at a sign, and, of course, they readily sell themselves for any well-paid villainy.

Do these creatures prosper? If so, Roman citizenship comes next. They change their names, assume the toga, and their sons or at least their grandsons will be borne along in their high litters toward the Senate House. There is

another large group of "Conscript Fathers" who, Calvus
angrily tells Gratia, are only crude Celts from Spain, Gaul,
or even distant Britain. Another group can only speak
Latin with a pronounced North African accent. There is
even a certain dark-skinned "Julius" (a good Roman name
surely), who wears his broad purple stripe proudly enough,
but who, — every one swears, — was born far up the Nile in
Egypt — "How did he get the Emperor's favor!" At first
thought, therefore, Rome seems one of the most democratic
cities socially in the world.

102. Strict Divisions of Society. The Régime of *Status*.
— But closer acquaintance discloses the fact that Roman
society is utterly undemocratic. Wealth to be sure can sur-
mount many barriers, but even a hundred-million sesterces
plus imperial patronage cannot *quite* do everything. The
whole Roman Empire is founded not on the basis of human
brotherhood and equality, but on "*piety*." "Pious Æneas"
is the hero of the national epic poem. But what in fact is
this piety? Not the rendering of due homage to the gods
merely, but the bestowing of exact justice upon every man
according to his *status* — the great stratum in society in
which the law has placed him, and whence he can neither
rise nor fall without important formalities. Are you brought
into court? Instantly the question is, "What are you?"
And on that answer, regardless of guilt or innocence, your
fate will largely depend.

The Roman Empire in reality is essentially *a régime of
status* — giving to every man a certain social and legal due.
This accent on *status* has been increasing ever since Augustus
founded his dominion ; and it will intensify even more rapidly
down to the very end of the Empire.

In the 1,500,000 odd people in Rome, there are these
six well-defined social classes, each with a distinct legal
condition: I. *Slaves;* II. *Freedmen;* III. *Free Provincials;*

IV. *Ordinary Roman Citizens, or "Plebeians";* V. *Equites;*
VI. *Senators.* In Rome the third class, of course, is necessarily small, being made up solely of visitors and resident aliens,
some of whom, if notables from such free allied towns as
Athens, enjoy excellent protection and privileges. Nearly
all the freedmen are technically Roman citizens but are
still under certain civil and social disabilities. The Plebeians,
Equites, and Senators are all reckoned officially as "majores," persons with superior legal rights, however much the
two upper orders may scorn the one inferior. Socially, however, there are many cross sections, with the upper slaves
of rich noblemen despising the petty tradesmen, who wear
moth-eaten togas, and the higher "Cæsarians" (slaves at
the imperial palace) have been known to patronize equites
and even senators.

103. Vast Number of Slaves. Universality of Slavery. —
The slaves, however, are always officially at the bottom of
the human ladder. Their number is great, making up
close to half, if not quite half, of the population of Rome.
They are not required to wear a special dress.[1] Some years
ago it was proposed to order this in the Senate, but the motion was voted down : " It would be dangerous to show the
wretches how numerous they really were." Ordinarily
they go about in sad-colored tunics and long cloaks like most
of the common citizens, or else they wear some bright livery
devised by their masters.

Only a few of these unfortunates have Italian countenances
and can speak Latin without some foreign accent. Plenty
of alien adventurers, it is true, drift to Rome as willingly, but
probably the great bulk of the cosmopolitan multitudes
everywhere observable, even if free at present, come to

---

[1] They could not, of course, wear the toga, or, if female slaves, the
matronly stola.

Latium involuntarily — as slaves imported to wait on the masters of the world.

Almost no one has questioned the rightfulness and necessity of slavery. Seneca, indeed, has written that no man can be enslaved beyond a certain point — his body is his master's, but his mind is his own. Horace has written grandiloquently "Who is truly free? The wise man alone; who is stern master of himself." This sounds well but does not alter the practical results of a situation wherein, for example, all farm implements are solemnly classified in the handbooks under three heads: I. *Dumb tools* — plows, mattocks, shovels, etc.; II. *Semi-speaking tools* — oxen, asses, etc., that can bellow or bray; III. *Speaking tools* — slaves useful as farm hands.

104. Power of Master over Slaves. — Until very lately, before Hadrian's time, these "Speaking Tools" have had rather less legal protection than may be granted to horses by the "humane" legislation of later civilization. The reigning Emperor, however, a remarkable innovator, and tinctured with the Stoic philosophy, has lately issued an edict that a slave cannot be killed outright by his master without some kind of consent by a magistrate.

Every owner of human bipeds has probably grumbled that "discipline is now made impossible," but the new law is of little practical help to the slave. His master can still order a punishment so brutal that death is certain, and if he should murder a servant, slave witnesses can give no valid testimony, and almost no citizen will turn traitor to his class and prosecute. Half of Rome, therefore, continues in the absolute power and possession of the other half.

105. The City Slaves and the Country Slaves. — Calvus and Gratia have a familia of about one hundred and fifty slaves in their city house. Scattered upon their villas there are always at least as many more, but between the *city slaves* and the *rustic slaves* there is a great gulf fixed. The first class utterly despises the latter. The city slaves are mostly soft-handed ministers to their owners' luxuries. The country slaves are toiling farm hands often under extremely severe discipline. When the master, attended by a great retinue from his town house, sojourns at a villa, squabbling and even fights between the two contingents are extremely probable. Let a serving boy become too insolent, or a tiring maid fail in her duty — the master or mistress can simply order, " Send him or her to the villa ! " The wretch will then beg instead to be flogged in sheer mercy. Banishment to the rustic slave colony seems a mere death in life.

106. Purchasing a Slave Boy. — In any large city familia, the purchase of new slaves to replace vacancies caused by death or otherwise is an everyday occurrence. Very lately a new errand boy was wanted by Calvus, who could not condescend to purchase such a menial in person; and he left the task to a competent freedman, Cleander. The latter conscientiously went through the great slave bazaars near the fora and especially along the Sæpta Julia, the great porticoes lining the Via Lata.

Here any quantity of human bipeds were on sale as in a regular cattle market. There were numbers of little stalls or pens with crowds of buyers or mere spectators constantly elbowing in and out, and from many of them rose a gross fleshly odor as from closely confined animals. At the entrance to these pens notices, written on white boards with red chalk, recited the nature of the slaves inside, and sometimes the hour when they would be sold at auction. Every nationality was represented among these vendable commodities — Egyptians, Moors, Arabs, Cilicians, Cappadocians, Thracians, Greeks and alleged Greeks, Celts from Gaul, Spain, and Britain, and a good many Teutons, fair-haired creatures from beyond the Rhine. They were of both sexes and of all ages, but with youths and grown-up girls predominating. As Cleander went about he heard a crier announcing that a new coffle of Jews was just being put on sale, the results of the latest success of the Emperor's generals in capturing one of the last rebellious strongholds in Palestine.

107. Traffic in the Slave Pens. — It avails not to dwell on the hideous brutality and degrading character of many of the scenes. The slave-dealers were men counted the scum of the earth socially, but the vast gains from lucky speculation in human flesh drove many shrewd scoundrels into the trade. At last Cleander found the stall he desired. Several •boys from the Black Sea region were about to be knocked down. They did not seem so very miserable. Truth to tell their barbarous parents had probably sold them in way of regular trade, and the boys looked forward to entering a fine Roman familia as a great adventure.

The lads stood in line on raised stones, stripped almost naked and with white chalk on their feet as a token that they were for immediate sale. Cleander and other would-be purchasers examined them as they might so many cattle; felt of their muscles, examined their teeth, and made them converse enough to be sure they could speak fair Greek and a little Latin. Another buying agent was accompanied by a physician to give the proffered merchandise a regular physical examination, and Cleander in his turn interrogated the selling clerks very specifically: " Did they warrant the health of a certain boy, especially his freedom from fits? Was he thievish? Was he prone to run away? Did he get despondent and attempt suicide? " [1]

---

[1] The ancients had intense fear of epilepsy, supposedly a visitation of the gods. The questions given were the points on which slave-venders had to give assurance, or formally to waive all responsibility.

One ill-favored youth was standing with a tall felt hat on his head. That implied he was being sold " as is," without the least warranty; " An incorrigible thief " went the whisper, and the great welts on his back betrayed repeated whippings. If the sellers failed, however, to " cap " their chattels, they had to answer all queries truthfully, and take back the slave if he developed various defects within six months. Such a liability, however, was hard to enforce. A slave trade involved all the points of shrewdness, hard bargaining, and smooth prevarication of the proverbial horse trade.

108. Sale of Slaves. — At last a bell rang. A boy whom Cleander had inspected approvingly was stood on a higher block. The glib auctioneer began his patter to the little group before him: " The lad's clear-skinned and well-favored from head to foot, a well-bred fellow carefully trained for good service. Has a smattering of Greek learning — you can educate him for a secretary if you want to. He can also sing a bit at dinners — not professionally, but enough to make you jolly over your wine. — All this is sheer and simple truth. You'll wait long for another such bargain. Just one point (with a deprecatory smirk) I am obliged to warn about — once he *did* have a lazy fit, and hid himself for fear of a lashing, — Well, he's yours for a mere 8000 sesterces." [$320.] [1]

" Take 2000," stolidly retorted Cleander, naming the standard price for male slaves of no extra qualities. Counter bidding and much chaffering followed. All ended when " Crœsus " (slaves were often given fancy oriental names) was knocked down to Cleander for 4000 sesterces ($160), a very fair bargain if the youth had not been praised too

---

[1] This is almost precisely the slave auctioneer's speech in Horace. (*Epistles*, bk. II, 1.) — If the dealer had failed to mention that the boy had once tried to run away, he would have been legally liable.

extravagantly. On the same errand the freedman also purchased for his master a stout Gaul, needed as an expert muleteer on one of the farm villas, — such a fellow if at all capable was well worth the 6000 sesterces asked for him.

The next day, however, it was announced by Gratia that she required a first-class lady's maid, a girl not merely versed in all toilet mysteries, but comely to look upon should she have to appear with her mistress in public. Such damsels commanded a high price, and Gratia and Calvus together condescended to do the shopping. Along the Sæpta Julia they visited special booths, from which vulgar idlers were carefully excluded, and where human chattels of the superior grades were shown to bona fide purchasers.

The dealer whom they visited had handsome slave boys to act as statuesque cup bearers and worth up to 100,000 sesterces ($4000) apiece; he also had a truly competent physician at the same price; a good private schoolmaster; two very expert dancers, and a remarkably fine cook just thrown on the market by a bankrupt ex-consul. Girls fit for kitchen service could be had in the common stalls as cheap as 1000 sesterces ($40); but Gratia and her husband had to pay a round 25,000 ($1000) for a truly pretty little Greek, who was a dexterous hair-dresser and who could read aloud to her mistress with a good Attic accent.

109. Size of Slave Households (*Familiæ*). Slave Workmen. — Thus the *familia* of the Calvi has been made up. People complain that owing to the surcease of great wars the supply of cheap slaves fit for farm service is running down. Great landowners are actually being driven to fall back on free hired labor or a system of tenantry; but kidnapping, the sale of children by their barbarian parents, the ceaseless petty wars in Africa, Asia, and along the Rhine, as well as the sale of slaves born and bred on the Roman farms or mansions themselves [1] keep up a sufficient supply for domestic service.

The very poor plebeians are, of course, slaveless and servantless, and plenty of small tradesmen or minor officials get along with only two or three slaves-of-all-work; but it is impossible to be a " somebody " and to exist in Rome without *at least ten slaves*. The social ladder and the size of the familiæ ascend together until we find senators and very rich equites who boast many more than two hundred in their city houses alone. " How many slaves has he got? " is the regular formula for asking " What's his fortune? " In Augustus's day there was a very wealthy freedman who owned 4116 slaves, although the majority of these were scattered on his numerous farms; but well known is the story of Pedanius Secundus, City Præfect under Nero: One of his slaves murdered him, and by the harsh old law making the entire familia liable for the killing of its master by one member, all of the slaves in his Roman mansion, almost 400 in number, were actually put to death, although his farm slaves were spared.

There are many slaves, however, in Rome that are not strictly servants. They act as craftsmen and tradesmen of every kind, sometimes hired out by their masters to contractors, sometimes working on their own account. Custom, though not law, entitles them to a part of their earnings; this is their *peculium* (" special property ") and only a very harsh owner will deprive them of it. Indeed it is clearly understood that an intelligent slave cannot be expected to do his best without a personal incentive. You can even find savings banks and really large commercial enterprises run by slaves, often put in positions of great trust, but such

---

[1] Probably, however, it would be counted discreditable to sell a slave born in one's house (a *verna*) unless the fellow was wholly reprobate, or the master was in great financial straits.

persons undoubtedly have an understanding about being manumitted if they are faithful and successful.

110. Division of Duties and Organization of Slave Households. — In Calvus' house as in every other great mansion one is impressed with the multitude of attendants. The master, mistress, and their friends are dependent on every kind of menial service. Before Calvus rises from bed, he is massaged every morning by an expert masseur, and some of his more effeminate friends insist on having not walking sticks but handsome slave boys of convenient height

SLAVES WORKING IN A BAKERY.

always at hand, on which to lean as they move about. In a well-ordered mansion, indeed, it seems needless really for the master to do much more than feed himself and draw his own breath — the servants can do all the rest for him!

A familia of one hundred and fifty slaves, such as Calvus's, requires a semi-military organization. Everything should run smoothly. At the head of all are the upper slaves, proud, arrogant beings with their own body servants, the commissioned officers of the army. The *procurator* (sometimes a freedman), who does the purchasing and outside business; the *dispensator*, who manages the storerooms; the *atriensis*, who acts as general chamberlain, and especially

the *sileniarius*, who enforces "silence" and general discipline form the heads of this category. They are often
petty tyrants, and the newcomer Crœsus will have far more
to fear from their harshness than from Calvus, who will
hardly know him by sight.

The staff at large is carefully split up into *decuriæ* (squads
of ten) each under its special chief. There are the house
cleaners, the table retinue, the kitchen force, the chamber
boys and maids, the keepers of the wardrobes, the master's
valets, the mistress's maids, the special attendants of Calvus's
children, the litter bearers, the corps of messengers — each
forming a separate contingent. The master, too, has several
secretaries, expert copyists and readers, and a librarian.
There are several slave physicians although their duties are
largely confined to the familia; the masters will call in fashionable free professionals for their own serious ills. The
two sexes are about equally divided, and a great many slaves
are respectably if informally married,[1] although a familia
is anything but a school of social virtue.

**111. Discipline in a Well-Ordered Mansion. Long Hours
of Idleness.** — In such a mansion the master and mistress
have little acquaintance with the lower run of the human
beings over whom they possess absolute power. Calvus,
however, knows his upper servants, his favorite valets, and
his first secretary, and being a genuinely kindly man has
come to esteem them and trust them familiarly; and it is the
same between Gratia and her confidential maids.

The other slaves they treat fairly humanely, all things considered, but absolutely impersonally — their presence is
to be taken for granted like articles of furniture, and their
personal problems are ignored. In the peristylium there is
always posted a bulletin board informing the slaves of the

---

[1] Slave unions had no legal status, but only a harsh and tactless master
would ordinarily break them up.

nights when their master is going out to dinner, and although Calvus does not imitate certain very haughty individuals by trying to give all his orders through signs and never addressing a menial, it is good breeding to speak to ordinary slaves as seldom and then as curtly as possible, just as one should not waste words addressing a yoke of oxen.

Roman house-slaves have their sorrows but they need not ordinarily fear two mortal evils — hunger, or overwork. They have, of course, their own dining quarters and are kept on sufficient, if simple rations of meal cakes, salt, oil, common wine, and a little fruit. Butcher's meat they seldom touch, except as the kitchen staff get the leavings from the banquets, although the upper servants naturally fare more sumptuously.

As for slaves' working hours, they are absurdly short. Every servant has some limited appointed task. When that is finished nothing else is expected of him, and to require other duties would not merely make the master unpopular with his servants, it would stamp him before his equals as an extremely mean and sordid man. Thus, on very many days, Calvus's six litter bearers have absolutely nothing to do. On the many nights that he and Gratia dine out the great kitchen staff is concerned mainly with the dice-box. The boudoir maids are usually idle from the time their mistress is dressed until she must dress again for dinner. All this makes for gossiping, gaming, and for the worst kinds of busy idleness.

112. Inevitable Degradation Caused by Slavery. Evil Effect upon Masters. — Are these "speaking tools" very miserable? Calvus's familia is not exceptional in that a tolerably kindly relation often exists between owner and owned. The Stoic philosophy is making its impression, and there are plenty of theoretical arguments that "a slave is also a man" and entitled to humane treatment. A master or mistress who is habitually cruel is frowned on socially as might be a man accustomed to abuse his horses.

Nevertheless, the status of a slave is always morally degrading. He feels himself a mere chattel. Whatever he enjoys, he enjoys merely on suffrance. Any sort of iniquity is condoned in his mind " if the master orders it," and he is likely to be honest and faithful more through the fear of harsh punishment than because of any high ethical motives.

On the other hand just because slavery has perforce its brutal, soul-destroying elements, it is almost equally evil for the master. It is seldom good for a man to have the lives often of hundreds of fellow beings in his power; or to be relieved of every possible kind of honest exertion by a swarm of officious menials. Furthermore, slavery being inevitably so brutal, masters often live in terror of a mutiny by the brutes themselves. " *So many slaves, so many enemies,*" is a standard maxim; not always true, but true enough to excuse many horrid practices.

The slave revolt led by Spartacus in 73 B.C. is now half forgotten in history, but that rebel gladiator had later several almost as successful imitators. Every now and then something happens which makes senatorial blood run cold. Only in Trajan's day there was one Lagius Macedo, an ex-prætor, a cruel and overbearing master, indeed, who was beaten to death by his slaves while he was bathing at his Formiæ villa. The wretches were all crucified, of course, but (as wrote Pliny the Younger just after it happened): " You see what we masters are exposed to; and nobody can feel safe because he's an easy and mild master; for it's sheer villainy, not premeditation, that prompts our murder."

Another danger, especially under evil emperors, comes from the incessant presence of slaves at the most private affairs of their lords, their willingness to tattle, to assist informers, and often to help ruin their masters outright in return for freedom and reward. " The tongue is the worst part of a bad slave," runs a familiar saying, and even an honest and high-minded man must shudder at the idea of having all his intimate doings passed on to delight his enemies.

113. Punishment of Slaves. — Under these circumstances, and with so many slaves who are undoubtedly by origin and nature unreliable if not incorrigible, every large house has its small private dungeon, and also a low-browed wolfish creature who serves as jailer and official " whipper." Even in Calvus's house he finds occupation, for in so large a familia some luckless boy or maid is often caught loitering or pilfering, and gets a dose of the many-lashed scourge — at the orders of the upper-slave managers.[1] Under-slaves, indeed, think nothing of a lashing beyond its mere pain ; there is no disgrace, it is all part of one's lot in life.

There can be much worse things than this in many houses. Servilia, one of Gratia's acquaintances, often beats her tire-women cruelly with the flat of her bronze mirror for the most trivial offenses. Ambustus, the new ædile, lately ordered a boy to get one hundred stripes merely for being slow in bringing hot water. The rich widow Lepidia so enjoys having her slaves flogged, that she makes the whipper actually do his pitiless work in her dressing room, while she is reading

---

[1] Of course, in a large slave household frequently there were unruly elements who often had to be punished privately, when, if free men, their actions would have landed them in the police courts. The stripes might be inflicted as a mild correction with the cane, or leather strap, or more severely with the terrific *flagellum* (loaded whip), usually with three chains set with metal. A sound lashing with this could cause death (see below, p. 137). The prejudice against brutal whipping and the like was growing steadily, thanks to the advance of the Stoic philosophy, even before the triumph of Christianity. Juvenal denounces those who inflict outrageous floggings for slight faults. "Does a man set his son a good lesson by calling in the torturer and having a slave branded for stealing a couple of towels? Does such a man hold that the bodies and souls of slaves are of the same elements as our own ? "

the " Daily Journal " (*Acta Diurna*, see p. 282) and having her face rouged. Many a slave has been whipped to death because of some small folly which sent his master or mistress into a rage, and noblemen have been known to keep huge flesh-eating carp in their fish ponds, and to toss in a recalcitrant slave occasionally to improve the flavor of the fish, although such actions disgust all decent people.

114. Branding of Slaves. *Ergastula* — Slave Prisons. — If a slave's offense is too great to be rewarded by a mere whipping, and yet does not provoke the death penalty, there are plenty of intermediate punishments. Toiling around Calvus's atrium is an ill-favored lad with the scars of branding barely healed on his forehead : " FVR " he is marked (" Thief ") [1]. He is taking the place of another youth who, to cure extreme laziness, has been sent for a month to the " mill gang " — chained to the great lever which turns the grist mill and forced to toil all day like a hard-driven ass — an excellent cure for idleness.

This fate is not so bad, however, as what befell one of the eques Pollio's valets, a bright clever lad, who foolishly became too pert to his master. In a fit of anger Pollio ordered, " Give him six months in the *ergastulum*." The soft-handed boy was, therefore, not merely shipped off to severe farm labor, itself utterly repulsive, but was obliged to work in the fields in a chain-gang along with the very scum of slave-criminals ; always in fetters, lashed by brutish keepers themselves slaves, and confined at night in underground prisons (*ergastula*) that were mere kennels.

115. Death Penalties for Slaves. Pursuit of Runaways. — If a slave really deserves death, there are, of course, two standard methods of capital punishment, both very degrading

---

[1] "Three Letter Man" or "Man of Letters" became a common taunt among slaves.

as well as fearful. Everybody knows about crucifixion with
its hours and perhaps days of hideous agony; but more
common and nearly as painful is death on the *furca*.[1] The
victim's head is placed at the opening of two " V "-shaped
beams and his arms tightly lashed upon them; then the
professional floggers strike the wretch with their loaded
whips, the leaden balls worked into the thongs making them
a terrific weapon, until death comes as blessed relief. It
has been a long day since there has been an execution at
Calvus's house, but some years ago a Spanish boy who murdered an upper-servant perished thus under the lash. There
is, however, a much simpler way of disposing of criminal
slaves, one bringing a certain return to their masters, —
namely, to sell them to the givers of public shows to train
as gladiators or merely to set in the arena to give sport to
the bears or lions.

Of course, under such conditions slaves will often try to
run away. They seldom really succeed, however, unless they
are persons of marked intelligence and can make off with considerable money. The Roman Empire is one vast police unit,
unattached strangers are everywhere scrutinized carefully and
when a slave disappears a reward is promptly offered. Only
now a crier has gone down Mercury Street, with a crowd after
him, as he proclaims: " *Disappeared from the public baths, a
boy aged about sixteen. Free and easy habits. Curly hair. Good-
looking. Answers to name of Giton. A thousand sesterces to
anybody haling him back to Aulus Sulpicius near the Temple
of Ops, or to anyone who will betray his whereabouts!* " [2]

If Giton is retaken, he can thank the gods if he is merely
flogged almost to death, and is not also given a year in the
ergastulum.

---

[1] A slave might be lashed to a *furca* for some hours, as a minor penalty
without desire to put him to death.

[2] An actual proclamation from Petronius.

Naturally slaves can only testify in court by their master's consent and under torture, although the reigning humane Emperor has just issued a decree limiting its use to the last resort. Hadrian, also, contrary to the usage in Nero's day, has ordained that if a man is murdered by his slaves, only the slaves near the actual scene of crime are to be tormented, and he has actually banished a certain matron, Umbricia, for "abusing her slave girls most atrociously for trivial reasons." All this perhaps dimly foreshadows a new day; but what human chattel can wait to see the abuses of slavery whittled down by the law across the centuries?

Have the slaves along Mercury Street any nearer hope? Possibly. The other day many of them saw in the front benches of honor at the Circus a man of dignity. His hands glittered with sardonyx rings; his lacerna was of Tyrian purple; his shoes were scarlet, his hair reeking with costly essences; a great train bowed and cringed to him. But his forehead was covered with "numerous white patches like stars"; "sticking plaster," everybody whispered, to cover up the FVR once branded on his countenance. He was an ex-slave, an exalted freedman, who, a couple of decades before, had stood on the auction block, but now was a mighty power in Roman high finance.

CHAPTER VIII

THE SOCIAL ORDERS: FREEDMEN, PROVINCIALS, PLEBEIANS, AND NOBLES

116. Manumission of Slaves Very Common. — A Roman slave's legal position may be miserable, but usually he is not under that fearful stigma of race and color weighing upon the slaves of another era. His complexion and his brain power do not differ essentially from his master's.[1] If he is a Greek or Levantine, often his mental acuteness may be greater than that of his lord. An intelligent slave under not too harsh a master will devote himself to the latter in every possible way, expecting pretty certainly the great reward for faithfulness and zealous service — freedom. Of course, many dull hardened wretches, especially upon the farms, will die as the toiling chattels they have lived; but freedom comes often enough to make manumission something for which to hope eagerly.

Often the death of a master is the signal for a grand enfranchisement of all the older members of his familia. It costs nothing thus to reward faithful service at the expense of your heirs; and it is a fine thing to have a long file of newly created freedmen, all wearing the tall red caps of "liberty," march in your funeral procession. Everybody will praise your "generosity," and the freedmen can be expected to cherish their lord's memory. Incidentally, also, there are few better ways of punishing a generally incompetent slave than having him ostentatiously *refused* freedom when all his comrades go about rejoicing.

[1] There would be just enough of negroes in Rome for them to cease to be great curiosities.

139

117. The Ceremony of Manumission. — Nevertheless, many slaves need not wait for their masters to die. They are perhaps suffered to work at a trade, and accumulate their " peculium," and then very likely to purchase their own and their wives' and children's liberty. With rich masters of the better sort, it is also a gracious act at certain intervals to select a few extra-deserving slaves and say to them the blessed words, " Come with me to the prætor ! "

When they are all before the magistrate a solemn legal formality is gone through. One of the official lictors steps forward, gives a light tap with his rod upon the head of each slave and says loudly, " I declare this man is free ! " The master laying hold of the slave and turning him around, replies, " And I desire that this man should be free ! " adding a slight blow on the cheek ; whereat the magistrate declares officially, " And I adjudge that this man is free." This completes the " manumission " ; then home the happy " freedman " (*libertinus*) goes to be greeted with the congratulations of his former fellow-slaves, showers of sweet cakes, dates, and figs and all kinds of humble rejoicings.

118. The Status of Freedmen. Their Great Success in Business. — Henceforth, the ex-slave is the freedman of his former master. He takes the first part of his master's name ; thus that Cleander, manumitted a few years ago by Publius Junius Calvus, now swells about proudly as Publius Junius Cleander. His children will henceforth be Junii, no less lawfully than Calvus's children ; with a result that the gentile names of some of the proudest houses in Rome are now also borne by families perforce acknowledging swart Africans or tow-headed Batavians as very near ancestors.

Once escaped from actual slavery a great career in life can open before an energetic freedman. If his ex-master is a Roman citizen, he also is now a Roman citizen without any naturalization process. True he is under a social stigma.

Not merely he, but his children also, are excluded from the Senate and all the higher offices of the state; but an ex-slave is not likely to suffer from thinness of skin. Compelled in his youth to use his wits and put forth all his energies, he now often possesses abilities, often not very refined or delicate, which carry him far in trade, general business, and finance.

Usually before a master manumits a slave it is arranged that he shall remain in the mansion as some kind of an invaluable " man of business " for handling a large estate. Many a senator is like Cicero, in all private affairs completely at the mercy of a confidential *alter ego*, a freedman like Cicero's able and beloved Tiro. Practically every dignitary in Rome will refer his business matters to " my freedman," a shrewd consequential fellow, probably of Græco-Levantine origin, who has the right to use his patron's seal ring, and who knows all the family secrets. Supple, obsequious, and indispensable, he is certain of a great legacy when his patron dies; and if the patron is childless, he often becomes his heir. There are, indeed, plenty of cases where a slave-boy who entered a house as a valet, first earned freedom, then became a general confidant, and ended not merely with inheriting the house itself but with marrying the late owner's widow.

119. Humble Types of Freedmen. — Of course, the bulk of freedmen have no claim to such expectations. They are petty shop keepers or skilled craftsmen. They make up the great bureaus of upper clerks in the huge government offices on the Palatine. Everywhere they compete, as a rule very successfully, with the free born, and, of course, they add to the cosmopolitan multitudes in Rome.

An ex-slave cannot avoid becoming substantially the client of his former master. He is supposed to show his patron and his patron's family constant respect and usually a cer-

tain amount of service without compensation. Thus a
while ago Calvus manumitted a very faithful slave-physician.
It was stipulated that he should continue to physic the familia
without charge. For a freedman to show himself neglectful
of these obligations, above all to do anything to injure his
ex-master, is the depth of depravity. The legal penalties
for such " ingratitude " are very severe, and in extreme cases
the actual act of manumission itself can be cancelled.

120. **Wealth and Power of Successful Freedmen.** — Nevertheless, top-lofty freedmen abound. Their ready wits bring
them riches — the power before which all the Empire bends.
Once more Juvenal describes an obnoxious type: " Though
I'm born on the Euphrates, a fact which the little windows
[holes for earrings] in my ears would prove if I denied it —
yet am I the owner of five shops which bring me in 400,000
sesterces [$16,000] per year. What better thing does a
senator's robe bestow? Therefore, let everybody give way
to one who but yesterday with the chalked feet of a slave
entered our city." Freedmen, of course, get ahead
marvellously because nothing is too sordid if only it promises
gain. " He [a certain freedman]," says Petronius, " started
with an *as* [large copper coin], and was always ready to pick
a *quadrans* [farthing] out of the filthy mire with his teeth. So
his wealth grew and grew like a honey comb ! "

Very probably, the ideal set before this species of persons
is that of becoming all-powerful imperial freedmen, such as
that pair, Pallas and Narcissus, who literally ruled the
Roman Empire through their patron, Claudius. Trajan
and Hadrian have, indeed, greatly reduced the power
of freedmen around the Palace, turning the great
secretarial offices over to equites, but there are still ex-slaves
in the service of " Cæsar," who have only a little less influence than that mighty Claudius Etruscus who died of old
age under Domitian after having served six Emperors. He

began life in Rome as a slave boy from Smyrna. Tiberius manumitted him. He rose to become practically the head of the Treasury. His wealth was great, but his integrity matched his vast power, and few senators had such commanding influence in the government as he possessed.

121. Importance of Freedmen in a Roman Family. — In such a house as that of Calvus there are neither imperial ministers nor miserly speculators. The freedmen are honored and trusted members not of the slave familia but of the actual "family." When they are sick Calvus and Gratia are greatly concerned, as was Pliny the Younger over the illness of his beloved reader, Zosimus. If there is any domestic crisis, their counsel is sought and they take a zealous interest in the education of their lord's children.

On the other hand, on the nearby Flora Street spreads the huge garish palace of the ex-slave Athenonius, who won his freedom by catering to a foolish master's worst passions, and then gathered enormous wealth by speculating in Egyptian corn. *" Freedmen's riches "* have become a proverb. Not all freedmen are by any means wealthy, but enough of them have risen to the seats of the mighty to make every toiling slave dream dreams and see visions of something better than a dishonored, servile grave.

122. The Status of Provincials. The Case of Jesus. — All freedmen are Roman citizens, albeit citizens under a formal handicap, but in a city like Rome there are always many free persons who are not citizens at all — visiting provincials. Every year the Emperors issue some edict granting the franchise to a new group of non-citizens, but the numbers of the latter in all the provinces of the Empire is still great.[1] At Rome their position is ordinarily comfortable

---

[1] It is impossible to estimate the proportion of the population "enfranchised" finally by the oft-discussed edict of Caracalla in 214 A.D. It must have been over one half of the entire total.

enough, although if arrested, they are liable to a more summary trial than Roman citizens and in case of famine or
public disturbance they are liable to sudden expulsion from
the city (as Claudius expelled the Jews) without any redress.
The real disadvantage which they endure is that they cannot be appointed to any kind of public office under the
Roman government.   They are also sometimes under a
legal handicap in making and enforcing commercial contracts; and last but not least in their own provinces they
cannot " appeal to Cæsar " (if in an " Imperial " province)
or to the Senate (if in a " Senatorial " province) against the
decision, however arbitrary, of the Roman governor.

If you search the public records at the great *Tabularium*
(Public Record Office) by the Forum, you can find for example
the report of the trial of a certain Jew, one Christus, who was
accused of sedition in Judæa, about a hundred years before
our visit to Rome.   The procurator Pilatus yielding to
popular clamor had him executed ignominiously by crucifixion.   This was, of course, within Pilatus's legal authority.   Christus was only a provincial and he could take
no appeal.

The status of the provincials depends much on whether
their communities enjoy any treaty with or charter from
Rome.   Athens and a few other favored places are nominally " equal allies " with full rights of self-government, and
their citizens can claim a favored position among the mass
of provincials.   Other places possess charters giving great
privileges but revocable in case of gross abuse.

The bulk of the provincials are mere " stipendiaries,"
often permitted local self-government, but subject to Roman
taxation, and to the complete jurisdiction of the Roman
governor.   Under the Empire these governors are only by
exception corrupt and arbitrary, but their decisions must
usually be final.

123. Great Alien Colonies in Rome. — Apart from the great alien slave population there are inevitably large groups of resident aliens in various parts of the capital. There is a Little Syria, Little Egypt, Little Spain, and a Little Greece as surely as in certain great cities of a later civilization, but the most famous and conspicuous is the great Jewish colony.

This exists mainly in the Trans-Tiber district under the shadow of the Janiculum, although Jews are allowed to settle and to do business in any section of the city. The total number of free Jews in Rome has been set at 35,000 in Augustus's day, and it received a great reinforcement through the captives of Titus, many of whom regained their liberty. The Jews are obliged to pay to the Capitoline Jupiter that tribute which they formerly paid to their Temple in Jerusalem, but otherwise they are not harassed by the government. For the most part, however, they are very poor; few of them are great bankers or merchants, but nearly all the rest are petty shopkeepers and peddlers — also a great many are alleged to increase their living by fortune-telling and by like dubious arts.

124. The Roman Plebeians, the " Mob " (*Vulgus*). — Greatly surpassing the resident aliens in number are inevitably the ordinary Roman plebeians. It is a fine thing in the provinces to boast, " *Civis Romanus sum*," but in the capital many a freedman, many an upper-slave of a magnate even, looks down with scorn on a large fraction of this " common herd " (*grex*) that still claims to form " the Roman People." However, if you are really a Roman citizen entitled to wear a toga, and to share in the grain doles and other public distributions, you can really live on very little. Somehow you must find means for the rental of a sleeping garret in an insula, but the daytime you can spend hanging around the fora, porticoes, or the entrances to the circuses

and gladiator schools, playing *morra* and checkergames
(see p. 205); idling in the great public baths; frequenting
every possible public exhibition in the theater or amphitheater and often getting a bare income by toadying most abjectly
to the rich.

Everybody despises this Roman " mob," and yet cringes
to it. Its yells across the circus send the blood from the
cheeks of very tyrannous emperors. The mild Italian
climate renders an existence amid dirt and sunshine, eked
out by very little labor, decidedly tolerable.[1.] Assuredly
very many of these " citizens " are simply honest thrifty
industrialists, trades people, or professional men, holding
their own stubbornly against the competing slaves, freedmen, and aliens. Nevertheless, the proportion of undesir-
ables is dangerously great. Many of the idle plebeians are
the sons of freedmen, who have inherited their parents'
non-Italian vices but who have not been under their necessity
of hard work and faithfulness; and when one examines the
moral and social qualities of the alleged heirs of the virtuous
old-time plebeians the idea of " restoring the Republic,"
still sighed after by a few aristocratic philosophers, appears
absolutely laughable.[2]

**125. The Desirability of Roman Citizenship. The Case
of St. Paul.** — It is as contrasted with the status of provincials that Roman citizenship still preserves its remarkable
value. A citizen can, indeed, no longer go to the Republican
assemblies to elect magistrates and vote on proposed statutes,
but he has his personal and property rights protected by
the best kind of " Quiritian " law. The government is
never, indeed, iniquitous enough to enact that, as between

---

[1] Apparently it was quite possible for impecunious persons to sleep
much of the year under the public arches and porticoes, and thus even
dispense with the need of paying rent!

[2] These hopes had practically died out by Hadrian's day.

Roman and provincial, the judge must always decide for
the former, nevertheless the advantages of the citizen are
great.

A Roman can command all sorts of protection not open to
provincials. The judge will almost inevitably be a little
prejudiced in his favor. If arrested, a citizen can ordinarily
demand the right to give bail. It is a gross outrage to " examine him by scourging." He cannot be put to torture.
If he is finally sentenced to die, he cannot be crucified, but
ordinarily must be beheaded — a very merciful end. Particularly, unless the case is extremely clear, in matters touching his life and status as a citizen he can appeal from the
decision of a provincial governor to " Cæsar " or to the
Senate (if in a province governed by that body).

If we visit the Record Office again, this matter is clearly
illustrated. About twenty-five years after the crucifixion
of Christus, one of his followers, a certain Paulus, was also
arrested in Jerusalem on much the same charges of attempted
sedition and inciting disturbance. But Paulus, when arrested, promptly pleaded his Roman citizenship. Vainly
the local mob clamored for his life even as they had demanded that of Christus. When the local procurator Festus
hesitated to set him at liberty, the prisoner demanded to be
sent to Rome — and thither at great trouble and expense
he had to be shipped; to be tried ultimately before the Prætorian Præfect sitting as Nero's deputy; and the charges
were dismissed and he was set at liberty.[1] If he had not
been a Roman, assuredly the weak-kneed governor of Palestine would have sacrificed him " to please the Jews " just
as Pilatus sacrificed Christus.

126. Clientage: Its Oldest Form. — Between the poorest
classes of plebeians, sleeping within porticoes and despised

---

[1] That St. Paul was presently released after trial at Rome is the con-
sensus among very many competent scholars.

by the superior slaves, and those dignified well-to-do gentlemen who have almost the means to pass as equites, there
are, of course, an infinite number of social strata.   The most
important section of the better plebeians is undoubtedly
to be numbered among the *clients*.

Clientage is a very old Roman institution.   The kings
and nobles of Rome in the very twilight of history had their
clients.   Those were the days when poor plebeians had little
or no legal protection unless they enlisted the patronage of a
magnate.   They entered his *gens* (inner-clan), followed him
in war, voted (when they obtained the vote) in his interest,
assisted him in certain money matters, in short, became
members of his household although very much better off
than the slaves.   In return the patron was bound to defend
their legal rights in the courts and to protect them from all
forms of outrage.   Men were proud to confess themselves as
clients of a Fabius or an Æmilius.   But by the end of the
Republic the institution had practically disappeared in its
original form.   There was little legal discrimination then
against poor citizens, and about all the real clients who now
remained were freedmen, who, as just seen, were bound to
be loyal and helpful to their *patroni*.

**127. The New Parasitical Clientage: the Morning Saluta-
tion**. — Now, however, a new and wholly parasitical clientage
has come into being.   Early every morning the clients can
be seen hurrying down Mercury Street in their hastily donned
togas.   Sometimes a patron lives a great distance across
the city; sometimes a fawning myrmidon hopes to visit
two patrons in the same morning and get a double reward.
Calvus does not rejoice in a great horde of clients, but being
a senator his dignity requires that he should maintain perhaps a score of them.

These clients are an assorted lot.   Some are merely cheap
hangers-on, some are adventurers visiting Rome and ex-

pecting to prosper by earning the favor of the great, there is also a mediocre poet who hopes for a tidy gift some day because of laudatory verses about his " Rex " and the latter's family, there are several distant relatives of the Calvi, poor relations to whom the doles are a form of pension ; and finally there are two or three men of good family and tolerable

CLIENTS GATHERING IN THE RAIN, BEFORE THEIR PATRON'S DOOR.
After Von Falke.

incomes who actually dance attendance on Calvus just to get a little extra pocket money.

The clients gather in the vestibule at dawn, rubbing their eyes, rearranging their hastily donned togas, and each trying to induce the not very civil porter to permit him to enter first. At last the word is passed to the door that, " The patron is ready." The valves open ; the clients swarm inside together. Publius Calvus dressed for the morning is standing in the rear of his atrium, just behind the pool of the impluvium. At his elbow is his nomenclator, the slave who "knows everybody," to whisper a name in case he should not connect it promptly with a face.

" *Ave, patrone, ave !* " cries each client coming up in turn. " *Ave, Marce !* " or " *Sexte !* " or " *Lucie !* " answers Calvus with a more or less formal smile.

If his mood is very gracious, each client is allowed to seize his hand, and two or three in extra favor are suffered to kiss his cheek. The nomenclator meantime prompts him in undertone, " Ask about his wife," " Congratulate him on his niece's marriage," etc. And if that evening there are not more important guests in view, the senator will delight the souls of several by saying affably, " Come to-night to dinner." The clients in any case congratulate themselves that their patron is not like some of those very haughty parvenus, who simply hold out their hands to be kissed and never speak a word, and who like to be called " dominus," as if their clients were merely slaves.

128. The Dole to Clients (the *Sportula*). — After the clients will appear more pretentious visitors — equites and fellow senators — who call to see Calvus on business. Their own clients are probably waiting listlessly in the street, while Calvus's dependents have to stand respectfully near their lord until an upper slave beckons them toward the office — the tablinum. He has a list in his hand and checks off all present as might a master the pupils in his school, and then comes the reward which brought all these toga-wearing gentry thither, a distribution of money.

In former years every client had received an actual portion of victuals, known as *sportula* from the " little basket " which everybody brought to bear the viands hence. But this custom of distributing actual food was inconvenient, and far more pleasing is an actual gift of money. Only regularly listed clients can receive this ; and no client, sick or lazy, can send a deputy.[1] He must appear in person or stand his loss. At length, to every lawful retainer present is carefully counted out a hundred *quadrantes*, small coppers (rather under 25 cents), and besides the clients entertain a few hopes of a fairly liberal present at New Year's Day, and at some other festivals, and as seen, in a kind of rotation they are invited at broad intervals to dinner.

129. Attendance by Clients in Public. Insults They Must Undergo. — After the sportula has been paid, the clients look anxiously toward Calvus. Will he tell them, as he does about half of the time, " Nothing more to-day," and let them scatter down the streets? Not so; " My litter " he orders. The clients are obliged to march before and behind, along with the slaves, helping to elbow aside the crowd, while the senator visits other senatorial houses, next his banker at the Forum, and then the law courts for a consultation, and so goes his round. If he detains the clients through the noon hour, he is obligated to give them some kind of luncheon ; but he can command the attendance of them all even up to the tenth hour, when he may turn them loose to refresh themselves in the public Baths of Titus, after they have left him perhaps at the more select Baths of Agrippa.

As for the clients invited to Calvus's dinner, if the fare is plainer than on the night of a high banquet, there is at least no insulting discrimination. A decent patron and patrona are bound to show themselves " friends " of their clients and to keep up a pretence of democratic manners. But as stated earlier (see p. 120), many a vulgar plutocrat, feeling that he has paid good money to get a proper retinue

---

[1] Women as well as men could sometimes be enrolled as clients. Comical stories abounded ; how a husband appeared with a litter claiming that his " sick wife" was inside — " and would the steward please hurry with the fee" — when, on brushing aside the curtains, the litter was found to be empty.

to follow him to the Forum, delights to insult his clients'
feelings when he invites them.   The host enjoys his fine white
loaf, while the client's is almost too hard to break; the host
a splendid lobster garnished with asparagus, the client " a
crab on a tiny plate hemmed in by half an egg "; the lord
" noble mushrooms," the client " toadstools of doubtful
quality," — and all other treatment is to match.   Yet such
is the servility and pettiness of many that they will endure
all this and worse merely in order to boast the next day of
" last night when I dined with my friend the senator ——! "
" You think yourself a citizen and the guest of a grandee,"
cries the indignant poet.   " *He* thinks, and he's nearly right,
that you've been captured by the fine smell from his kitchen."

Clientage then is a typical institution of imperial Rome —
a means for letting rich men flatter their desire for a huge
company of obsequious attendants by trading on the wretched
ambition of so many to appear to be on familiar terms with
the great.   It multiplies the horde of shabby-genteel persons
around the city, and the vast number of those who flee from
their greatest aversion — honest work.

**130. The Decurions: the Notables of the Chartered
Cities.** — Above the run of clients or even of the better
plebeians is the actual nobility.   Strictly speaking only the
senators and equites are reckoned in this group, but always
in Rome are sojourning a certain number of other men who
hold themselves decidedly better than any plebeians — the
decurions from the enfranchised towns covering all Italy
and dotted over the entire Empire.[1]

The decurions are the notables of the smaller chartered
cities.   In their own communities they are local senators
and enjoy in a small way the position of an actual Senator

---

[1] Especially in Gaul, Spain, and North Africa; in the Eastern provinces the city governments were not run so strictly in the Roman mold
and often kept their native characteristics.

in Rome.[1] Nobody can be elected decurion without a reasonable property qualification, in many cities 100,000 sesterces ($4000), and from their body of wealthy dignitaries the local public assemblies still elect (even under the Empire) city magistrates, duumvirs, ædiles, etc., who take the place in each community of the old consuls and censors of Republican Rome.

Since the loyalty of the population and the popularity of the imperial régime often depends on this very influential class of decurions, the government makes much of them; allows them high-sounding titles and tinsel honors, and any who visit Rome are given social precedence directly behind the actual equites. Furthermore, many high Roman nobles themselves are proud to be enrolled as patrons and *honorary* decurions of the Italian towns, looking after the interest of their client communities in the capital, and, if they visit the smaller cities, being received as particular guests of honor. The number of decurions, however, in Rome itself is always small, although their importance everywhere else in the Empire is vast, and they virtually form a third order of nobility.

131. The Equites: the Nobles of the Second Class. — Everywhere around the metropolis you meet the second-class nobles — the Equites.[2] This " Splendid Order " dates, of course, from the oldest days when to keep a cavalry horse implied having considerable property. The equites sank to unimportance in the prosperous era of the Republic, but were revived to great power by Gaius Gracchus; they were later reorganized and made an effective part of the new imperial régime by Augustus.

---

[1] Hence they were often called *Curiales* from their seat in the local Senate House (*Curia*).

[2] This name is not wisely translated as "Knights," unless there is complete disassociation from the idea of the mediæval baron in armor.

The dividing line between Senators and Equites is not always sharp. Young men of senatorial family who renounce a political career have to " make narrow their purple stripe," as did Ovid, and without disgrace appear henceforth as second-class nobles. Supposedly no persons but the sons of free-born men are eligible for enrollment as equites, but the members of the old-line families fume vainly at the way the Emperors (who have complete dispensing power) will grant " the right of the gold ring," not merely to the sons of freedmen, but sometimes even to downright ex-slaves. There are in truth very few equites in Rome who do not reckon a slave among their not remote grandparents.

The equites are all carefully enrolled in a public bureau under imperial control, and one of the surest holds which the Emperor possesses upon the government lies in the fact that he can refuse enrollment arbitrarily to any young man and thereby practically exclude him from any kind of high public office except in the municipal towns, or from any military rank above that of centurion. The senators, all the more important officials, and all the commissioned officers of the army are equites, although their greater honors cause them to ignore the lesser, while if the Emperor has an eligible son or heir, he is often proclaimed the *princeps juventutis* (" Chief of the Roman Youth ") and is nominally the first member of the Equestrian Order.

132. Qualifications and Honors of the Equites. — To be enrolled as an eques one must possess besides unstained birth (with exceptions above noted), a good public reputation, and taxable property worth at least 400,000 sesterces ($16,000) ; sufficient therefore to pass for a tolerably rich man. The honor comes for life, subject to demotion, however, for disgraceful conduct, or lapse into poverty. A son normally inherits his father's status, if his own share of the patrimony comes to over 400,000 sesterces ; and of course, to make up that magic figure many plebeians pinch and slave.

The honors of an eques are great in any age laying such stress on outward praise and glory. Besides the right to the plain gold ring, the narrow purple stripe running down the front of the tunic proudly proclaims the fact, " I am of the nobility." The equites also enjoy fourteen rows of seats in the public games and theater directly behind the four front ones reserved for the senators. They provide a large fraction of all the jurors in the great civil tribunals which handle most of the litigation.[1] Very many of the great imperial ministries and superintendencies are reserved for them, for the Emperor does not like to trust the senators too implicitly, and some of the smaller provinces have equestrian " Procurators " as their governors, as also does the enormously wealthly province of Egypt.

The majority of the equites, however, are in private life. Senators ought not (except through convenient middlemen) to engage in commerce and trade. Not so the equites — the powerful bankers with whom the imperial treasurer may confer; the owners of the peaceful armadas that enter Puteoli or Ostia; the proprietors of the finer retail establishments along the Sæpta Julia as well as of the huge wholesale houses; the directors of the vast brickyards, and other highly developed industries; the owners of so many of the squalid but profitable insulæ — nearly all will show their " Angusticlave " — their narrow purple stripe. Equites appear at banquets with senators without the least awkwardness; and they like to be addressed by fine booming titles : *insignes, primores, illustres,* or, if holding high office, *eminentissimi,* but in most cases as *splendidi;* and " splendid " they appear to the envious slaves and plebeians.

---

[1] Apparently at this time two thirds of the jurors were equites and one third senators, but the point is not quite certain.

133. Review of the Equites. Pretenders to the Rank. —
The equites are still in theory a military body.   Every 15th
of July, unless the review is deliberately omitted, all members
who are physically able are supposed to procure horses and
take part in a grand parade before the Emperor.   Sometimes
there are at least 5000 equites in the procession.   The
Emperor still has the right of the ancient censors to brand a
man as a bad citizen by the public command, " Sell your
horse ! " as he rides by the reviewing stand ; [1] but the parade
has now become merely an unpleasant formality for portly
men unaccustomed to horseback, and old gentlemen are
usually excused.

In so large a body of " gentry," however, imposture becomes fairly common.   Nearly every Emperor issues an
edict for the purging of the order, and every now and then
some adventurous nobody is divested of his " narrow stripe."
Calvus came home lately from the Flaminian Circus laughing
heartily.   Just behind his senatorial tier a perfumed and
beringed fellow set off with a splendid lacerna sat down saying loudly, " Now at last, thanks to our Cæsar, due honors
have come to the Roman equites, and the vulgar are kept
away " ; but hardly had he spoken ere a lynx-eyed usher
identified him and amid the jeering of hundreds " forced
that very fine lacerna to get up ! "

134. The Senatorial Order. The First-Class Nobility. —
The first class in the nobility is the Senatorial.   The actual
functioning of the Senate which is still a most venerable and
powerful council will be told later (see p. 334) ; here we
have to see its members merely in social and unofficial life.
They number six hundred and entrance into their gilded circle
comes usually by a kind of hereditary right.   The sons of a

---

[1] The Republican censors could also give the order, " Sell your horse"
without stigma to equites who appeared in the review when too old or too
fat !

senator can almost always count on becoming senators themselves if the family fortune is not too impaired and they have not fallen under imperial disfavor. To win the honor you must either be elected (by the Senate itself) to some one of the old Republican offices — quæstors, ædiles, prætors, consuls, etc., — which carried a life seat in the Senate with them, or be appointed outright by fiat of the Emperor. The latter, furthermore, is always pushing forward his favorites by " inviting " the senators to elect them to office, and the " Conscript Fathers " never disregarded such a broad hint from " Cæsar."

135. Social Glories of Senators. — Senators alone are eligible for the highest commands in the army, for the governorships for the more important provinces, except Egypt, and for most of the other exalted offices which do not involve a vulgar handling of money. The Emperor himself ranks as the head of their noble body. Even when he is at bitter odds with them, he must not forget that they share part of his glory. Still is told the story of how one of Nero's parasites raised a laugh from the tyrant one day. " I hate you, Cæsar ! " he announced. " And why is that ? " " Oh, just because you are a senator."

All the senators are officially the " friends," *amici*, of the monarch.

These great nobles are entitled to visit the Emperor in the palace somewhat as clients visit their patron. He is expected to extend his hand to them ; to treat them as a kind of social equals ; and to allow the more important of them to kiss him. They and their wives must be invited to all the greater palace banquets. Finally all the better monarchs are expected to take oath at the beginning of their reigns that they " will never put any senator to death " — that is, that the Senate shall be the supreme judge over its own members.

Although parvenus are promoted by even the best **of**

emperors, the senatorial families average much older than do the equestrian; and it is still a very desirable thing to boast of " ancient blood and the painted visages of one's forebears."

136. The Senatorial Aristocracy Greater than the Senate. — The " Senatorial Aristocracy," nevertheless, is something greater than the actual membership of the great council itself. Not merely the sons but all the male descendants of a senator to the third degree are reckoned as equal socially to the actual " Conscript Fathers," though many such connections dress merely as equites with the narrow stripe. This may be from " lack of ambition " or it may be from desire to engage in trade. Gratia has two brothers. One is a senator, his wealth invested in lands, and at present he is imperial legate over part of Britain. The second is technically only an eques, busy with enormous financial transactions with Alexandria; but the second is the richer and probably the more influential man of the two. Of course, all the wives of senators rank with their husbands, and every cousin, niece, or nephew of the latter feels a reflected luster. The six hundred senators are, therefore, the center of an upper aristocracy with at least six thousand actual members.

137. Insignia, Qualifications, and Titles of Senators. — The actual senators make no concealment of their honors. They have their special shoes (see p. 95), and most important of all they have the broad purple stripe running down the front of their tunics, the precious *laticlave*, distinguishing them instantly from the equites. Nobody, furthermore, can be enrolled as senator unless he possesses the taxable fortune of at least 1,000,000 sesterces ($40,000); and this insures that he is a passing rich man, above petty bribes and able to live with the dignity becoming a Lord of the Empire.

The public glories of these dignitaries match their fortunes. At all the public games and spectacles the senatorial tiers are directly behind the Emperor's loge. In the public feasts the senators are not merely entitled to the seats of honor, but frequently to extra-generous portions of the food. If a senator tours the provinces, he can command every kind of servile attention, even if the Emperor refuses him the " right of free legation " — the privileges of traveling with the honors of an ambassador. Finally if he is arrested, not merely is he ordinarily tried before his peers — in the Senate ; he is subject to much lighter penalties than the run of citizens in case of conviction.[1]

Finally the senators have a title of nobility which they are able to command practically as a formal right [2] — *vir clarissimus* — " Very distinguished Lord " or " Your Magnificence." Gratia, like every senator's wife, is a *femina clarissima;* even her small sons can be addressed pompously as *pueri clarissimi.* To the multitude who make way for their litters, the rank of *clarissimus* appears the acme of attainable happiness.

The political power of the Senate has waned, but emperors are only mortal individuals. They come and go ; the existence of the great, proud, wealthy, landed aristocracy seems to go on forever. Emperors usually succeed so far as they win its loyalty and favor ; they somehow fail, and are branded across history as tyrants (often cut short by dagger thrusts) when they earn its hate. In an Empire of nigh one hundred millions the six thousand of the Senatorial Order form the normal apex of the human pyramid. It is a fine thing to be a senator.

---

[1] By the age of Hadrian we see signs of that rigid separation between upper-class citizens (*majores*) and lower-class (*minores*) which marked the Later Empire. The equites tended to be mingled with the senators in the *majores*.

[2] Marcus Aurelius confirmed this legally about 170 A.D.

CHAPTER IX

PHYSICIANS AND FUNERALS

138. Scanty Qualifications and Training of Doctors. —
People fall sick in Rome quite as much as in every other great
center of humanity, but the healing art has not really pro-
gressed a great deal beyond that in Athens in the days of
Hippocrates nearly five hundred years earlier.[1] A great proportion of even the most fashionable doctors are freedmen,
and nearly all of these have Greek (or sometimes Egyptian)
names. There is no medical examination. Anybody who
has made a failure in other callings is welcome to pose as a
physician and try to extract money from the unfortunate.
There are many " surgeons " and " therapists " around the
city who, a little while ago, were shoemakers, carpenters, or
smiths, and who, perhaps, keep up their old handicraft on
the side. Six months is time enough to learn a little medical
jargon while serving as " disciple " to some experienced
doctor; after that, let the invalids beware.

Under such circumstances the glory of the medical profession suffers. Rightly did Pliny the Elder complain of
doctors : " Any voluble person has powers of life and death
over us, just as though thousands of persons did not live on
without doctoring, as Rome existed for six hundred years
[before the first physicians came]." Such gentry inevitably,
if they fail at quackery, can then drift off to something else,
and very familiar is Martial's epigram : " Diaulus has been
a surgeon and is now an undertaker. At last he's begun to
be useful to the sick in the only way that he's able."

[1] See "A Day in Old Athens," p. 77.

139. Superior Class of Physicians. — Nevertheless, the physicians of Rome are by no means all of them charlatans. If their theories are grossly imperfect, many of them are men of wide experience and keen insight. A sick man able to command the best, need not give up in despair unless his case is really complicated and difficult. Great cures are recorded, as that of Augustus, whose life was saved in a most critical illness by the " cold-water treatment " ordered by his doctor, the wise freedman Antonius Musa — a cure which by saving an all-important life affected the world's history.

Whatever their qualifications, physicians, if not highly educated, assuredly abound in large numbers. Every chartered city maintains a corps of them for the free treatment of the citizens, and keeps up public *hiatreia* — well-lighted, spacious halls for offices and dispensaries.[1] Every cohort of the army has four physicians attached, with superior medical officers over the larger divisions, and camp sanitation has been worked out excellently by the Roman military experts.

In the Imperial Court, the *archiater* (" head physician ") is a well-paid and very important dignitary. Between him and the miserable slave doctors who bleed and physic their fellows in the private familia there are any number of gradations. Most of the doctors, of course, practice for fees, although in Rome, too, a system of free clinics and dispensaries is coming in, with a special public physician for each of the fourteen regions of the city.

140. A Fashionable Doctor. — A doctor of the superior kind is Symmachus whom Calvus summons whenever any of his own family are seriously ill. He has one of the most fashionable practices in Rome, and his annual income is not

---

[1] Antoninus Pius, the ruler succeeding Hadrian, formally enjoined the remission of civic burdens for "community physicians" in the Province of Asia; five in small cities, seven in larger ones, and ten in the largest.

much under that of Quintus Stertinus whose fees in Claudius's day brought him 600,000 sesterces ($24,000) per year. A high-grade physician does not render a monthly bill. He expects to be paid once annually — on the first of January. Besides he counts on receiving a substantial legacy whenever a regular patient at length escapes him and dies. Lower

INVALID WITH ATTENDANTS.

grade doctors, however, are less delicate. They are charged with being greedy for unreasonable fees and with prolonging illnesses easily curable, demanding outrageous sums for common medicines, and taking every sordid advantage of the needs of the sick.

Symmachus is apparently above all such *gaucheries*. He has been trained to bear himself as a polished gentleman. His visits are long or short according to the desires of his patients. He never blurts out unpleasant truths and he always repeats the Hippocratic maxim, " A cure depends on three things, the sick man, his sickness, and the physician " ; and that the physician's business is to help the sick man to cure himself.   The result is that while his anatomical theories would distress a later age, and some of his medicines are very crude, he often effects excellent results especially in those cases where mental therapeutics can avail a little.

Such a doctor possesses a set of surgical instruments quite as good as any available in a later age until at least the time of the French Revolution, and assuredly he knows how to use them very skillfully.   He can dull pain for operations or induce sleep by juice of mandragora or atropin, and he can operate for cataract by distending the eye-pupil by anagallis. Delicate surgical operations, however, he will probably turn over to specialists.   There are such surgeons who operate, no doubt with reasonable success, for hernia and fistula, who take out gall-stones, and deal with very dangerous fractures. There are also lesser specialists who can remove or fill aching teeth and can banish superfluous hair, and there is one shrewd old fellow who commands a princely income — he can really erase the degrading marks of branding upon slaves, after they become lordly freedmen.

141. Medical Books and Famous Remedies. — Symmachus affects to be a man of professional learning.   He possesses and claims to have studied carefully the great medical treatises of Hermogenes of Smyrna in 72 books, and that of Tiberius Claudius Menecrates in 156 books.   To impress his patients he will talk learnedly of the jangling theories of the " Dogmatics," and " Methodics," " Pneumaticists," etc., although professing himself to be an " Eclectic."   However, his own shrewd common sense is usually of greater avail than all his books.

A large part of a popular physician's gains come not from regular fees, but from supplying his patients with medicine.

There are many shops selling crude drugs in Rome but no regular prescription pharmacists.[1] Public opinion avers that the more costly remedies are always the best, and Symmachus does not discourage that idea too much, although telling his select patients that cheap medicaments often are as effective. It is often hard, however, to get pure drugs, and genuine ingredients.[2] Even the best doctors will be deceived by oriental drug dealers palming off false balsams, and similar commodities.

Many physicians consider it professional to keep their remedies secret, and boast of private formulas, which they will not share with their rivals. In Tiberius's day there was a Paccius Antiochus who prepared a marvellous powder, a kind of panacea for many ills. He compounded it behind locked doors and mystified even his assistants as to its nature; but on his death he had the decency to bequeath his formula to the Emperor who had it deposited for inspection in all the public libraries; and Hadrian has just done the same with some formulas left by the great Marcellus of Side.

142. Absurd Medicines. Theriac. — Some of these remedies are of an extraordinary nature and so intelligent a man as Symmachus can have no confidence in them. Still plenty of good doctors will tell you that a piece of hyena-skin is an excellent remedy for mad-dog bites, and that certain very filthy substances make good poultices for swellings. The imperial government actually employs several slaves to catch adders, whence are derived several important medicaments; and it is claimed that medicines to cure gall-stones must be pounded with a pestle that contains no iron. There is no need to dwell on the absurd articles foisted on the gulli-

---

[1] Establishments selling ready prepared salves, plasters, and other standard remedies were not unknown, and must have supplied many doctors.

[2] Chemical analysis was, of course, unknown.

ble by the quacks ; pills made from dried bugs and centipedes are among the very least obnoxious.

There is supposed to be a specific medicine for every disease, and Symmachus's office is crammed with little chests bearing such labels as " *Drug from Berytus for watery eyes. Instantaneous* "; " *Ointment for gout. Made for Proculus, imperial freedman. Safe Cure* "; "*Remedy for scab. Tested successfully by Pamphilius during the great scab epidemic,*" or " *Eye-salve tried by Florus on Antonia, wife of Prince Drusus, after other doctors had nearly blinded her.*" [1] There is also a large box of a famous compound to be used whenever diagnosis is uncertain. *Theriac* is a mixture of sixty-one different elements including dried adders. Whoever takes it is sure to find at least *one* substance that will assist his disease ; and it is prescribed by almost every physician at the opening stages of a malady, before he can attempt diagnosis.

143. Fear of Poisoning. Popularity of Antidotes. — A large part of the doctor's drug collection is, however, made up of *antidotes* for poisons. Everybody dreads being poisoned. Many peculiar deaths which ought to be diagnosed as caused by natural illness are charged up to venomous drugs [2] and indeed a deadly dose rather than a deadly dagger seems a favorite means for murder. People still whisper stories of that awful poison-vender, the woman Locusta, who probably supplied Nero's mother Agrippina with the fatal powder she sprinkled on her husband Claudius's dish of mushrooms, and then another dose to Nero himself to kill his stepbrother, Britannicus, with a highly spiced goblet.

---

[1] These titles and much more of the data here given are from the writings of the great Galen — the master physician of the imperial age ; who wrote his books under Commodus about 185 A.D.

[2] As in the case of the death of Cæsar Germanicus (19 A.D.) whose death at Antioch was probably natural, but which all his friends attributed to poison given by his personal enemy, the Pro-consul Piso.

If a man has many deadly foes, he is likely to take a potion of the precious theriac daily — because antidotes for so many poisons are carried in the compound; and all histories tell how Mithridates of Pontus, that famous adversary of Sulla and Pompeius, used to take antidotes so constantly that he became entirely immune to the venoms prepared by all his enemies. Symmachus, as part of his stock in trade, therefore, keeps the proper antidotes for all such familiar poisons as hemlock, opium, henbane, gypsum, white lead, etc., as well as for many obscurer foods of evil. Rumor says that not long since he had to use several of them on the old ex-consul, Annæus, whose spendthrift sons seemed very anxious to get their inheritance.

144. Medical Students, " Disciples," Beauty Specialists. — Symmachus like all responsible physicians keeps an office on a good street, but although patients can visit him there, the place is mainly for the compounding of medicines by various slaves under the direction of several " disciples." There are no medical schools in Rome,[1] and these young disciples follow their master about, study a little, and learn by watching him. They are kept away from his most select patients; but are allowed to troop into the sick room of the poorer, feel of the pulse, examine the wounds, etc., in a manner most distressing. People, in fact, dread to call in a doctor — it often means being felt over not by one but by a half dozen clammy hands, usually when one is very ill.[2]

In addition to the men of medicine are the " beauty specialists " — persons who claim to have reduced the supplementing of nature to a science. A court physician Crito once wrote four books of standard authority on the com-

---

[1] Probably there were such in the eastern provinces.

[2] Without clinical thermometers or second-watches, the taking of temperature, timing of pulse, etc., must have been a very tedious and disagreeable as well as uncertain process.

pounding of cosmetics. Every physician is called upon to prescribe skin washes, depilatories for rendering the bodies of young dandies perfectly hairless, and formulæ for fragrances for clothes or chambers; but it takes a specialist to know the intricacies of rouge and enamel, and otherwise to assist the ladies. The dividing line also between the physician and the hairdresser is not always easy to mark. Petronius tells about the dames who not merely have abundant false hair, but " take their eyebrows out of a little box " and " put their teeth away at night just as they do their silks."

145. Cheap Doctors: No Hospitals. — The inferior grades of doctors do a great deal of office work. In mere booths or small shops opening upon the street they receive patients, sometimes even standing by the door and bidding the hesitant " Step in! " Their surgeries are decked out with a display of ivory boxes, silver cupping glasses, and golden-handled lancets, — the more incompetent the leech the greater often being the display.

To advertise their skill practitioners of this class will often set bones and perform minor operations before a gaping crowd just outside in the streets — actions denounced by men of Symmachus's caliber; and all their patients are examined with great publicity. Lower still are the itinerant quacks who will diagnose diseases on a street corner and vend alleged theriac and other " medicines " from a pedlar's pack. There are other unlovely members of the profession who grow rich by performing criminal operations, and to whom unfaithful wives or legacy-seekers can appeal, begging them to " put the patient out of his misery! " — with results deliberately murderous. More legitimate of course are the numerous women who attend to the maladies of their own sex. Some of these women are said to be physicians of high capacity and able to command generous compensation.

A serious handicap to medicine exists because there are no public hospitals in Rome, although sick strangers are probably allowed to lie around the Temples of Asculapius or of other healing deities.[1] The control of epidemics is very imperfect. Rome has been visited severely by the plague, and in the reign of Marcus Aurelius it will be ravaged yet again. The age is a brutal one. Much is done to keep the populace amused and to delight the eye; relatively little to preserve precious human lives. In the great slave familia, however, self-interest if no better motive impels the owners to try to keep their chattels healthy. As already explained nearly every slave household has its special slave physicians, men of tolerable competence; and there is also the *valetudinarium*, the infirmary — a detached building or a large room in which sick slaves can be properly tended, and also isolated to prevent infection.

146. Suicide as Escape from Hopeless Disease. — Symmachus, despite his reputation for " wonderful cures," has just lost a wealthy patient. The circumstances were somewhat unusual but by no means unprecedented. Quintus Gordianus, an elderly senator, had been suffering from a very painful internal disease. Symmachus assured him the case was incurable, but that he might, nevertheless, live for years. Thereupon Gordianus announced that he would commit suicide.

The right of a sane man voluntarily to surrender his life is undoubted. Philosophers have written fine essays on the desirability of suicide; only it must be entered upon discreetly and not as a cowardly means of escaping the duties of life. Many of Nero's and Domitian's noble victims ob-

---

[1] Apparently the organization of *public hospitals* in the fourth century of our era, was among the earliest and worthiest of the distinctly Christian charities, after the toleration of Christianity by the Roman government.

viously obeyed the mandate " Open your veins " more because they were tired of existence than because a desperate
attempt to overthrow the tyrant would have been hopeless.
Many a Roman aristocrat has sucked all the sensual pleasure
so completely out of life that the latter has become one great
boredom, and no religion commands " Live on ! " when it is
evident that the remainder of existence must merely be
months or years of helplessness and pain.

As soon, therefore, as Gordianus was satisfied that his case
was hopeless he declared to his relatives that, " He would
starve himself to death." They pleaded with him faithfully
and caused most tempting food to be always within his reach,
but later they took pride in telling of his iron will which re-
jected all their efforts. At last the end came, and all his
circle remarked that Gordianus died as became a Roman
senator and a true philosopher. Suicides for more trivial
reasons than the above are, of course, reported every day.[1]

**147. Execution of Wills. Numerous Legacies Custom-
ary.** — Before Gordianus became too weak, he called in a
group of friends to witness the revision of his will. The right
to execute a will is a precious privilege for Roman citizens,[2]
and the law allows wide options in disposing of one's property. A Roman gentleman makes his will many times and
is constantly revising or adding codicils to the same. Slaves
are not supposed to make testaments — their small *peculia*
must legally revert to their masters ; but the more decent
owners allow even slaves to bequeath their belongings to
fellow-slaves.

---

[1] Two similar cases are recorded in Pliny the Younger ; in one of them
the person contemplating suicide, on being assured by the physicians that
his case was not quite desperate, "agreed to fight on a little longer."

[2] The legal status of women made it needful to resort to various legal
fictions when they drew wills, but they could execute effective testaments also.

A will implies much more than merely distributing one's property among near kin. Gordianus's widow and son were in fact well content when they found not more than two-fifths of the large estate was to pass outside the family. It is a deadly insult — all the more deadly because the departed are beyond retaliation — to fail to remember a familiar acquaintance with a sizable legacy.[1]

"When the tablets are opened" all Rome knows how a man has paid his social debts, usually to people who have no blood connection.

Was the ex-ædile Numerius angry because he only received 10,000 sesterces ($400)? And why was that ill-mannered old eques Albinus left 20,000? And why was the banker Velocius, once such a confidant, left nothing at all? Did Gordianus wish to brand the last-named as a scoundrel? The list of slaves enfranchised, and also of those specifically refused enfranchisement is carefully scanned; as well as various legacies to certain great advocates who have evidently rendered Gordianus service in tight law-suits, and above all a sum of 100,000 sesterces ($4000) to "Our Lord Hadrianus Augustus Cæsar." Gordianus had been by no means a great intimate at the palace, but it would have been most untactful to fail to remember the Emperor. Under bad rulers such a slight would probably involve the actual setting aside of the will, posthumous charges of treason, and the ruin of the heirs by the confiscation of the entire property. Under a good Emperor such an insertion puts the donor's son in good odor with the government, and insures that the imperial procurators (who guard their master's property) will assist in defending the will if disgruntled kinsmen should try to break it.

---

[1] Still greater revenge could be taken by making insulting references in wills to old enemies, making them bequests of no value, or burdened with unwelcome conditions, or even explaining at length, without fear of a slander suit, why no bequest was left to them at all!

148. Regular Incomes from Legacies. Professional Legacy Hunters. — The granting of legacies is in fact so ordinary a part of Roman life that distinguished men like Cicero and Pliny the Younger can almost count on a steady flow of bequests (often from people whom they know but slightly) as part of their income. Gordianus is leaving a mature and proper son to take over his great name, clients, and a good share of his property. His bequests therefore are relatively small, and that fact robs his will of most of its interest. If, however, he had been childless, all Rome would have been agog as soon as people knew that he was dying. Great, if evil, are " the advantages of childlessness." The rich bachelor is sure of obsequious service from innumerable quarters. The more he coughs and the paler he grows, the more the presents he receives and the more do loudly condoling friends press to his bedside. They reach the very depth of servility, and sometimes they are rewarded.

Years ago Horace gave directions to the successful legacy hunter. " If a man hands you his will to read, be sure to refuse and push the wax tablets from you — yet take a side-glance to catch the second line of the first table [below the preamble]. Run your eye quickly along to see whether you are the *sole* heir or one of many." If the prospective victim has a " crafty woman, or a freedman looking after the dotard, strike a partnership with them and praise them to him, that they may praise *you* behind your back." Then when the testator at last dies lament him loudly, as a " worthy and true friend," shed as many tears as you can, and don't grudge a splendid funeral

Thus fortunes can be and often are won, but not invariably. In Trajan's reign there died a rich Domitius Tullus. He allowed the legacy hunters to fasten upon him; to shower him with all kinds of favors — then he actually left everything to a niece and to grandchildren. All Rome was

divided: "Perfidious hypocrite!" some gossips buzzed in
the great baths; but others praised him for "cheating the
hopes of the rascals."

149. Public Bequests. — Gordianus, besides these legacies
to friends, also makes some public bequests. This is an age
when the rich are expected to justify their good fortune by
showering favors upon the community. If the rich testator
had lived in a municipal town, he would have been expected
in his life time to have provided feasts, public games, new
civic buildings, and probably to have repaired the city walls.
As it is, he leaves the cost of a good gladiator fight to an
Italian town that once elected him patron; increases the
endowment for a public library which he had earlier founded
at another such town near one of his villas; and institutes a
trust fund to provide an annual feast in honor of his "Manes"
to be shared in by all the freedmen of his family and by their
own descendants.

**150. Great Funerals Very Fashionable. Desire to Be
Remembered after Death.** — Before he died, Gordianus
also gave particular orders about his funeral. Every Roman
seems to look forward to his obsequies with a melancholy,
but an enormous interest. If he is poor, he hoards his money
and joins a coöperative burial society to provide for final
rites that will be long remembered. If he is rich, he will
leave nothing undone to succeed in impressing the entire city
that it has lost an important citizen. Under the Republic
the funerals of great personages were really public pageants,
deliberately calculated to teach young nobles the glory of a
long career spent in the service of the state. Under the
Empire these customs are still maintained, although often
they are nothing more than vulgar displays showing forth
the wealth of the deceased.

The age does not believe earnestly in immortality. Epicureans deny it outright, and Stoics more than doubt. Sometimes a very gross view of death is taken, that it is merely the careless end of a round of sensual pleasures. You can occasionally read on tombstones inscriptions like this: *" Bathing, wine, and love-affairs — these hurt our bodies, but they make life worth living. I've lived my days. I revelled, and I drank all that I desired. Once I was not; then I was; now I am not again — but I don't care!"* [1] But most persons, especially grave Stoics like Gordianus, view death otherwise. Death means a going out into the dark; a process of being forgotten by those who once loved or admired you. If, by a splendid funeral, you can make your memory last a little longer, who would fail having one? Hence the excuse for very costly obsequies, often for unimportant individuals.

151. Preliminaries to a Funeral. — The moment Gordianus seemed to be breathing his last his son bent over his face as if to catch his final sigh. Then immediately the young man called his father three times " Quintus! Quintus! Quintus! " partly to make sure he was dead; partly as a signal to start off all the expectant slaves and freedmen in loud and frenzied lamentation through all the wide domus. A messenger promptly summoned a fashionable *libitinarius* (funeral director) who undertook to conduct everything in the best possible style. While the house rang with outcries, professional experts washed the body in warm water and took immediately a waxen impression of the features.

The dead was thereupon dressed in an embroidered toga, such as he might have worn when a magistrate, and was placed on a gilded couch in the atrium with the feet towards the door, beside which was set a bunch of cypress or pine, in token of the sorrow in the house. Skillful embalmers

---

[1] An actual tomb inscription.

were available and the actual funeral could have been delayed as much as a week.   This was not necessary, however, and the ceremony took place in two days — time enough to arrange the great pyre and other necessary matters.

The old practice was for every funeral to be held at night, and " funeral torches " were once about as common along the streets as the more festive marriage torches.   But under the Empire the greater display can, of course, be made by daytime, although by a peculiar survival a few torch bearers will solemnly march along in the procession as if to outvie the sunlight.

The mustering of a large funeral procession calls for no mean executive skill.   If the deceased is from an old family, persons must be hired to wear all the death masks found in his atrium, and costumes improvised or rented so that the wearers can appear as consuls, prætors, etc., and all the various articles and exhibits needful for the procession must be assembled.   Above all there must appear at the house of mourning a clever Greek actor, selected partly because of some physical resemblance to the dead.   This is the *archimimus*, who carefully confers with Gordianus's freedmen and even with his son to learn the speech, mannerisms, and the personal foibles of the departed.

152. The Funeral Procession.   The Display of Masked " Ancestors." — At last at a time sure to command the best attention, the criers begin going about all the streets where Gordianus is likely to have had friends.   They shout a formula in quaint, archaic Latin.   " This citizen, Quintus Gordianus, is being surrendered to death.   For those who find it convenient, now is the time for his funeral.   He is being borne from his house! " and the procession sets forth commanded by a master-undertaker — the pompous *designator*.

At the head marches a band of players, their flutes, lyres, and dulcimers keeping up a most melancholy music.   Then unavoidably follows a whole platoon of professional clowns and buffoons singing ribald songs and shouting very coarse jokes to the thronging spectators. Next, apparently, there walks Gordianus himself — it is the archimimus dressed like the ex-consul, imitating his gait, gestures, and voice, and even making broad personal jests at the expense of the deceased. Then follows the really imposing part of the display, and the bereaved widow and her son thrill with aristocratic pride at the thought of it. Theirs is a very old house, and a hundred actors are needed to wear all the wax *imagines* (often battered and blackened) from the great cupboards in the atrium. All his " curule ancestors " going back to the Gallic invasion seem to be accompanying Gordianus to the grave. The spec- tators are checking off the " consuls " and " ædiles " on their fingers, and at last some cry " a censor," and presently even more admiringly a " dictator." [1] One can almost feel that it is no misfortune to die, if only one can look forward properly to this moment of posthumous glory.

153. The Exhibits in the Procession. The Retinue around the Bier. — Behind the procession of death-masks come slaves bearing on poles large crudely sketched pictures upon boards, showing incidents in the Dacian wars where their master commanded as one of Trajan's legates. Gordi- anus also had dabbled in literature, and copies of his essays and poems are now tied on tall rods and carried along con- spicuously by the marchers. Next comes the corpse itself — exposed to view, upon a couch decked with purple, fretted with gold, and carried aloft upon the shoulders of eight picked bearers. All can see that Gordianus wears the "triumphal

---

[1] A hundred imagines of curule ancestors would be a very respectable but not an extraordinary showing. When young Marcellus (Augustus's nephew) died, *six hundred* imagines of noble ancestors were borne in his procession.

ornaments," the laurel wreath as well as the toga prætexta
awarded the favorite generals in the army.[1]

After that follows the family procession. Young Gordianus is robed in black, and leads by the hand his mother, a
venerable matron, who wears the mourning color for women,
white, and who lets her gray locks stream in disorder over
her shoulders. If he had possessed sisters, they would now
tear their hair, dig their nails in their cheeks, and utter piercing cries of grief. This clamor is produced sufficiently by a
group of slave women led by two or three professional female
wailers who, at intervals, set up a shrill chant of lamentation
for the dead. Next follow a great company of Gordianus's
more distinguished friends, all walking with down-cast looks
and clad in black or sad-colored togas. After them is the
large retinue from the familia, first the older freedmen, then
groups of ex-slaves wearing tall caps — token of manumission
by will, and trying not to appear *too* exultant in their new
freedom, then bringing up the rear the whole group of actual
slaves, supposed to be torn with grief at the loss of " so good
a master."

154. The Funeral Oration in the Forum. — The procession
heads at first not toward the place of the final pyre but toward
the Old Forum. The honor of a public funeral oration is
granted to practically every distinguished citizen, including
many noblewomen. Indeed, this use of the Forum is an extremely common occurrence. The space around the orator's
stand (the *rostra*) has been cleared of idlers, and an array of
suitable " curule chairs " has been set out for all the wearers
of the death masks, as if they were again sitting like the
magistrates of old.

After a suitable delay a kinsman of the deceased, a senator
somewhat vain of his reputation as an orator, mounts the

---

[1] Under the Empire only the Emperor could actually ride in a triumph;
but his lieutenants could enjoy the "triumphal ornaments."

rostra and delivers a fulsome culogy. It is notorious that
such " laudations " never stick closely to the truth. The
audience is made to understand that Gordianus was a very
Cato the Elder in personal virtue and a Scipio Africanus in
his success as a general. When that ceremony is completed
the whole company sets forth again — this time toward one
of the gates beyond which is the funeral pyre.[1]

155. Family Tombs. The *Columbarium* and the Garden.
— Burials are not unknown in Rome, but most bodies are
disposed of by cremation. Even persons of very modest
means will try to provide money for a good pyre. This is
partly because the very poor, the worthless slaves, and the
lowest of the plebeians, are not burned, but their bodies simply
are dumped in hideous open pits not far from the Esquiline
itself. Nothing is done to the bodies thus exposed except
to leave them to the dogs and ravens, and only the favor of
Jupiter averts from the city an incessant pestilence in consequence. Long since, however, Gordianus's family has
erected along the Appian Way (though another frequented
highroad could have been selected) a stately tomb, calculated
to attract attention from all passers.

Handsome tombs can take many forms; there is even a
good-sized stone pyramid, 116 feet high, erected to guard the
ashes of Gaius Cestius, a great man under Augustus. That
of the Gordiani is of a more modest character; a circular
masonry tower, about fifty feet in diameter and rather higher,
surmounted by a castellated battlement adorned with life-
sized marble statues of famous members of the family. Inside there is no huge chamber for a sarcophagus, but simply
a series of arched vaults the walls of which are honey-combed
with little niches, each intended to receive a funeral urn.

---

[1] The granting of an actual funeral pyre inside of Rome was an extraordinary honor — reserved only for emperors and other unusually favored
personages.

This kind of interior, therefore, is not unhappily called a *columbarium* — a " pigeon-cote "; and here will be placed not merely the urns of all the regular scions of the family, but (in inferior niches of course) those of all the freedmen and even of all the better loved slaves.   The ashes of the Gordiani, mighty or humble therefore rest all together.

SCENE ALONG THE APPIAN WAY: showing the tombs and the gay crowds passing.

Outside this massive tower there is a considerable open compound, laid out as a pleasant garden, with shrubbery, flower-beds, and a little lodge for the slave in residence who acts as caretaker.   There is even a small but handsome building, where members of the family can meet for the periodic feasts in honor of the dear departed.   Handsome statues and fine bas-reliefs on the inclosing walls abound, and the place in short seems much more like a small pleasure park than a cemetery.   This mortuary compound, however, is one of the better types of inclosures.   The taste displayed

in some adjacent is execrable. Already across the Appian
Way opposite, a rich freedman has purchased a large lot and
is erecting in his own life-time a tall central statue of himself,
flinging money from a bag to the populace, with the base
surrounded by bas-reliefs showing his favorite small dog,
some gladiator fights, and deep-laden craft under full sail —
to explain how he made his money.[1]

PYRAMID — TOMB OF GAIUS CESTIUS: Ostia Gate of the Wall of Aurelian
(built *circ.* 275 A.D.) in background.

For many miles out into the Campagna around Rome extend these strange cemeteries — not in seclusion, but passed
by incessant traffic. Some of the monuments are magnificent, some simple; they illustrate almost every type of sculpture — but the object of nearly all is the same, to remind
the living of the one-time existence of the dead, and so to

[1] This, of course, was the monument which Trimalchio, Petronius's
famous character, arranged for himself.

provide a kind of spurious immortality often for very commonplace persons, in an age when the immortality of the soul
seems no favored doctrine.

156. The Funeral Pyre and Its Ceremonies. — At last
the funeral procession has reached the great mausoleum of
the Gordiani. The pyre of choice wood, sprinkled with
perfumes, unguents, and costly spices is ready at a safe dis-

VIEW ALONG THE APPIAN WAY SHOWING FUNERAL MONUMENTS.
Restored after Von Falke.

tance. The sides of the pile have been covered with dark
leaves, while cypress boughs have been set upon the top.
Amid these the bier and the corpse, just as they have been
borne, are now planted and various articles of clothing,
jewelry, trinkets, etc., used by the deceased are next placed
upon the pyre. If the ex-counsel had been a younger man
fond of hunting, deer nets and boar spears might have been
added; or favored horses and dogs slaughtered and their
carcasses added to the pile.

At length all is ready.   Young Gordianus is handed a
torch, and with averted face he touches it to the wood im-
pregnated with perfumed oils.   Instantly a great blaze shoots
up, the smoke from the aromatic wood smelling most sweetly.
The company waits in mournful silence until the tall pyre
collapses and the bier has been utterly consumed.   Then as

STREET OF THE TOMBS AT POMPEII, SHOWING TYPICAL MONUMENTS OF THE
SMALLER CLASS.

the fire glows away, several loyal freedmen dash forward
and quench it with great jars of chilled wine.   Certain cal
cined bones and ashes are collected, wrapped in fine linen
cloths and placed in a superb funeral urn, blue and white
glass cut into exquisite designs, showing boys piping and
treading the grapes in a festival of Bacchus.   The last mortal remains of the departed senator are, therefore, at rest
amid scenes eminently cheerful.

157. Funeral Monuments.   Memorial Feasts to the Dead.
— The ceremony is over. " *Vale!* " — and again " *Vale!* "
cries all the company ere departing.   The urn will now be
placed in one of the niches in the columbarium; but in
Gordianus's honor they will erect a special statue, at its base
chiseled a peaceful ship gliding steadily toward a distant
shore; the son and widow evidently recalling the peaceful
thoughts of Cicero in his essay " On Old Age " — " I find the
nearer I come to the time of death the more I feel like one
who begins to see land, and knows that sometime he will
enter the harbor after the long voyage."

On Gordianus's birthday, on the anniversary of his death,
and also for eight days in February sacred to the honored
dead, his heirs and loyal freedmen will visit the spot, deck his
statue with wreaths of roses, violets, and other flowers, sacrifice a black sheep or pig to the " Manes," and indulge in a
feast in his honor.   This will be kept up, perhaps, until his
own son is placed on the pyre and the fame of the " great
Gordianus " has sunk to the barest memory.

158. Funerals of the Poor.   "Funeral Societies." —
We have witnessed obsequies of a rich senator.   Less favored
persons, of course, are buried with ever-increasing degrees of
simplicity.   There is almost no religious element in Roman
funerals.   The bodies of unfortunates can be disposed of with
brutal abruptness and lack of decorum, but the great host
of plebeians and of those freedmen who cannot hope for an
urn in the columbarium of a noble family have a recourse.
They often club together in a " Funeral Society."   Everybody pays a fixed assessment into a common chest; out of
these funds space is hired in one of the great public columbaria
which are often erected as legitimate speculations.   When a
member dies he is assured of a respectable procession of buffoons and weepers (imagines being out of the question), a
private harangue in his honor, and a thoroughly adequate

funeral pyre.   Funds not needed for this purpose are spent
on feasts once or more a year in which the names of dead
members are solemnly commemorated.

Some of these funeral "colleges" are really elaborate
affairs, with considerable ritual, a permanent hall, and a
corps of elective officers, "prætors," "curators," etc., whose
tinsel pomp makes the wearers forget that most of the time
they are humble plebeians or even slaves.   The collegia, in
other words, appeal to those who in another age may find a
certain inferior type of "lodge" very congenial.   They are
grandiloquently named for some patron god, calling themselves "The Worshippers (*cultores*) of Apollo," or perhaps
for an Oriental deity, "The Servants of Serapis"; but their
fundamental purpose is the same; to insure against the horrid
thought of having one's body flung into the open pits of the
potter's field and then perhaps having one's ghost wander
in misery over sea and land instead of finding a calm oblivion
in Hades.

CHAPTER X

CHILDREN AND SCHOOLING

**159. Theoretical Rights of Father over Children. The
Patria Potestas.** — When a child is born into a Roman home
the father has complete legal rights even as in Athens to
determine whether it is to live or to die.[1] If theoretically
he has the terrific power as *pater familias* to kill his children
in later life if they merely displease him, how much more can
he claim the right to decide that " This boy will be one too
many," or " We can afford no more girls," or " This child
will be sickly and deformed." If his decision is adverse,
mother and nurse may beseech in vain ; the babe is simply
" exposed " — that is, carried by a slave to some spot
by the highway and left to perish. This harsh old law is
unrepealed.

Possibly such deserted children will be taken up by those
whose homes are desolate and who require consolation.
There is a greater and fouler chance that such babes will be
carried away and reared by human harpies who raise boys
and girls to sell as victims of gross wickedness among the
rich, or who even mutilate the children to convert them into
grotesque buffoons or pathetic beggars to wheedle the coppers
from the tender-hearted. Perhaps some of those horribly
deformed creatures who cry " Give ! Give ! " behind the
litters of the senators are blood relations to the gilded lords
themselves. This is physically possible, if we can believe
many ugly stories.

---

[1] Compare "A Day in Old Athens," p 57.

Legal right and actual custom can often, however, stand miles asunder. No Roman gladly will see his house dying out, despite the " advantages of childlessness." In fact to keep up the family name, resort is often had to *adoption*, sometimes of mature adults, to an extent quite unknown in other ages. The upper classes under the Empire are dwindling so rapidly, thanks to many causes, that rare indeed is the house where a lawful child is unwelcome; and in the lower classes fathers are fathers still. In short though the cruel old " right of exposure " exists, it is not exercised often enough to make its practice a wholesale evil, and a man of distinction who exposes a babe (unless his family is remarkably large and expensive) will fall under social ostracism; in fact the Emperor may even be advised to strike him from the list of senators or equites as " a bad citizen."

160. Ceremonies after Birth of a Child. The *Bulla*. — The birth of a child in a good family is, therefore, the signal for no common rejoicing, and thanks to the favored position of Roman women, girls are not a serious discount as against boys. Then comes the grand celebration — the *lustratio*, the name-day for the babe.

This occurs nine days after the birth of boys and the eighth after that of girls; the idea being not to name the child prematurely lest it die in first infancy. The ceremony takes place in the atrium. The mother cannot, perhaps, be present, but there is a general gathering of the near friends, kinsmen, clients, etc., before whom the nurse solemnly presents herself and then lays her little bundle of swaddling clothes at the feet of its father. With equal solemnity the father bends and takes up the infant and with his formal " lifting up " the whole company raises a shout of joy.[1]

---

[1] The father might have "taken up" the child earlier to indicate his intentions not to expose it, but some later act of legal acknowledgment before witnesses was necessary.

Henceforth, the babe is of undoubted legitimacy, a member of the family, entitled to the protection alike of the family lares and of the public law, and a new citizen of the Roman state. Then the father, turning to the company, if the child is a boy, announces in clear voice his *prænomen*, *e.g.*, " Let the lad be called Marcus ! "

After these formalities are ended the kinsmen and also the favorite slaves rush forward and throw around the neck of the infant cords bearing little metal toys, tiny swords, axes, flowers, or even dolls, all called *crepudia*, from the manner in which they clank together.   Most important of all, however, is the golden *bulla*, an elaborate locket containing charms, which the father himself hangs about the child's neck.   If the family is poor, one of painted leather may answer, but a bulla there must be.   It will never be laid aside permanently until the proud day when the grown-up lad " assumes the manly toga," or when the girl leaves her parents' house as a bride.

161. The Roman Name : Its Intricacy. — It is no slight thing, this matter of the Roman personal names, and they are far more complicated than are the Greek.   Under the Republic names were so standardized among the upper families, that those of a young nobleman were practically determined the moment he touched the cradle.   How many " Appii Claudii " figure in the history of the Commonwealth !   Omitting technicalities, practically every Roman citizen then had three names : his *prænomen*, a personal designation something like the Christian " John " or " George," his *nomen*, fixed on him by his *gens* (special clan) such as Cornelius, Fabius, Julius, etc., and finally his *cognomen*, which marked the particular family of the gens to which his father belonged.   Cæsar, Sulla, Cicero, Scipio, and the like were all cognomens corresponding closely to later-day surnames, and were anything but the individual property of certain famous holders of the same. Thus even a cognomen could have many bearers, and sometimes a second cognomen was added — such as Publius Cornelius Scipio *Nasica.*

This is all very well, but how few are the options left to the parents in selecting the prænomen! There are only eighteen regular Roman prænomens, of which Marcus, Gaius, and Lucius are perhaps the most common. Certain families confine themselves to a very few prænomens. Thus no Cornelian ever names his sons anything but Gnæus, Lucius, and Publius unless the gods bless him with a fourth boy. The Domitii were nearly all either Gnæus or Lucius. Rare was the Claudian eldest son who escaped being called Appius.[1]

These cases simply register what is true in most of the old families. The rule is to name your first son always after your own father. Thus Publius Calvus's young Titus is the grandson of a Titus and the great grandson of a Publius. His younger brother, however, was not thus named by rigid precedent. He could be named Decimus.[2]

162. Irregular and Lengthy Names under the Empire. Names of Slaves. — Things are far more irregular, however, since the Empire has brought the Roman name along with the Roman citizenship to hordes of freedmen and foreigners. They Latinize their alien names, or they take an altered form of their ex-master's names, for example, Claudianus Licinianus; or often, being complete upstarts, swell around with absurdly long names often meaning nothing at all. This is true even of some high officers, and there is now ruling as proconsul of Africa a senator calling himself pompously Titus Cæsarinus Statius Quintius Statianus Memmius Macrinus, while that of the governor of North Britain, a

---

[1] And hardly anybody outside the Claudian gens was ever named Appius.

[2] Literally "Number Ten"; but that meaning had disappeared.

certain " Pollio," has *nine* names if you give him his full title.[1]

As for slaves they were ordinarily called in simpler days of the Republic merely " Marcipor," or " Lucipor," etc., — " Marcus's boy," or " Lucius's boy "; but such descriptions in the days of the great familiæ become impossible. Most house slaves are either named for Greek deities or heroes, or else for some Oriental potentate, precisely as " Cæsar " and " Pompey " will figure on slave plantations of another day. " Mithridates," " Pharnaces," " Cyrus," and the like appear in every atrium. There are also plenty of handsome boys answering to such fine names as " Eros," " Polydorus," " Xenophon"; or who are named for their native country as " Syrax " for a Syrian, and " Cappadox " for a Cappadocian.

163. Names of Women. Confusion of Roman Names. — When a girl is born in an old family her chance of a distinctive name seems even less than that of her brothers. There are really no recognized prænomens for girls, and until lately there have been hardly any regular cognomens. Calvus's daughter should have been merely called Junia for her gens : " The Junian Woman." If it is needful, however, to separate her from her cousins, she can be called *Junia Calvi* — " Calvus's Junia." If she had a younger sister, she would be simply " *Junia Prima* " as against " *Junia Secunda* " — Junia No. 1 and Junia No. 2.

This kind of effacement is, however, becoming very displeasing to high-spirited Roman women. They are now asserting their personality by demanding special names. The result is that they are getting a kind of irregular cognomens. Calvus's daughter is, therefore, known as Junia *Gratia* (from her mother), and should the house be favored

---

[1] Very many such lengthy names are found under Hadrian.

with another young mistress, she will probably be Junia *Calva* in compliment to her father's cognomen.

Nevertheless, with every explanation, the names alike of men and women at Rome are utterly confusing. Duplication seems incessant and anything like a complete directory of the city would apparently carry many pages of identical entries. Of course, a ready use of nicknames (constantly invented by Italian ingenuity) overcomes the actual difficulty. Among near friends or dependents it is quite proper to cry "Hail, Spurius!" or "Well said, Tiberius"; but it is an impolite familiarity to employ the prænomen except for intimates. Ordinarily the cognomen is the proper form, used, be it said, without any "Sir" or "Mister," and in the Senate the archaic usage requires that the Conscript Fathers should be summoned by prænomen and gentile name only. *"Dic, Marce Tulle,"* "Speak, Marcus Tullius," was the form by which Cicero was often called before he began his great orations.

164. Care of Parents in Educating Children. — So a Roman child receives that great thing, his name. What is the course of his life if he grows to manhood? Very much the same as in other civilized lands, where most parents are loving and where most children bring joy to the house. Boys and girls, until school age, are largely in the hands of the womenfolk. Gratia's old nurse, brought with her to Calvus's house, is still more of a beloved mentor and tyrant to Gratia's children, usually bribing her charges to be good "with honey, nuts and sweet-cakes." But as soon as boys, at least, begin to pass out of early childhood their fathers are expected to take them in hand, and even a man of high rank is criticized if he leaves his sons too much to the guidance of paid tutors and of slaves.

This paternal discipline may be harsh but it is seldom negligent. Boys are taught to go with their fathers almost everywhere; to watch and listen in silence, but to ask intelligent questions afterward. Thus young Titus is already old enough to accompany his father Calvus to the sessions of the Senate itself. On a seat reserved near the door for senators' sons he listens through many a solemn debate. Presently the routine of business is so familiar to him, that he presumptuously thinks he can correct the consul on certain points of order. He and his companions of like rank already are playing " prætor's court " — with one of them on the tribunal and the others (like their parents) the orators in the great basilica. As the good old customs have waned this companionship of fathers and sons has perhaps somewhat waned also — but it still remains one of the worthiest features of the Roman training.

165. Toys and Pets. — Roman children lack nothing in playthings. All but the elaborate mechanical toys of a later age are at their disposal. Little children have their rattles, balls, and carts. Small Junia plays with very life-like dolls of ivory, wax, and painted terra cotta, often fashioned by exceedingly skilful Greek craftsmen. She and her brothers rejoice in swings and hobby horses, while Titus and young Decimus also make glad in a finely painted " century " of wooden soldiers and in tops, hoops, and marbles — such as are transmitted almost unchanged across the ages, and they receive somewhat suspiciously (as soon as they are of proper age) a gift of a carefully carved set of wooden letters, a sly device for teaching the alphabet.

Much more welcome than these last are, of course, the New Year and birthday presents of tame nightingales, talking parrots, and caged blackbirds, of dogs, large and small, of that somewhat rare animal from Egypt — a delightful furry cat, and best of all — when they grow a little older — being children of a senator, each a well-broken pony — of little use in Rome, but a splendid comrade when the family goes to its villas.

As they get older still a decent allowance of pocket money is added and an earnest attempt is made to teach the children financial responsibility, to add accounts, to save their sesterces, and not to run up bills. It is not ungenteel, however, for a youth of family to be an easy spender, and Pliny the Younger has scolded a friend as outrageously severe for "thrashing his son because he was too lavish in buying horses and dogs."

166. The Learning of Greek by Roman Children. — Even before formal schooling begins, the young Calvi, like all other Romans of the better class, have begun an important part of their education — the learning of Greek. The Athenian education was a single-language education with no studies outside those of the mother tongue.[1] The Roman education is a bi-lingual education.

Without Greek everybody confesses that a full half (probably more) of the world's entire wit and wisdom is locked away. Without Greek not merely must a man refuse to claim the least real culture; he is handicapped in all the professions and in most forms of business. He can have no commercial dealings with the Levant. If he travels anywhere East of the Adriatic, he can hardly make himself understood outside of the governors' prætoria and the camps. Even into the literary Latin there have crept an enormous number of Greek terms, mostly having to do with matters of learning or luxury. In short without the mastery of Greek a Roman of any ambitions is hopelessly lost.

A scholar need not, however, bother about any third language. Practically all Levantines can jabber *some* Greek, even though their accent be abominable, and their native tongue Syriac or Coptic. As for Spaniards, Gauls, and Britons doubtless interpreters are needful if you visit their

---

[1] See "A Day in Old Athens," p. 63.

crude villages, but all their upper classes are now busily learning Latin just as they are learning the joys of Roman baths, circus races, and cookery. With Latin and Greek you are ready to meet the world.

Greek is taught in the schools, but hardly as a painfully acquired foreign language. From infancy Titus, Decimus, and Junia have had Greek-speaking attendants, and their own parents (very fair Greek scholars) take pains to talk in good Attic part of the time while they play with them. As the children grow up about half of all the more elegant and refined conversation they must hear will be in Greek — and so through all their education. The result will be that Junia may turn out to be a learned lady like the poetess Julia Balbilla, the Empress Sabina's friend, who has written some very fine Greek elegiacs,[1] " worthy of Sappho, " say her friends; or Titus if he dabbles in philosophy, may write a long treatise in good Attic prose as well as can his contemporary the destined emperor, Marcus Aurelius.

167. Selection of a School. — In the good old days a father was expected not merely to give his son moral and practical lessons, but actually to be his schoolmaster — to flog reading, writing, and a little arithmetic into him; even as Cato the Elder (234–149 B.C.) boasted that he did with his own son. But that stage has long passed, and the main question now for every boy or girl is, " tutors or school? " No doubt families of the highest rank find private tutors fashionable and convenient; thus such a personage as Augustus employed the skilful freedman, Verrius Flaccus, to teach his grandsons; but the advantages of contact with other children of about the same social class are clearly understood. The young Calvi, therefore, have been sent to

---

[1] These verses have been preserved to the present age by being inscribed upon the foot of the colossal statue of the "Speaking Memnon" in Egypt, during the visit there of Hadrian and Sabina.

a carefully selected school.   This arrangement is exceptionally good because their father's colleague, the ex-prætor Aponius, owns a remarkably gifted slave, one Euganor, who is allowed not merely to teach his master's children but (by a recognized custom) to take in others; their fees going toward his *peculium* saved up to buy his freedom.

168. Extent of Literacy in Rome.   Education of Girls. — Schools exist everywhere in Rome, and there are all sorts and conditions of schools.   There is no system of public education, and probably a good many poor plebeians and slaves are barely literate enough to spell out the gladiator notices and to jot down a few accounts or memoranda; but public opinion condemns parents who deny their children at least a little schooling, and absolutely illiterate persons are rare.[1]

Girls in poor families are rather less sure of instruction than boys, and in superior families they seldom pass on to the upper and the rhetoric schools; but apparently in the ordinary schools they frequently go with their brothers on terms of perfect equality.   There seems to be no prudish separation of the sexes, although when the grown boys go off to learn the tricks of orators and philosophers, nobly-born girls spend the years just before their marriages under good tutors learning the poets, and being taught a graceful proficiency in harp playing and also enough of dancing to give them the erect carriage and the stately, calm movements of destined matrons.

169. Schools for the Lower Classes. — Between the select establishment of Euganor in a side apartment of Aponius's great mansion and the cheapest type of school along Mercury Street there is a great gulf fixed.   Any kind of a

---

[1] Of course, there would be many lower class Italians who, although fairly at ease with Latin, would be entirely unfamiliar with Greek.

shelter will do for a low-grade school, and any kind of a half-educated fellow can set up as a school teacher.

Take for example poor Platorius who, having failed as an inn-keeper at Ostia, is trying to earn a living by leasing a vacant shop near the Insula Flavia. The shallow room opens directly upon the noisy street, and the passing throngs divert

BOY STUDYING.

the children, while the clamors of the children distress all the semi-invalids in the big insula. Every thrashing by the master attracts a knot of brutal idlers just outside. Platorius's school is of the lowest grade, but he has to make a certain pretence of learning by setting up a few chipped busts of Homer, Virgil, Horace, etc., and erecting a high seat (*cathedra*) for himself. His class sits before him on long backless benches. There are no desks, and every child holds his smudgy wax-covered tablets uncomfortably upon his knee, as he copies or erases with his stylus.[1]

To all the better schools the children come each accompanied by his or her " pedagogue," much after the Greek manner; a private slave being especially assigned to each boy or girl, and obligated to lead his charge to and from school, help with the lessons, guard the child's morals, and even assist in chastising.[2] But few of Platorius's pupils come

---

[1] The writing end of the stylus (bone or metal) was sharp. The opposite end was blunt and flattened for erasing on the soft wax.

[2] See "A Day in Old Athens," p. 64.

from parents who can afford the luxury of a pedagogue for their children. They appear by themselves so early in the morning in winter time that they have to bear smoky lanterns; the most self-sufficient of them being " the sons of centurions, with satchels and tablets hung on their left arms, and carrying every Ides (middle of the month) their fee of eight brass pieces each." [Horace.] Each boy has devoured a crust before leaving home and the school continues without recess until noon when there is an intermission of fair length to get the prandium or at least to buy some sausages from the street dealers, and perhaps to indulge in a short siesta. After that the deafening study is resumed, and there is relief in the neighboring tenements only when the school is dismissed towards dusk.

170. Scourging, Clamors, and Other Abuses of Cheap Schools. — A school is no asset to the neighborhood. Vainly do the satiric poets implore a teacher to " be kind to his scholars " and to " lay aside his Scythian scourge with its horrible thongs " and his " terrible cane, the schoolmaster's scepter." Poor Platorius knows well enough that the type of parents who employ him believes the old maxim " he who is not flogged is not educated." The Romans are a military people and the ideal of a school is always somewhat the stern discipline of the centurion with his vine-stock (see p. 323). Precepts in many a classroom are enforced with curses and blows, and Seneca has declared in disgust that it is a common thing " to find a man in a violent passion teaching you that to be in a passion is wrong."

The children, too, are often permitted to study their lessons aloud even as in the schools of the Orient. All this adds to the buzzing confusion, so that it is claimed that a school causes more noise than a blacksmith at his anvil or the amphitheater applauding a favorite gladiator.

The teaching and the flogging keep up through a long

season. The school year begins on March 24th, when Platorius painfully counts the entrance fees brought by each scholar, reckoning himself lucky if he does not have to split his gains with the pedagogues who attend a favored few of the

SCHOOL DISCIPLINE.

children. There is a considerable holiday in summer when it is too hot to study, and children of good family are likely to be attending their parents in the country. There is another interval of about a week at the Saturnalia and over New Year's Day; another just before the new school year begins in March. Otherwise, except for the more important religious festivals, and the " Nones " (5th or 7th days of each month), the studying and the beating go on, with rather fewer holidays than in the twentieth century.

Platorius is near the bottom of the educational ladder. His fees are only about four sesterces (16 cents) per month per pupil, and he is none too sure of prompt payment. The miserable room costs something for rental. If his pupils fail to progress, their parents storm at him and promptly shift to another master. In short he leads a dog's life. The green grocer and the copperpot monger who have stalls opposite the school despise him as entirely beneath them.

171. A Superior Type of School. — Quite different is the atmosphere of Euganor's schoolroom. He is technically a slave, but a slave of very superior class. The children come to him accompanied not merely by extremely genteel pedagogues but by subordinate slaves, *capsarii*, who carry their books and tablets, and the establishment has a convenient ante-room, where all these gentry can foregather and match gossip, " My master says " — while their charges are being instructed.

The school itself is held in an elegant chamber adorned with fine frescos of historical events such as the campaigns of Alexander, speaking statues of great literary figures, and, conspicuous upon the wall, an elaborately painted map of the Roman Empire, " for," affirms Euganor, " the boys should have daily before their eyes all the seas and lands, and all cities and peoples comprehended therein; for the name and position of places, the distance between them, the source and outflow of rivers, the coastline with all its seaboard, its gulfs and its straits are better taken in by the eye than by the ear." [1] Euganor, too, has his rod and does not bear it in vain, but he never allows his discipline to degenerate into stupid cruelty. He is, in short, an extremely competent man who studies each of his charges carefully and who would prove an excellent teacher in any schoolroom in any age.

172. Methods of Teaching. — All Roman schools are small. The idea of vast " graded " establishments where year after year pupils are passed from teacher to teacher and at last " graduated " has occurred to no man. Platorius conducts his school entirely alone. Euganor has a couple of efficient monitors, but neither he nor Platorius tries to handle more than say thirty pupils. Many of Euganor's pupils came to him while little more than babies and will only leave him when actually ready for the rhetoric schools. He is largely responsible for their entire elementary education, although many of the higher class children know the Latin and Greek alphabet and can spell a little before being put under his charge.

---

[1] These are the words of Eumenius, a teacher of about 300 **A.D.**, but they would have been equally proper in the age of Hadrian.

This is no place for a real discussion of the actual forms of education. First there comes the mere teaching of reading, writing, and simple arithmetic, with very little use of books, the master dictating sentences and correcting the tablets whereon the children write them down. Such a teacher as Platorius may have a few musty rolls of papyrus which his charges are allowed to handle gingerly, but " First Readers " as understood in later schools are unknown. Euganor is better off, and a considerable library is at his disposal, although barring a few books of fables it contains little that is directly appealing to children.

In the poorer schools the average master congratulates himself if his charges stay long enough to become fairly literate, but the better establishments, of course, accomplish far more.   When a child can once read with tolerable fluency, and can write the characters on his wax tablets without wandering from the traced lines or needing too many corrections, he begins to have the great poets, especially Virgil and Horace in Latin and Homer in Greek, pounded into him. He is compelled to learn very long passages of such authors by heart,[1] and as an especially desirable exercise he is forced to translate both from Greek into Latin and also from Latin into Greek.

Since many of Euganor's pupils will presumably become orators, they are furthermore aided to improve their diction also in every possible manner, to acquire a good stock of metaphors, and to have on hand a great supply of apt, pungent quotations.   All the possible meanings in the literary texts are explained, likewise the mythological, historical, and geographical allusions, etc.   The study of literature thus becomes what is really a form of a " General Information " course.

---

[1] Persons who could recite the whole of the Iliad and Odyssey from memory were not unknown, although they were usually learned slaves, not Romans of the higher class.

173. Training in Higher Arithmetic. — Before the children leave Euganor they are also taught the higher forms of arithmetic. Prior to the coming of Arabic numerals this is pretty serious business, yet every Roman of property must be able to keep elaborate accounts, and not be too dependent upon his stewards. Indeed, in some superior schools a special arithmetic teacher is called in ; a *calculator*, who is entitled to demand extra large fees, although one suspects that most of his pupils are equites' sons who will probably engage in commerce. One thing, however, Euganor does not have to bother about — physical culture. The Greeks can send their sons to the *palæstra* and to the harpist to learn gymnastics and music. The Romans try merely to see that their boys get exercise enough to keep them in good health, but they cannot grasp the practical value of a training that neither makes the lads better soldiers nor better men of business. Many Romans, of course, learn also about the fine arts, but never in the regular classroom.

174. The Grammarians' High Schools. — By their early teens, however, even Euganor's pupils begin to forsake him. They are passed on to a higher teacher, a regular " grammarian " (*grammaticus*), who assumes that his charges are well grounded in the fundamentals, and who endeavors to instruct them in the real niceties of Greek and Latin literature. Sometimes also there is a specialist in each of the languages.

In these high schools great stress is laid on proper pronunciation and elocution. Euclid's theorems in geometry are studied, and a good deal of history is fluently if not very critically taught. Much of the learning is superficial, for it is a fine thing in many circles to *affect* to be erudite,[1] and more

---

[1] A tombstone for a boy who died at the age of ten boasts that its subject "knew the dogmas of Pythagoras and the teaching of the books of the learned." He was also alleged to have read all of Homer and to have studied Euclid "tablets in hand."

stress is sometimes laid on absurd problems of mythology
than upon learning sober facts.   Grammarians who teach
the sons of the parvenu rich are liable, indeed, to be scolded
if they cannot themselves explain instantly " Who was
Anchises's nurse? "   But the better grammarians' schools

GRAMMARIAN INSTRUCTING TWO UPPER PUPILS : an attendant (*capsarius*)
standing at one side.

turn out pupils who are not perhaps men of deep learning but
who have a great fund of information, who can write a clear
accurate Latin (and often a Greek) style, and generally
carry themselves as cultivated young gentlemen.   Those,
however, who aspire to pass as highly educated will inevitably go on to the still higher school of the *rhetor*.

175. Oratory Very Fashionable. — Oratory seems the
keystone to success.   True, the fall of the Republic makes
it impossible to harangue the assembled Comitia in behalf of
favorite candidates or proposed laws.   Even in the Senate
there are now grave limitations upon free eloquence.   Nevertheless, the desirability of " fame " as an orator seems incalculable.   To win your cause in the courts; to make a

crowded hall resound with applause at your set orations seems the height of peaceful triumph. Never will another age set more store on high-soaring formal *talk* than this age of the Roman Empire. The actual performances of professional orators and " readers " we can glance at later, and, of course, space lacks for any presentation of the " Science of Eloquence "; but mention must be made of the rhetoric schools in which by ardent anticipation young Titus and Decimus Calvus are already winning laurels.

176. Professional Rhetoricians. — No slave or ordinary grammarian can hope to conduct a rhetoric school. The masters are either Romans of such rank that they can mingle with senators, or are distinguished Greeks fresh from the schools of Rhodes or Athens.[1] Not many years ago in Trajan's reign, a certain Isæus came to Rome from Greece. He dazzled the noblest circles by his proficiency; his diction was the purest Attic; his sentences sparkled with epigrams. He called on his audience to name any mooted subjects it liked for discussion and to state on which side it wanted him to argue. Instantly he would rise, wrap his gown around him and " without losing a moment, begin, with everything at his finger tips no matter what subject was selected." Presumably his thoughts and the information behind them were very superficial; no matter, the flow of his logic, learning, and language set his audience into ecstasies. Calvus only hopes he can find an equally distinguished master for his own sons.

177. Methods in Rhetoric Schools: Mock Trials. — Rhetoric schools are arranged rather as halls of audience

---

[1] Senators, degraded and banished for reasons good or bad, could earn a living in the provinces by opening rhetoric schools. Thus Lucinianus did so in Sicily in Trajan's time. Pliny the Younger records that he began his first set oration by declaring: "O Fortune, what sport you make to amuse yourself! You make professors into senators, and senators into professors."

than as ordinary classrooms. The students are expected to
sit in a proper manner, " to look steadily at the speaker, not
let their minds wander or to whisper to their neighbors,
yawn sleepily, smile, scowl, cross their legs, or let their heads
drop." The training in its earlier stages, however, seems
decidedly academic. Great models in Greek and Latin
oratory are examined and discussed. Then the young
advocates-to-be are put to work preparing their own orations. They are not, however, allowed to take any live
and fresh topic. Instead they must seek one in distant
history.

Every day the streets of Rome resound with noise from the
rhetoric schools — some youth is laboriously inciting the
Athenian patriots, Harmodius and Aristogeiton, to screw
up their courage and to free their country by slaying the
foul Hipparchus. Still more threadbare are the ceaseless
orations urging Hannibal to advance (or not to advance) on
Rome after his victory at Cannæ. There are a number of
stock subjects of a more private kind. Mimic prosecutors
work themselves into a passion against " The Ravisher,"
" The Poisoner," or " The Wicked and Thankless Husband."

Often a couple of pupils a little more advanced can be pitted against one another in an imaginary law-suit. Suppose a
father orders a son to kill the youth's brother, whom the
father suspects of intending to turn parricide. The boy
pretends to have obeyed the order, but the second lad really
escapes. The father at length discovers the facts and prose-
cutes his first son for " The Crime of Disobedience," [1] —
what endless opportunities now for " eloquence " either
proving that a parent must be obeyed at any cost, or that no
one can be compelled to commit fratricide!

[1] An actual case for young orators as explained by the Elder Seneca.
Less advanced pupils could be pitted in arguments as to "Whether country life is better than city life," or "married life better than celibacy."

Again it is supposed that a young girl has been kidnapped, but rescued and her ravisher later arrested. Imagine now that the law gives her the choice — either the kidnapper must marry her and give her the status of an honorable wife or she can require that he be put to death. The rhetor will put two of his best pupils to prepare counter exhortations to the perplexed girl: " Marry the fellow to assure your social future! " or " Let justice be done — summon the executioner! " It is all very ingenious, but equally unreal, and it is often hopelessly artificial. Angrily wrote Seneca of such debates that by them " we are learning not for life but for school."

178. Enormous Popularity of Rhetoric Studies. — However impractical this study, the upper classes at Rome assuredly dote upon it. When each youth in turn mounts the orator's stand in the school and begins his *suasoria* (set oration) or his *controversia* (pretended legal argument) all his fellows are duty bound to cry in Greek, " *Euge!* " or " *Sophos!* " at every booming sentiment or well-rounded climax. At least once during the oration it is good form for them to rise from their seats and join in a salvo of applause — they will all get like courtesies when their own turns come.

When the young declaimer has finished the master will arise. He will show how to gesture, making his garments fall in picturesque folds. He will take the subject just handled and repeat the argument showing how each point can be better developed; how new matter can be brought in; how allusions to the gods, the worthies of old, and perhaps to the reigning Emperor will improve the effect; how to use one's voice at each particular turn, etc., etc. If the only object of oratory is to tickle the ear, the result is magnificent. The students dutifully applaud their master even more loudly than they do their fellows, and each goes home wondering anxiously, " When can I argue my first case before the prætor? "

179. Philosophical Studies : Delight in Moralizing. — A good many Roman nobles of intellectual type advance a step further than the rhetoric schools. They study philosophy; and even go to Athens (now a quiet, delightful university town) to listen to lectures by the alleged successors of Epicurus or of Zeno the Stoic, but to Greece one need not follow them. It is proper to say, however, that a certain dabbling in philosophy is extremely fashionable.[1] There are plenty of stories about noblemen who have treatises on philosophy read to them while they are being carried to and fro in their litters under the porticoes of their villas; or even of ladies who listen to lectures by a professional philosopher every morning while their maids are arranging their hair.

Such personages, needless to say, never improve upon the familiar guesses at the riddle of human existence; but sometimes their desire to moralize becomes worse than comical. People still repeat stories of Agrippinus, a high-born victim of Nero. When he caught a fever he immediately dictated a panygyric on the moral excellencies of fever. He was ordered into exile; he wrote a treatise on the benefits of exile. He was made a high judge; he added to the anguish of those he condemned by giving his victims long orations to prove that he passed sentence on them only for their own good!

180. Children's Games. " Morra " and Dice. — It is a long cry from child-rearing to philosophy. One must return

---

[1] The zeal for philosophy and rhetoric, or at least for the patronage thereof, is shown by the story of how Trajan, a very simple-minded soldier, used to invite the great rhetorician Dion Chrysostom to visit him and take long journeys with him. The Emperor, greatly impressed by the other's learning, openly declared to him, "I don't in the least understand what you keep talking about, but for all that I love you like my own soul!"

to the first topic enough to notice the games played by young Romans and also by their elders. Tag-games, blindman's buff and its refinements, and like sports, can be seen in every street and dusty area in Rome. A favorite game is that of " King "; when a group of children elects a *Rex* who commands them to perform all sorts of fooleries. Time fails to tell of all the contests with tossing knuckle bones and at " odd and even," guessing at concealed pebbles, shells, and nuts. The later-day Italian game of " morra " (*micare digitis*) in which both players hold out a hand with a certain number of fingers extended, and then each one tries to shout out the correct number of his rival's fingers before the other can do the like by his, is a highly popular if noisy method of killing time. At the eating houses and taverns it is regularly used among friends to settle who shall pay the score.

All too early boys, and likewise girls, learn also to rattle the dice box. Some of the dice are ordinary six-sided cubes, some are oblong, with the numbers " 2 " and " 5 " omitted from the narrow ends. Almost always three dice of bone or fine wood are used; and the familiar expression " three sixes or three aces " is the same as saying " all or nothing."

181. Board Games of Skill: " Robbers " (*Latrunculi*). — Altogether too much time and money are wasted at dice even by fairly grave people, while professional gamblers abound; but the Romans have two games in which men are moved on a gaming board according to rules involving very high degrees of skill. You can play *Duodecim Scripta* very much like later-day backgammon; fifteen white men and fifteen black men are shifted about on a board marked with twelve double lines (whence the name) according to the casts of the dice. More abstract and learned is *Latrunculi* (" Robbers "), a game without dice and seemingly very much like later-day checkers or chess. Some of the pieces are called " soldiers "

and others " officers " — and the moves are very elaborate.[1]
Of course, such games are far removed from a mere youthful
sport.   Consuls and Emperors delight in them, and while
playing forget everything but the problem involved.   Devotees cite with pride the story of Julius Kanus, one of the
mad Caligula's victims.   He was in prison but was allowed
to have a friend visit him, and the two were busy over
" Robbers," when a centurion came in to say he must be
immediately executed.   Kanus at once arose unmoved, but
carefully counted the men on the board; then said to his
friend, " Mind you, don't tell a lie after I'm dead, and say
that you won "; then turning to the centurion, " Please bear
witness for me that I was one man ahead," — and so did
Stoicism find its way even to the gaming table!

182. Out-Door Games. Ball Games, _Trigon_. — Among
out-of-door amusements, we find that young Romans and
some of their elders enjoy fairly elaborate games of ball.
There are various exercises which show that the world is on
its way to handball, tennis, and even to polo, but hardly any
contests foreshadow such things as baseball, foot ball, or
cricket.   The most common game is _trigon_, when three
players stand at the corners of a triangle, and at least three,
or even six balls, are kept flying around the circle with great
rapidity;   the points being made on catching and throwing
with as few misses as possible.   The players stand close
together, and the whole sport is more a mild form of juggling
than it is any real field exercise.

---

[1] It is impossible to recover the exact details of these two games. We
know of " solitaire " forms of these games, with the board made of tere-
binth wood, and with crystal pieces, or with gold and silver coins in place
of the common black and white counters.

CHAPTER XI

BOOKS AND LIBRARIES

183. Letters and Writing Tablets. — The multiplication of schools presupposes the constant use of books, correspondence, and other forms of writing. What are these like?

"Tablets" are seen everywhere. Upper-class people delight in scribbling down memoranda. The story even runs that Augustus wrote out his intended conversations with his wife Livia " lest he should say too much or too little," a testimony at once to the need of circumspect dealings with the lady and to a great mania for writing. Ordinary tablets are made of two or three thin strips of wood joined together like

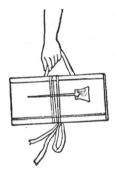

WAX TABLET WITH STILUS ATTACHED.

later-day book-covers, and spread over the inside with a thin coating of wax. On this wax, often black and dingy, day accounts and business messages can be scratched with facility. But really important fashionable letters demand something better. The leaves can be made of fine citrus wood or even of ivory. As for very special correspondence, love letters, and the like, these are written on very small tablets in contrast to the broad slabs carrying the merchant accounts.

If you want a handsome note book, you can buy one with a number of folding leaves and with outside covers of finely chased ivory, silver, or gold, and such handsome note books make very convenient presents among friends. By a convention attached to the high office, when Calvus became prætor, he presented his intimates with tablets adorned with his own portrait in low relief on ivory, and with scenes of the prætor's tribunal. If he had been consul, he would have been expected to give around bunches of tablets even more elegant.

When a letter is written no envelope is needed. The tablets are folded over upon themselves, fastened with crossed thread and then at the point when the ends are knotted is placed a round piece of wax, stamped before it can cool with a signet ring. The name of the person to whom the letter is going can be written on the outside, and then the communication is ready. Letters can be transmitted to distant places usually only with

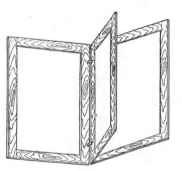

WRITING TABLETS AND STILUS.

tedious difficulty, but around Rome delivery from writers of any high position is extremely prompt. The carrying of letters is one of the commonest duties for otherwise idle slaves, and from a mansion like Calvus's it is easy every morning to send off ten packets each by its own hurrying messenger.

184. Personal Correspondence and Secretaries. — Calvus, like every man of distinction, has a heavy correspondence. It is a fine thing to be a good letter writer, to make your epistles seem easy, natural, gossipy, and yet in such faultless language that they can be collected presently and published in a book. To a few special correspondents, especially to absent relatives, Calvus writes almost daily in his own hand.

But he dictates even more frequently. He has a couple of slave *amanuenses* who are with him constantly; they can take down his dictation in a kind of abbreviated long hand; then write it out in handsome script, always submitting the final text to their master not for his signing but for sealing. As a consequence of all this correspondence, the demand for new tablets in Rome is prodigious. The wax, indeed, can be melted upon letters which one does not care to preserve, and the wood used a second time, but the waste inevitably is great.

185. Books Very Common: Papyrus and the Papyrus Trade. — Nevertheless, the activity of such secretaries is vastly less important than that of another set of scribes, the makers of books. Poor is the tenement suite that does not contain a few musty papyrus scrolls, while a parvenu freedman will inevitably acquire a large library (which he may never read) just to show himself a man of fashion. Books are so common that their divided sheets are wetted, and used in kitchens to keep fish in fresh condition, or, if dry, to make wrappers for incense and spices.

BOOK CUP-BOARD.

Paper is unknown, and parchment although not unknown is used mainly for very important correspondence, public documents, and the like, which require extremely durable material. Practically all books are written on papyrus arranged in rolls.[1] The papyrus is strictly an Egyptian monopoly, and if the importation of this precious article should cease, apparently all Greece and Italy would be doomed to partial illiteracy.

The papyrus plant grows in the swamps by the Nile to a height of about ten feet. The pith of its tall stalks is first cut

---

[1] In very early Roman days public records seem to have been kept on books of *linen;* but these soon disappeared.

into strips ; next the latter are placed one by another upon a wetted board and smeared over with a paste.   On these there is next laid a second layer forming a cross pattern or kind of net work.   Then the whole combination is pressed and beaten

down into a solid sheet and smoothed with an ivory knife or a shell.   After that it is ready for export from Egypt and to be put to proper use.

The papyrus trade is well standardized.   There are eight well-recognized grades of the commodity.   The best is

BOOK CONTAINER.   *hieratica*, so called because it is fine and firm enough to be used by the Egyptian priests for their sacred books.   The cheapest is *emporetica*, not fit for writing but only for wrapping parcels.   The intermediate qualities answer for the run of books.   When the papyrus sheets are ready separately, either they can be pasted together at once into a long scroll making a complete volume, or first the book can be written off and the sheets pasted later.

186. Size and Format of Books. — Books can, therefore, be of all sizes but everybody usually agrees with the Greek saying, " *Big book, big evil!* "   It is an indescribable nuisance to fumble over a roll of more than a certain length hunting for a desired passage.   Not many volumes run over 100 pages,[1] and many are much smaller.   Each sheet constitutes a separate page (varying between six to twelve inches high), with the writing usually in a single column, four to six inches broad, on each page, and a blank space crossed by a red line before the next page begins.

DOUBLE INKSTAND.

[1] We hear, however, of a single copy of Thucydides that required 578 pages, making a roll about 100 yards long — a most cumbersome volume.

It is impossible to read with any convenience writing on more than one side of the papyrus prepared in this manner. The result is that discarded books are often used for school-boys' exercises or for mere scribbling " paper"; although, if the papyrus is very firm, often the writing can be sponged out and a whole new work can be written over the vanished sentences. Books being of this character, it is impossible really to prepare the " ponderous tomes " of a later day. " Volumes " are very short. The Iliad of Homer is ordinarily in twenty-four separate rolls, one for each of its " books," and the same arrangement obtains for other standard works. Very many " books " in the Roman libraries, therefore, are really little more than pamphlets.

For writing on parchment, of course, one cannot use the stylus. Reed pens skilfully cut may suffice, with a thick ink made of lampblack and gum for ordinary purposes and also a red ink, rich and permanent,

PEN AND SCROLL.

for ornamental lines. In Calvus's library, as in almost every other, are two large beautifully wrought ink wells, made of bronze with silver chasings, and attached together — one for the black ink and one for the red.

187. Mounting and Rolling of Books. The mounting of the papyrus long roll is a great art, especially if the book is intended for a fine library. First, the whole long strip of papyrus is dressed with cedar oil to repel worms — thus giving the pages a pleasing yellow tinge. Then the last leaf is fastened to a thin cylinder of wood or of rolled papyrus called the *umbilicus*. The ends of the roll itself are carefully cut and smoothed with pumice stone, and the ends of the umbilicus are often gilded. Next a strip of solid parchment bearing the title of the book in handsome red letters is attached by a string at one end, where it will hang down when the volume is rolled.

After the book itself is ready a neat cylindrical cover or case must be made of parchment, colored red or yellow, and also marked with the title.   For really fine volumes additional elegancies are possible; for example, a handsome portrait of the author can be painted or pasted upon the first page, and the edges of the entire scroll can be colored.   Handsomely illustrated works grace every good library.

BOOK SCROLL.

To read these books will seem to persons familiar only with *codexes* (flat opening books) extremely cumbersome.[1] You have to take the volume in both hands, unrolling with the right while you roll up with the left.   It seems nigh impossible to " run through " such a volume, and hard to trace down a passage; and there are apparently no indices.   However, practice can make almost perfect.   Calvus can roll and unroll his books with remarkable dexterity and by a kind of instinct hit promptly upon almost any allusion.   It will be a real gain for the world, nevertheless, when the roll is supplanted by the many-leaved book.

188. Copying Books: the Publishing Business.   Horace's and Martial's Publishers. — Books abound, although of course all are multiplied by painful human effort.   This is because slave copyists are relatively cheap.   Atticus, Cicero's

[1] The use of flat opening books of the style later so familiar came in before the fall of the Roman Empire, but they were apparently used only for merchants' ledgers, etc., in the time of Hadrian.

friend, seems to have made a real fortune in the publishing business — that is, he owned a great corps of skilful slaves incessantly busy transcribing manuscripts. The finest copies must be made deliberately one by one, but ordinary volumes can be multiplied more summarily. As you go about Rome you will perhaps come on large rooms where a great number of scribes are seated in a kind of lecture hall desperately following word for word some reader who, in a smooth, monotonous voice, is giving out the text either of an established classic or the newest essays or epigrams of the successors of Pliny the Younger or Martial. In this way what is really an " edition " of say a hundred or even two hundred copies can be produced in a remarkably short time, without the aid of the printing press.[1]

The publisher, and even more the authors who try to live by their literary genius, are, however, under a grave handicap. There is no copyright. What you " publish " today, may be flagrantly recopied and sold under your very nose tomorrow — possibly with errors and interpolations calculated to drive an author frantic. The average aspirant for literary fame unless he has personal means is therefore constrained, as were Horace and Martial, to hunt up a rich patron who for the joy of being " immortalized " will keep him from starving.

However, every aspiring author tries to find some bookseller, who will turn his works over to a corps of competent slaves, and then vend the products. There is a regular booksellers' quarter in Rome down by the Forum of Cæsar in the heart of the commercial district. Here Horace's old publishers, the Sosii, had their stalls; and Martial's publishers, the firm headed by the clever freedman Allectus, are still there in the business.

---

[1] This was the probable method of multiplying popular books, but we lack very precise knowledge.

At Allectus's shop they will tell you how the epigramist used to drop in with pardonable vanity to see how from " the first or second shelf they would hand down a ' Martial,' well smoothed with pumice stone and adorned with purple — all for five denarii (80 cents)." On the columns by the entrance to this and the rival shops are plastered up long lists of new publications — often with sample extracts to prove their wit or learning; or announcement of new or old copies of standard works from Homer down to that clever Greek litterateur Plutarch, who has recently died in Bœotia; or in Latin from old Nævius and Ennius to the recent biographies of the Cæsars by the imperial secretary Suetonius.

Considering the labor of copying, the price of books is moderate; a small volume of poems by a popular writer can be had for as little as two denarii (32 cents), although such a scroll would probably be only equivalent to a thin pamphlet of later-day printing, and the works of a really voluminous author like Pliny the Elder might appear ruinously expensive.

189. Passion for Literary " Fame." — Expensive or cheap, by men of education a certain number of books must be had. Perhaps the Age of Hadrian will fail to leave a great mark in the history of either Greek or Latin letters, but that will not be because *literary fame* is not passionately sought after. Everybody is anxious to dabble in authorship. Everybody (in the upper circles) seems incessantly compounding formal " epistles," memoirs, essays, rhetorical and sentimental histories, and last but not least great quantities of verses which pass as " poetry." Pliny the Younger (not long dead) was incessantly urging his correspondents to write: " to mould something, hammer out something, that shall be known as yours for all time." The same pathetic desire for immortality which leads to ostentatious funeral monuments and to endowed funeral feasts, perhaps puts a premium upon this mania.

The fine gentlemen and ladies who share these tastes boast
that nothing can interrupt their furious pursuit of " letters."
Senators like to inform their friends that even while hunting
boars in the Apennines they keep their writing tablets and
stylus near them when watching for the beaters to drive the
game into the nets — what precious sentences might escape
them otherwise! They like also to have freedman or slave
" readers " always at their elbows to keep up a flow of poetry
or philosophy apparently all the time when they are not
eating, exercising, or conversing.[1]

It is also a kind of etiquette for all members of the gilded
literary circle to keep sending their unpublished effusions
around among their friends with demands for " entirely
frank and severe criticism "; the response always being a long
letter of praise even for very mediocre efforts. " Terse,
lucid, brilliant, stately," or even " keen, impassioned, graceful " — these are grievously overworked adjectives, although
perhaps at the end of the answers there are a few polite hints
suggesting a slight improvement.

The Latin-speaking provinces are said to follow Roman
literary celebrities intently. Nothing delights the latter
more than to learn that their fame has spread to distant
parts. Tacitus was certainly a great historian, but he was a
man of his time and also a very warm friend of Pliny the
Younger. Oft repeated is the story of a conversation he had
in the circus, where on the front benches for notables he met a
" certain learned provincial." The twain, without introduction, fell into a delightful literary conversation, until the
stranger who manifestly was very up-to-date asked: " Are
you from Italy or the provinces? " " Ah," said Tacitus,

---

[1] Pliny the Younger had a favorite reader Eucolpus. When he fell ill
his master was sadly tormented: "Who will read my books and take
such an interest in them? Where can I find another with so pleasant a
reading voice?"

"you know me very well from my books that you've read." "Then," cried the other, "you are either Tacitus or Pliny!"

190. Zeal for Poetry: Multiplication of Verses. — Prose compositions in smooth and fastidious Latin, or in very passable Greek are common enough, but even the authors of genuinely superior histories or literary essays, often desire to become something more magnificent — they wish to be

OLD FORUM: looking towards northern side, with the Curia shown behind the high columns in foreground ; restoration by Spandoni.

poets. Very famous Romans have put forth their energies over iambics, elegiacs, or hexameters ; Sulla, Cicero, Hortensius the Orator, Julius Cæsar, Brutus, Augustus, Tiberius, Seneca, Nerva — the list of such celebrities could be made much longer. Of course, every loyal subject knows that the reigning Hadrian is the author of clever epigrams, which would really deserve a certain fame even if their author had lived in the Subura and not upon the Palatine.[1]

---

[1] Hadrian's famous and pathetic poem "To his own soul" was not of course, composed until he lay on his death bed (138 A.D.).

Probably if there could be physical measuring rods where-with to determine it, the sheer quantity of Latin, and also of Greek verses, being thrust upon the world every year would seem prodigious. At Allectus and Company they will tell you that Romanus has just brought out some very acceptable " Old Comedies " in the style of Aristophanes, and some other " New Comedies " in iambics worthy to be classed with Plautus and Terence. The noble Caninius, too, has at last completed and published a remarkable Greek epic : " The Dacian War " — celebrating Trajan's victories in a manner quite worthy, let us say, of Homer and Hesiod. True, the uncouth names of Dacian barbarians do not fit well into the hexameters, and especially that of their king, " Decebalus," is metrically almost impossible, but ingenious poetical license has overcome the difficulty. Who can doubt that Caninius's " long poem " will live across the ages ? [1]

Such a practical man of affairs as Calvus does not take all the smooth compliments proffered his efforts over-seriously ; but even our friendly senator can feel a thrill of pleasure when he dashes off a dozen elegiacs in praise of his mountain villa, and hears the " *Euge! Euge!* " (he hopes not *too* insincere) of his guests as he reads them at a dinner party.

191. Size of Libraries. — With such an affectation for books and literary fame there are inevitably great libraries. Long ago the old Hebrew gloomily recorded, " Of making of many books there is no end," and his sighs would have in-creased could he have seen the collections in Rome. The small size of the volumes indeed makes it hard to compare these libraries with those of other ages. The largest library in the world is that at Alexandria with some 400,000 rolls, but there are public collections in Rome not very much smaller. As for private libraries, a certain rich and learned

---

[1] These men were well-known poets according again to Pliny the Younger. The world undoubtedly gained when their verses perished.

senator has about 60,000 rolls.[1]   Calvus and his friends make
no such boast, and he contents himself with some 4000
volumes.   This is respectable, but nowise an unusual collection for a man of refined tastes, and it has plenty of counter-
parts all over the city.

192. A Private Library. — The library in the house of Calvus is small but sumptuously furnished.   Around a large part
of the walls extend great tiers of large pigeonholes made of
finely carved wood, and in each hole is a group of rolls, either
the complete works of a voluminous author, or a collection of
smaller books on a single subject.   The bright red lettering
on the dangling labels, the gilt ends of the rolling rods, the
pleasing soft yellow of the end of the papyri (if these are not
also colored red) give a luxurious appearance to the collection.

Set above the tiers of books in such a room is a long array of
fine busts in bronze and marble of nearly all the distinguished
literary figures of Greece or Italy.   Calvus has just added a
handsome bronze of the comedian Menander.   The careful
frescos on the exposed walls have to do with learned mythological subjects;   there is also a fine life-sized statue of
Minerva the patroness of letters, and on a long shelf stand
really beautiful silver statuettes of all the Nine Muses.
Along one side of the library there are also tables where
Harpocration, Calvus's truly learned and capable freedman
librarian (*librarius*), who assists in all his patron's studies,
can spread out rolls for patching, rewinding, or even for re-
copying;   also a convenient writing couch for the senator
himself when he wishes to take his tablets and compile those
fine " extracts " which the literary world delights to cull
from every possible author, or to try his own hand at original
composition.

[1] The record for a private collection — 62,000 rolls, owned by the
senator Serenus, dates about 235 A.D., but there is no reason to suppose
that there were not libraries equally large under Hadrian.

Calvus is not a virtuoso, however, and does not imitate such wealthy enthusiasts as the poet Silius Italicus who collected all kinds of rare editions, crammed his house with every imaginable writer, and " kept Virgil's birthday more carefully than he did his own." For all that Harpocration has been commended for hanging a small wreath around the bust of Sophocles, this day being the reputed anniversary of the death of the great tragedian.

193. The Great Public Libraries of Rome. — Into the Public Libraries of Rome we cannot enter. They exist nevertheless as great and beneficent institutions although probably only a favored few are permitted to read their treasures except inside their ample halls.[1] The oldest public library is that founded by Asinius Pollio (an officer of Julius Cæsar) and is located on the rather distant Aventine. Cæsar himself projected two very grand Greek and Latin Libraries but did not live to create them; Augustus founded a very fine library in the Temple of Apollo on the Palatine (making it virtually the imperial palace library), and his sister Octavia created another. There is still a fourth good library in the Temple of Peace founded by Vespasian; but all these are now overshadowed by the relatively new " Ulpian Libraries " established by Trajan at his new Forum. These enormous collections of Greek and Latin rolls make Rome by far the greatest repository of literary treasures in the entire world, barring always the famous collection in Alexandria.

[1] Concerning the actual arrangement of these public libraries we know very little.

CHAPTER XII

ECONOMIC LIFE OF ROME: I. BANKING, SHOPS, AND INNS

194. Passion for Gain in Rome. — Much has been said about Roman trade and riches, but this is no place for an economic survey of the realm of the Cæsars. It is impossible, however, to ignore the outward side of that commercial activity which is everywhere in evidence around the imperial capital.

The desire for gold, doubtless, had its potence in old Egypt and Babylonia, and most certainly in old Tyre and Carthage, but never has the fierce passion burned much keener than along the Seven Hills. Go into many a pretentious vestibule; in the mosaic pavement are set as mottoes, " *Salve Lucrum!* " ("Hail, Profit!") or " *Lucrum Gaudium!* " (" Profit is pure joy! "). Hearken also to the cynical poets of society, for example, to Juvenal : " No deity among us is held in such reverence as *Riches;* though as yet, O baneful Money, thou hast no temple of thine own ! Not yet have we reared fanes to Money in like manner we have to Peace and Honor, Virtue, Victory, and Concord." And he speaks again : " No human passion has mingled more poison bowls, none has more often plied the murderer's dagger than the violent craving for unbounded wealth."

His less sedate but not less cynical contemporary, Martial, echoes his words. He recommends that an honest friend should leave Rome; he cannot succeed for he is neither a rake nor a parasite; he cannot tell lies like an auctioneer, wheedle old ladies out of their property, sell " smoke " ("empty rumors," in other words political, gaming, or commercial tips), nor otherwise earn a corrupt living. Martial tells us too of despicable misers who, as their vast fortunes increase, let their togas become even more dirty, their tunics still worse, their wine mere dregs, and their main diet one of half-cooked peas.

Perhaps such sordid creatures, however, are no worse than the others who struggle for riches simply to enjoy gross material vanities; who desire "that their Tuscan estates may clink with the fetters of innumerable toiling slaves in order that they may own a hundred tables of Moorish marble supported pedestals, that gold ornaments may jingle from their couches, that they may never drink anything but Falernian cooled with snow from large crystal goblets, and that a crowd of clients may follow their litters; etc., etc." And long before Martial, Horace has asserted, " All the arches ot Janus [the typical Latin deity] from end to end teach one lesson to young and old 'Oh, fellow citizens, fellow citizens, *money is the first thing to seek — virtue after money!* '"

195. Life in Rome Expensive. Premiums upon Extravagance and Pretence. — With every deduction from such charges Rome is undoubtedly an extremely expensive city to dwell in, probably the most expensive in the whole Empire, and in all but very limited circles the pressure for wealth is inconceivable. A typical man-of-affairs is represented as boasting to his cronies, " Coranus owes me 100,000 sesterces ($4,000); Mancinus 200,000; Titius 300,000; Albinus 600,000; Salinus a million; Soranus another million; from the rent of my insulæ I get three million ($120,000); from the flocks on my pasture lands 600,000." On any night at half the triclinia, the mighty equites and senators can be heard talking about investments, real estate transactions, government contracts, and foreign trade prospects, far more vigorously than concerning either the wisdom of the Emperor's policy in building the wall across Britain, or the philosopher's doctrine of the immortality of the soul.

The very life of the city puts a premium in fact on getting and spending. A youth inheriting a modest fortune in the provinces comes to Rome. In a few months his patrimony has drifted away on fish-mongers, bakers, luxurious baths, ointments, and garlands, not to mention fine clothes, gamesters, and dancing girls. In many circles an outlay of 40,000 sesterces ($1600) is " a mere pinch of poppy seed for an ant-hill." You must at least *seem* rich or you amount to nothing.

Half the young men of fashion are therefore, good authorities aver, up to their ears in debt; but anybody with a little ready money can put on a bold countenance to make an impression. Many is the apparent aristocrat who is swung along in a fine litter, his violet robes trailing, and with a long train apparently of clients and slaves following him, who has actually hired litter and attendants, nay, the gown which he wears from a ready contractor — in order perhaps to carry his part in some business conference at the Forum. And if you are to plead a case as advocate but are unluckily a poor man, nevertheless be sure to hire a fine toga and a couple of handsome rings to wear through the morning, or the jurors will assume you are a nobody and promptly vote against you.

196. Rome a City of Investors and Buyers of Luxuries. — Everybody declaims against this scramble for wealth and yet joins in it. Even Martial and Juvenal, it is peevishly averred, would have held back their jibes if their financial hopes had prospered. Be it said also that this struggle in Rome is probably not much more sordid than it can become in other capitals in other ages. The standards of business honesty are relatively high. Most bargains are faithfully kept. A great credit system has been built up — itself a witness to the fact that most traders are honorable.

The business life of Rome flows in many channels, but in general the Eternal City does not compete with Alexandria, or even with certain smaller Græco-Levantine cities, as an industrial or distributing center. Rome *receives* much. The great incomes from investments in the provinces and from the expenditure in the city of the imperial revenues, make it possible to pay for enormous quantities of luxuries for which no corresponding articles are exported in return. There are many petty industries but they exist mainly for local needs. Rome exports legions and law-givers, so her inhabitants assert proudly, — is it not right, therefore, that she should wax fat upon the tributes of the world, when she can repay them with the blessed *pax Romana?* [1]

197. Multiplicity of Shops. The Great Shopping Districts. — But if the industrial life of the city is relatively weak, never before has there been such a " wilderness of shops " as spreads itself along the streets of Rome. A certain type of shops can be found everywhere; hardly a street but has grocers' stalls; the terra cotta plaque with a goat, the sign of a milk dealer; the stone relief of two men tugging a great jar slung up on a pole, the sign of a wine shop, and the like.

There are nevertheless certain great retail quarters to visit if you are seeking for articles of *vertu* and price. The fashionable fish-mongers have their odoriferous stalls under the great porticoes and basilicas by the fora; the fruit sellers are along the ascent from the Old Forum to the top of the Velia (a spur of the Palatine flung out toward the Esquiline); while the jewelers, goldsmiths, and makers of musical instruments as well as the great bankers have their headquarters directly along the Sacred Way itself. The perfumers' shops in turn are well concentrated under the southeast brow of the Capitoline.

---

[1] Of course, by Hadrian's time an increasingly large proportion of the privates of the army was being recruited in the provinces.

In addition to these, however, there exist two grand shopping districts for Rome outside the Fora themselves: for
the cheap trade, where elbowing plebeians struggle for
bargains, we find that the little shops are wedged all along the
swarming Tuscan Street (*Vicus Tuscus*) going south from the
Old Forum toward the Circus Maximus and the adjacent cross

streets; but for the more select purchases high-born ladies and gentlemen
order their litters to take them northward along "Broadway" (*Via Lata*),
where by the Sæpta Julia and the vast
series of porticoes adjoining or opposite
are the finest retail shops in the entire
world.

**198. Arrangement of Shops.
Streets Blocked by Hucksters.** —
What the inferior shops were like has
been already seen in the local survey
of Mercury Street. They are almost
countless in number but are very
small, the bulk of their wares being
on sale upon the open counters facing
the street, and often you can make all

TRADESMEN'S SCALES   your purchases without going inside.
AND BALANCES.   The proprietor and his wife with a
slave or two manage the entire business, unless, indeed, they
manufacture, let us say, the shoes which they retail; in
which case a workroom directly in the rear keeps busy a few
more slaves or free wage-workers.

The shop fronts are protected at night and on holidays by
heavy wooden shutters which, when raised, project into the
street serving as a kind of awnings. They are the more
necessary to guard against thieves and also against a riot.
Shop-keepers are proverbially timid folk, and to say " all

the shutters are being closed down " is practically to say that a brawl or a tumult seems possible. The small size of these shops makes their owners encroach upon the streets whenever they can. The counters thrust out over the scanty sidewalk, while pedestrians trip over the boards with placards set in front of the shops advertising the wares inside.

In such narrow streets a little knot of bargain hunters can readily halt all traffic. Every now and then, indeed, the City Præfect orders his deputies, " Enforce the shop edicts ! " A few offending hucksters are hailed into court and the rest draw back their counters. " Now the city is Rome again and not one vast bazaar," rejoice the poets of the hour. Then, after a little, official zeal abates, and the streets are as badly cumbered as before.

A great deal of the trading, however, goes on without any permanent shops at all. In almost any cross-street or little square one can get a license to locate a table and to set thereon a small stock of such articles as copper or iron pots, the cheaper grades of women's and men's shoes, or pieces of cloth, probably woven by the huckster himself, not to mention all kinds of edibles, also the stands of menders of old pots, and others of public letter-writers for the illiterate. Through the midst of all these, beggars glide whining for alms, and children dash about playing hide-and-go-seek.[1]

199. Barber Shops and Auction Sales. — An institution almost as familiar in Rome as in Athens [2] is the barber shop. Not that a shop is really needful. Many a dirty tonsor will put down a low stool in the middle of the crowd in the very street and ply his shears or razor upon any poor wight who

---

[1] All these hucksters' stalls as well as the beggars and the playing children are depicted in certain very informing frescos in a house at Pompeii, showing life in the forum of that little city.

[2] See "A Day in Old Athens," p. 24.

can find a *quadrans* (small copper).   The finer barber shops, however, are really elegant establishments, fitted to please the fastidious.   Here men of parts and fashion can meet to hear the latest gossip, and perhaps to read a copy of the " Daily Gazette " (see p. 282).   A complete manicure service is afforded; · superfluous hairs are removed with tweezers or depilatories, and nails polished and faces massaged very skilfully;   although some inferior barbers are railed at bitterly, and it is charged that their patrons " may count the scars on their chins like those on an aged boxer, or those marks produced by the nails of enraged wives."

Another institution much frequented is the auctioneer's room.   Auction seems at Rome an ideal method for realizing quickly upon property, and bidding is often keen.   The auctioneers are past-masters in stimulating the bidders, and in praising-up worthless articles.   An auction sale is the normal end for the career of a spendthrift when his creditors seize his plate and furniture.   A dozen times around the city one can see placards like the following, tactfully worded to save the pride of the unfortunate debtor :[1]

GAIUS   JULIUS   PROCULUS
WILL   OFFER   FOR   SALE
CERTAIN   ARTICLES
HERE-UNDER   NAMED
FOR   WHICH   HE   HAS   NO   FURTHER   REQUIREMENT

200. Superior Retail Stores. — However, besides the petty shops and street traders there are the really magnificent stores, especially toward the Campus Martius where articles of *vertu* attract the wealthy.   If you have wealth, you can delight yourself in splendid establishments offering citrus-

---

[1] This form of advertisement is given in Petronius.

wood tables, veneered with ivory and gold, with other articles of furniture to match, or candelabra that are massy works of art, or vases and mirrors of every possible style and elegance, and where all kinds of fine pottery, plate, and bric-a-brac, as well as gorgeous upholsteries, tapestries, and carpets, can be had for a price.

To thrust into these places that welcome only the most aristocratic clientele is the delight of those professional shoppers, which abound in Rome as in many another city. Martial's Mamurra will have many survivors in the next generation. This worthy fellow put in his days at the richest bazaars along the Sæpta Julia. He would force his way to inner rooms where the handsomest and most expensive slaves were on private exhibition. He made obsequious clerks uncover fine tables " square and round, and next asked to see some rich ivory ornaments displayed on the upper shelves." He measured a tortoise-shell veneered dinner couch five times, then sighed, " It's not long enough for my citrus table." He smelled of rare bronzes " to see if they were real Corinthian "; criticized a statue by Polycleitus, had ten porcelain cups " set aside " to be taken by him later, examined some splendid antique goblets, made a jeweler let him inspect some emeralds in a splendid gold setting, also some valuable pearl ear pendants, and complained aloud that he was seeking " *real* sardonyxes." At last, just as the shops closed for the day, utterly wearied, " he bought two earthen cups for one small coin and bore them home himself."

201. Numerous Banks and Bankers. — All this trade implies the handling of great sums of money, and for its care banks and bankers are everywhere in evidence. The Romans naturally run to finance. It appeals to their keen sense of the practical. Even before Cæsar's conquest it was boasted that rarely a large sum changed hands in Gaul without its being entered in an Italian account book ; while in

Nero's day a serious revolt in Britain was said to have been precipitated by the act of the millionaire philosopher, Seneca, in calling in his British loans, thereby reducing certain tribes to beggary.

Stocks, bonds, and long-time government securities do not indeed exist, and there is no regular stock exchange, but in many respects about all the other financial conveniences of a later age can be found by the Tiber. There are two kinds of money handlers — mere coin-changers, dealing in foreign mintages and often no doubt accepting sums merely for safe keeping in their strong boxes; and above them are the real bankers acting under a kind of state license and doing business on the largest scale.

202. A Great Banker and His Business. — The highest classes of these *argentarii* are men whom the Emperor will gladly consult if the Parthians break loose in an expensive war, or great public works have to be undertaken in Africa. They are strictly under government supervision, their business honor is high and bankruptcy is a great disgrace.

On this day in question Calvus must needs visit his own personal banker, Sextus Herrenius Probus, head of the firm of the Probi, one of the oldest houses on the Via Sacra. Probus is an eques, though his wealth surpasses that of most senators. His father helped such personages as the philosopher Seneca to make and to manage their huge fortunes, but the real origin of the firm went back to Augustus's settlement of Egypt, when the successful liquidation of the royal estates of Cleopatra provided enormous and lawful commissions. Probus now is practically the custodian of many of the noblest patrimonies in Rome. He is all the time consulted concerning investments, and Calvus has particularly desired to-day to ask whether his own freedmen are wise in urging their patron (acting, of course, through themselves as middlemen) to put 300,000 sesterces into a transaction in Arabian frankincense.

Probus, of course, runs a regular banking business. Besides several junior partners he has a great corps of clerks, some freedmen, and some slaves. His office has all the signs of a well-ordered commercial establishment. Every item of his business is entered in an elaborate system of ledgers, which are regularly brought into court as the most reliable kind of evidence.

Such a banker issues bills of exchange on correspondents in such places as Athens, Alexandria, Antioch, Lugdunum, Gades, and even on distant Londinium in Britain. Money is deposited with him, then withdrawn by personal checks (*perscriptio*) in a manner very familiar to another age. On long-time deposits he pays interest; and, of course, he is always loaning money for long or short terms on what seems good security.

On the day that Calvus comes to him Probus has just loaned 200,000 sesterces on a mortgage on a well-rented insula, at the standard rate of 12 per cent; and also a sum to a merchant planning a trading voyage to Spain at the heavier rate of 24 per cent until the ships are safe in harbor.[1] Probus, too, exchanges foreign moneys at a fair commission, although by the reign of Hadrian the coinage of all the Mediterranean world has become decidedly Romanized; one seldom now has to change drachmas and shekels into sesterces and *aurei* (gold pieces), although the old Græco-Oriental coins have not quite disappeared.

203. Trust Business: Savings Banks. — Besides its strictly banking business Probus's firm also does much that could at another time be referred to a " Trust Company." It makes sales or purchases for its clients, undertakes to close

---

[1] 12 per cent (one per cent per month) was the lawful and normal rate of interest. Greater interest could be demanded on risky ventures, especially those by sea. Rates of 36 and 48 per cent, heard of under the Later Republic, were excessive, and usually unlawful.

up estates, attends to legal business, collects debts, and above all conducts auctions of large quantities of goods in the most responsible manner possible.   Somewhat on the side the firm also maintains several small savings banks to attract the sesterces of the humble.

These modest savings institutions, paying the depositors a fair interest, are numerous all over the city ; and such concerns also make loans for small sums on chattel mortgages — in short, doing a business that is sometimes highly legitimate, sometimes griping and usurious.   Probus's savings banks, like many others, are intrusted to slave managers (*institutores*) who are expected to invest their own *peculium* in the business to insure their watchfulness and honesty.   The management of such small establishments is naturally held in little social esteem, and the heads of Probus and Company affect to ignore their savings banks just as much as possible, although the gains from them are, perhaps, almost as great as from the dealings with the lofty *Clarissimi* of the Senate.

204. Places of Safe Deposit: The Temple of Vesta. — At all the banks there are very strong brass-bound treasure boxes carefully guarded and protected by elaborate locks. These boxes if not actually " safe deposit vaults " can defy any ordinary burglars.   However, objects of great value, caskets of jewels, large sums of bullion, and the like, can be deposited in the Temple of Castor at the Old Forum, where (under the double sanctions of law and religion) the government undertakes their storage for a moderate fee.   There is also a second government deposit vault at the Temple of Mars Ultor on the Augustan Forum, but this unfortunately "lost its helmet" (*i.e.* its reputation for inviolability) when it was successfully entered by burglars some years ago.

There exists, however, a still safer place than the Temple of Castor, although obviously it can only give room to pro-

tect very small packets and highly precious documents. The
Vestal Virgins in their House of Vesta, sacrosanct and absolutely guarded, have now in their keeping the wills of half of
the Senators and of many other distinguished men. There
they are safe from tampering not merely by common criminals, but by designing heirs
and even by greedy Em-
perors; but this service, of
course, is only at the disposal of the aristocracy.

**205. Inns: Usually Mean
and Sordid.** — The very nature of a city like Rome
presupposes an enormous
floating population. The
metropolis is always full of
strangers. The more dis-
tinguished of these almost
inevitably find hospitality
at least as " paying guests "
in some private quarters, so
that large hotels for the gentry are almost non-existent;
and as stated (p. 112) the

MONUMENT OF A HOSTLER.

universal custom of either dining at home or being a dinner
guest of friends largely obviates the need of luxurious restaurants. But all visitors cannot command noble hospitality;
and many a plebeian, freedman, or slave cannot go home
from his work either to the noon-time prandium or to the
regular evening dinner. Besides there are plenty of loose
fellows who desire congenial places for tippling and carous-
ing. The result is that Rome is provided with inns and with
eating houses; although nearly all of both types are sordid
and held in little aristocratic favor.

The inns (*tabernæ*) usually combine the reception of travelers with the providing of meals for chance visitors. Since driving in the city is seldom permitted, nearly all wagons have to unload near the gates, and around these there

GATEWAY AT POMPEII : present state. Note the small entrance for foot passengers, available after the main gate for beasts and wagons has been closed.

is a perfect sprinkling of inns primarily for the accommodation of teamsters.

A few of these establishments are very large but the most are decidedly small. Take for example the " Inn of Hercules," just outside the Porta Capena, where the Appian Way commences. It is kept by one Proxenus, a sly-eyed, strong-limbed fellow, who pretends he is an Athenian Greek, but who probably comes from somewhere much nearer the Orient. His inn stands side by side with a number of competitors, all much alike. There is a broad entrance through

which wagons can drive; and on either side of this passage
are rooms, one for the proprietor's personal use, the others
for serving meals, drinking, and idling. On the walls are
coarse frescos, showing besides the Lares (the serpent
Genius of the place, and the god Hercules) views of the wine
trade, perhaps of a man pouring wine from a large jar into a
still larger earthen hogshead. In the rear of these rooms
there is a fairly large court for wagons, a stable, and a water-
ing trough. Near these are three small chambers for teamsters who have to sleep near their beasts; but most of the
guests are accommodated in small, dirty cubicles in the story
above the wine-rooms.

206. Reckonings and Guests at a Cheap Inn. — Proxenus
is not more filthy or extortionate than the majority of his
kind. He takes it as part of his perquisites to hear his
tavern cursed as " dirty," " smoky," " vermin infested " —
or things much worse, and laughs heartily when he finds that
a departing guest has scratched upon the walls of his sleeping
chamber such doggerel verses as

> "Landlord, may your lies malign
>   Bring destruction on your head!
> You, yourself drink unmixed wine
>   Water sell your guests instead!" [1]

He can at least claim that his ordinary charges are moderate. His regular bill to a driver is likely to be:

> "Bread and a pint of wine 1 as;
> Meat dish   2 asses;
> Mule provender   2 asses;
> Night accommodation   2 asses."

The bronze *as* is hardly more than 2 cents; and the whole
charge, including the mule, is thus about 14 cents later-day
reckoning. The real profit, however, comes when for example

---

[1] These verses are from the wall of an inn in Pompeii, and the fore-
going description is that of an actual Pompeian inn.

a burly soldier off duty tramps in with his hob-nailed boots, swings back his military cloak, and orders, " Come, mine host (*copus*), some really good wine with a little water ! " If congenial spirits, male and female, are now ready, such may be the beginning of a long sousing evening, when the dice will clatter furiously and the soldier will awake in the morning with not one sesterce in his pouch.

207. Noble Frequenters of Taverns. — Sometimes Proxenus rejoices in still more exalted company. Certain fast young nobles enjoy " doing the rounds " of low taverns ; and the Inn of Hercules has fairly regular visitors of this very profitable type. When Proxenus sees Gnæus Lollius, Gratia's black sheep of a cousin, entering, he makes haste to anoint his own locks with pungent musk, and runs to greet his visitor as ' Dominus ' and ' Rex,' — while the young profligate, boasting that he has come to enjoy a perfect " Liberty Hall " (*æqua libertas*), commands the host at once to call in all the loose rascals in the neighborhood and insists that they drink with him from the same goblet. At last they are all sprawling about the tavern, the noble Lollius " cheek by jowl with cut-throats, bargees, thieves, runaway slaves, hangmen, and coffin makers." [1]

All Rome has been laughing in loyal glee at the retort in verse which the clever Hadrian has just made to a certain Florus, who wrote some lines saying " he would rather not be Cæsar " because the latter was always gadding off to outlandish places. Florus is notoriously a frequenter of all-night taverns, and the Emperor instead of imitating Nero and sending him a centurion with a death message, has hit back roundly :

"Florus would I never be,
Now a-tramp to taverns he,
Sulking now in cook-shops see
Victim of the wicked flea!"

[1] This scene is a familiar one from Juvenal.

208. Respectable Eating-Houses. — But not all people are teamsters seeking a lodging, or rascals seeking a carouse. Honest hard-working men and women must buy their meals every day. The simplest method, if you care nothing for

CHEAP GROCERY AND COOK-SHOP. *After Von Falke.*

appearances, is to halt before one of the cooks who station themselves in the open street with caldrons over small charcoal fires. At the end of copper sticks they attach little cups with which they bring up boiled peas, or some form of stew to be eaten on the spot. Of better grade are the

cauponæ (eating-houses) ; these are ordinarily arranged with
a long counter open to the street whereon is arrayed a tempting display of dainties, and above this are marble shelves
set with cups and glasses. We see also a place for heating
liquids over a charcoal fire.

On going inside a typical restaurant, one comes to a long
room filled with small tables and backless stools for the use
of the guests. The walls are covered with tolerable frescos
showing scenes of eating and drinking, while from the ceiling
dangle strings of sausages, hams, and other eatables. Really
good meals can be ordered here, also good wine at reasonable
prices. Most of the guests are honest, quiet tradesmen who
go about their business, and every sign of a brawl is promptly
repressed. When two youths in servile dress begin to exchange blows over a cast of dice, the strong-armed proprietor promptly gives them a push toward the door with
the firm injunction, " Please fight outside." [1]

209. *Thermopolia* — " Hot-Drink Establishments." —
Such places are genuine restaurants where more attention
is given to the food than to the beverages. Hardly any
eating-house, however, can really be popular unless it does
business also as a *thermopolium*, a " hot-drink establishment." Coffee and tea are unknown ; but hard-working
folk around the city find *calda* very refreshing especially after
the toil of the morning. Calda is a kind of diluted wine mixed
with spices and aromatic herbs, and heated up into a sort of
negus. It is in constant demand. In fact a cup of calda and
a little bread and peas make up the average poor laborer's
luncheon ; therefore the samovar (*authepsa*) is continually
steaming in all the Roman eating-houses.

Needless to say most inns and even the better restaurants
enjoy such an evil reputation among the high and mighty
that the latter never frequent them save, as does Lollius, for

[1] Another scene taken from an actual bas-relief and inscription.

the naughty " experience." Even when traveling through Italy, so general is the custom of extending hospitality, that only rarely will a great man like Calvus have to lodge with his retinue at an inn. The result is that country inns are hardly more select than those in the city, with sometimes the additional reputation of being the holds of unabashed robbers. Ladies and gentlemen, and even their more fastidious slaves, groan when they have to put up at country taverns, and what Cicero, Horace, Propertius, and other writers have thought of inns and inn-keepers has passed into literary history.

CHAPTER XIII

ECONOMIC LIFE OF ROME: II. THE INDUSTRIAL QUARTERS. THE GRAIN TRADE. OSTIA. THE TRADE GUILDS

210. Industrial Quarters by the Tiber. — We have said that Rome was not primarily an industrial or commercial city. A million and a half people cannot, however, exist without a great deal of local manufacturing and an elaborate organization for importing staples and luxuries. If we go down the Vicus Tuscus or some other streets leading near the Tiber and toward the southern part of the city, the fine mansions grow fewer, the insulæ become more squalid, and even these last are interspersed with dingy structures of concrete which by the noise and smells proceeding thence are obviously factories.

These industrial plants are for the most part small according to the standards of another age; there is also a marked absence of complicated machinery and a conspicuous dependence simply on patient man-power; but some establishments are really on a great scale. The noble House of Afer, for example, has a practical monopoly of the brick industry.[1] Its products are used all over the city, as may be proved by the name stamped on almost every brick, and in the Afer yards and kilns are employed several thousands of slaves and free workers.

211. Conditions of Industrial Labor. — Slave labor has crowded free labor hard but has not actually destroyed it. You can never get quite the same efficiency from a " speak-

---

[1] Marcus Aurelius belonged to this rich family on his mother's side.

ing tool " as from a man to whom life affords honest prospects. Furthermore, the supply of slaves is unsteady. While the legions were overrunning helpless kingdoms, it was easy enough to buy a hundred more hands for your pottery works or metal factory; but now the campaigns of Trajan (the last period, it will prove, of the great conquests) are over. There are barely enough prisoners in the slave market at present to provide a fair supply of servants.

There are other drawbacks to servile labor : though a slave worker cannot " strike " against terms of employment, his employer cannot cease to feed and clothe him during slack times, when he will gladly lay off free labor. As a result the average industry employs slaves and free men side by side; the latter are a little more self-sufficient, but seemingly they do not object to having slaves as fellow workmen. In any case the hours of labor are long and the conditions hard. A denarius (16 cents) is apparently wages enough to provide an artisan with a few rooms in a dingy insula and to keep his wife and children from starvation — especially if they can get the government grain doles; greater reward he dares seldom to demand.

212. Great Trade through Ostia and the Campanian Ports. — But Rome, as stated, imports more articles than she manufactures. The commerce from the interior of Italy, down the Tiber and along the main roads from the north, the Via Cassia and the Via Flaminia, is not of first impor‑ tance — mostly garden produce, stone, and timber. Not so that from Ostia, the harbor town, or that coming by the famous southern highways, the Via Appia and the Via Latina. Navigation along the Italian coast to Ostia has its dangerous features, and a great many merchants try to unlade at such south-Latin ports as Antium or preferably at the busy harbor of Puteoli in Campania. The result is that the southern roads are often black with great trains of

heavy wagons bumping over the hard pavement all the hundred and fifty odd miles from Puteoli to Rome.   However,
a very large fraction of the entire commerce of Rome passes
up the Tiber from Ostia, and is set down on those long arrays of wharves southwest of the Aventine, known as the
Emporium.

213. The Emporium and Its Wharves: the Tiber Barges.
— The Emporium is not the most beautiful section of Rome,
but it is one of the most important.   From its murk and
bustle many a lordly eques is swung away every night in his
litter for the quiet, aristocratic Quirinal or Esquiline; but
it is the Emporium trade which makes possible his great
mansion with its hierarchy of soft-footed slaves.   To reach
the Emporium we go down the Vicus Tuscus past the upper
end of the tall gray masses of the far-stretching Circus
Maximus, then turn down narrow lanes where the Aventine
crowds closely toward the Tiber.   Immediately the river
opens before us with a scene of teeming life.

We are now below all the regular bridges and at the head
of deep-sea navigation.   In truth the Tiber is too shallow
and uncertain a river to be very practical for large ships,
even of the Græco-Roman type.   Only small vessels, mostly
of the coasting variety, come up to Rome on direct voyages.
But the regular procedure is to unload the deep-sea craft
at Ostia and then bring up their lading along the twenty odd
miles of the crooked river, in light-draft barges.   These
barges — some worked by long oars, some towed by their
crews walking along the shore — are constantly coming and
going.   To-day as every day the river is alive with them, and
many others are moored closely, prow following stern, all
along the magnificent stone embankments which serve as
quays.

Approaching one of these ungainly flat-bottomed craft,
we see it has a little cabin on the poop, and its name, the " Isis

of Geminus," [1] is marked in large red letters upon the black hull. The captain is now standing by the mooring cable passed through a sculptured lion's mouth, directing a great gang of porters carrying sacks of grain down a bank to the wharf, where Geminus, the owner himself, assisted by a government clerk carefully checks off every sack upon their bills of lading. A little scrutiny reveals that while all kinds of commodities abound on the Emporium two take

RIVER BOAT LOADED WITH HOGSHEADS OF WINE.

wide precedence over all others — *grain*, from Egypt and provincial Africa; and *marble*, from Numidia, Greece, and Asia Minor.

214. The Marble and Grain Trades. — The marble trade, indeed, demands a special section of the wharves. For the government buildings the imperial procurators in the marble-producing provinces are constantly sending in valuable cargoes, and for monolithic columns and extra large blocks specially constructed barges are used to bring them from Ostia. Even now a great labor gang is painfully

---

[1] The real name of such a vessel.

disembarking a splendid column of Egyptian porphyry for the new Temple of Venus and Rome.

Behind the Emporium stretches an ugly complex of offices, warehouses, porters' barracks, and the like, but most conspicuous and ugly of all are the public *horrea*. These are tall gaunt storehouses for the keeping of grain, enormous fabrics of dull gray concrete, " elevators " in fact, carefully maintained by the government for the victualing of the capital. There are said to be more than three hundred horrea, and the largest are named for the emperors who built them — the Horreum of Augustus, of Domitian, and the like. Thousands of men are employed around them, and the state of their contents can give anxious nights to the Imperial Council. Unlovely as they seem, they are vital to the life of Rome.

It is no small task to provide grain for so huge a city, and that, too, without the aid of railways or steamships. Even a top-lofty Emperor like Domitian can fear the howls of the crowds in the circus if the price of wheat becomes high and the customary free distributions are not forthcoming. Hence these horrea must be large enough to supply a large margin against possible delay in the annual arrival of the " Alexandrian " or " African " fleets on which the provisioning of the capital depends.

215. The Public Grain Doles. — All the world knows that one of the most precious prerogatives of a plebeian in Rome is the right to receive about 5 *modii* (about 10 gallons dry measure) of grain every month at government charges. Is it not only right that the wearers of the toga should live on the bounty of the subject world?

In the past there have been, indeed, efforts to make the populace pay *part* of the price of their grain, with the government simply discharging the balance. This half measure has broken down because of unpopularity. All that the au-

thorities can do now is to see that the list of recipients is
limited to genuine citizens, and that the alien riffraff of the
great city is strictly excluded.

DISTRIBUTING BREAD.

There are now, as since the time of Augustus, about 200,000
citizens upon the precious " Frumentary Lists."   The recipients are not paupers, but include very many " small
citizens " of the worthier kind.   It is an honor in many circles
to win the precious *tessera* (metal or bone ticket) entitling

one to stand in line at the numerous grain dispensaries all over the city and get the monthly allowance.[1] Every adult male Roman in the city receives this privilege, but under some circumstances the tessera can be alienated. You hear of persons selling theirs or even bequeathing them by will; and some of the holders are thus not merely freedmen but even ex-criminals.

216. Distribution of the Free Bread: Extraordinary Bonuses (*Congiaria* and *Donativa*). — For a long time this food has simply been portioned out unbaked at the numerous grain stations all over the city; after which it has to be made into bread at home, or to be handed over to private bakers who will return so many loaves per measure, deducting a commission in kind. There is a growing tendency, however, towards government bakeshops as a new means of pampering the " Sovereign People " and towards passing out the food in the form of handsomely baked bread.

The custom nevertheless is not yet universal.[2] The private bakeries continue to flourish, and since each baker must grind his own flour, no sound is more common all over the city than the rasping of the millstones worked either by long-suffering donkeys, blindfolded to keep them from eating, or by the most recalcitrant and sodden class of slaves.

These distributions of free grain are part of the normal life of Rome. Inevitably they multiply the number of parasites, busybodies, and sheer beggars. Ever since Gaius Gracchus started the evil system, thoughtful men have groaned over its consequences, but all have been helpless, and the demoralization increases when an Emperor, to insure

---

[1] The expression "Sharer in the Public Grain Doles" appears on many tombstones of worthy burghers, to indicate that they enjoyed the full rights of citizenship.

[2] It became so under the Later Empire.

popularity at the beginning of his reign, or to confirm it later, orders a special *congiarium* to all the citizens.

This gift can take the form of special distributions of oil, wine, and meat to all the lucky holders of the tesseræ; but presents even more lavish are possible. When Trajan died in 118 A.D. and Hadrian was proclaimed, the latter, not quite

OVEN AND GRIST MILL IN A BAKERY. *After Von Falke.*

certain of public favor, put all the insulæ to roaring in his praise by proclaiming a gift of three aurei (gold pieces of $4.00 each) to every " frumentary citizen " in Rome. What wonder that later *donativa* (bonuses) become necessary at dangerously frequent intervals to prevent even the most loyal plebeians from praying for a new reign! [1]

[1] When Commodus became Emperor in 180 A.D., the congiarium came to the ruinous sum of 725 denarii per citizen. This was $96.00 each, if the coins were of full weight and fineness, which probably at that period they were not.

217. The Trade in Sculptures and Portrait Statues. —
But it is time to return to the region about the Emporium.
Near the marble wharves are naturally the huge establishments where all the day long the chip, chip of many mallets
and chisels indicates that great masses of sculptured stone
are being turned out — magnificent capitals, pediment groups,
bas-reliefs that are splendid works of art, for all the needs of
the government buildings and the mansions of the wealthy.

Many large concerns devote themselves to manufacturing
single statues, life-size or miniature. Standing around in
their courtyards are rows of sculptured deities, mostly copies
of good Greek masterpieces, representing the whole host of
Olympus from Jupiter down to the inferior demigods; there
are also numerous statues displaying orators posing in their
togas, magistrates in their official robes, and generals in their
armor, but with the features left in the rough — to be finished up on order at short notice to adorn some atrium or
small-town forum.

A great array of statues of the Emperor are also kept in
stock. These are needed in every government building, and
the demand is constant; but it must be admitted that
Hadrian's handsome bearded features are often outrageously
distorted by the careless journeymen, so that loyal folk protest even as does the governor of Pontus, Arrianus, who has
just written his master, " Your statue at Trapezus [on the
Euxine] is beautifully placed, but it is not the least like you.
Please send on another at once from Rome! "

Special markets and warehouses also exist for almost
every other major commodity. Near the Circus Maximus
there is the noisy, fetid cattle market where horses, kine,
and asses change hands amid coarse chaffering very much as
in the trade for slaves. There are likewise great repositories
for oil, flax, lumber, wool, spices, etc. — some private, some
under government supervision; the clang from all kinds of

smithies and metal workshops is incessant, and the factories
for manufacturing bronze statues are almost as large as those
for the stone sculptures.

218. The Tiber Trip to Ostia : the Merchant Shipping. —
If, however, one would learn the real sum of Roman industry
and commerce, it is needful to charter a slim swiftly-pulling

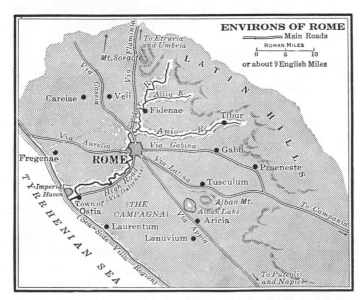

wherry and to glide down the yellow Tiber to Ostia. All the
way the craft has to dodge the enormous barges, but the
shores are covered with delightful villas, small villages, or
with prosperous farms raising poultry, flowers, vegetables,
and the like for the city trade. In the distance across the
level campagna can be seen the impressive array of the solemn
arches of the great aqueducts, reaching back into the hills
and bringing their supply of pure water to Rome. Ostia
itself, however, is strictly a harbor town, with an elaborate

series of breakwaters, dredged basins, naval docks, mercantile docks, and a perfect jumble of shipping.

The vessels have come from all parts of the Mediterranean, and there is even a battered trader that has coasted all the way from Britain with a cargo of tin ore. The smaller craft can trust sometimes to their oars in a calm, but all the larger must depend on their unwieldy lateen sails which swing from two or three long yards crossing as many masts.

By far the largest merchantmen are the Egyptian corn ships, and one of these, that is just being moved to the quay by a gang of shouting half-naked stevedores, is of somewhat unusual size. We are informed she is fully 180 feet long and 45 feet in beam.[1] She is provided with elaborate and decidedly comfortable cabins for many passengers, so that it is easy to believe the story that when the Jew Paullus (previously mentioned) on his compulsory trip to Rome was wrecked off Malta, 276 persons were rescued from the Alexandrian merchantman whereon he and his guards had embarked.

219. Imperial Naval Vessels. — At Ostia, too, can be seen a few triremes of the Imperial Navy. Enemies to the Roman dominion have practically disappeared from the seas, but there is still a certain danger of pirates or local insurrection; therefore, although the clumsy four- and five-bankers of the Punic War periods disappeared soon after the battle of Actium, small patrol squadrons of swift triremes, pulling about 170 oars, or of smaller craft are maintained by the government. These ships are extremely like the Athenian triremes of the golden age of Greece and call for no special description here.[2] The Romans are not naturally a seafaring people. Nearly all the larger merchant ships are manned if not owned by Greeks or Levantines; and it has

---

[1] Figures given by Lucian for a craft of this type.
[2] See "A Day in Old Athens," pp. 125–134.

been with real satisfaction that the Emperors have felt that they could allow their navy to dwindle down to insignificance. With the army, as will be seen, things are very different.[1]

220. The Harbor Town of Ostia. — Ostia has all the accompaniments of a busy port: a great mass of squalid lodging-houses for sailors, innumerable taverns overrun with dirty loiterers of both sexes, a great many uncouth faces along the quays, ear-ringed Syrians, and even quaintly jabbering negroes. There are, however, some good houses for the rich merchants and directors of the shipping, and a forum flanked with handsome temples and government buildings befitting the harbor town of the Mistress of the World.

In the outskirts of Ostia one can quickly get out into delightful country stretching all along the seashore. The villas of city magnates look forth upon the blue Tyrrhenian Sea, or are bowered in lush groves surrounded by rich gardens and fruitful orchards. The melons raised around Ostia are in demand by every epicure in the capital. Who can believe a prophecy that this active bustling port, with its enormous shipping, and all these villas, groves, and gardens will some day vanish like a dream, and that Ostia will lie in a desolate fever-stricken country, — with hardly a house in sight along the deserted shores, and with the harbor town of the Eternal City reduced itself to a few miserable cabins?

221. The Roman Guilds (*Collegia*). — Ere turning one's glance from the economic life of Rome it is needful to regard the organization of industry. Nearly all free workmen are members of " guilds " (*collegia*) which nominally exist for the purpose of worshiping some patron deity; thus the bakeries are the special votaries of Vesta the hearth goddess, the fullers

---

[1] There was practically no naval warfare worth mentioning in the whole course of Roman history from the battle of Actium (31 B.C.) to 323 A.D., when considerable naval fighting took place at the time Constantine captured Byzantium from his rival Licinius.

of Minerva the protectress of wool-working, the smiths of Vulcan, and so with others.

These " colleges " are not labor unions for the protection of the wage-earners against exploitation ; they are more like the guilds that are to be developed in the Middle Ages. The chief members are the employing " masters," and paid journeymen and apprentices have little share in the control of the organization. However, most industries in Rome are on so small a scale and the situation is so complicated by the competition of slave labor that the friction between wage-earners and their employers seldom becomes dangerously acute.

The trade guilds are carefully watched by the government lest they become the hotbeds of sedition and disturbing intrigue,[1] on the other hand their existence is often useful in helping to mobilize industry in behalf of the army and to keep up the public works in general.

They have a fairly tight organization, with their own officials, " prætors " and " presidents," and the like, and the election to such a post by one's fellow craftsmen is no slight honor. The guilds, too, have their special corporate property; and many of them possess elaborate guild halls for their feasts and meetings.

222. Very Ancient Guilds: the Flute-Blowers. — Some of the colleges are of decidedly recent origin, but eight of them boast that their history goes back to the very early days of Rome. These are the fullers, cobblers, carpenters, goldsmiths, coppersmiths, dyers, potters, and last but not least, the flute-blowers, so important at funerals and all public festivals.

From the " good old times " come many quaint stories about these guilds, and everybody remembers especially the tale concerning the flute-blowers. About 314 B.C. the cen-

---

[1] As at Ephesus where Demetrius used the guild of the silversmiths to start his riot against St. Paul. (Acts, 19 : 25.)

sors saw fit to forbid these somewhat riotous and irregular gentry from joining in the sacred banquets to Jupiter in which they had formerly participated. In anger the whole college struck and retired in dudgeon to the friendly city of Tibur. Soon the Senate found it difficult to conduct the religious rites properly without the aid of the flute-players, and endeavored to cajole them home, but the strikers had found their fare and quarters in Tibur very pleasant and refused any reasonable terms. The people of Tibur, however, wearied of their guests and to get rid of them gave the whole corporation a generous banquet, during which all the members became so drunk that they could be loaded into wagons, trundled back to Rome and then laid down in a helpless stupor in the very Forum. The next morning the entire guild awoke, rubbed its collective eyes and found a vast crowd of jeering friends pressing around. The result was an honorable compromise. The censors relented, and the flute-players, in return for giving solemn attention to their religious duties, were awarded the right to three days of high carnival, with songs, dances, and every kind of coarse gayety.

223. Importance of the Guilds. — The complete list of the guilds is very long. Besides those mentioned, among the more prominent are the barbers, perfumers, fruit sellers, garment cutters, pack carriers, mule drivers, gig drivers, and fishermen, not to mention the great guild of the bakers. There is as yet no formal compulsion upon a craftsman to join a college, but in fact any " non-union " workman is subject to discrimination and sabotage which make his life unhappy. Cases are known of funerals being halted amid an unseemly scuffle when a non-member of the guild of bier-carriers has been discovered helping to carry the litter for the dead.

Certain crafts have perforce to be distributed all over the city but inevitably fellow guildsmen like to flock to-

gether. In the industrial quarters each craft tries to concentrate upon a certain street which is then called by its
name. Well known is the case of how Catiline's gang had
its rendezvous at Marcus Læcas's house on Scythemaker's
Street. There is no annual " labor day " when all the guild
members of the city hold festival together. On the contrary
each college has its own separate festival, when the united
craft is entitled to parade through Rome with horns, pipes,
cymbals, and gaudy banners; its officers appearing in
the guise of magistrates. The whole company with their
families ordinarily head for the outskirts, where, beside convenient temples and hospitable taverns, the good people can
spread themselves for picnics under the trees, join in vulgar
dances, and very often spend the night under improvised
tents of leaves — everybody sleeping the sounder because
of much strong wine.

224. Multitude of Beggars. — To these honest plebeians
must be added another less noble multitude. Rome literally
swarms with beggars. The parasitical habits taught by
slavery and by the grain doles go far to make begging somewhat respectable. At every turn you can run on whining
wretches often repulsively mutilated in order to excite sympathy. They have their regular stand, however, upon the
bridges, where they crouch on dirty mats shouting their
" *da! da!* " " Give! Give! " and at the gates where travelers take or leave their carriages they are thicker than the
flies. Near Ostia and along the Emporium may also be
seen real or pretended sailors escaped from shipwreck, identifi-
able by their heads, which are shaven because of vows made in
peril, and who hold out their caps for coppers while " delight-
ing in garrulous ease to tell the story of their perils."

Downright thieves, professional robbers, and petty pil-
ferers are held in reasonable restraint by the active police,
but the absence of street lights makes it risky business to

go about after dark without torches and a good escort. Serious burglaries are often reported, and every now and then the body is found of some wayfarer who was stabbed while resisting a hold-up. As for certain districts going down the river toward Ostia, or along the Via Appia toward the Pomptine Marshes, their reputation is so bad that even in daylight a company of armed slaves is desirable.

CHAPTER XIV

THE FORA, THEIR LIFE AND BUILDINGS. THE DAILY JOURNAL

225. The Fora, the Centers of Roman Life. — Hitherto in our prolonged " day " in Rome we have carefully avoided visiting those famous quarters or buildings which are the glory of the imperial city. These can only take on true sig-

GENERAL VIEW OF OLD FORUM AND CAPITOL : a simplified restoration.

nificance when we have first seen the ordinary life of rich and poor. It is now time, however, to visit the " Heart of Rome " — the splendid system of fora in that great hollow where five of the " Seven Hills " almost come together just north of the Palatine, and then to visit the Palatine itself with its abodes of official majesty.

The renowned and original " Forum " is known technically

OLD FORUM: present state, looking towards the Capitol.

as the *Forum Romanum*, or the Old Forum, and down to
Julius Cæsar's time it was the only great plaza inside the
official limits of the city.   Under the emperors it is still revered and famous, but the needs of an enormous metropolis
have caused first Cæsar, then Augustus, Vespasian, Nerva,
and finally Trajan to add other wide public squares surrounded by buildings far more magnificent than most of those
around the ancient rallying spot of the men of the Republic.

All these fora are closely connected together, sometimes by
no very sharp lines of demarkation.   You can start in near
the Flavian Amphitheater and follow down the Sacred Way
across the Old Forum, with one soaring edifice, triumphal
arch, or memorial column succeeding another until at the
Temple of Trajan you find yourself on " Broadway " (*Via
Lata*), upon the great avenue leading through the select
shopping districts, and then past the Campus Martius, and
onward to the northern suburbs.   " Going to the Forum "
means visiting any place in this crowded, swarming district,
where every public and private interest seems to have its
stronghold, and where the litters of Senators go past so
frequently that nobody stops to count them.

   **226. Incessant Crowds at the Forum.   The Centers of
Gossip.** — If driving is impossible in the ordinary Roman
streets by day, it is doubly impossible in this congested region where only those who delight in crowds should endeavor
to force their way from one building to another.   Nevertheless, with that informality so characteristic of Mediterranean countries, all the fora are allowed to be overrun with
idlers.   Ragged boys are scampering between the columns
fronting the most sacred temples, and on the steps of the same
adult idlers from morn till eve are playing " Robbers "
on boards scratched upon the stonework,[1] or rattling dice

---

[1] Such improvised gaming-boards have been discovered by the archæologists.

(nominally forbidden) if the police are not too near. The foul and the elegant therefore are often in amazing juxtaposition.

For the average senator or eques a morning visit to the Forum, after he has received his own callers or clients, is almost a required act of the day. All his associates are doing the same thing; he can easily meet almost any friend without making an appointment, he can read that " Daily Journal " presently to be described (see p. 282), hear the latest tittle-tattle from the palace and get all the trade reports — all this even if he has no real business at the Senate House, the government bureaus on the Palatine, or the Record Office on the slopes of the Capitol.

If the great men do this, all the lesser fry and above all the genteel idlers must do the same. The women frequent the fora almost as much as do the men. If there is nothing else to busy one, one can always wedge into the crowds listening to the distinguished advocates in the Basilicas (Court Houses). It is quite a proper thing to imitate Horace who put in many days simply wandering around the business quarters. " I go on foot (said he) and go alone. I ask the price of kitchen-stuff and grain. I often stroll down toward the cheating [gambling] Circus and around the Forum; then perhaps I stop toward evening at the fortune tellers. Presently I go home to my supper of leeks, pulse, and macaroni."

Across the fora will parade all personages who wish to put men's tongues to wagging. People laugh at a certain pretentious senator who likes to pass for a great hunter and who is incessantly sending his slaves around the plazas at the crowded morning hour, bearing nets and spears and driving a mule apparently bearing home a wild boar " which we all know," whisper the cunning, " he has just bought in the game market."

Here in the fora also the magistrates with their lictoral fasces pass so often that it is really inconvenient the number of times you have to bow your head to them, or, if in a litter, to dismount and stand at polite attention : and in such frequented places the kissing nuisance takes on its greatest bane. The merest chance acquaintance, if only he is a citizen, will thrust his damp salute upon you, little heeding whether you have a vile cold or his own lips be ulcered and his breath foul.

227. Grandiose Architecture : Vast Quantities of Ornaments and Statues. — In viewing these great public squares and buildings instantly one is impressed by a single fact — the grandiose character of the ornaments and the architecture. All the enormous public buildings are literally overladen with adornments. The architects seemed to have abhorred the idea of blank spaces. There are no reposeful vistas. Everything seems striving to be magnificent and ornate. Statues, singly or in groups, occupy all the gables, roofs, niches, intervals of columns, and even the stairways. The Triumphal Arches are surmounted by equestrian figures or by prancing four-horse chariots. Reliefs and medallions cover all the friezes. If there is any space that cannot be seized for the mounting of sculptures or at least for bas-reliefs, it can be used for painting designs in stucco or colored mosaics. Every detail down to the gutters is highly decorated.

Very different, therefore, are these fora from the chaste elegance of the public places in Athens. On the other hand much of the effect is splendid as well as startling. The utilization of concrete permits the erection of vast soaring domes, often covered with gilded tiles. The elaborate Corinthian pillars before many of the buildings are often simply superb polished monoliths of colored marbles. The use of the arch (practically unknown in Greece) permits new effects often graceful and pleasing.

The sculptures permitted in such public places are, of

course, always of the highest order. Sometimes they are
original Greek masterpieces carried as spoils to Italy. Often
they are excellent copies of those masterpieces but with small
variations, not inelegant, which give the reproductions a real
character of their own. At every turn one sees these triumphs of bronze and marble, Apollos, Minervas, Victories,
Winged Mercuries, Centaurs, Homeric Heroes, and all the
legendary host of Græco-Roman mythology — now singly,
now in groups. Interspersed with these gods mounted on
pedestals or on the entablatures of the buildings are the
honorary statues of the worthies of Rome. Hardly a great
leader is absent from Romulus to the reigning Hadrian.

A mere walk about the fora with an explanation of their
portrait statues becomes therefore a detailed lesson in Roman
history. Besides the images of the truly great and good,
there are so many others of sheer mediocrities or worse that
one is left wondering whether the honor of a " statue in the
Forum " is so important after all. Even in old Cato's day
the abuse was such that he remarked sarcastically that
" he would rather that men asked why he had *not* a statue in
the Public Square, than whisper questioning why he had
one."

228. Use of Color on Sculptures and Architecture. —
Needless to say, in Rome as in Athens very many of these
buildings are brilliantly painted.[1] The great columns of
colored or of snow-white Carrara or Græcian marbles are
usually left in their natural aspect, but nearly all the back-
grounds, architectural members, and details are colored in
brilliant greens, reds, and blues. The nude statues are nearly
all tinted in flesh color, and the hair darkened, and there is
perhaps an overplus of gilding.

Under a bright Italian sky these color combinations make
the vast succession of enormous buildings stand out with in-

[1] See "A Day in Old Athens," p. 216.

describable grandeur; and to this spectacle must be added
the huge crowds incessantly moving about the fora, great
masses of soft white togas giving to the wide areas all the
exuberance of teeming life.   There can be many other great
plazas in the future capitals of the world; there will never
be any more clearly marked out as the veritable center of
an enormous Empire than the succession of fora in Rome.

We are not concerned with archæological descriptions.
The arrangement of the fora in this reign of Hadrian must be
sketched over lightly or explained completely, otherwise the
result is not knowledge but confusion; here a very brief survey will suffice.   If we are following Publius Calvus's litter
as it traces the Esquiline on routine business of a senator,
a series of convenient side streets probably will bring it past
the great baths of Trajan and then down the slope to the spot
where the vast bulk of the Flavian Amphitheater rears itself arrogantly.   The baths and the Amphitheater both will
be visited later (see p. 361 and p. 394), and we can, therefore,
ignore them.   Then the litter bearers swing west and slightly
north — and before us lies the veritable Heart of Rome.

**229. Entering the Series of Fora: the Temple of Venus
and Rome.** — To avoid being overwhelmed by details only
the most conspicuous objects and buildings will be mentioned.   Some structures are obvious at the very first.   To
the left, lifting vauntingly above the visitors' heads, rise tier
upon tier the domes, balconies, and pinnacles of the Imperial
Palace upon the Palatine, sustained at their base by an enormous mass of arches and buttresses of masonry and concrete.
The lords of the palace at any moment can look down from
a gilded balcony upon the Old Forum and its bustling life, and
they need only descend an inclined plane in order to mingle
with the mob, or cross the Plaza to visit the Senate House.
Directly ahead — at the end of the vista, rises the Capitol,
crowned by the rebuilt Temple of Jupiter Best and Greatest

(*Jupiter Optimus Maximus*), its roof flashing with the gold tiles; its enormous pillars proclaiming it the most splendid fane in Rome.

At the head of the Via Sacra (for this famous route of the great Triumphators now opens before us), upon our right,

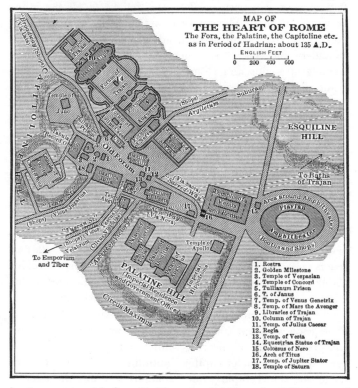

MAP OF
THE HEART OF ROME
The Fora, the Palatine, the Capitoline etc.
as in Period of Hadrian: about 135 A.D.

ENGLISH FEET
0   200   400   600

1. Rostra
2. Golden Milestone
3. Temple of Vespasian
4. Temple of Concord
5. Tullianum Prison
6. T. of Janus
7. Temp. of Venus Genetrix
8. Temp. of Mars the Avenger
9. Libraries of Trajan
10. Column of Trajan
11. Temp. of Julius Caesar
12. Regia
13. Temp. of Vesta
14. Equestrian Statue of Trajan
15. Colossus of Nero
16. Arch of Titus
17. Temp. of Jupiter Stator
18. Temple of Saturn

is the new and indescribably splendid Temple of Venus and Rome, a building just completed by Hadrian. This edifice has been reared by demolishing the last of the ruins of the impossibly extravagant " Golden House," the architectural monstrosity of Nero.

In order to get sufficient room for his new structure Hadrian also was compelled to move the colossal statue of Nero (99 feet high) located near the site and to set it nearer the Flavian Amphitheater. This had been a great task, executed by the clever architect Decrianus, with the aid of twenty-four elephants — performed to the delight of all the idling crowds in Rome. The statue now towers upon its new pedestal, with Nero's unworthy head sagaciously lifted from its shoulders and one of the Sun God substituted. The new Temple of Venus and Rome is a truly magnificent object; rising as it does upon a terrace 26 feet high, 500 feet long, and 300 broad, and surrounded by an enormous portico of 400 columns each 40 feet high. The versatile Emperor boasts that he has been the architect himself, and whatever are the real facts no vestibule to the fora could well be more impressive.

230. The Arch of Titus : Continuation of the Sacred Way. — With the Temple of Venus and Rome to our right and the substructures of the Palatine to the left we go straight ahead to the Arch of Titus. Everybody recognizes the shape of that impressive but relatively simple structure. Its bas-reliefs showing the spoils of Jerusalem — the "Golden Table" and more particularly the "Seven Branched Candlestick" — are destined to be reproduced countless times.

Old men in Hadrian's day can still recall the Triumphal Procession when the son of Vespasian returned in glory; how the great throng of cheering soldiers and citizens swept up toward the Temple of Jupiter Capitolinus, then halted at the portal of the Temple while Simon Bar-Giora, the captive Jewish leader who had been dragged in the procession, could be taken to a high place overlooking the Forum and deliberately scourged to death. At the news that he had perished all the vast company made the crags and columns quake with their brutal " acclamation," and Titus entered the shrine to

sacrifice and to bear witness how much mightier was Latin
Jove than Palestinian Jehovah.

And now the Via Sacra turns at right angles, or, to be more
accurate, its thronging ways divide. Go to the left and you
will come upon a high street passing under the brow of the
Palatine. It runs a considerable distance toward the Capi-

SPOILS FROM JERUSALEM: Arch of Titus.

tol, receiving several sloping avenues or broad staircases
leading down from the Palatine. This is "New Street"
(*Nova Via*), the most convenient route to certain buildings
on the southern side of the Forum.

It is better, however, to follow the denser crowds which are
swerving somewhat to the right, and then by a second turn
go straight onward again between magnificent structures,
with the gilded roofs of the Capitol ever looming ahead more
clearly. We are now on the Via Sacra proper; and caught

in the eddying throngs of litters, litter bearers, running footmen, following clients, elbowing plebeians with now and then

VIEW THROUGH THE ARCH OF TITUS, SHOWING THE FLAVIAN AMPHITHEATER
IN DISTANCE.

a masterful squad of Prætorians in gilded armor, we find it
perhaps impossible to get more than the names of the structures in passing.

231. House and Temple of Vesta : the Regia : the Temple of the Divine Julius. — The venerable temple near which the ways divide is that of Jupiter Stator where Cicero convened the anxious Senate when he delivered his great assault on Catiline. Next comes to view a long high wall broken only by narrow doorways until you see a stately portal at the western end, nearest the Old Forum. From above the wall can be glimpsed the tiles and marble of an elegant mansion inside, also the foliage trees of a really fine garden. This is the House of the Vestals, the abode of the six sacrosanct virgins who are the most revered personages in all Rome, hardly barring the Emperor.

As we advance there come next to view two buildings — one a small round temple of antique and simple structure; the other a handsome arched building of no great size. The first is the Fane of Vesta itself, where burns the eternal hearthfire of Rome, guarded by the Vestals, and the most sacred structure in the entire city. The second is the Regia, the official home of the Pontifex Maximus, the head of the Roman religion, and actually occupied (since that official is now the reigning Emperor) by various clerks and administrative bureaus relating to the upkeep of the State cultus. To the right of these buildings are government warehouses and offices ; [1] and then, closing off the Old Forum proper from these structures just named, stands another extraordinarily magnificent Temple, that of the deified Julius Cæsar.

232. The Old Forum (*Forum Romanum*). — We are now close upon the actual Forum. It can be entered by two methods : you can go between the Temple of Vesta and that of Cæsar, very likely walking through the triumphal arch of

---

[1] Later than the age of Hadrian this area was occupied by such famous structures as the Temple of Antoninus and Faustina, the Basilica of Constantine, etc.

Augustus, in which case you will see the pillared façade of
the stately Temple of Castor and Pollux (the divine helpers
of Rome at the half legendary battle of Lake Regillus), and
then across that busy shopping street, the Vicus Tuscus, before reaching the quieter portico of the great Basilica Julia ;
or you can take a better way by keeping on past the northern
side of the Temple of Cæsar and coming out pretty directly

OLD FORUM : looking west towards the Capitol. Restoration by Nispi-
Landi.

upon the Forum.   In so doing you will have the second great
court house, the old but capacious Basilica Æmilia to the
north on your right.   Let tribunals and litigants, however,
wait — before the visitor at last is opening one of the most
famous areas in the entire world — the *Forum Romanum.*

Of the Old Forum well may one say what Cicero declared
of Athens, " On whatever spot we tread we awake a memory."
There is hardly an event connected with the long reaches of
Roman history which is not also connected in one manner
or another with this public square.   The first impression, to

be sure, may be one of disappointment : the whole open plaza
barely measures 300 by 150 feet. It seems the more confined
because a large part of the southern side is hemmed in by the
huge Basilica Julia, while directly above the square rise the
two hills of the Capitoline and the Palatine, their summits

OLD FORUM, LOOKING TOWARDS CAPITOL FROM BEFORE THE TEMPLE OF
CASTOR : the building on the left, with statues beneath its upper arches,
is the Basilica Julia. Restoration after Von Falke.

crowned with lofty and noble buildings looking down upon
the Forum as a kind of common center.

As one advances, however, the impression deepens as to
how earnestly the Romans have tried to concentrate their
whole life around this beloved square. If statues abound elsewhere in the city, they seem here more numerous than even
the surging throngs around their pedestals. Every kind of
human activity is apparently going on simultaneously.
Along the north side, as we have seen, are the offices of those

great bankers who hold the nations in fee from the Euphrates to Hibernia, yet pedlers are now wandering about, almost under the feet of the consul's lictors, hawking hot sausages, strings of garlic, and pots of eye salve, while a snake charmer has obtained the license to exhibit two stupid serpents on the actual steps to the Temple of Janus just beyond the Basilica Æmilia.

233. The Forum Area: the Posting of Public Notices. — Walking out into the area itself, we find it solidly paved with rectangular blocks of travertine. The days are gone when closely packed throngs of quirites stood for hours upon this pavement listening to the orators bidding them vote upon peace or war, or for or against some proposed law, as lay in their right as free citizens. Gone, too, is the day of that great funeral pyre of garments, ornaments, trinkets, tables and benches, which the frenzied mob heaped around the corpse of Cæsar after Marcus Antonius had thundered his invective against Cassius and Marcus Brutus. But not gone is the Senate House (the *Curia*), looking out across the plaza from the northern side of the square, just beyond the Temple of Janus. And around the orator's stands, the Rostra, at the western end of the area there is still another elaborate funeral in progress; the wearers of the imagines sitting in their curule chairs, and the orator pompously lauding " the noble departed."

Truth to tell the Forum is frequented every morning largely to get the news. Not merely can you meet the bearers of all sorts of public or confidential information; you can spend an hour merely reading the great " white boards " (*albums*) bearing official and private notices which stand around everywhere. The "Daily Gazette" is here posted, and we shall consider its contents presently; but apart from that, whether you wish to know the price of grain or the day set for a lawsuit; whether Syphax the Moor will race his

four in the next circus, or Epaphroditus the Athenian will
lecture to-morrow on the nature of the soul, the Forum placards will tell you everything. Gossip incalculable, often of
a kind which no man dare put in writing, you may also pick
up, as well as accost half of your acquaintance. A visit to
the Forum, therefore, is almost as important to a Roman of
parts and activity as in another age will be the perusal of the
paper.

**234. Western End of Forum: the Rostra: the Golden
Milestone: the Tullianum Prison.** — At the extreme western end of the area, more temples are seen rising on the slopes
of the lofty Capitol. Here is the Temple of Saturn; and
higher still the Temple of the deified Vespasian, the Temple
of Concord, and the great " Public Record Office," the Tabularium, and the Rostra are reached just before you quit the
level area and take the winding ascents towards the Capitol.

These famous stands for the orators constitute an elaborate
platform, with a fine marble balustrade which is adorned
with exceptionally good bronze statues of notables such as
Sulla and Pompeius; although all these ornaments were
added by Julius Cæsar and know not the days of the Old
Republic. Some of the original " beaks " (*rostra*) from captured warships which gave the famous pulpit its name are
still in position, however, with others from such battles as
Actium added.[1] Even if the Republic is dead, the place
remains of decided utility not merely for funerals, but also
for formal speeches on state occasions; and sometimes an
emperor will still condescend to harangue the loyal quirites
from its platform.

Close by the Rostra and near its southern end rises a tall
stone pillar coated with gilded bronze. This is the " Golden

---

[1] A difficult archæological question is connected with the exact site of
the Rostra *before* Julius Cæsar's time. Probably its original position
was nearer the other end of the Forum.

Milestone " whereon Augustus inscribed the names of the great roads leading out of Rome, and the distances to the chief towns along their course.   " *All roads lead to Rome,*" and leading to Rome find their convergence in the " Golden Milestone."   It comes close, therefore, to being the " Hub " of the entire Roman Empire.

OLD FORUM : present condition, western end looking east. In foreground pillars of Temple of Saturn.

Near the other, the northern end of the Rostra, when one goes a little of the way up to the Capitol, there is quite a different landmark, far more venerable — the old prison of the city, the Tullianum, prepared, according to the story, by King Ancus Martius.   It was originally nothing but a kind of well let into the damp rock, with an upper and a lower compartment; this second chamber is only accessible by means of a hole in its vaulted roof through which prisoners were lowered by a rope.

The Tullianum has long since been discarded as the public jail, but state prisoners are sometimes confined or executed there. Familiar is the story of how Jugurtha, the luckless Numidian, was starved to death in the lower dungeon; and how Lentulus and the other Castilinian conspirators were strangled in the upper. Since then, if one accepts the story told by those very despised creatures, the Christians, their great leader, Peter, one of the associates of Christus, was kept there in chains before he was taken out to be executed by Nero's orders. It is assuredly a gloomy and fearsome enough place to strike terror even into such " Haters of all Mankind," as official documents assure us these Christians must be.

235. The Basilica Æmilia : the Temple of Janus : the Senate House (*Curia*). — But to return to the great buildings lining the Forum. The Basilica Æmilia on the north side was erected as early as 179 B.C., and, though often repaired, it is a substantial monument of the great days of the Republic. It is so like the greater Basilica Julia, however, that one description will do later for both. Directly by this court house stands the venerated Temple of Janus, a structure with many arches and sacred to the most characteristic if not the greatest of all the gods of Rome.[1] The gates of the shrine, one notices, are standing carefully open, as a token that some petty frontier wars are still raging. When absolute peace prevails these doors, however, will be carefully shut. The Romans are thrifty and practical people. Why waste good sacrificial victims and incense on the god when his help against the foe is not needed? It would be like paying a doctor when one is feeling entirely well.

Leading away from the Forum and this Temple is a series of vaulted passages also called *janus*, which form a large

---

[1] Janus was about the only Latin deity for whom there could not be assigned a Greek counterpart.

part of the banking district. Here, because the Sacred
Way is too limited, many great financiers have their offices;
here countless clerks are busy with their account books;
here great loans are negotiated or investments are placed
hourly. It is almost a regular exchange and the scene of
many speculations. Regularly one hears of fortunes made
or lost " between the janus," *i.e.* by the workings of high
finance.

Beside the Temple of Janus rises the magnificent porch of
the *Curia* (Senate House). The Conscript Fathers are not
yet in session, and a visit to the interior can wait. The
structure is very splendid, but it is not the grand old Curia
Hostilia, built according to legend by King Tullus Hostilius,
and the scene of nearly all those famous Senatorial debates
across the long annals of the Republic. That ancient building was burned in 52 B.C. during the riots following the murder
of the idol of the populace, the demagogue Clodius. Julius
Cæsar, therefore, had a good excuse for building a stately
new Senate House. This in turn was damaged in Nero's
great fire, but Domitian carefully repaired it — and with its
fine pillars, bronze doors, and galaxy of statues, it forms
a worthy meeting place for what is still a venerable and
powerful body.

**236. The Basilica Julia, the Greatest Court House in
Rome; the *Lacus Curtius*.** — The Basilica Julia on the southern side of the Forum is a building into which it is best to
enter. The structure was begun by Julius Cæsar to meet the
imperative need for a larger court house. More important
business is transacted under its roof and ample porticoes,
perhaps, than in any other building in Rome; and in bad
weather nearly all the Forum loungers take refuge beneath
its ample shelter. Its size is worthy of its important functions; it is 270 feet long and in addition to the regular exterior
colonnade has a fine inner colonnade.

These double porticoes are the special lounging spots of
fashionable idlers of both sexes. Young men of fashion
seeking to meet congenial ladies of easy habits have only to
loiter around and stroll about a little — their hopes are
gratified. Assuredly Venus can hardly reckon up the love
affairs that here have ripened. The pavements are even more
marked up for gaming boards than elsewhere and some of the
players, we note, actually wear the equestrian stripes, while

INTERIOR OF A BASILICA: restored.

there are senatorial laticlaves in the interested throngs standing around them. Along the sides of the building are roomy
offices, where a large corps of city officials and clerks conduct
the various municipal boards and bureaus.

The glory of the Basilica Julia, however, is its great hall,
used for the chief courts of justice, barring always those of
the Emperor and the Senate. The hall is paved with colored
marbles of price; the pillars running down either side are
splendid monoliths of still rarer marbles, and the ceiling is
heavy with gilt fretting and painting. In every possible

niche rise statues of famous jurisconsults and advocates. The light streams down abundantly through the windows in the upper clerestory, and in this second story at the present moment there are standing or sitting groups of very respectable men and women listening to the orator pleading before one of the tribunals below. Any guide will tell how the mad Emperor Caligula used to delight to stand in these upper balconies, fling down money, and roar with delight when the crowds trampled one another struggling to get the coins.

So large is this hall that not one but *four* tribunals have been set up in different quarters of the building, and litigation often proceeds before all four of them simultaneously, although in the absence of partitions strong-lunged advocates sometimes interfere with their neighbors; they tell of a certain stentorian Trachalus who once while speaking before one tribunal not merely was heard by but drew applause from the audiences in the other three. Here Quintilian, Pliny the Younger, Tacitus, and other orators of the generation just departed, won their fame, and at present every windy amateur in the rhetoric schools dreams of the day when he can wave out his toga in the Basilica Julia before a crowded and cheering balcony.

These are some of the more famous monuments in and around the Forum Romanum. Were one to descend to particulars the task were endless. Perhaps there should be mentioned a certain modest altar in the very center of the open plaza. This marks the so-called *Lacus Curtius*. Antiquarians give one several stories concerning it, but the accepted version is this. — Once in the good old days a yawning gulf opened at this very spot, the portent, perhaps, of the devouring of the entire city — when lo! the brave youth, Marcus Curtius "devoted" himself for his country and plunged unflinchingly into the abyss. The earth closed over him, he was seen no more, but Rome held his name in eternal remembrance. Doubtless he had thus taken upon himself the anger of the infernal gods and had saved the state ! [1]

237. The New Fora of the Emperors: the Temple of Peace. — After surveying the Forum Romanum we are

THE TARPEIAN ROCK: on slopes of the Capitol. (From this traitors were hurled in the time of the Republic.)

told that five other fora — the creations of high-minded Emperors — still await inspection. Truth to tell, however, these great plazas — not marking the growth and events of centuries, but the mandates of wealthy despots — give one a

---

[1] Later visitors to the Forum would, of course, be impressed with the fine, if ornate, *Arch of Septimius Severus*, erected about 211 A.D. at the northwest corner of the plaza.

sense of anticlimax. Of them it will be properly written:
" The fora of the Empire were as much superior in magnificence to the Forum Romanum as they were inferior in
historical interest and association."

They are the work of master architects mobilizing armies
of laboring slaves, stone cutters, and artists. The eye becomes weary with the incessant sheen of costly marble; the
equestrian statues, the forests of ornate Corinthian pillars,
the great reaches of tessellated pavements, the quantities of
colored paint, enamel, and heavy gilding. At first these
imperial fora appear to the visitor as a hopeless complex
of pretentious splendor; but after a little, a clever method
appears in their arrangement by which one great plaza or
system of public buildings joins itself to another.

Four of these public squares join closely together, but the
fifth stands a little apart. This last is located near the northeast end of the Old Forum, verging toward the Subura and
the Esquiline, and is the " Forum of Peace," constructed by
Vespasian about 75 A.D. The open area, however, is relatively small, for its center is occupied by the imposing
"Temple of Peace." This temple is adorned with a perfect
gallery of sculptures and paintings, nearly all of them masterpieces by the Greeks. These works of art had formerly
occupied Nero's Golden House until that grandiose structure was destroyed by the thrifty Vespasian. In this Temple of Peace likewise are kept those precious Jewish spoils
shown on the Arch of Titus, and there is not merely a fine
library but a hall for the savants and scientists when they
meet for their learned conventicles.

238. The Fora of Julius, Augustus, and Nerva. — In
dealing with the four connected fora it profits little to multiply detailed descriptions; one glittering marble edifice
succeeds another around each square. Nearest to the Old
Forum lies the Forum Julium. Julius Cæsar paid out

100,000,000 sesterces ($4,000,000) merely for the land which it occupies, and its buildings are worthy of the costly soil whereon they stand. In its center rises the great Temple of Venus Genetrix, "mother" of the Julian line. Here at times the Senate can convene, while the shops under the porticoes around are among the finest in Rome.

Directly north of this Forum Julium is the Forum Augustum. When young Octavius went forth to avenge his

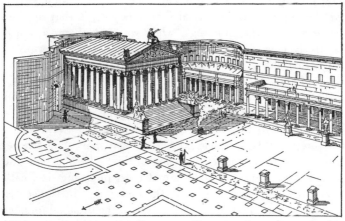

FORUM OF AUGUSTUS AND TEMPLE OF MARS THE AVENGER: restored.

adopted father against Brutus and Cassius he vowed a temple to Mars Ultor ("Mars the Avenger"). Later as the Emperor Augustus, most splendidly he fulfilled this vow. The porticoes around the plaza are of Numidian marble, and variegated marbles compose the pavements; the open area is covered with bronze *quadrigæ* (four-horse chariots), triumphal arches, and, of course, numerous statues, some of precious metals, while the Temple of Mars Ultor itself matches all its rivals in magnificence.

To the southeast of the Forum of Augustus and joining it

to the Forum of Peace is the smaller Forum of Nerva.   This
plaza was really begun by Domitian, but when that tyrant
perished ere completing the task, it was finished and named
by the eirenic Nerva.   It is really a kind of broad thoroughfare leading down from the Subura district, although upon
it fronts a fine Temple of Minerva.   One of the features of
this square is a stately avenue of statues of the deified Emperors.

   239. The Forum, Column, and Libraries of Trajan. — By
far the finest of the imperial fora, however, is that of Trajan — and all the buildings, when we visit them, are still
relatively new.   It opens to the northwest of the Forum of
Augustus, and is not really a single square but a genuine
series of squares.

   To get the level space for their great areas, it was needful
to cut away a whole spur of the Quirinal, excavating to a
depth equal to the height of Trajan's Column (128 feet).
On entering this precinct, if one has been marveling before,
it is right to be astounded now.   First there comes the
Forum Trajani proper, a square of most imposing size, with
lofty porticoes, semi-circular at the ends ; and in the center
stands a remarkable equestrian statue of the imperial founder
himself.   Then there is the vast *Basilica Ulpia*, the third
great court house of the city, which spreads lengthwise across
the northwestern boundary of this forum.   It is 300 feet
long, 185 feet broad, and five lines of pillars divide it into
four separate halls for different kinds of business ; in fact
it is really a finer building than the older Basilica Julia.

   Going through this enormous but very open structure, we
come to a second smaller plaza, and here rises one of the noblest sights of Rome — a monument that will draw the admiration of all ensuing ages — the *Column of Trajan* itself.
The bas-reliefs telling in picturesque detail the whole story
of the Dacian Wars, the 2500 human figures executed with

An Imperial Forum, near the Column of Trajan: restoration after
Von Falke.

infinite fidelity and care, wind spirally from the top of the 18 foot pedestal clear to the summit. This last is crowned by a colossal bronze-gilt statue of Trajan looking down upon the sculptured record of his military glory.

This column is, perhaps, the worthiest monument of the whole imperial age.[1] The marvels of Trajan's forum-system, however, are not exhausted. North and south of the Column are two fine buildings of moderate size; these are the *Bibliothecæ*, the two public " Libraries of Trajan," one Latin, one Greek — containing on the whole the finest collections of books in Rome; and directly facing the Column and the Libraries across another open area of considerable extent is the *Temple of Trajan*, where the priests daily offer their sacrifice to the deified manes of the terror of Dacia and of Parthia.

240. The Park System of the Campus Martius: the Pantheon. — These exhaust for the moment the structures we can survey around the fora: and it were well to stop lest sheer confusion may follow. With time, however, we could wander after the throngs again northwestward along " Broadway " past the great porticoes and fine shops of the Sæpta Julia, and saunter about the great park system of Campus Martius.

The public baths there located and such structures as the Theater of Pompey and the Flaminian Circus can, perhaps, be explained later; but a word must be spoken for the one great temple which is here situated away from the center of Rome. The *Pantheon*, dedicated to Mars, Venus, the deified Cæsar, and to all the other deities of the Julian line was the erection of Marcus Agrippa, the mighty coadjutor of Augustus. It has just been rebuilt from its very foundations by

---

[1] The column of Marcus Aurelius, erected about 180 A.D. in much the same style as that of Trajan, although a magnificent monument, is not equal in execution to the older column.

INTERIOR OF THE PANTHEON: restoration according to Von Falke.
281

Hadrian.[1] Its noble dome shines with the golden tiles. The soaring rotunda inside is encircled with stately altars to the gods the building honors. Already one can stand and look upward 143 feet to that patch of blue 18 feet in diameter through which sun and stars will shine down across at least eighteen centuries of changing history — making the Pantheon the one great building, not a ruin, which shall link the Rome of the Cæsars with the Rome of another day.

241. The Daily Gazette (*Acta Diurna*). How Rome Gets Its News. — One thing, to avoid complexity, we omitted while crossing the old Forum Romanum. It behooves us to return and to explain it. Before a series of tall white boards set up against certain pillars is gathered an elbowing, gesticulating throng. Many of the company have tablets and seem copying vigorously. The crowd is always receiving additions, while others are departing. The white boards (" albums ") when we get near enough are seen to be covered with somewhat fine writing. There is a special rush and flutter in the crowd when a petty official sets up still another white board, and a hundred styli instantly become busy. It is easy to learn the excitement caused by these notices : they constitute the publication of the new *Acta Diurna*.

Even without the Acta Diurna (" Daily Doings ") a city like Rome would have its supply of news. There are professional gad-abouts who make themselves desirable guests at dinner-parties merely because they are " very well informed." They have picked up all the stories about the Parthian king, the new chiefs of the Germans, the number of legionaries mobilized on the Rhine, and the corn prospects in Africa and Egypt, as well as every kind of commercial information.

---

[1] He magnanimously allowed Agrippa's name still to appear as the builder of the temple. The Pantheon apparently owed its preservation through the Middle Ages to the fact that it was early consecrated as a Christian church, and hence was exempt from profanation.

Other wiseacres of a less reliable cast are known as " *subros-trani*," — " Rostra-haunters," — for at the Rostra all gossipers have their tryst. These people specialize in rumors of calamity, reports of great military disasters, of the sudden death of magistrates, etc., and take a peculiar glee in circulating vile stories about the Emperors — the danger of repeating such rumors only adding spice to their game. Usually, however, they are too insignificant fry for the government to consider worth prosecuting.

242. Contents of the Acta Diurna. — The Acta Diurna, however, is issued by a government bureau, and a certain degree of official responsibility is attached to the more formal statements. The editors, nevertheless, are allowed to add racy anecdotes of a personal nature, especially concerning the higher aristocracy. The relations between the senatorial nobility and the freedmen and equites in the imperial government bureaus are none the best; and Hadrian himself is not on perfect terms with the Conscript Fathers.[1]

Official circles, therefore, are never careful to suppress spicy bits about the aristocrats. The public record offices and dispatches from the provinces supply most of the items, but some of the material can only have come from direct reportorial activity. In any case the interest in this Daily Gazette is enormous. Its single copy will be multiplied many times, copies being made of the copies, and the same sent to wealthy people in all parts of the Empire. A month from now groups will probably be gathering in Spanish Corduba and Syrian Antioch to read the items published to-day in Rome.

Owing to the limitations of space, despite the use of many " white boards," the Acta Diurna has to maintain a very

---

[1] At the end of his reign the Senate so disliked him that (although he had been in the main an excellent ruler) his successor Antoninus had much trouble in getting him voted a "*divus*," as were all good Emperors

dry journalistic style indeed. The lively Italian imagination, however, can provide most of the details, even if they
are not at once eked out by quantities of that " smoke," oral
rumor, which is passed about amid the copyists the moment
the new gazette is posted. This is a very commonplace issue, and the albums read something like this : [1]

" Records for the tenth day of June. Yesterday —— boys
and —— girls were born in the city of Rome. —— bushels of
grain were landed at the Emporium. —— head of cattle [and
other commodities specified] were also brought into the city.
On this same day the palace slave Mithridates was ordered
crucified for blaspheming the guardian genius of his master
the Emperor. At the imperial treasury —— million sesterces,
which it proved impossible to loan out at interest, were ordered returned to the public funds. A fire broke out in the
insula of Nasta in the Viminal district but was extinguished."

243. Miscellaneous Entries and Gossip in the Gazette.
— The entries go on to give the doings in the petty police
courts, the copies of important wills with especial mention
of any bequests that were left the Emperor, the statement
that a certain eques had caught his wife in gross misconduct
and divorced her ; that a procurator for a large trading house
was being prosecuted for embezzlement, and a summary of
the evidence in a great violation of contract case between two
marble importers now on trial in the Basilica Æmilia. Then
follow magisterial edicts, lists of judicial appointments, and
careful entries about all the doings of the Emperor and of
his progress back toward Rome. Next is given a rather
elaborate summary (evidently made by shorthand reporters)
of the latest debate in the Senate, with careful entry of the
applause and interruptions which the orators received.

---

[1] We have no copy of the Acta Diurna. We possess, however, what
seems a pretty literal parody of its style and contents in Petronius, and
can reconstruct part of an issue with some confidence.

All this is more or less " official "; but the newsmongers
are really more interested in "human interest stories "
added by the publishers' private authority. Thus it makes
good reading to tell how a frantic admirer of a certain " Red "
charioteer who was killed in the last races, cast himself on
the funeral pyre of the beloved jockey, in order not to survive his idol; or to relate how a citizen of Fæsule has
just visited Rome and sacrificed to Jupiter along with
" eight children, thirty-six grandchildren, and nineteen great
grandchildren." [1] Furthermore, the report of love affairs
among the noble and mighty is never omitted — how a senator's wife has eloped with a gladiator, and how a certain oft-
mentioned lady is about to wed an eighth husband. Finally
(perhaps the most copied of all) there are, of course, the
announcements for the coming exhibitions in the theater,
amphitheater, and circus, with lists of the actors, gladiators,
and charioteers, and other data, which can enable all Rome to
arrange its wagers and its holidays.

The Acta Diurna therefore goes about as far as is possible
to create a real newspaper in the days of mere penmanship.
Its vogue is immense. Many a fine lady sends her slave or
freedman to the Forum every day to bring home a special
copy. Its items will focus the conversation at a thousand
dinner tables.

Finally this publication will enjoy a certain degree of his-
toric importance. After each issue has served its daily purpose, fair copies are deposited in the Public Record Office,
and here they can be consulted many years later by the
learned. It is from the files of the Acta Diurna that Tacitus
and Suetonius have apparently drawn a great many of
their anecdotes about the days of the early Emperors.

---

[1] Both of these are actual cases from the reign of Augustus.

CHAPTER XV

THE PALATINE AND THE PALACE OF THE CÆSARS. THE GOVERNMENT OFFICES, AND THE POLICE AND CITY GOVERNMENT OF ROME

244. History of the Palatine: its Purchase by Augustus. — There is one other great quarter of Rome, from the political standpoint the most important of all, the Palatine.

The Palatine originally was a hill of modest height, in shape fairly rectangular, some 1400 feet on the side. Here according to firm tradition was that first settlement by the Alban shepherds led out by Romulus. The hill seems to have been encompassed by its own crude wall, and presently it figured as the earliest " Rome," often called from its squarish configuration *Roma Quadrata*. Time fails to count the various memorials such as the " House of Romulus," alleged to have survived since this primitive time. Note should be made, however, of certain small but very old temples such as those of Victoria, Viriplaca, and Orbona,[1] which are now carefully preserved amid surroundings of artificial magnificence.

After the growth of the Republic the Palatine became one of the most fashionable residence sections of the city. Public leaders liked to mount the roofs of their mansions and see the whole Forum with the familiar Senate House spread out at their feet. Here were erected the earliest of those sumptuous mansions wherein the aristocracy invested their spoils from the great conquests. Marcus Scaurus had his pretentious dwelling on the Palatine, and so did Catiline,

---

[1] Old Latin goddesses.

and Marcus Antonius, and Cicero. Last but not least, Hortensius the Orator, Cicero's professional rival, erected an extremely fine dwelling here shortly before his death in 50 B.C., which mansion was later purchased by Augustus when he had assumed the government and desired a suitable

ARCH OF TITUS: part of Palatine visible to the left.

residence; and thus it was that the Palatine became the " Palace " of the Emperors.

245. Extension of the Imperial Buildings: Central Position of the Palatine. — Augustus, posing merely as the " First Citizen " among his fellow Quirites, and with a studious abhorrence of the outward forms of monarchy, had avoided establishing anything like an Imperial court; but he was, of course, entitled to a large senatorial mansion. In addition to his private residence elaborate offices had also to be provided for the great corps of secretaries and clerks through whom he governed half the provinces and controlled the army. This corps of bureaucrats has grown with every new accretion to imperial power; furthermore, Augustus's pretence of democratic simplicity has been utterly discarded following the extravagances of Caligula and Nero.

One enormous building has, therefore, been added to another. The last private dwellings upon the hill have been condemned, and the Cæsars now control every inch of the Palatine, making it so completely the abode of majesty that " palace " will remain across the centuries as the name for any seat of princely authority.

246. Commanding View from the Palatine Hill. — This is the smallest of the Seven Hills, but it is the real focus of the other six, which " seem to surround it with their homage, as being their king." It is so close to the Capitol that the crazy Caligula erected a bridge (now long demolished) leading from his mansion clear over to the Temple of Capitoline Jove, in order that he might frequently " go and visit his friend Jupiter." The view from the crest of the palace structures is superb: northward across the Forum, and all the thickly clustered roofs on the slopes of the Quirinal, Viminal, and Esquiline, westward to the Capitol where the magnificent temples seem within a stone's toss, southward across the great hollow of the Circus Maximus and then across to the densely covered Aventine. Whether the Emperor desires to harangue the Senate, to sacrifice to the greater gods, or to grace the chariot races — Curia, temples, or circus are all close at hand; with the Flavian Amphitheater to the northeast, almost equally near.

247. Magnificence of the Palatine Structures. — But the Palatine itself is perhaps the most glorious sight of all. It rises above the city two and three hundred feet to its upper parapets, lifting itself on several tiers of arches and pillared stories which gleam with marble below and present a perfect

treasure house of gilded tiling above. Under the morning
light with the sun flashing the gold of the multitudinous domes
back into the clear azure the whole effect is incomparable.
The natural foundations of the hill are covered with enormous substructures of masonry and concrete, and these are
continued by long tiers of many-arched buildings which house
the great government bureaus and ministries. Crowning
these can be seen equally long forests of columns, upbearing

PALATINE AND PALACE OF THE CAESARS: restoration by Spandoni.

a whole complex of gabled roofs covered not merely with the
gilded tiles, but with a whole legion of gilded or richly toned
bronze statues. Here and there show forth bits of greenery and foliage betraying the gardens and the parks reserved for the Lords of the World.

The effect of this entire mass is overpowering. The eye
wearies of counting the sweeping porticoes, tall monoliths,
colossal statues, and quadrigas. The result is also enhanced
by the use of great numbers of huge awnings, hung over
nearly every opening and window, usually made in brilliant

colors, with the imperial purple very conspicuous. There
will never be another Palatine in the history of the world.

**248. The More Famous Buildings on the Palatine:
Enormous Display of Art Objects.** — This vast residence
compound — it cannot be called a single building — can
be reached by a number of inclined planes or stairways upon
all four sides.   Access is easy enough and crowds of slaves,
plebeians, and nobles are incessantly coming and going, al-

ROMAN URN: typical art object.

though a couple of Præto-
rians loll carelessly on their
spear-shafts beside each in-
gress.   Possibly the easiest
entrance is by the *Clivus
Victoriæ* (" Ascent of Victory ") which starts upward
from the edge of the Old
Forum very near to the
Shrine of Vesta.

To find one's way about
the Palatine is, however, far
more difficult than about
the fora.   It is not, of
course, an area but a jumble
of buildings, all splendid, but often thrust upon one another
without any real system.   Augustus added extensively to
the old house of Hortensius, and particularly he built
a very pretentious Temple to Apollo.   Tiberius, the next
Emperor, added a new wing, the *Domus Tiberiana*, almost
doubling the bulk of the former structures.   Caligula thrust
on more buildings still.   Across the ages will be pointed
out that *Cryptoporticus*, the twisting underground gallery
connecting parts of the palaces, where the stout tribune
Cherea struck down and slew the insane despot, January
24th, 41 A.D., to the great profit of the entire world.   Nero

added other wings and structures, some of which had to be rebuilt after his great fire. Finally, Domitian added a whole series of enormous halls, baths, banqueting rooms, and government offices. The Palatine is now virtually complete: Trajan and Hadrian have erected their monuments elsewhere, and so will most of the later Emperors.[1]

We do not propose to explore all these buildings in so vast a complex. It is enough that one superb court or façade follows another; that almost every hall and anteroom is of sumptuous splendor; that veined marbles, porphyry, elaborate bas-reliefs, and profuse gilding seem multiplied until they become commonplace. All the artificiality and over-elaborate art of the age seems concentrated around the Palatine. Within the great substructures and the arched terraces which bear up the more important buildings, even in the cells for the slaves and the offices for the toiling clerks there are fine frescos and handsome stucco reliefs.

249. The Triclinium and Throne Room of Domitian. — As for some of the special areas and chambers, they justify the praises of the servile court poets: " Olympian " is the mildest word which they can use. Take, for example, the porticoes of Domitian. On the inner side of their vast length, they are lined throughout with marble so highly polished that it shines like mirrors. What matter if the original cause for their use was the desire of the suspicious tyrant to have a promenade wherein nobody could glide upon him without warning from behind. The result is indescribably brilliant. But let us go rather into the " House of Domitian " itself, and inspect the great banqueting hall, the Triclinium. " The gods themselves might quaff their nectar there ! " cried the enraptured Martial.

---

[1] The only important addition after Domitian was made by Septimius Severus, who, about 200 A.D., built the very lofty *Septizonium*, a new palace at the southeast corner of the hill.

This magnificent apartment leads off from a marvelous peristyle-court of more than 10,000 square feet in area. The chamber itself is not huge, but is arranged so that three tables (each for nine guests) can be placed laterally along the walls, with the third, opposite the door of entry, for the Emperor and his chief guests. Twenty-seven dignitaries thus can dine together. On each side of the hall five large windows are separated by massive columns of red granite.

As the guests of majesty repose on their silken cushions they can see between the columns still another court where water is softly gushing from a fountain, and purling in a small cascade over steps of marble, verdure, and flowers. The ornamentation may be grievously overdone; the taste of some of the reliefs and wall pictures is questionable, but the effect of the sheen from the many colored marbles, the gilding, and the heavy fret work around the lofty dome undeniably justifies all the enthusiasm of the verse-mongers.

Equally striking is the Throne Room built by Domitian. It is called the tablinum as in humbler dwellings, but it is actually used for great state audiences. It is a hall of imposing size. You enter past the guards, and directly across the broad area is a niche where sits "Cæsar Augustus" upon a gilded dais and curule-chair, every whit as truly a throne as that of the Great King of Parthia. The walls of the room are covered with extraordinarily costly marbles, and around the circuit rise twenty-eight Corinthian columns of intricate workmanship. Eight large niches contain as many colossal statues wrought of adamantine basalt, and a Hercules and a Bacchus are particularly noteworthy. The entrance door is flanked by two enormous columns of *giallo antico*, deep yellow marble flushed with pink, imported from Numidia. The threshold is a single immense slab of a whiter marble brought from Greece.

Words thus exhaust themselves describing these grandiose,

overpowering, magnificent courts, halls, and apartments. We can perforce ignore such features as the separate hippodrome and the luxurious gardens reserved for imperial amusement or recreation. Better it is to concentrate attention upon the human life wherewith the Palatine ordinarily abounds.

250. Swarms of Civil Officials Always on the Palatine. — All the Palatine revolves around the Emperor. Rome is not yet governed by an unabashed despotism, yet it would be hard to name a deed that a king of old Babylon could perform which a *Princeps et Imperator* could not perpetrate if his heart really desired, although certain restraints and decencies make this absolutism endurable save under a Nero or a Domitian.

The thousands of persons who dwell upon or are employed upon the Palatine are all employed with one of two things, the imperial court or the imperial public service. Since Hadrian (despite the grumblings of his Italian subjects) is still absent from Rome the court ceremonial has practically ceased. A few of the Emperor's relatives dwell in gilded ease in certain wings of the palace, but except for the care-takers the great army of self-sufficient slaves and still more self-sufficient freedmen who act as valets, cooks, waiters, musicians, chamberlains, and in every other menial capacity, can eat, play dice, and discuss the races in idleness.

Now as always, however, the imperial public service which sends its impulse to the remotest borders of Dacia, Syria, or Britain is functioning actively, and most of the vast bureaus and ministries have huge offices upon the Palatine. The Prætorian Præfect, as high judge for the Emperor's half of the provinces, daily mounts his supreme tribunal. The four Imperial Secretaries for Finance, for Petitions, and for Official Correspondence (one for the Greek provinces and one for the Latin) direct their great corps of subordinates. The chief Procurators (Superintendents) of the enormous

Imperial Estates all over the Empire are receiving reports
and protecting their masters' interests; and so with a great
body of other high officials.

The huge administrative machine perfected by the practical
Roman genius is running steadily — so steadily that even
under a very bad Emperor, even a Nero, it will function for
years with no great harm to the governed millions.   The
only condition is that the tyrant will reserve his cruelties for
the nobility and refrain from tactless interference with the
secretaries instead of indulging merely in vicious personal
pleasures.[1]

   251. The Emperor Center of High Social Life. — Into
these high political concerns we dare not enter, but the social
life of the Palace cannot be so well ignored.   Already the
imperial freedmen are busy planning the great receptions and
state banquets which Hadrian must give soon after his
return.   In half the atria of Rome men and women are dis-
cussing vigorously, " When ' Cæsar ' returns will he have
any new ' Friends,' and will he have discontinued any old
ones ? "

Already it is rumored that certain freedmen (supposedly
in their lord's confidence) have received a great bribe to
get them to induce the " Dominus " (so loyal etiquette
calls the monarch) to summon back to favor a certain Jallius,
an indiscreet senator whom, on his last sojourn in Rome,
Hadrian had ordered excluded from his personal receptions.
Rome is a city of rumors, but nowhere do these abound more
than about the Palatine, always centering on the doings,
words, and even the health of the Emperor.   " Smoke "
from the valets, barbers, and table-servitors of the Augustus

---

[1] As is, of course, well known, such emperors as Tiberius, Nero, and
Domitian were popular with the provinces, which were usually well
governed under them.   Their cruelties smote mainly upon the senatorial
nobility.

can often be sold for precious aurei. Self-respecting monarchs punish the tale-bearers pitilessly, but the latter can seldom be caught in the act.[1] Every Emperor knows that he is the constant victim of outrageous tattling.

252. Friends of Cæsar (*Amici Cæsaris*). — But an Emperor's company is not confined to menials; neither does he spend all his time at council with his ministers. Being a Roman among Romans he is forced to spend a good deal of his day receiving the social attentions of those who proudly list themselves as his " Friends."

To be an *Amicus Cæsaris*, to be entitled to greet as a kind of social equal the personage who is worshiped as a god in all the Oriental provinces, who is (by adoption in Hadrian's case) the son of a Divinity, the " Deified Trajan," and whose own " divine genius " (guardian spirit) receives prayer and incense in every government building — this honor seems almost dazzling. Every Emperor ranks his " Friends " in two classes — " *First Class Friends*," great secretaries, ministers, and generals who must have constant access to his cabinet, certain very distinguished members of the Senate, certain near relatives, and also a few congenial personal companions — poets, and philosophers, with great Emperors, or jockeys, gamesters, and debauchees with the bad; and " *Second Class Friends*," which great catalogue includes all the rest of the Senate, many of the more distinguished equites, and a select sprinkling of such plebeians as Cæsar delights to honor.

The First Class Friends, it is true, pay for their glory by a heavy obligation — to appear at the Palace every morning usually before daylight, and greet the Lord of the World

---

[1] About 230 A.D. Alexander Severus caught a palace menial selling gossip, and had him executed by being burned in a fire of damp wood. "He is punished by smoke," said the irate monarch, "who sold 'smoke.'"

while he sits up in bed and is dressed by his valets.[1] Very much of state business is then transacted, but the obligation to appear merely to say an *"Ave"* is imperative provided the Emperor is in his residence. Sometimes merely to avoid giving gouty ministers great inconvenience Hadrian has been known considerately to pass the night away from the Palace in order to dispense with the ceremonial in the morning.

253. The Imperial Audiences. — After the Emperor has been clad with due ceremony, has conversed with his intimates, and perhaps has sealed some urgent rescripts, he is ready for the morning audience. A full cohort (1000 men) of the Prætorian Guard is always on service at the Palace and a platoon of these without armor, but in magnificent cloaks, stands by the entrance to the hall of state. Only men as a rule are admitted.[2] Under certain evil or very suspicious Emperors such as Claudius there has been the humiliating custom of searching every visitor (whatever his rank) for weapons, ere admission; but that abomination has ceased at last, beginning with Nerva.

In the broad courts before the audience chamber some dozens of senators dismount from their litters every morning when the monarch is in Rome, and sometimes the delay ere the doors are opened is so long that much personal business can be transacted and philosophical disquisitions indulged in. Second Class Friends do not have to appear every morning, but it is a serious error to fail to use your entrée fairly often.

254. Social Ruin through Imperial Disfavor. — The process resembles that with the clients in the noble lords' own

---

[1] The ceremony was not unlike that of the *levée* of French kings like Louis XIV, under the Old Régime before 1789.

[2] The Empresses would give a similar reception, however, to the wives of their husbands' "Friends."

houses a little earlier in the day, although with greater solemnity and formality.[1] A group of gorgeously dressed " admissioners " (*admissionales*) keep the doors, and scan every applicant closely, but besides the regular Friends they frequently admit certain distinguished visitors from the provinces, especially members of those provincial delegations that are always junketing to Rome to proffer the homage of their district to the Emperor, or to present some kind of a public petition.

The last day that Hadrian gave audience ere leaving Rome, when our friend Calvus waited upon him, there was an awkward happening. A very roistering and immoral young nobleman, Calvisius, presented himself when the doors were opened, whereupon an imperial freedman took him by the arm, announcing: " You are no longer admitted to the palace." Calvisius instantly slunk away, overwhelmed by his calamity. He would have suffered less if he had forfeited half his fortune.

Even worse was in store for the aforementioned Jallius, who was said to have mocked at Hadrian's pretentions as an art critic (a tender point) while over-drunk at a dinner party. He was suffered indeed to enter and to approach the imperial seat: " *Ave, Cæsar!* " he called out boldly, hoping that his indiscretion had been unnoticed. " *Vale, Jallie!*"[2] (" Good-by, Jallius ") answered the monarch, turning his face from him. The insult was offered in the presence of at least

---

[1] Sometimes, with an affectation of democracy, almost any decently clad person would be admitted to present petitions or merely to pay respects. Servile prostrations before the Emperor were not encouraged under the Early Principate ; once when a petitioner went through great bowings and scrapings while presenting a scroll to Augustus, the latter cried testily, "You act as if you were presenting some money to an elephant."

[2] This was the form used by Augustus in announcing to Fabius Maximus the withdrawal of imperial favor.

fifty tale-bearers and that night it was over Rome.   Under a
bad Emperor, Jallius's life would have been in sore jeopardy,
and as it was he was socially ruined; every time-serving
nobleman closed his house to him and his innocent wife and
children shared his ostra-
cism.   His only hope now
is that when Hadrian re-
turns he can be induced to
let Jallius call again, and
will answer affably " *Ave!* "
to   the   visitor's   greeting.
Then the poor senator can
hold up his head in the
world.

CÆSAR AUGUSTUS: showing costume of a Roman general.

**255. Enormous Value of
Imperial Favor.** — On the
other hand Calvus returned
walking on air from this particular audience.   The Emperor answered his greeting
by calling him " My very
dear Calvus "; then asked,
" And how are your Gratia
and the boys? " and actu-
ally added, " Do you think
Gallinas, the Thracian, is
going to be a good match
for Syrus in the arena? " — finally, throwing in the sage advice, " These morning frosts now are sharp if you don't
dress warmly." [1]

When Calvus quitted the hall all his friends swarmed
around congratulating him on " the remarkable favor of the

[1] Polite chatter, as reported by Horace, such as was vouchsafed by
Augustus and his great associate Mæcenas, to their social favorites.

Emperor," and intimating that he was surely destined to be Consul within a few years and then the imperial legate of a great province. He can hardly persuade them that he has received no private information about the boundary settlement with Parthia and the terms being offered the chiefs of the Quadi. In fact the imperial looks and moods are studied as carefully as is the weather. " Did *he* frown or look pleased when so and so was mentioned? " " Did he offer his cheek graciously to be kissed by that ex-consul? " " Did he invite the chiefs of the delegation from Provincial Asia to dinner? " " Did he cast down his eyes gloomily when they said N—— was about to be tried to-morrow in the Senate? " No marvel if bad Emperors are easily persuaded that they are gods on earth, and even good Emperors have to strive hard not to allow their heads to be turned!

Hadrian is still away from Rome, and both First Class Friends and Second Class Friends are probably a little relieved not to have to play the client to him. If the days of bloody tyranny seem past, the fate of poor Jallius can still overtake almost any of them.[1] But though the vast hall of audience stands vacant save for gaping sightseers, there are plenty of distinguished visitors upon the Palatine come to transact business at the imperial ministries, or very likely at the great offices of the City Præfect (*Præfectus Urbi*), who is essentially the Mayor of Rome.

256. City Government of Rome: the City Præfect (*Præfectus Urbi*). — It was one of the greatest sins of the defunct Republic that it permitted Rome to grow until it became an enormous metropolis without providing any

---

[1] Hadrian, although not a bloody man, was so averse to being opposed in argument that the philosopher Favorinus, with whom he took issue on a point in etymology, promptly announced that "Cæsar was correct," and so ended the discussion amiably. "But *you* were really correct," protested Favorinus's friends afterward. "Ah!" replied he with a laugh, "the master of thirty legions must be allowed to know better."

respectable police force, fire department, or other efficient means of securing law, order, and public safety. The old *ædiles* (commissioners of public works) were overburdened men, with imperfect authority, few constables, and great political interests. In the days of Cicero great fires, great riots, and serious crimes occurred almost daily. In self-protection many prominent men had actually to arm their slaves in regular companies and even to hire the assistance of armed bands of gladiators. Augustus ended all this. Thanks to him, Rome has become one of the best policed and protected cities in the world.

The old ædiles [1] are now supplemented and largely superseded by a corps of officials all named by the Emperor, for indefinite terms and removable by him at pleasure. At their head is that high " Clarissimus," the City Præfect. He is always a senator who has held the consulship, and who often has governed great provinces. To be named City Præfect is almost the highest civil honor in the gift of the Cæsars, and it ordinarily comes to a veteran nobleman of approved experience and integrity. He is really in part a military officer because at his command stand the " City Cohorts," the regular armed garrison of Rome, four Cohorts of reliable troops, one thousand men in each, ready to assist the ordinary police in repressing rioting.

The City Præfect is responsible for the general good order of the metropolis; it is his business not merely to punish evil, but to take measures to prevent it, *e.g.* by breaking up illicit societies and assemblies, such as those of the " debased " Christians. In conjunction with the other magistrates he also takes measures to keep down the price of provisions. In addition he is the high judge in most cases arising around Rome, which are not especially reserved to other tribunals.

---

[1] These old "Republican" officers, now six in number, retained a certain control of the public markets, baths, taverns, etc.

Particularly he and his deputies have jurisdiction over cases involving outrageous usury, betrayal of trust by guardians, unfilial conduct of children, and disrespect shown to patrons by freedmen. And to his court go all the charges of serious crimes sure to arise in a great city, barring, however, lesser police court cases — these last falling to his colleague, the Præfect of the Watch.

257. The Municipal Superintendents and Commissioners (*Curatores*). — Aiding the City Præfect are several high superintendents or commissioners usually of at least prætorian rank among the senators. The two " Curators of the Public Works " obviously have to look after the municipal buildings and especially the temples and the considerable endowments often attached to them. The Præfect of the Grain Supply (*Præfectus Annonæ*) is a magistrate who — in view of the importance of his function (see p. 242) — will often be chosen with almost as great an eye to his efficiency as the City Præfect.

Besides the corps of agents collecting grain in the provinces, the special deputy at Ostia, the " Official Grain Measurers," the " Grain Magazine-Keepers " (*horrearii*), and the staff of clerks and porters, all the bakers of the city also are under the Præfect of the Grain Supply, and he can sit as high judge in all cases, criminal and civil, where the provisioning of the city is affected. As for the Tiber, it is so often bursting its levees and flooding the lower city that a special board of five senators, " Commissioners for the Tiber, River-Banks, and the Sewers," attends alike to the care of the dikes and also to the great sewer system which drains the capital.

258. Excellent Water Supply of Rome. — An official board with duties of the first order is that of the " Curators of the Water Supply." There is a chief curator and two assistants, and since the task calls for expert professional knowledge, these are not senators but imperial freedmen, or at the highest only équites. No sinecure, however, is their task. Justly are the Romans proud of the excellent water supply of the imperial city. As early as Augustus's time Strabo the geographer warned his fellow Greeks that while they could boast that their cities excelled the Roman in artistic adornments, Rome rejoiced in a far better water system, in better

RUINED AQUEDUCT IN THE ROMAN CAMPAGNA.

pavements, and in better sewers. Certain of the latter, he declared in admiration, were " arched over with hewn stone and were so large that in some parts hay wagons can drive straight through them ! "

By Hadrian's day the aqueducts supplying the city have become wholly admirable. Time fails us to go out into the Campagna or to the distant hills and see how, by gravity alone, and without the aid of pumping engines, " copious streams are conducted great distances despite the obstacles presented by mountains, valleys, or low-lying level plains, sometimes rushing along in vast subterranean tunnels, at other times supported on long ranges of lofty arches, the remains of which [in after ages] will still be seen spanning the waste of the Campagna." [Lanciani.]

There is difficulty in making very large iron pipes capable of standing high pressure over long distances; and as a result the Roman engineers prefer to carry the water in channels lined with solid cement and borne across the open ground on a vast series of arches. Besides, most of the good water near Rome leaves a calcareous deposit; and it is much easier to clean out large channels than an underground piping system.

259. The Great Aqueducts. — When we try to understand the water system of Rome we come upon astonishing figures for the great aqueducts. There are nine of these huge conduits in constant use. The oldest is the *Aqua Appia*, built in 312 B.C. by that tough old censor, Appius Claudius, and it starts only about eleven miles from the city, with nearly its entire bed underground; but when this supply proved inadequate the engineers had to reach much farther back into the hills to find powerful jets. An increasing proportion of the channels of the newer aqueducts has also to be on arches; for example, the *Aqua Julia*, built by Agrippa in 33 B.C., has to go back fifteen and a half miles, and six and a half of these are on arches; while the *Aqua Claudia*, built about 40 A.D., is no less than forty-six miles long with nine and a half on elevated arches. There are two others, the older *Aqua Marcia* and the slightly newer *Aqua Anio Novus* (taking water from the river Anio), that are not much shorter either upon the ground or in their elevated sections.

Once inside the city this enormous volume of water is distributed in a most scientific manner according to a scheme worked out by the mighty Agrippa. There are 700 public

pools and basins and 500 public fountains drawing their
supply from 130 collecting heads or reservoirs. Only the
poorest or tallest tenement houses, consequently, are bereft
of a water supply, clear, sanitary, and abundant, such as
most later cities can desire in vain until close upon the
twentieth century.

260. The Police System Instituted by Augustus. — Almost as important, however, as the excellent water supply
came the blessing of the firm police system instituted by
Augustus. There was an end at last to the fearful riots and
even private wars of the later Republic, as when those
cheerful desperadoes Clodius and Milo played at being the
" Hector and Achilles of the Streets," and ordinary crime
soon became comparatively rare.

The city has also been divided into 14 " regions " (*regiones*)
and these into 262 " precincts " (*vici*) distributed among the
" regions." Each vicus is in theory a religious unit. It has
its own little *ædicula* (petty temple) containing the images
of the two guardian Lares of the neighborhood plus inevitably
a statue of the Genius of the Emperor. Each vicus also has
its two special curators, worthy tradesmen usually, elected
by their fellow wardsmen and clothed with enough importance to make the office desirable. Their chief official duty
is to keep up the sacred rites at the central shrine and to help
to compile the census lists, but they are also a kind of local
arbitrators or justices of the peace who assist the police and
look after the general weal of the precinct.

**261. The Police-Firemen of the Watch (*vigiles*): the
Præfectus Vigilum.** — However, the actual security of Rome
is not intrusted to any such unprofessional guardians. Augustus understood clearly the need of an effective police
force apart from a mere armed garrison ; besides he had to
protect the capital against the fearful and incessant fires ;

as a result his new *vigiles* (" watchmen ") were a combination
of policemen and firemen. The fourteen regions of Rome
have now been coupled together into seven police districts,
each possessing a regular police station (*excubitorium*) and
two subordinate watch houses.

Each district is intrusted to a separate cohort of vigiles
about 1000 men strong, thus giving Rome a total force of
some 7000. The vigiles are not actually soldiers, and not
being honorable legionaries they are recruited almost entirely
from the freedmen. However, after faithful service they
can be transferred to the army. They are under a rigid
discipline, nevertheless, and are divided into " centuries,"
each under a centurion, with a tribune over the entire cohort.
They have various weapons for an emergency, but the crowd
usually mocks them for the fire-fighting apparatus with which
they often hurry down the streets — hooks, ladders, axes,
simple hand-pumps, and above all, many buckets made of
rope rendered water-proof with pitch.

By their promptitude, discipline, and daring, even with
such inadequate apparatus, these patrolmen can often stop
very dangerous fires, and their familiar equipment gives
them their nickname. " The ' *Bucketmen* ' are coming ! "
is the yell that frequently disperses a knot of thieves or of
turbulent bullies.

At their different police stations the vigiles when off
duty scribble many things upon the walls,[1] which give a
vivid idea that life " on the force " is much the same in
every age. At night these " Bucketmen " go out in little
groups bearing tallow lanterns and patrol the pitch-black
streets, rounding up evil-doers and detecting incipient fires.

At each station there is a good-sized lock-up which never
wants its unhappy occupants, also, it must be added, a pro-

---

[1] As discovered by modern archæologists.

fessional torturer (*quæstionarius*) to wring confessions out of slaves and other non-privileged prisoners without any tedious "third degree" process. Petty offenses are tried summarily before the Præfect of the Watch or his deputies in police court at these stations; and for great crimes the alleged offenders can be conveyed to a central jail, or admitted to bail, prior to a formal trial before the City Præfect.

The Præfect of the Watch (*Præfectus Vigilum*), the head of this very important organization, is really the most important municipal official in Rome except the City Præfect. Since he has to do with much sordid detail, he is not a toplofty senator, but only an eques; nevertheless, his honor and dignity are great. The subpræfect under him is also a highly respected officer. The entire force of the vigiles, although, of course, incessantly criticized and jeered at, is a very capable body of men, whose faithfulness and energy go far to make life and property better protected in Rome than in most great cities at any age.

So with this glance at the municipal government of a metropolitan community of 1,500,000 we quit the Palatine. A new opportunity has presented itself: we can visit the **Prætorian Camp.**

CHAPTER XVI

THE PRÆTORIAN CAMP. THE IMPERIAL WAR MACHINE

262. The Army the Real Master of the Roman Empire. — The Romans beyond all else have been a military people. Their great abilities as law givers, administrators, disseminators of civilization through Western Europe apparently would have been almost in vain if the legions had failed against Hannibal, against Mithridates, against Vercingetorix. Furthermore, the power of the Cæsars is primarily that of war chiefs. Let the army revolt, and Senate, plebeians, and provincials can protest their loyalty ever so frantically — the Princeps, the " First Citizen," nevertheless is a lost man.

Every Emperor knows this fact. His memory goes back to those two fearful years 68 and 69 A.D. when first a revolt in Gaul and a mutiny by the Prætorians in Rome overthrew Nero and set up Galba, then a second mutiny of the Prætorians set up Otho, then a revolt of the Rhine legions set up Vitellius, then a counter-revolt by the Danube and Syrian legions set up Vespasian; with the civilian population looking on helplessly, and being almost as helplessly plundered, while decidedly small bodies of professional swordsmen settled the fate of the Empire. Still later they remember how after Domitian's murder, the Prætorians (whom that despot had caressed and corrupted) forced his successor Nerva to punish the very conspirators to whom Nerva himself owed the throne.

Hadrian, in turn, who passes for a very " constitutional " ruler, when his kinsman Trajan died (117 A.D.), allowed himself to be " proclaimed " immediately by the soldiers in the East where he then was. Next he wrote with studious modesty to the Senate begging the Conscript Fathers to " excuse " the zeal of the army and to ratify its action in choosing him Imperator. Every senator knew the blade might soon be at his own neck if he openly opposed confirming the mandate of the legionaries. The army, in short, is the final authority in the Roman Empire. Presently there may even be an Emperor [Septimus Severus about 210 A.D.] who will give his sons direfully blunt and effective counsel: " Enrich the army and then you can do anything."

263. Army Held under Stiff Discipline and Concentrated on Frontiers. — Nevertheless at present the army is under a tight rein. Trajan and Hadrian by a mixture of donatives and severity have restored firm discipline. The Roman world functions freely and normally behind the frontier barriers held by the legions, with the great chaos of barbarism tossing harmlessly outside. Furthermore, this army, if very formidable, is, we shall see, decidedly small. It is distributed mainly along the northern and eastern frontiers, with a sizable garrison and guard-corps at Rome.

In the arrangement of the army, most of the provinces seem absolutely divested of regular soldiers save those in transit, and their governors only require a good constabulary to arrest brigands and rioters. The collapse of the Jewish insurrection has practically ended the last serious attempt to cast off Roman authority, and the provinces submit not simply because of fear, but because they are now bound to the imperial régime by great cultural and economic interests.[1]

[1] For the attitude of provincials under Roman rule the student can with interest read the speech put in the mouth of King Agrippa, the descendant of Herod, by Josephus (" Jewish War " : book II, ch. 16) in which he tells the Jews of Nero's day, (1) that on the whole the Roman rule is so reasonable and tolerable they have no real cau?e to revolt against it ; (2) that all nations, including the most warlike such as Sparta,

In Rome itself, thanks to the presence of the imperial guard, soldiers are frequent sights upon the streets, but in many other great cities of the Empire they are comparative rarities. Their duties are in the frontiers, and their officers know well the demoralization wrought by keeping their men in city garrisons.

When Augustus found the world at his feet he also found himself with armies which were very expensive and somewhat ready to mutiny against him. Very promptly, therefore, he reduced his 45 legions to only about 18. This number proved too few, and by the end of his reign they had risen to 25; these in turn have been gradually increased to 30; and this will be the ordinary number for a good while longer.[1] The legionaries are the regular troops of the line, on whose disciplined fighting the safety of civilization may well depend. There are, however, no ordinary legionaries stationed in Rome, although we can, of course, obtain full information in the capital about them. Their place is taken by a magnificent and arrogant guard-corps — the Prætorians.

264. The Prætorian Guard of the Emperors. — The Prætorian guards are the successors of the old *Prætoriani*, picked men, who guarded the Prætorium (general's residence or tent) in the armies of the old Republic. But the new Imperators were entitled to a much larger and more permanent guard, and they also desired to have a reliable body of troops always in or near Rome to protect against an uprising. Augustus, therefore, organized nine " prætorian cohorts," although keeping only three directly in Rome; his successor, Tiberius, however, boldly concentrated

Macedonia, the turbulent Gauls and Spain, have long since submitted; (3) that these have not merely submitted but keep obedient with only a trifling local display of armed force; (4) that resistance to Rome is so hopeless in any case that a revolt would be impious suicide.

[1] About 200 A.D. they were raised to 33.

them all in the imperial city, and built for them an enormous camp behind the Viminal hill, on the northeast side of the metropolis.

Here they have remained as the dreaded engine of the Cæsars. Disguise the fact as he may, every senator knows in his heart : " If the Senate defies the Emperor, the Præto-

PRÆTORIAN GUARDSMEN.

rians can and will sack the Curia." So long as the Prætorians are obedient no Emperor need tremble overmuch at stories of a provincial uprising. When the Prætorians desert he had better, as did Nero, slink away to commit suicide.

The guard-corps is jealously regarded by the frontier legions who sometimes turn against it, but thanks to its position at the capital its power is tremendous. Even the privates walk down the streets with a confident swagger — can they not make and unmake Emperors? If the army really controls the Empire, the Prætorians go far to control the will of the army.

265. The Prætorian Præfect and the Prætorian Camp. — Such being the case, there is one high official whom the Cæsars will always select with greater care than any other — the *Prætorian Præfect*. On this general rests responsibility for the military efficiency and loyalty of the corps. If he is a scheming bloody man, he can, like Tiberius's præfect Sejanus, almost place himself upon the throne; and if he is simply a faithful competent officer, his public services excel that of any civil functionary.

Since curiously enough the Emperor usually intrusts to the Prætorian Præfect the task of hearing legal " appeals to Cæsar " from the imperial half of the provinces, it is not unusual to name two præfects, nominally of equal authority but with one of them often a trained jurist, and the other more concerned with the military management of the corps. This has the additional advantage of making it harder to start an insurrection, — each Præfect will keep watch upon his colleague.

Inasmuch as the Emperor is now absent from Rome a detachment of the guard is away with him, but the world being in general peace there is no need (as in a major war) for the entire corps to go forth to reinforce the frontier legions. The Prætorians are therefore on duty as usual; one cohort at the Palatine, the remainder barracked at their great camp.

The *Castra Prætoria* [1] is more than a mere cantonment; it is a real fortress, only to be stormed after desperate fighting. We enter it from the central gateway (*Porta Prætoria*) which looks straight westward upon the city. A lofty wall of ma-

[1] Its site to-day is occupied by the chief railroad station of Rome, by which most foreign visitors enter the city and depart.

sonry, brick, and concrete, crowned by suitable battlements, surrounds a vast rectangular area about 1400 feet wide, and 1100 feet deep. The greater and lesser gates are crowned with fine marble sculptures almost worthy of the Palatine. In the center of the area rises a mass of office buildings, a residence for the Præfect and a small temple to the military gods such as Mars, and especially to the deified emperors. The side walls of the inclosure are extended on the inside by an enormous system of arches and vaulting, making many deep chambers where thousands of men are easily barracked.

In the open area fountains are playing, and the sun is sending a flying glory from the burnished armor of a cohort standing at rest, while certain officers affix medals of honor, or bestow spears and banners of honor upon various men who have lately distinguished themselves during some detached duty in Mauretania. Everything about the place betrays a perfect " police "; all commands are executed with extreme promptness; and every individual seems absolutely to know his part, as being one cog in an enormous war machine, into the making of which has entered an almost inconceivable amount of skill and energy.

266. Organization and Discipline of the Prætorians. — The Prætorians are organized much as the ordinary legionary troops with certain proud modifications. The regular legions can be recruited from all over the Empire; the Prætorians are still drawn only from Italy. They receive twice the pay of the legionaries, and their term of service is only sixteen years as against twenty with the regulars. Besides these advantages, and the joy of living near to the pleasures of Rome, their discipline is said to be much easier.

The emperors, who fear the mutterings of the guard-corps much more than they do those of the Senate, often shower special bonuses upon the Prætorians. Their centurions and still more their tribunes are welcome guests in the most aristocratic houses in Rome. Their weapons are the same as the legionaries', but, of course, their armor is of the finest; and on gala occasions when the whole corps is ordered out with gilded or silvered helmets and cuirasses over purple military cloaks, the sight of these thousands of tall powerful warriors marching in perfect rhythm is astonishing beyond words.

In one important respect the organization of the Prætorians differs from that of the regular legionaries: their nine cohorts number 1000 instead of 600 men each and the whole guard-corps therefore amounts to about 9000 men. Considering that these troops are chosen for their splendid physiques, and are trained for years in every military accomplishment, remarkable will be the foe of like numbers that can withstand them. As for the city of Rome, its whole raging populace is like mere chaff and straw if the trumpets sound through the camp, and the centurions thunder down their files, " Open the gates and clear the streets ! "

267. The City Cohorts (*Cohortes Urbanæ*). — The Prætorians, however, have some humbler comrades in Rome, in addition to police-firemen, the vigiles. Sometimes the guard-corps must follow the Emperor on campaign, but nevertheless the capital needs a fixed garrison. The City Præfect (see p. 300), therefore, commands four additional cohorts (*cohortes urbanæ*) also of 1000 each, in a special camp in the northern part of the metropolis. These " City Cohorts " are organized much like the Prætorians, and in a grave emergency would act with them ; but they have longer terms of service, lesser pay, severer discipline.

It is far less of an honor to belong to this force than to the Prætorians, and there is little " fraternizing " between its members and the haughty guard-corps. However, they make 4000 more armed men always available for the defense and control of the city. Added to these can, of course, be the vigiles (7000 strong), easily changeable into genuine soldiers in a crisis. This makes the total garrison of Rome, while the Prætorians are in the city, around 20,000 men, plus usually some marines detached from the squadrons at Ostia and Misenum.

The frontiers are far away, but the central direction of the great imperial war machine is inevitably at Rome. From the Prætorian barracks issue those orders which can set the legions marching against the Caledonians of North Britain or the Arabs of the Syrian deserts. There can be no better place, therefore, for inquiry about the organization and discipline of that grim efficient engine which maintains the Pax Romana and makes possible the splendid, artificial Græco-Roman civilization.

High officers are constantly passing through Rome. Some of these men have had long and distinguished careers, and among them is a certain Aulus Quadratus, a gray and grizzled veteran, now in the capital for honorable retirement, after an unusual term of service. By tracing his experience, a good insight can be gained into the organization and duties of the legionaries.

268. A Private in the Legions: the Legionary Organization. — Quadratus was born in South Gaul (*Gallia Narbonensis*), a country that has already been well Romanized, and from which the government draws many excellent legionaries.[1] He was a poor free laborer on a great estate, but when he was only about eighteen an enrolling officer appeared and demanded a certain number of recruits of his master. The latter naturally suggested taking several of the youngest and least valuable of the hands. Quadratus was strong, courageous, and adventuresome, and he did not object to this informal type of " selective draft." Thus he soon found himself a private in the camp of the " Second Augustan Le-

---

[1] An ever larger proportion of legionary troops had to be enlisted in the provinces, although preferably in the parts somewhat Romanized.

gion " (*legio secunda augusta*) stationed in a great fortified camp guarding the Rhine somewhere near later Mayence or Strassbourg in " Upper Germany " (Alsace and the Rhenish Palatinate).

Once enlisted, Quadratus realized that at least twenty years of unremitting service lay ahead of him. Home life and marriage were forbidden the soldiery, and their whole lives revolved around the army. The Roman discipline caught each man, and each became a valuable and contented soldier only so far as he submitted to this discipline and merged his personality in the vast organization.

Quadratus was, therefore, promptly " put under the vine-stock," the stout cudgel of twisted vine twigs with which the centurions vigorously corrected their tyros. At first he was a very ignorant and unimportant part of

A SLINGER.

the " Second Augustan," but soon he understood its organization and became proud of its history. Every legion consisted of ten *cohorts*, each in turn divided into six centuries.[1] Each century contained in theory a hundred infantry, making 6000 for the entire legion. Besides these, there was a small cavalry force for scouting attached to each legion, four *turmæ* (squadrons) of 30 horsemen each. The various con-

---

[1] In Hadrian's time a change was taking place whereby the first cohort in a legion contained about twice as many men as there were in any of the other nine; but this alteration became only gradually effective.

tingents, however, were seldom quite full.   When the Second
Augustan went to battle it reckoned, therefore, somewhere
under 6000 men.

269. Training of the Legionaries: the *Pilum* **and the**
Gladius. — Quadratus, under very severe drill masters,
learned the use of weapons.   Nothing could take the place,
so he was taught, of cool proficiency with sword and javelin.
It was the trained valor of the average Roman legionary,

ROMAN SIEGE WORKS: restoration of Caesar's siege works at Alesia.

not the skill often of his commanders, that had given to the
Cæsars the mastery of the world, and while the discipline
was strict, and the training incessant, pains were taken not to
destroy the young man's self-respect, or those powers of
initiative which were the glory of his profession.

He was taught furthermore to despise those enemies, who,
like the old Macedonians, were so lacking in personal re-
sources that they had to go into battle wedged together
shield to shield with long spears bristling in front — the
rigid "phalanx" formation.   This is excellent on level ground
when the foe is all ahead, but often becomes a source of

danger to itself because the closely packed soldiers are deprived of any chance to display personal valor, and are almost helpless to change position if attached on flank or rear. Quadratus in his training was taught to stand five feet from his comrades on either side with plenty of room to swing his shield and javelin.

Long exercise made him a master of his two weapons. The heavy javelin (*pilum*) is a devilish missile, as every foe of

STORMING A CITY WITH THE *Testudo.*

Rome has learned to his cost. It is about six and a half feet long with a heavy wooden butt and a long blade-like head, usually barbed and razor keen. Flung by a practiced soldier at short range it can knock down any adversary who is not firmly braced, even if it does not pierce his shield. Once lodged in the shield it is no light thing to draw it out and not expose oneself to a second deadlier blow.

The pilum, they told Quadratus, was what had really made the Roman Empire possible; but it is duly supplemented by the Spanish short sword (*gladius*). This is a weapon borrowed, perhaps, from Spain but thoroughly Italianized. The blade is about thirty-three inches long, two-edged, sharp-pointed, and always used for thrusting. The instant a legionary has flung his pilum, and while his foe if not wounded is at least utterly demoralized from the shock, he whips his gladius from his thigh and leaps upon him. A single good thrust will disembowel a man, and he who is thus assailed by a trained Roman swordsman should pray to his native gods — he will need all aid possible.

CATAPULT.

270. Defensive Weapons. — These two very simple weapons Quadratus was taught to handle to perfection, until across the years their use became simply mechanical to him. Meantime he was learning to march, leap, and fight in his heavy defensive armor. He wore a stout metallic cuirass of fish-scale plates, and a solid helmet of brass upon which in parades and in actual battle he set a nodding plume of horse-hair. This helmet had brow- and cheek-pieces giving very perfect protection, but was so heavy that while marching he was allowed to carry it swung from a strap upon his breast.

Of course, however, his chief defensive weapon was his shield. This capital piece of armor is a rectangle of solid leather about four by two and one half feet, rimmed with iron and with handles for carrying on the left arm. A trained legionary knows how to fend and lunge with his shield with marvelous agility, and by means of the solid metal base in the center he can strike a tremendous blow. Almost no weapon can penetrate the shield, and thanks to it and his

cuirass and his helmet, a soldier can march unscathed amid
a perfect shower of arrows. Every technical point about his
armor has, of course, been worked out scientifically. Simple
as it appears, it represents a triumph of human skill.

271. Rewards and Punishments for Soldiers. — Thus
accoutered Quadratus gained his first experience when the
Second Augusta was or-
dered over the Rhine to
punish a tribe of Ger-
manic raiders in later-day
Hessen. In the fighting
that ensued he so proved
his skill and courage that
he received his first deco-
ration, the right to wear
a small banderole upon
his pilum when his co-
hort appeared on parade
ground. Discipline was
severe, but rewards for
faithfulness and valor
were prompt and conspic-
uous. He had long seen
his older comrades march-
ing about with "spears
of honor," banderoles,

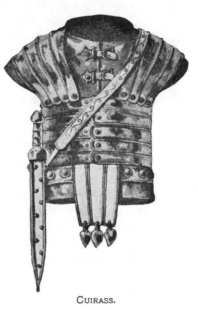

CUIRASS.

and above all with huge medals and medallions, which, upon
gala occasions, they wore upon their breasts.

Long before Quadratus's career was ended, he, like many
others, had a perfect collection of these medals, which hung
jangling over his cuirass almost like a second coat of armor.
Everybody knew the honors awarded his comrades, and
there was constant emulation to deserve like decorations as
well as more substantial rewards. No system could be better

devised to call out the valorous service of simple-hearted and often very uncultivated men.

While Quadratus, without too many blows from his centurions' vinestock, was thus on his way to promotion, he could witness the punishment of less fortunate comrades. Stripes, docking of pay, and extra duty were the standard penalties; but sometimes there were worse inflictions. Once a whole century acted in a cowardly manner. It was sentenced for one month to bivouac outside the camp and to eat bread of barley, — not of wheat, the food of brave and obedient troops.

Sometimes, of course, capital penalties were demanded. Once a private was guilty of gross insubordination; he had to "run the gantlet" (*fustuarium*) between two long files of soldiers who beat him with cudgels while he dashed vainly down the line, perishing ere he could reach the end. Once a detachment of half-drilled auxiliaries fled in an outrageous manner before the enemy. To teach a stern lesson these irregulars were "decimated"; being forced to stand disarmed before the whole legion, while lots were cast selecting every tenth man, who was forthwith dragged from the ranks and beheaded.

JAVELIN: *pilum* of the legionary.

SWORD.

272. Pay and Rations in the Army: Soldiers' Savings Banks. — While a private Quadratus, of course, drew the private's pay, 1200 sesterces ($48) a year,[1] out of which, however, was deducted a certain part of his upkeep and equipment. Even as it was, however, this gave fairly ample spending money, and every soldier was required to deposit a part of his wages

---

[1] In the earlier Empire it was only 900 sesterces ($36).

in the legionary savings bank, accumulating against the day
of his happy discharge, and protected from barrack-room
gambling and squandering. Besides this, brave service often
won an increase of stipend, more valuable than many medals;
and Quadratus was presently a *duplarius*, a "double-pay
man," to the great envy of certain comrades.

Army rations would have seemed to another
age extremely monotonous, a mere succession
of huge portions of coarse bread or of wheat
porridge. There were also distributions of
salt pork, vegetables, etc., but the legionaries
did not care greatly for meat. There were
even cases when they protested against "too
much beef and too little wheat." As for drink,
everybody in camp enjoyed plenty of *posca*
— the dilution of cheap wine and vinegar.[1]

HELMET.

273. The Training of Soldiers: Non-Military Labors. —

Drilling went on incessantly. Even soldiers versed in their
spear play seemed forever under arms merely to keep up the
camp routine and morale. Every man was trained to be a
good swimmer, to run, jump, and indulge in acrobatic feats
like the *testudo* (when one group of men climbed upon their
comrades' heads) so useful in storming walls. Thrice a
month the whole legion went on a forced practice march,
going at least twenty miles at four miles (or more) per hour,
each man bearing, besides his heavy armor, an elaborate
baggage kit, half a bushel of grain, one or two tall intrench-
ing stakes, a spade, axe, rope, and other tools — a weight of
sixty pounds.

If strictly military work failed, there were endless civilian

---

[1] It might be added that Roman legions appear to have had a medical
department under a *medicus legionis*, which cared efficiently for the
health of the troops. Camp sanitation was well understood, and epidemics in the army were rare.

labors. Quadratus learned to use his spade almost as well as he could his pilum.   He assisted in making and in repairing the great network of magnificent military roads leading to the frontiers.   He worked in the legionary brick kilns, making bricks for the camps and the numerous small *castella*

used to hold back the onthrusting Germans. He helped also to rebuild a temple of Jupiter at the garrison town of Mogontiacum (Mayence), and later to tug up the stones for a new amphitheater in that city. If he had been attached to a Syrian legion, he and his comrades might even have been ordered out to repel an invasion not of Parthians but of the more devastating locusts.

274. Petty Officers in the Legions. — All this experience came to him while he was earn-

SHIELD OF THE LEGIONARY.

ing his first promotions.   Everybody in the legion — except those lowest and highest — had somebody, indeed, whom he could command while some one else could command him, and there was a very ingenious division and interlocking of power and responsibility.

Petty officers abounded, and having approved himself, Quadratus became one of the *principales* (high privates, and corporals) — first he became a *tesserarius*, " bearer of the watchword " for his century; then the " horn blower," responsible often for important signals, then the *signifer*, the bearer of the small red flag (*vexillium*), surmounted with a small image of Victory, which was the standard of the cohort; then he was named *optio* (" chosen " man by a centurion), a centurion's deputy and assistant, entitled to rank as a real officer and responsible for the control of a large squad of men.

At last came one of the most important days of his life. At a general parade of the legion the commanding general (*legatus legionis*) announced that Quadratus was appointed centurion and sol-

MILITARY TRUMPET.

emnly intrusted him with the terrible vinestock. There was no danger he would show mercy to the raw recruits!

275. The Centurions: their Importance and Order of Promotion. — Quadratus was now a member of that group of officers to which the Roman army owed the greater part of its entire discipline, morale, and efficiency. There were sixty centurions in every legion. They were usually self-made men, sturdy peasants' sons like himself, who had risen from the ranks and then been selected by the general on account of merit.

The six military tribunes of each legion were, indeed, of higher rank, but they were often untested young noblemen, obliged to get a certain " military experience " before returning to Rome to sue for seats in the Senate and the favor of the Emperor. The centurions, however, were a permanent body. They had enlisted in the legion, and their whole life was tied up with it. If their methods were harsh, they prided themselves on showing an example of daring yet scientific valor in every battle. They were intensely devoted to their corps, its honor, and the honor of their comrades. With good centurions a motley host of raw recruits soon became formidable legionaries; without them the most skilful general might strive in vain to organize an army.

As centurion Quadratus found a straight line of promotion before him. He was obliged to begin as the sixth centurion of the tenth cohort, and by process of seniority he was entitled to rise to first centurion of the first cohort. He was making fair progress but advancement was discouragingly slow, and he might have ended (as did most of his fellow officers) only part way up the ladder before he reached the retiring age, when a great good fortune came to him.

LEGIONARIES (REGULAR TROOPS-OF-THE-LINE): one soldier is carrying his equipment upon a "Marius's Mule," a staff arranged to serve as a knapsack, invented by Marius about 110 B.C.

While only a private he had won the " civic crown " (*corona civica*) of oak leaves for saving the life of a comrade in battle; he had also gained the golden " mural crown " (*corona muralis*) for being the first in a desperate storming party over the parapet of a crude fortress held by the Germans. But now, while acting as senior centurion of a large detachment, with the commanding tribune absent, he learned that a Roman garrison somewhere in the heart of the Black Forest region was hard pressed by a horde of Chatti. He led up his men suddenly and skilfully, broke through and dispersed the Barbarians and saved the garrison when it was at last gasp. For this

he was awarded the " siege crown " (*corona obsidionalis*), a
remarkable honor given by the rescued garrison, and plaited
out of grass and weeds plucked on the spot of battle,[1] to the
leader who had saved them.

276. The *Primipilus*: the Great Eagle of the Legion. —
This distinction made it inevitable that when the post of
first centurion in the legion fell vacant, Quadratus should be

jumped over the heads of many
others and made *primipilus* ("first
javelin ") — the head of the whole
corps of centurions, entitled to
participate with the tribunes in
a council of war, and — being,
of course, now a man of great
practical experience — allowed to
speak very openly to the Legate
of the Legion himself. Quadratus
was now in some respects the
most important man in the Second Augustan. His war pay was
considerable, and he added to it
by the permitted usage of taking
fees from the men for certain ex-
emptions from duty.

ROMAN OFFICER.

As primipilus he had the weighty responsibility of taking
charge of the great golden eagle of the legion. In battle he
would sometimes pluck it from the ordinary bearer (*aquilifer*),
and electrify his comrades by dashing ahead with the full-
sized golden eagle with outspread wings, surrounded by brilliant streamers, now borne on its pole high above his shoulders.
Where the eagle went, there honor and devotion made every
legionary follow with the fury of a man possessed. In a

---

[1] The only materials for a crown assumed to be available in a rescued
fortress.

certain shrewd tussle with the Hermunduri, the valor of the whole phalanx of those Barbarians was snuffed out when they saw the glistening *aquila* bearing down on them heading a six-thousand-man wedge, with all the ten cohort flags like obedient retainers thrusting on behind, and when next came the pitiless beat of the pila succeeded instantly by the rush of the expert swordsmen.

277. Locations and Names of Legions. — Having become *primipilus* while still a fairly young man, Quadratus was not at the end of his promotion. He had carefully saved his money, and presently he gained official nobility as an *eques*. Now he was appointed to an independent command not in the legionary regulars, but in the " auxiliary cohorts."

Only about one half of the imperial forces are in the legions. These are for the heavy fighting; they are kept in large garrisons and are used for secondary work as little as possible, nor are they moved from province to province except in serious emergencies.[1]   The Second Augustan has always been in Upper Germany and there presumably it will stay for generations more.   The same is true of the Third Augustan in North Africa, of the Fourth Scythians on the Danube, of

------

[1] The distribution of the legions varied somewhat from one period to another according to the probable dangers on the exposed frontiers, but the largest armies were always stationed along the Rhine, the Danube, and the Euphrates.   In Hadrian's time apparently the main forces lay thus :

Britain, 3 legions.
Germany (Rhinelands), 4 legions.
Danubian lands and Dacia, 10 legions.
Syria and Palestine, 5 legions.
Cappadocia, 2 legions.

In all the other provinces requiring legionary troops at all (*e.g.* Egypt, Spain, Numidia, etc.), only one legion.

Apparently in the second Christian century the greatest danger point seemed near the Danube, and the second greatest along the Euphrates, with the Rhinelands relatively more secure than earlier, when more legions had been stationed near them.

the Twelfth Thunderers in Syria, and of a good many others. The result is that each legion, largely recruited in the near-by provinces, has small desire for distant service; and there is little love between, say, the " Twenty-first Ravagers " in Upper Germany and the " Sixth Ironclads " stationed along the Euphrates.[1]

278. The Auxiliary Cohorts: the Second Grand Division of the Army. — But it is absolutely necessary to have a mobile force, composed of troops of many kinds, especially cavalry, archers, slingers, and light spearmen for scouting. These men are often enlisted in the un-Romanized provinces, and are allowed to keep their native arms and discipline. As a rule they are organized in unattached cohorts, either in " large " cohorts of 1000 men with ten centuries, or " small " cohorts of 480 with six so-called centuries. Their commander is regularly a " Præfect,"

LIGHT-ARMED SOLDIER.

commonly an officer who, like Quadratus, has graduated from the stern school of the centurion in a legion.

Auxiliary cohorts are often embodied and disbanded, they have no such glorious history and traditions as the legions, but they have a distinctive name and a number. Quadratus was assigned to the command of a new " large " cohort made up of tall blonde Germans who were glad to

---

[1] Some legions were named for their organizers: Augustus, Claudius, etc.; some for real or alleged martial qualities, "Ferrata," "Fulminata," "Victrix," and the like; one, the "Alauda," from the lark's wings worn on the helmets; several which were made by dividing existing legions were known as "Gemina," and some from their place of original recruiting, "Gallica," "Italica," etc.

forget their feuds with the Romans, cross the Rhine, and take the Emperor's pay, swearing to him the great oath of implicit military allegiance (*the sacramentum*). The government is far too wise, however, to leave such aliens too near their homes. Quadratus was, therefore, promptly ordered to march his " Sixth Nervan " (so named in honor of the then Emperor Nerva)[1] to the Danube.

The day the new Præfect quitted his old comrades of the Second Augustan he drew from the legionary chest all the savings from his pay, plus the sums deposited there after each bonus or donation wherewith the Emperors were always conciliating the army. He had also long since joined a self-help organization among the officers whereby he was to receive a fixed sum for his outfit whenever he received promotion.[2] He thus started upon his career as an upper officer a tolerably rich man.

279. The Præfect of the Camps and the Legate of the Legion. — As Præfect of the Sixth Nervan he won the good opinion of Trajan in both of the desperate Dacian Wars and then in the campaign against Parthia. As the next step, he was appointed by imperial patent " Præfect of the Camps " — the second in command of a legion, not responsible, indeed, for its conduct in battle, but with almost complete authority over its management and discipline while in its great permanent garrisons, subject only (in extreme cases) to the final authority of the commanding legate.

This was as high ordinarily as even a very fortunate soldier, who had enlisted as a mere private, could advance. Even

---

[1] The centurion to whom St. Paul's custody was intrusted (Acts XXVII, 1) was of the "Augustan band," *i.e.* one of the somewhat numerous cohorts named for Augustus — the special number not being given.

[2] Also we know from the by-laws of these soldiers' benefit clubs that every member was entitled to a fine funeral, to an allowance for travel money if obliged to go on a long journey, and finally to a fixed sum as consolation money in case he was demoted !

as Præfect of the Camp Quadratus was looked down upon socially by the six young military tribunes, scions of senatorial families, who hung around the headquarters (*prætorium*), wrote verses, patronized the centurions, and boasted of how " they commanded the legion." But Quadratus was, we repeat, an extraordinarily lucky officer. Grizzled now and battle-scarred, he impressed Hadrian as absolutely to be trusted. The Emperor, therefore, raised him to the rank of " Legate of the Legion," which carried with it a seat in the Senate, and for the past few years accordingly Quadratus has been on the Rhine in chief command of that same Second Augustan where once he had " submitted to the vinestock " as a raw recruit.

He has now returned to Rome to be honorably retired and to end his days in a luxurious villa in the hills, having enjoyed every honor possible in the Roman army save that of being Imperial Legatus over an entire province, a post ordinarily combined with the command of several legions. It is men like Quadratus, hard and fit soldiers of absolute faithfulness, coolness, courage, and efficiency ; steeped in the traditions of the army, and obeying automatically the call of military duty, that have been the soul of the Roman war-machine. Perhaps some day there will be degeneracy in the camps, even as in the luxurious city. Then the perils of the Empire will draw nigh — but not in the reign of Hadrian.

280. Care for Veterans : Retiring Bonuses and Land Grants. — Few enough of Quadratus's messmates kept near to him in his upward career. To the average recruit, the most to be hoped for is that, before the end of his twenty years' enlistment, he can be somewhere near the rank of centurion But many men learn to enjoy the military life even as privates, and when the time for honorable discharge comes, will often be glad to reënlist in picked corps of *veterani*, bronzed and hardened warriors who make invaluable scouts and bodyguards for the upper officers, and who have quite forgotten the modes of civilian life.

If, however, they elect to be mustered out, not merely are there accumulations of pay and donations given them from the legion's savings bank, but along with the *honesta missio* (honorable discharge) they receive either a grant of land for a modest farm, or a lump sum (some 3000 sesterces — $120) to start them on a peaceful career. If they become sick or disabled while in service, reasonably good care is taken of them. In any case the constant award of honorary spears, pennons, and medals appeals to the soldier's vanity, and helps to reconcile him to a very long enlistment and an equally stiff discipline.

281. Barrier Fortresses; System of Encampments; Flexible Battle Tactics; Siege Warfare. — Into the details of the Roman war machine we cannot enter. We cannot discuss the wonderful system of barrier fortresses along the junction of the Rhine and Danube upon which the northern tribes beat in vain, nor the newly completed " Wall of Hadrian " sundering peaceful and guarded Britain from the stark savagery of Caledonia. We cannot explain the scientific system of temporary encampments, whereby every night — when a legion is on the march, — it occupies a square of ground fortified by solid palisades and with every tent in precisely the same spot as in the old camp of the preceding night — a method insuring that every camp becomes practically a fortress, almost impregnable in case of a defeat in the field. We cannot visit the permanent garrison towns, such as Colonia Agrippina (Cologne) on the Rhine, or Vindobona (Vienna) on the Danube, where extensive cities, with all the paraphernalia of civilization, have grown up around the cantonments on the very edge of raw barbarism.

It is still less possible to offer here a discussion of the flexible legionary battle tactics, whereby each particular foe is

met with the formations most formidable to his special arms
and weaknesses ; and of the carefully adjusted order of march
whereby an army can move with all its baggage train through
a hostile country defiant of any ordinary harassment and
flank attack. We must pass over also the system of siege
warfare, and the use of long-range casting engines — a genuine artillery ; and finally the wonderfully scientific engineer-

STORMING A BESIEGED CITY : casting engines in foreground.

ing service, building high-roads through deserts, and throwing strong bridges even across such mighty streams as the
Rhine, and — on Trajan's Dacian campaigns — the Danube.

**282. Limited Size of the Imperial Army : its Great Ef-
ficiency.** — Two or three things about the army, however,
call for particular comment. The size of these forces seems
decidedly small, considering the vast extent of the Empire,
the slow communications, the careful demilitarizing of the
provincials, and the absence of any reserve corps or efficient
militia. The thirty legions (5000 to 6000 men each) reckon

perhaps 175,000 troops of the line. The Prætorians at Rome, the heterogeneous and scattered auxiliary cohorts, the small naval force, and other armed groups at the command of the government, in all reckon, perhaps, as many more; 350,000 men, however, is a very limited number when spread out from Britain to the confines of Arabia and the Nile cataracts, although only along the Rhine, the Danube, and the Euphrates are there now enemies creating serious military problems.

Except at Rome, we have seen that the bulk of these troops is held in the frontier garrisons, with all their corps kept on edge in full battle efficiency. Let a frontier be in real peril, however, and there is no means of reënforcing the local legions save by calling off other legions from posts at great distance. Governmental policy has not merely disarmed the provincials, it has systematically discouraged maintaining the military virtues.[1] If the frontiers are forced and the legions fail, the civilian population of the Empire (possibly some 80 to 100 millions) will be nigh helpless before a Parthian raid or Germanic invader; they can only call on the gods and the distant Emperor for aid.[2]

---

[1] The process of demilitarizing the population went so far that Trajan even discouraged the organization of regular bands of firemen in cities of Bithynia "lest they become the prey of factions" — *i.e.* somehow start a movement against the government.

[2] The Roman Empire has been rightly called a "military monarchy," but was such only because the disarming of the civilian population and the extreme efficiency of the professional army put the former at the mercy of the latter. The imperial army and navy hardly exceeded 350,000 men, and *may* have been as small as 300,000. At the time this book was written the United States, with a population not greatly exceeding that of the Roman Empire, had a total of some 250,000 men in its standing forces (army, navy, and marine corps) not counting any organized militia. Almost nobody would have pretended that the addition of some 100,000 men to this force could have rendered a "military monarchy" possible in America except as very peculiar conditions favored it — as they did in the Roman Empire.

However, as yet, the legions have not failed. The Roman armies, never large, but unsurpassed in quality and composed of highly expert soldiers steeped in martial tradition, and organized and commanded with scientific skill, lie as a solid barrier around the Mediterranean world, and in Hadrian's day they are holding back possible invaders by the mere terror of their name. When one looks, marveling, upon the huge, luxurious, sophisticated capital, let it not be forgotten that Rome is imperial Rome because far away on the frontiers thirty brigades of iron-handed men night and day keep watch and ward.

CHAPTER XVII

THE SENATE: A SESSION AND A DEBATE

283. Apparent Authority and Importance of the Senate. —
Powerful is the army and powerful its Emperor, yet there is
a body to which they both pay lip-service, and which still
enjoys a prestige and moral authority that stamps itself upon
the imagination of every man in the Roman Empire —
the " venerable Senate."

Theoretically the Senate shares the government with the
Emperor, controls the state when there is a vacancy in the
palace, selects the new ruler and bestows on him the " proconsular " and ":tribunician power," — the legal bases of his
authority. It must be consulted by him in every important
act, and when he dies it decides whether he is to be deified as
a god, or suffer the awful " damnation of memory " (*damnatio
memoriæ*) branding him for all time as a tyrant. It can also
declare him suspended or deposed from office, set a price on
his head and order the armies to refuse him obedience. Its
formal decrees (*senatus consulta*) constitute, now that the
old public assemblies have been abandoned, the most binding
kind of law.

The Senate also governs directly all of those provinces
(about half of the whole Empire) which do not require any
army for defense or control. It has its own treasury, and it
can strike copper money, although gold and silver are reserved
to the Emperor, making a considerable profit on the seignor-
age. It acts as supreme court of appeal on all cases which rise
in the provinces under its government. By the vote of its
members are elected all those " old Republican " magistrates

from consul down to *quæstor* (treasury supervisor) which carry along with the temporary glories of office the right to a life seat in the Senate itself — making the latter practically a self-perpetuating body. A good Emperor swears at the beginning of his reign, " I will never put any senator to death" — *i.e.* the Senate shall judge all capital charges against its members, even those involving treason.

Besides these prerogatives senators alone are eligible for the highest military commands and the governorships of all the larger imperial provinces. As already stated (see p. 156), the senators in addition constitute the highest aristocracy; they must each possess at least 1,000,000 sesterces ($40,000) taxable property, and they enjoy all the influence that comes to vested prestige and wealth in an age that cringes to titles and fortunes. On this showing, the 600 senators apparently constitute the most powerful organ in the government.

284. Actual Weakness of the Senate. — Unfortunately much of this brave showing is only a glittering mask. The Senate has not one swordsman in Rome or in any of its provinces to obey the summons, " Resist the Emperor and his Prætorians." It ordinarily has to stand helpless while the army decides who is to be the next Cæsar in case of a contested succession.

After Caligula's murder in 41 A.D. the Conscript Fathers debated earnestly: " Shall we restore the Republic? If not that, which aspiring nobleman can we elect as Emperor?" Meantime, the Prætorians, pillaging the palace, found the terrified and demoralized Claudius hiding in a closet; they dragged him forth and discovered a survivor of the Cæsars whose dynasty they greatly wished to perpetuate. "*Ave Imperator!*" rang their shout. Soon the senators were informed that their debates were unnecessary — Claudius was being proclaimed in the Prætorian Camp. The Fathers made haste to bestow on Claudius full imperial powers and to congratulate him on his succession. Nobody doubted after that where the real power lay.

Besides all this, without mentioning the army, the Emperor has every senator personally within his grasp. He can strike any member from the *album* (Senate List) by use of his irresponsible Censorial Power. Through that same power he can appoint any favorite to the order by his mere fiat. In the elections held within the Senate, he can control the choice for any office by announcing that he favors the aspirations of such and such a friend; the " Candidates of Cæsar " are always elected. In the debates it is a bold senator who dares to face the unpopularity of opposing the Emperor's suggestions;[1] and once let the monarch indicate the slightest wish, a whole pack of servile favor-seekers will instantly champion the proposition with fervent loyalty. Finally by his " tribunician authority " the Emperor can veto any senatorial proposal which he dislikes. The power of the " venerable Senate " seems, therefore, to have vanished in thin air.

285. Amount of Power Left to the Senate.—This last is not quite true, however. The Cæsars do not, as yet, represent an unvarnished despotism; they need a cover for their autocracy,[2] and they have to leave to the Senate a certain show of power. No new Emperor's throne furthermore is secure against pretenders until, after the army has proclaimed him, the Senate has confirmed him, and no Emperor likes to feel that his sole refuge is with the irresponsible swordsmen.

---

[1] Bad Emperors, *e.g.* Domitian, made it a practice to *speak first* in the Curia; any senator who later opposed their opinions was liable to charges of disloyalty. If, however, an Emperor spoke last he also left the groundlings miserable because they might unwittingly have opposed him.

[2] The last avowedly constitutional "Princeps" was Alexander Severus (murdered 235 A.D.); then followed the military monarchy. Aurelian (270–275 A.D.) took on practically all the trappings of a despot, and with Diocletian (284 A.D.) the absolute monarchy existed without concealment.

Besides all this, the moral prestige of the Senate is still so great that even a Nero or a Domitian hesitates to flout that famous body too openly. Finally, be it said, the task of governing the enormous Empire is a tremendous burden. A reasonable monarch is glad enough to throw upon the Senate a great many problems over which the " Fathers " can exhaust their eloquence and which they probably can settle quite as wisely as he. If they fail and the case is then dutifully referred back to " Cæsar," his own importance becomes all the greater. If they succeed, he gains a reputation for moderation and liberality. The senators, on their part, have long since ceased to dream of restoring the old Republic. Since the accession of Nerva, 96 A.D., an era of good feeling and equilibrium on the whole has existed. The Senate therefore still vaunts itself as a coördinate branch of the Roman government.

286. Organization and Procedure of the Senate. — The Senate of the Empire exists in form and procedure very like its predecessor under the Republic. Its debates are the talk of the capital and are duly reported in the Acta Diurna ; and at present, with Hadrian out of the city, its supreme presiding officers, the two consuls, affect to be the most powerful personages in Rome, although some of the great permanent ministers on the Palatine, and especially the Prætorian Præfect, have firm doubts on the subject.

When Publius Junius Calvus is compelled to attend sessions of the Senate, he has ordinarily been informed a couple of days in advance by a *viator* of one of the consuls bringing a personal notice to his home, although urgent meetings can be summoned on much shorter notice merely by sending forth a crier. There is no fixed quorum for the Senate; although there are 600 lawful members, many of these are high government officials absent in the provinces, others are retired, elderly dignitaries very loath to quit their luxurious ease in

their Etruscan or Campanian villas.   Since the post of senator is ordinarily for life, the body contains an undue proportion of superannuated, doddering old men who will only appear on great occasions.

Sessions can thus be held with only a very thin number,
say fifty,[1] although if the gathering is disgracefully small,
those attending can shout to the presiding officer, " *Numera!
Numera!*" (" Take the number!") and insist on adjournment
until the consul's tipstaffs and bailiffs have rounded up a
respectable fraction.   On this day in question, however, there
is no danger of a slim attendance.   Every member in Rome
is sure to be present, including certain invalids who have to be
helped out of their litters and led inside by their freedmen.

Sextus Annius Pedius, ex-proconsul of Asia has been im-
peached by Publius Calvus and a fellow senator, Titus
Volusius Atilius, for gross extortion and malfeasance in his
government.   The case has been referred to the Senate by
Hadrian as lying within its special competence.   Pedius is of
the highest aristocracy, but like most great men has made
plenty of enemies.   Every possible social influence has been
mobilized for and against him.   A great state trial, with an
abundance of soaring oratory is consequently in prospect.
Every senator is in his element.

**287. The Curia (Senate House) and Its Arrangement of
Benches.** — On days when the Senate convenes, the clients
can stream into the empty atria of their noble patrons, col-
lect their money doles and depart — the patrons themselves
have set off at first dawn for the council, accompanied very
probably (if it is not summertime) by link-boys to guide them
through the still darkened streets.   They gather thus at
prima luce in the rebuilt Curia at the Forum, although sessions
can be held in almost any other duly consecrated spot, and

---

[1] The law required, however, a minimum of certain specified numbers
for the passing of various important kinds of decrees.

Pompey built a special Curia near his own mansion in the
Campus Martius for use when he wished to deliberate with
the Fathers.[1]

The Curia Julia has a magnificent hall with tiers of comfortable and highly carved benches (*subsellia*) curving in a
semi-circle not unlike the legislative chambers of other times.
The six hundred senators sit fairly close together, so that the
debates can be in easy voice. At the entrance the consuls'
viatores and lictors check off the Fathers entering to exclude
interlopers, but there is no real secrecy. The doors are
numerous and stand wide, and a curious crowd is permitted
to linger around them; especially are the young sons of a
good many senators seen there, eagerly following all the proceedings wherein they hope soon to have a part. (See p. 190.)

Facing the benches rises a low dais whereon is a line of
curule chairs for the consuls and prætors, also a long solid
settee whereon ten of the younger senators sit down solemnly
together. These ten are the tribunes of the Plebs, — shorn
now of nearly all their ancient authority, but still maintaining the "shadow of a great name," a name surviving from
the time when, as in the days of such personages as Gaius
Gracchus, a tribune could be mightier than a consul.

288. The Gathering of the Senators. — The Fathers drop
into their seats. No law adjusts their precedence, but etiquette gives the front row to the ex-consuls, the next banks
to the ex-prætors, behind them the former ædiles, tribunes,
and quæstors with the *pedani*[2] (senators who have never
held elective office) modestly in the rear. The defendant

---

[1] He did this because as holder of the military power it was unlawful
for him to come inside the consecrated city limits (*pomerium*); so he
built a suburban Senate House outside of these confines.

[2] So called because, being last on the Senate list, and seldom called
upon to speak, they could express themselves with their "feet" only
— *i.e.* by voting when they walked out in divisions of the house.

Pedius attended by several distinguished senators, his relatives, all clad in the gray togas of distress and mourning, and also by his two advocates both in conventional white, take seats in the front benches. As they do this it is noted as of ominous significance that several ex-consuls, who had come in first, promptly shift to the other side of the hall.

At the center of the platform is observed a majestic, gilded statue of Victory, with expanded wings, flowing robes, standing upon a globe, and stretching forth a laurel crown.[1] Before it, upon a little altar, a few coals are smoking. Presently a door at the side of the platform opens, and a lictor signs with his fasces. The chatter across the now crowded hall ceases instantly; all the toga-clad figures rise together, while the presiding consul, Gaius Juventius Varus,[2] leads in the array of magistrates, each in the ornate toga prætexta.

289. Opening the Session: Taking the Auspices. — Gravely this official company seats itself in the curule chairs; gravely Varus casts a handful of incense upon the altar before the Victory, and a cloud of fragrance fills the hall. Then Varus, a tall and very majestic figure, signs to the senators; they also are seated, next his voice sounds clearly: " Bring forth the chickens!"

Not a lip twitches in all that sedate audience as two attendants appear upon the platform setting down a small coop containing a few barnyard fowls. The consul rises and stands beside them; next to him takes station an elderly senator also wearing the prætexta and holding a staff with a pecul-

---

[1] Under the later Empire this statue (originally set up by Augustus) came to be looked upon as the "Palladium" of Rome and its removal from the Senate House in 384 A.D. by Valentinian the Second, despite vigorous protests by the pagan party, was looked upon as an official announcement of the triumph of Christianity.

[2] The other consul in 134 A.D. was Gaius Julius Servianius. The consuls would settle as to their presidency from day to day either by mutual agreement, by taking turns in rotation, or by the casting of lots.

iarly shaped spiral head, a *lituus* — the badge of office of an *augur*, lawfully entitled to proclaim the will of the gods. In a dead hush the servitors pass a small dish of grain to the consul who carefully scatters the grain within easy reach of the chickens. The latter, carefully starved since yesterday, snap up the grains eagerly.

They even devour so fast that the wheat drops from their bills, a most excellent sign. The augur bends forward intently, watching their action, then motions with his staff : *" There is no evil sight nor sound ! "* he announces in solemn formula.

A mutter of relaxation passes around the Senate. The servitors carry out the chicken coop. The consul shakes his great draperies around him with studied dignity and turns to the waiting

COOP OF SACRED CHICKENS USED IN DIVINATION.

assembly. " Affairs divine " have been attended to ; " affairs human " can now begin.

290. Presentation of Routine Business : Taking a Formal Vote. — Even under the Empire it is a glorious thing to be consul, with the twelve lictors, the temporary colleagueship with the Emperor, and the right to preside over the most magnificent council in the world. Varus carries himself with the dignity of a nobleman who has enjoyed a long career in the Senate and now is at the summit of his aspirations. Every tradition of the ancient body has been cherished ; and the solemn forms still differ little from those in the great conclave that piloted the overthrow of Carthage.

The chief business of the day is the trial of Pedius, but a

certain lesser matter demands prior disposition.   The consul
has received a dispatch from the propraetor of Sicily (a
" senatorial " province) asking if he can be empowered to
remit the taxes of certain peasants near Agrigentum, whose
crops have suffered from the blight.   Varus begins with the
time-honored formula, " That it may be well and fortunate to
the Roman people, the Quirites, we refer this thing to you,
patres conscripti."   Then in well-chosen words he gives the
substance of the governor's request, and reads certain correspondence explaining the plight of the peasants; having thus
finished his *relatio* — the " presentation of the problem " —
he ends with another formula, " What is it your pleasure to
do concerning this matter?"

If the business be contentious, now might begin a vigorous
debate; but the governor's request, based on wise policy, is
not worth questioning and almost everybody wants to proceed to the trial.   The consul, therefore, after a pause, demands, " Is it your will to grant this thing?   Let then all the
Conscript Fathers favoring pass to the right!"

One garrulous old senator anxious for a chance to speak,
indeed begins shouting *"Consule!   Consule!"* (" Take counsel!" — *i.e.* start a debate.)   If many others join him, Varus
can be forced to permit a long-winded discussion; but the
troublemaker is without a second.   The senators with one
accord seem rising and passing to the right side of the Curia.
Nobody ventures to go to the left.   The motion thus carries
unanimously.   The company resume their seats; then all
eyes are again upon the consul when with clear voice he commands: " Let the accusers of Sextus Annius Pedius stand
forth."

291. Presenting an Impeachment at a Senate Trial. —
Publius Calvus rises from the front benches opposite the
defendant, allows the many folds of his toga to fall magnificently around him, thrusting them back just enough to reveal

the purple laticlave running down his tunic, and carefully adjusts a ring so its great emerald will give precisely the correct flash as he gestures. Directly behind him, inconspicuously garbed stands a favorite freedman, avowedly to pass him papyri and tablets which he will read, but really quite as much to whisper, " Drop your tones ! " " Speak louder ! " or " Not so shrill ! " and like promptings as the oration progresses.[1]

The Senate, of course, cannot be expected to put in weary days listening to intricate and sordid testimony. All this has been taken before a special board of judges, and on their report there is no real doubt of Pedius's guilt. He has taken a bribe of 300,000 sesterces ($12,000) to banish a Roman eques from his province and has put seven less-protected provincials, friends of this eques, to death; worse still, he has taken still another bribe of 700,000 sesterces ($28,000) for committing the unspeakable outrage of causing yet a second eques to be first beaten with rods, next hustled off to the mines, then actually strangled in prison. The prominent provincials from Asia have, therefore, presented an absolute case against their evil ex-governor. The lesser culprits have mostly confessed and received appropriate penalties — and the only question really before the Senate is fixing the punishment of Pedius.

He is a great noble with great connections. Ought a senator who has held the consulship be banished and ruined even if he *has* misgoverned his province, taken bribes and done to death an eques — one of those upstart half-nobles whom every true senator should scorn ? Pedius does not lack friends who have told him to brazen it out, and that no severe

---

[1] This trial follows closely the account of the prosecution of Marius Priscus, proconsul of Africa, before the Senate by Pliny the Younger and Tacitus the historian ; but in Priscus's trial the mere oratory actually took three whole days ! (See Pliny the Younger : Book II, 11.)

penalty can befall him; and he glares defiantly across to Calvus as the latter begins his argument.

292. The Water Clocks; Methods of a Prosecutor; Applause in the Senate. — Just as the chief prosecutor commences, the servitors reappear and set close beside him a large glass vessel upon a wooden stand, perforated to empty slowly into a second vessel beneath, and when thus emptied the upper container is promptly refilled. Calvus has been informed he can have " only four water clocks " (about two hours) — an outrageously insufficient number in his opinion, when many an advocate can get twelve — but time must be given the other orators and after that the Senate must discuss and vote.

Speedily Calvus warms to his task, and in long periods of sonorous Latin his voice resounds through the Curia. He delights to expand upon the enormity of the crime of putting to death not a mere provincial, not a simple Roman plebeian, but a Roman eques. His speech abounds with elegant and apparently impromptu allusions, metaphors and similes — duly practiced half a month before. He goes out of his way to pay an extended and fulsome compliment to the benignity and liberality of the Emperor in condescending to let the Senate settle the issue. Words at length almost fail him when he calls on the Fathers in the name of Justice, Virtue, Heavenly Vengeance, and all the other guardian deities of the state to punish the hideous misdeeds of such a criminal as Pedius.

As he proceeds the Senate kindles at his eloquence. First his personal friends who are sitting directly behind him begin to shout " *Euge!* " and " *Sophos!* " Then the applause re-echoes from all over the hall. Presently the occupants of the curule chairs on the platform begin to clap, the consul half rises from his seat as if transported by the oratory, and even Pedius's own advocates politely join in that applause which

Calvus is professionally bound to return with interest as soon as they begin to speak in turn.

Soon, all too soon, for the orator, and for those senators who love " the good old times," when an advocate could thunder all day long, the four water clocks are exhausted. Calvus subsides, to be immediately surrounded by his friends who compare his efforts to those of Cato, Hortensius, Cicero, and such later masters as Cornelius Tacitus; while the freedman immediately speeds off to inform Gratia of the " wonderful triumph " of her husband — a triumph of oratory, whatever be the actual verdict.

293. Speech for the Defendant: Methods of a Professional Advocate. — After order is restored a grave old senator — Quintus Saturius — arises to answer the prosecutor. He is a professional advocate of fame, but evil report has it that in his youth under Domitian he was a *delator* (professional accuser), and won a fortune by prosecuting the innocent victims of that bad Emperor's disfavor. Since then he has never been squeamish in accepting doubtful causes. The law only allows him 10,000 sesterces ($400) as the fee from each legal client, but the latter has plenty of indirect means of showing his " gratitude," and Saturius's wealth now is enormous. This morning he has carefully smeared eye-salve above his left eye — a token that he is to speak for the defendant, not over the right as if for the plaintiff. His toga also floats in billowy folds, his hands flash with costly rings, and his powerful voice soon booms through the Curia.

Saturius does not waste time denying that many of Pedius's misdeeds have been proved, but he praises at great length his client's " glorious ancestry " and distinguished social connections. As for the accusations, — what if he did abuse his office? Was a member of the great house of the Annii to be held down to the sordid rules befitting mere plebeians and freedmen? What if an *eques* *had* been wrongfully done to

CICERO DENOUNCING CATILINE BEFORE THE SENATE: painting in modern Senate House in Rome.

death? Was not the fellow by birth a Phrygian who had
gained first citizenship and then the " narrow-stripe " merely
by the use of his wits? How could so great a man as the
Proconsul of Asia be expected to live on a beggarly salary of
1,000,000 sesterces ($40,000)?

At this point Saturius's voice begins in fact to tremble with
pathos. How can the Conscript Fathers bring themselves
to disgrace all the defendant's distinguished relatives who just
now are sitting behind him in the gray togas of public mourning? Think of his distressed wife whose father and all three
uncles were at least prætors! Think of his brother who had
been killed bravely fighting the Parthians! Think of his two
sons whose public careers would be blighted by the disgrace
of their father! Think finally of the Senate itself — what
contempt upon the " Venerable Order " if one of its most
prominent members should be ruined on the testimony of
mere provincials and upstarts! etc., etc.

**294. Concluding Speeches; Interrupting Shouts; Per-
sonal Invectives.** — Saturius, ere concluding, works himself
into a fine passion. He also gets sallies of applause — mostly
from the self-same men who have just cheered Calvus. But
at some of his assertions there are murmurs of dissent, and
even open shouts such as " Drop that argument!" " Don't
insult our intelligence!" Finally, however, he sits down,
having exhausted his four water clocks. More cheers, more
congratulations, everybody swears to his neighbor the day is
proving an intellectual feast.

The consul proclaims an interim; and the Conscript
Fathers adjourn to stretch their limbs, snatch a hasty colla-
tion provided by their attendants and discuss the arguments.
Then all resume when Marcus Petreius, Pedius's junior advocate, continues for the defense. The hostile attitude of the
Senate has impressed the defendant's counsel, and Petreius
enters into an elaborate appeal for mercy, with many fine

invocations of the " Divine Clemency," and reminders of how any senator might some day find himself in Pedius's horrid predicament. Petreius is allowed " less water " than Saturius; he gets considerable applause, however, when he finishes, but knowing members shake their heads: " They cheer his oratory and not his cause."

In fine mettle therefore Titus Atilius, Calvus's associate, next sums up for the prosecution. Atilius is a relatively young man, as yet only an ex-quæstor; and to-day is his glorious opportunity. Carried away on a flood of invective, he allows himself, as is permitted by usage, to cover not merely Pedius but even Pedius's advocate with a storm of bitter personalities. When he thunders against Saturius's sycophantic career there are wild shouts of applause from all over the Curia; and more applause follows when he ridicules certain physical infirmities of the miserable defendant.[1] Pedius rises with supplicatory gestures and appeals loudly to the ten tribunes, " Oh, very noble tribunes protect me! " — but the ten sit stolid and silent upon their bench and he subsides with blenching cheeks. His advocates, exchanging knowing glances, are seen to be gathering up their tablets.

295. Taking the Opinion of the Senate. — At last Atilius's " water " has likewise ended. Amid another whirlwind of applause and rush of congratulating friends he takes his seat. The consul Varus rises with extreme dignity, and beckons with his hand. Every senator instantly is tense and silent.

" We do now," proclaims Varus, " take the opinions (*sententiæ*) of the Conscript Fathers concerning that which it befits should be done in the case of Sextus Annius Pedius this day arraigned and tried. You have heard his accusers and his advocates. I shall call the album of the Senate."

---

[1] Any student interested in the coarse and violent personalities permissible in speeches before the Senate, should read Cicero's speech "Against Piso."

He holds up tablets whereon are listed the senators in order of official rank and precedence; then turns to the members seated directly before him, the magistrates-elect for the ensuing year, summoning first the senior consul designate, Appius Lupercus:

" *Dic, Appie Luperce!* "

Appius Lupercus, an elderly aristocrat, the head of an ancient family, rises amid a portentous hush. The " right to speak first," possessed by the Emperor when present, is invaluable. All the orators for either side have really aimed their best arguments toward Lupercus, knowing his prerogative, but his " cold looks " toward Pedius have already fallen as ice upon the friends of the defendant. His voice now carries through the expectant Curia.

" Conscript Fathers: — It is true that Sextus Pedius is a man of exalted birth; the more shame, therefore, that he has disgraced the name of a *clarissimus* of the Venerable Senate. It is true his victims were either provincials or citizens of provincial origin: — the law is impartial, the Roman Empire has been established upon the inflexible rule of ' piety ' giving alike to gods and to men that which is lawfully their due. If he has outraged provincials the case is clear; long ago the Emperor Tiberius expressed the ruling policy when he said, ' A good shepherd shears his sheep but does not flay them.' If Pedius has also outraged citizens, much more equites, wherein lies the boast ' *Civis Romanus sum!* ', if these men, whatever their original birth, cannot demand lawful vengeance at our hands?

" My opinion, therefore, is this: let the defendant's ill-gotten bribes be confiscated to the treasury, and let Pedius himself be banished from Rome, and Italy; let his lesser confederates be banished from Rome, from Italy, and also from the Province of Asia. Since also Publius Calvus and Titus Atilius have pleaded the cause of the provincials with diligence and fearlessness, let them receive the thanks of the Senate.   Such is my opinion!"

A great murmur rises — applause with some shouts of dissent.   "Hangman!" "Butcher!" rise from the little knot of Pedius's relatives.   Then Varus calls on the second consul designate, Atticus, who, rising stiffly, says with clear voice, "I agree with the most noble Lupercus," and promptly takes his seat.

One by one the ex-consuls, each summoned by turn, announce that they also agree with Lupercus, until one cynical old aristocrat, the ex-consul Gavius, notorious for his own sensual life and the manner whereby he enriched himself in Africa, yet powerful through his vast wealth and influential connections, announces that he is confident the Senate should show mercy.   "Let Pedius disgorge the money and forfeit the priesthood of Mars which he holds — that will be punishment enough.   A good lesson has been taught and the unfortunate man has been disgraced enough already."

296. An Uproar in the Senate: an "Altercation." — Instantly the Senate is in an uproar.   The short-hand reporters[1] can hardly take down all the interrupting shouts that are tossed back and forth: "How now, Marcus Æmilius Gavius, will you let such a scoundrel go?" "What are those provincials but scum anyway!" etc., etc.   A violent "altercation" follows, several senators rising and demanding that Gavius explain himself.   The old reprobate however cleverly stands his ground, and is vigorously cheered by many who will not actually support his proposal.

At last the house cools down.   The taking of the opinion now proceeds among the prætors-designate and the ex-præ-

---

[1] Short-hand reports of the Senate meetings were taken, and seemingly embodied everything said, including even the applause and the unfriendly interruptions.   We do not know, however, whether they were taken by senators or by reporters brought in for the purpose.

tors. No senator can speak twice, but each man, when on his feet, has great liberty of action — several of the younger men half ironically support Gavius, and one senator earns unpopularity by insisting on his right of the floor and calling attention to the embezzlements reported in the African municipality of Utica — a matter quite beside the question. Two or three long and eloquent speeches are delivered in favor of Lupercus's stern proposal. It is growing late and nobody wants to call on the ex-ædiles and other junior senators,[1] and cries are rising, " *Divide! Divide!* "

297. Taking a Vote of the Senate. A Sentence of Banishment. — Varus again rises, " Conscript Fathers : you have heard the opinions of these very noble men of consular and prætorian rank. Two propositions are before you. Those who favor the penalties for Sextus Pedius proposed by Appius Lupercus let them walk to the right ! Those the lesser penalty proposed by Marcus Gavius to the left."

The hundreds of togas rise together. Gavius is not without a certain minority of supporters who start with him to the left, but most of these, seeing how many ex-consuls of birth and character are following Lupercus, desert Gavius, who is left with only a trifling band around him. There is no need for Varus to count the result. Even while the Senate is dividing the luckless Pedius, with his kinsmen and advocates, is seen gliding through a side exit. It is the defendant's right thus to anticipate sentence and to slip away with as little ignominy as possible into exile.

At a word from the consul the senators return to their seats. The long shadows of evening are stretching through the doors of the Curia, as Varus announces that Sextus Pedius having been convicted of high crimes is banished from Rome and

---

[1] Apparently men not of prætorian rank rather seldom got the floor, although in highly important cases the presiding officer had to call for *sententiæ* down through the ex-quæstors.

from Italy. He must quit the city to-morrow. He must quit
Italy in twenty days. Should he tarry or return he will be
" cut off from fire and water," and dealt with " after the
ancient custom " — *i.e.* he will be scourged with his head in
a forked stake, then sewed in a bag with a cock, a dog, and
a viper, and flung into the sea.

Everybody is anxious to be gone. In the great mansions
six hundred expensive cooks are fuming over the delay to six
hundred expensive dinners. The terrible fate of Pedius will
make talk for all Rome through ten days. Varus raises his
hand and at length pronounces the sonorous ancient formula,
" *Nihil vos moramur, patres conscripti* " — " We detain you
no longer, Conscript Fathers."

Publius Calvus and Titus Atilius are escorted homeward
by groups of fellow senators as if they were triumphant generals. Their skill, eloquence, pathos, and legal learning are
praised to the skies. Each is assured that " he has rendered
himself and his friends immortal ! " Each to-morrow will
begin rewriting his speech, introducing many fine arguments
which he has had no time to utter.[1] These will be embalmed
in his published works which will be presumably carried some
day, tied to poles, in a conspicuous place in his funeral
procession.

So ends a typical meeting of the Senate under the Empire ;
noble forms, much dignity, a perfect river of eloquence, a
judicial decision in this case conforming with justice, but
handling no great issues of diplomacy, high finance, or peace
or war. Already Pedius's friends are consoling him, as he
drearily prepares to retire to Macedonia : " In a few years
at worst we can get your pardon from the Emperor."

---

[1] As did, of course, Cicero in his " Orations against Verres," and in
other orations.

CHAPTER XVIII

THE COURTS AND THE ORATORS. THE GREAT BATHS. THE PUBLIC PARKS AND ENVIRONS OF ROME

298. Roman Court Procedure Highly Scientific. — If Publius Calvus does not have to attend the Senate, two places will assuredly devour a great part of his normal day — the courthouse and the public baths. Even if he is not plaintiff, defendant, or witness, like every man of his class he delights in listening to oratory, and etiquette requires that, whenever one of his numerous friends argues a case, he, with as many other senators and equites as possible should sit in the front of the audience, to "lend their distinguished influence," to lead the salvos of applause, and even to stand up conspicuously behind the orator at critical points in his argument.

Roman courts are not like the Athenian dicasteries, huge juries of many hundreds,[1] with tumultuous appeals from the letter of the law to the emotions of the members. Personal influence has its part, but everything is regulated, orderly, scientific. Cases which do not involve the safety of the state or the fate of distinguished personages are usually argued coldly, and with a nice attention to technicalities. Your Roman jurisconsult (expert in the law) is as much superior to an Athenian in developing the science of formal justice, as another Athenian might be to a Roman, in breathing life into chiseled marble. The administration of law is intricate. There are courts behind courts, with final appeal either to

---

[1] See "A Day in Old Athens," p. 135.

the Senate (as we have just seen) or to the Emperor.[1]   The
" law's delays " are perfectly well understood by adroit advocates ;   and Martial records a case that took twenty years
while dragging through three successive courts — to the ruin
of both sets of litigants.

299. The Great Tribunals in the Basilicas. — If we visit
the great basilicas, we find two kinds of tribunals steadily
functioning.   For much civil business there is the great
" Court of the Centumviri," a board not of " One Hundred "
but actually of one hundred and eighty distinguished citizens, who sit sometimes all together, sometimes divided into
four groups for conducting trials simultaneously.   Their
stronghold is the Basilica Julia.   It is a great honor to argue
before the Centumviri, and every advocate exhausts his
wiles to induce the grave judges to pay him the highest compliment (as they did to Pliny the Younger) by " suddenly
leaping to their feet and applauding him as if they could not
help themselves."

The most of the higher litigation, however, goes before
judices.   A *judex* may be one of the great panel of 4000
citizens, — senators, equites, and plebeians of substance who
can be called upon to serve as a kind of jury for ordinary
trials of importance.   The size of such a jury depends on the
nature of the case as provided by statute, — you can have
from 32 members up to a full 100.   There is a high judge
over the entire body, either the prætor, or a professional
expert in the law, the *judex quæstionis*, who controls the
presentation of evidence and the strictly technical parts of
the trial.

---

[1] Very few civil cases involving merely private rights would be heard
by the Emperor, although they might by his deputy, the Prætorian
Præfect.   Claudius sometimes seems to have sat on the tribunal, out of
a pedantic sense of duty, but often falling asleep until the advocates
bawled " O Cæsar !" loudly enough to wake him.

After the evidence has been submitted, orally or in writing, and the orators have exhausted themselves, the jurors take small wax-covered tablets and vote, each man marking simply letters: A = *absolvo*, "Not guilty," C = *Condemno*, "Guilty," N.L. = *Non Liquet*, "No verdict." A bare majority can either acquit or condemn, but, of course, no man is condemned on a plurality, and a tie means acquittal. If "No verdict" is the decision, the case can still go to another trial. Roman juries, therefore, do not have to be locked up for days to compel them to agree.

However, this jury system is often inconvenient and does not adapt itself to that very technical justice in which the Roman jurisconsults increasingly delight. More and more cases are being tried by a single *judex*, or a small bench of *judices*, men highly trained in the law, and especially appointed by the prætor or other high official, to investigate a given case and report their findings. Under the later Empire the large juries will disappear altogether, and a few professional judges will become arbiters alike of the law and the evidence — an excellent system from the standpoint of scientific jurisprudence, but not so excellent if these judges become corrupt, pliable, or subject to class prejudices.

300. Great Stress on Advocacy. — Whatever the tribunal may be, great is the stress laid on the arts of the advocate. Calvus has served a long probation arguing in the basilicas before his day of glory came in the Senate. All the young Ciceros in the rhetoric schools dream of the hour when they can stand in flowing togas before the high raised platform of the judices, wave their arms, throw out their voices, and plead the cause of some widow, or arraign some embezzler or extortioner. The mere fact that senatorial speeches have to be extremely careful, lest they trench upon imperial prerogative, puts a greater premium upon private argument in the courts where usually " Cæsar " has no interests.

The rewards of successful eloquence are great;[1] and if the legal fees are small, rich clients, at least, never fail with big New Year's presents, and with legacies in their wills. Besides there are no governmental prosecuting attorneys. Criminal actions can be started by any citizen against any possible offender. To reward such zeal, a good part of the fines or confiscated property of convicted criminals goes to the self-appointed prosecutor. It is thus easy to see how, under Tiberius, Nero, and Domitian, the delators (" professional accusers ") grew fat prosecuting wealthy senators for " treason." These good days for the profession seem over, but the incomes of certain of the leading advocates are princely, some almost vying with those of the earlier Vibius Crispus and Epirius Marcellus, who had over 200,000,000 sesterces ($8,000,000) apiece.

301. Cheap Pettifogging Lawyers. — On the other hand Rome is infested with starving pettifoggers, pretentious wretches, sleeping in dirty tenements, and with hardly a decent toga to wear when they argue on petty cases in the præfect's court. Sometimes they get a better class of client, hire a good robe and ring to wear at the trial, and win the case in the Basilica. Their client will very likely decorate the stairs to their tenement with palm leaves, but as the only fee[2] send them a quantity of uncertain edibles — " a dried-up ham, a jar of sprats, some veteran onions, or five flagons

---

[1] "Eloquence" was looked upon as indispensable for everybody expecting any kind of a public career. Even in the army there was much speech-making prior to a pitched battle. Tacitus speaks of how an army was so utterly surprised that its general " could neither harangue his men nor draw them up in battle array" — two operations apparently equally necessary. (Tacitus, " History," iv, 33.)

[2] Litigants were required by law to take oath that before the trial they had not promised any sum to their advocates or entered into any bargain with them. After the trial they were "allowed" to "offer" their lawyers not over 10,000 sesterces if they wished.

of [very cheap] wine that has just sailed down the Tiber!"
If any money is actually paid, lucky the advocate who does
not have to split his fee with some agent who has secured the
case for him!

302. Character Witnesses; Torture of Slave Witnesses.
— One thing more concerning these trials must be noted:
the testimony of Roman citizens carries much greater weight
than that of aliens, and the unreliability of Græco-Levantines
is notorious. Freeborn men, Roman or provincial, testify
under oath. Only accusers have the right to compel the
attendance of unwilling witnesses, but the defense can bring
not merely voluntary witnesses to the facts, but can present
as many as ten *laudatores*, character witnesses, and if men of
high standing are vigorous in their friends' praises, their
opinions will offset very many ugly facts in the testimony.

Frequently enough, however, the statements of slaves have
to be taken. These wretches, having little better status
before the law than animals, can only testify under torture.
No master, nevertheless, except in cases of treason, can ordinarily be compelled to let his slaves testify *against* him, but it
is assumed that torture is necessary if a master voluntarily
offers his slave as witness, — for what slave would dare
uncompelled to say anything unwelcome to his master in
view of the terrific flogging waiting after he gets home? The
situation in short as to slave testimony is substantially as in
Athens.[1] This use of the rack and flogging post is one of the
worst blots upon the highly scientific and usually reasonable
and humane judicial system of Rome.

**303. Written Evidence; High Development of the Advo-
cate's Art.** — On the other hand much weight is given to
reliable written evidence. Public documents from the record
office, and the careful entries on bankers' ledgers are contin-

---

[1] See "A Day in Old Athens," p. 138.

ually being introduced as testimony. Much of the forensic oratory also is of a high order. The rhetoric schools have not taught their better pupils in vain; despite much silly display, " appeals to the emotions," and artificiality, the art of advocacy has never completely lost touch with the promotion of justice; and usually the verdict goes still to him who best meets Cato the Elder's pungent definition of the true orator, *vir bonus, dicendi peritus* ("the good man versed in the art of speech"), and who recalls that great republican's classic injunction for all advocates — *rem tene, verba sequentur* ("Grasp the subject and the words will follow").[1]

In all matters not touching certain high interests the Roman courts are perhaps as disinterested and clean as human tribunals can well be, and the average judex is charged with a passionate desire to do that which is formally right. In the courts the spirit of Rome is often to be seen at its best.

304. Popularity and Necessity of the Baths. — As the afternoon advances, however, unless the case is extremely urgent, or the advocates unwontedly skilful, the impassive toga-clad figures upon the high seats of the tribunals begin to show signs of uneasiness. The pleaders themselves reach in turn a suitable climax, as the last filling of the water clocks runs out; — if necessary they can finish their castigations or their excuses to-morrow. The courts are adjourned, and judges, litigants, advocates, spectators, all hasten from the Basilicas possessed with the thought which is common to

---

[1] Space lacks for a discussion of the formal training of the Roman lawyer-orators, or concerning those public recitations which sometimes were the means of winning even greater reputation than any ordinary successes in the courts.

Some of these recitations in hired halls, with the audience carefully sprinkled with a paid claque, were worse than pedantic and artificial. Pliny the Younger, although he denounced the use of a claque, repeated with pleasure how he gave a reading from his own works and plays which lasted two days, "necessitated by the applause of my audience"; and boasted how he "had not allowed himself to skip one word."

nigh every man in Rome not of the most unfortunate class —
" To the Baths ! "

The warm Italian climate makes frequent ablutions not
merely comfortable but necessary, but in the stern old days
of the earlier Republic Seneca specifically assures us that the
fathers of Rome were not wont to wash all over oftener than
once a week (*nundinæ*).[1] Long before the age of Hadrian,
however, a daily bath became a personal necessity. No
dinner can be enjoyed without it. No respectable man can
feel comfortable deprived of it.

As the bathing habit grows, its luxury and elaboration
grow correspondingly.   The daily bath becomes a social
ceremony, and the bathing place becomes almost as indispensable as the forum, or the triclinium.   Other peoples and
ages may equal or surpass the Romans in actual cleanliness ;
none can develop institutions really corresponding to the
enormous public *thermæ* scattered over the capital.[2]

305. Luxurious Private Baths. — Probably every senator
and all the more pretentious equites have sumptuous private
baths in their own mansions.   Here they can go when visits
to the public thermæ are inconvenient, or to refresh themselves between the long courses of their great dinner parties.

The luxury of these private baths can be so prodigious as to
afford constant texts for the Stoical philosophers.   Seneca
has waxed almost frantic telling how an aristocrat feels
somewhat poverty-stricken unless " the walls [of his bath]
shine with great costly slabs, and marbles of Alexandria

---

[1] The Roman week, *nundinæ*, had eight days — seven working days,
then a market day.   The Jewish week of seven days (*hebdomas*) became
known to the Romans by the time of Pompeius Magnus, but it was not
generally adopted until Christianity became the state religion.

[2] Undoubtedly along with this incessant bathing there often went the
presence of much squalor, dirt, obnoxious insects, etc. which seem ines-
capable in Mediterranean countries.   Probably many persons injured
their health by excessive and debilitating bathing.

tricked out with reliefs in stone from Numidia, and with the whole ceiling elaborately covered with all varieties of paintings, and unless Thasian marbles inclose the swimming pool, and the water gushes out of silver taps " ; likewise " how many a rich freedman adorns his baths with fine collections of statues and a multitude of pillars supporting nothing but serving only as ornaments." Essential, too, are such private baths for those so devoted to the enjoyment that they insist on bathing several times a day.

306. Government and Privately Owned Public Baths: Both Very Popular. — Even great nobles, however, enjoy the society and recreations afforded by the public establishments ; and there is often no better way for a rich senator to display pomp and circumstance than to enter one of the huge thermæ followed by a long train of slaves, freedmen, and clients. Men of business, and, of course, mere toilers must visit the baths when their duties give temporary leisure, but for everybody who can control his time there is one preferable period — the eighth or ninth hour, two or three P.M. It is around this time that the bath attendants heat all their huge tanks to boiling and make ready with an endless supply of anointing oils and " strigils " (metal scrapers) to care for the onrush of the multitudes.

There are about sixteen enormous public baths in Rome owned by the government, although often their care is leased to contractors. Small baths, privately owned, opened to anybody at a tolerable fee and managed solely for profit, exist in addition all over the city, and nearly nine hundred stand licensed on the City Præfect's books. Some of these privately owned baths are elegant establishments, offering great luxuries at corresponding prices.

The keepers of a bath-house (*balneatores*) rank low in social estimation, for many of their places are the scenes of gross reveling and debauchery ; but there is excellent money in the business. Their baths have names something like inns, and going about the metropolis, we have noticed the " Baths of Daphne," "The Æolian," "The Diana," "The Mercury," or they are simply called from the names of the owners, as " Faustinian Baths " or " The Crassian." On a signboard one can read that the " Thermæ of Marcus Crassus " offer both salt- and fresh-water baths.[1]

307. The Great Baths of Trajan: Baths, Club-House, and Café. — However, if one would see and meet the world, a visit to the great public baths is absolutely necessary. Some of these are located on the outskirts of the capital; for example, the magnificent Baths of Agrippa stand near the Pantheon in the Campus Martius; but only a short distance from Publius Calvus's mansion on the Esquiline rise what are, perhaps, the finest public thermæ as yet existing in Rome, those of Trajan, which were rebuilt on the site of a similar establishment earlier erected by Titus.[2]

The Baths of Trajan constitute more than a vast establishment where perhaps a thousand persons can bathe in the various tanks and pools simultaneously. They supply many of the needs which another age will meet partly by the club-house and partly by the café. They are frequented by women as well as men, although the former are expected to make their visits particularly during the morning hours and certain special rooms are set aside for their use. These rules, however, are often violated, and scenes can take place at the

---

[1] An actual inscription. From the small provincial towns we have other inscriptions, advertising bath-houses "in city style (*more urbico*) and fitted with every convenience."

[2] The great Baths of Caracalla (built *circ.* 215 A.D.) and those of Diocletian (*circ.* 300 A.D.) were not in existence, of course, in the days of Hadrian. Their ruins are at present among the most imposing in Rome, and they were probably somewhat larger than the Baths of Trajan, which are to-day nearly demolished, but their aspect and general arrangement were hardly different.

Baths of Trajan which from the standpoint of a later time are simply indescribable.

308. Heterogeneous Crowds in the Great Baths. — One of the glories of the great thermæ is their apparent democracy. Any freedman is entitled to make use of them, although there are doubtless special recreation and reposing rooms reserved for the rich elect. In theory the public baths are free, but except on gala occasions when the Emperor wishes to win popularity, there is usually a standard charge for admission of a *quadrans*, a small copper coin (about $\frac{1}{4}$ cent). This simply covers the expense of the attendants who look after one's clothes, and provides the oil for anointing — the use of the magnificent building goes for nothing.

In such a place persons of every station can be seen min-gling together, social barriers partially break down, and a delightful informality prevails. It is recorded of Hadrian that when he is in the city, he proves his " liberal " habits by frequenting the public baths and bathing in the great pools along with the meanest of his subjects. Every afternoon, therefore, the thermæ are the scenes of intensely bustling life. The noise rising from their great halls is terrific — the shouting, laughing, splashing, running, exercising, going on continuously.[1]

The Romans are preëminently a sociable people. They delight in the free and easy contacts of the baths. What place has witnessed more financial bargains struck, quarrels started or abated, lawsuits arranged, marriage treaties nego-tiated, philosophical theories spun, artistic points discussed, or even matters of imperial policy promoted than the thermæ of Trajan? At the thermæ are continued all those matters you talked over in the Forum this morning and which you

---

[1] Houses near private baths were counted undesirable for residence or investment purposes on account of the noise, which, in private baths, often kept up late into the night.

will finish on the supper couches to-night.   The place, however, to a stranger is utterly bewildering in its hugeness,
its noise and the hurrying of its crowds and its complexity,
and few scenes in Rome could be more novel to a visitor from
another civilization.

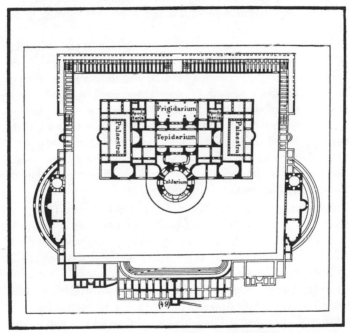

PLAN OF ROMAN PUBLIC BATHS : partly conjectural.

309. Entering the Thermæ. — We can follow Calvus as
he approaches by the great southern portal which looks down
from the slopes of the Esquiline upon the great gray cylinder
of the Flavian Amphitheater.   Before us stretches an enormous portico, fronting a high masonry wall, of course crowned
at many points with statues.   The entrance is relatively

narrow in order to control the thousands of persons streaming inside, each passing his copper to the attendants at the gate. But once past the barrier, we see before us the vista, apparently not of a bathing establishment, but of an ample, inclosed park, girded on every side with handsome porticoes, scattered with trees, bright shrubbery, and groups of sculpture, but with the domes seemingly of a magnificent palace rising from the middle of the area.

This park is teeming with life; young men in the scantiest of costume are running races on a long sandy track, others are tossing ball, others engaged in a wrestling contest, Greek fashion, before a crowd of spectators wedged upon seats along a kind of stadium. In a kind of kiosk, or small temple, in a remote corner behind the shrubbery a venerable man with the long beard of a philosopher is expounding the theory of atoms to a small but select audience. We are told that there are also *aulæ* for learned conventicles, likewise excellent libraries within the central building.

310. Interior of the Baths: the Cold Room (*Frigidarium*). — This building itself is an enormous mass of brick and concrete, formed into correspondingly enormous vaulted apartments and domes, their entire surface covered with polished marbles or at least with brilliantly colored stucco. At every point there are statues, singly and in groups, historical and mythological, in the round or in high reliefs, in stone and in bronze. Particularly to be noted is a marvelous if overrealistic Laocoön group destined to be celebrated through the coming ages.[1]

It boots little to describe all the special chambers and features of the Baths of Trajan; we can only notice those prime features common to all public thermæ even in the provincial cities. The great mass of visitors makes for the hall of the

---

[1] The famous group of Laocoön and his sons, now in the Vatican, was found in the ruins of these Baths of Titus and Trajan.

frigidarium (" cold room "), a vast unheated space, albeit comfortable enough on a warm Italian afternoon. Here they toss off their garments, to their own personal slaves if they are visitors of consequence, although there is a great force of regular attendants (*capsarii*) whose prime business it is to take charge of togas and tunics. For all their pains, thefts of clothes in the baths are very common and give rise to frequent uproars.

Once stripped, even the gravest and oldest visitors are likely to indulge in all kinds of gymnastics and horseplay. If they do not go outside to limber themselves with tossing ball at trigon (see p. 206) or with amateur races in the stadium, there are plenty of diversions in the frigidarium itself. One can behold the " Very Noble " Varus, the presiding consul, forgetful of all official dignity, competing with an imperial legatus, both with their hands tied behind them and trying by leaning backward to touch their heads against the tips of their toes ; while a prætor, an hour earlier an austere judge in the Basilica Æmilia, is leaping up and down " murdering a good song by trying to sing it." [1]

311. The Great Swimming Pool and the *Tepidarium*. — All this is usually preliminary to a splashing plunge into the clear cool *natatio*, the great swimming pool of unheated water, which is nearly 200 feet long by 100 broad, and in which scores of Rome's noblest dignitaries now are to be seen splashing, swimming, and cavorting, with perfect self-respect beside a much greater number of the plebeians. For the many who do not prefer a warm bath, this is sufficient refreshment on a summer day, and presently they will call their attendants to bring towels, strigils, and ointments and hasten home. But your true *habitué* makes almost as much of his baths as of his dinners. He delights in hot baths and all the refreshments

[1] Petronius's "Satyricon" gives a vivid and informing picture of the amusements and horseplay in the thermæ.

that go with them. "People want to be parboiled," once declared Seneca disgustedly.

A hot bath involves an elaborate process. Often one will omit the frigidarium with its cold shock, or take it later. In any case one goes on to a second enormous chamber, perhaps the finest in the whole building. A majestic dome soars over broad pavement. The pillars and the fretwork on the ceiling and vaulting groan with heavy gilding. The groups of statues flanking each of the huge marble-incrusted piers are themselves of heroic size. The light streams down over the polished marbles of the walls and pendentives, upon hundreds of persons lolling about on stone benches, conversing, or lazily meditating. A warm mist is rising; one feels as if in a plant house of tropical exotics, while the elaborate mosaic designs are pleasantly warm under one's bare feet.

Such luxury of course is enjoyed in the *tepidarium* where the bathers are gently warmed before the actual hot bath. It is an oblong hall, nearly as large as the great cold swimming tank,[1] and, as stated, the decorations are almost overpowering in their richness. Anybody will explain that the floors are composed largely of hollow tiles through which warm air of just the right temperature is being continually forced from the great system of charcoal furnaces ("hypocausts") located in the substructures of the thermæ.

312. The Hot Baths (*Caldaria*): Their Sensuous Luxury. — At intervals some person rises from the couches and hastens away to one of the smaller chambers located at the four corners of the tepidarium. These are the actual *caldaria* (hot baths), wherein a perpetual fine steam is rising. The water here is so hot that only experienced bathers can find a plunge in the large prophyry tanks enjoyable. If one can

[1] The tepidarium in the later Baths of Diocletian was about 300 feet long by 92 feet wide, but probably that in the Baths of Trajan was somewhat smaller.

endure the heat, however, soon it becomes a kind of stupid bliss to lie back motionless in the heated water, gazing upward to the vaulted ceiling which is skilfully painted in a deep blue interspersed with trees, foliage, birds, and gilt stars, as if one were dropping off to slumber in the forest some summer evening! If the acme of life is merely sensuous enjoyment, what can existence offer greatly surpassing this!

After you have lain quiescent in the caldarium until its pleasure has begun to pall, the proper thing next is to pass to the *laconicum*. Here the hypocausts have heated the floor and walls with an intense dry heat. The bathers loll again upon marble slabs, and first are dried off and then burst into a profuse perspiration. The ceremony of the bath is at last over.

Your slaves or the regular attendant now will scrape you down with the thin flexible bronze strigils, rub you thoroughly with towels, and anoint you with unguents, the more costly and highly perfumed the better. In the numerous small chambers around the great laconicum, open for special fees, there is a greater luxury still; — here such elderly magnates as Varus, or even young noblemen of the more effeminate type, will be elaborately massaged and finally rubbed down with very soft woolen blankets, by at least three expert masseurs working together. After such an experience surely body and mind ought to be prepared for the pleasures of the dinner party.

313. Restaurants, Small Shops, and Sports in or around the Baths. — Very much more might be added about the Great Baths. For those people who wish to linger until the edge of meal time, there is no need to go hungry. Close by the entrance are numerous restaurants (*popinæ*) of more than ordinary elegance. Here you can send your slave for sweet cakes, slices of toasted honey bread, sausages, eggs, and like viands; and in the great frigidarium and tepidarium the peddlers from these restaurants are always going about with trays of such food, crying their wares and making the ordinary bedlam so much the greater.   Directly in the thermæ them- selves are small shops for the sale of fine perfumes and un- guents ; and often in the corridors and antechambers you can find crowds gazing at special displays of paintings, or of new statuary — for the public baths are practically the art gal- leries of Rome.

As for the frequenters of the baths, here even more than in the fora are the trysting spots for parasites. Let an ap- proachable nobleman be seen lolling at ease in the tepidarium and he is instantly spotted by some dinner hunter.   Innu- merable are the attentions that can then be paid him.   Does he wish to play handball ? — The parasite retrieves for him. Does he lay aside a fine garment ? — At once " his remarkable taste " is praised to the skies. Does he lie perspiring in the laconicum ?   His " friend " tries to anticipate the slaves in wiping the sweat from his brow.   No act is too obsequious — all in hopes of hearing those delightful words, " Come home and dine ! "   In the halls of the women similar scenes are enacted, but we cannot pursue them.

At last the sun dials that stand in every open spot around the thermæ indicate that the afternoon is well spent.   From the laconicum the refreshed bathers return to the milder tepidarium, to recover from the shock of the intense heat and to resume their garments.   Then the crowds all hasten out again.   Some of the privately owned bathing-places may remain open all night, but the great thermæ, lately the scene of such boisterous life, stand vast, dark, and empty.

314. The Great Porticoes along the Campus Martius. The Park System towards the Tiber. — The public baths are not the only places for daily enjoyment which a solicitous government has provided for the quirites. The fora are limited and the city proper is very closely built, but around its outskirts and especially to the north and west there is a genuinely magnificent park system. The beginnings of this are reached after you go through the Forum of Trajan and follow along " Broadway." Here are the great porticoes and promenades of the Sæpta Julia. The famous stores (see p. 228) are mostly on the east side of the avenue verging off towards the slopes of the Quirinal, but the west side, going clear across the broad Campus Martius to the Tiber, is more strictly public property.

This wide level area formed by the great bend in the river has long since ceased to be a mere parade ground for the army. There are broad masses of greenery, grateful shade trees, spreading over neatly graveled walks, as well as literally miles of lofty porticoes stretching in every direction and giving comfortable places for strolling in bad weather. The greatest of these porticoes is, of course, the long Sæpta Julia, but there is a succession of others, so that you can almost wander from the Column of Trajan across the Campus clear to the Ælian Bridge completely defiant of any rain.

In the open pleasure grounds there are always people exercising without the restraints inevitable at the thermæ, playing ball, wrestling, exhibiting horses and chariots, as well as very many children chasing about with hoops. If legionaries are passing through the city, their leathern tents probably stand here, and here, too, can be held all the vast open-air pageants which cannot accommodate themselves inside any building.

315. Public Buildings upon the Campus Martius. — Out of the lofty trees, however, there rise still loftier structures. Two of the great public thermæ, those of Nero and Agrippa, are here upon the Campus Martius. In this region, also, are three of the principal theaters, that of Pompeius, accommodating some 25,000 people, and two others (Theaters of Marcellus and Balbus) only slightly smaller. Here is the Flaminian Circus and the Amphitheater of Taurus for those horse races and gladiator fights which do not demand the huge Circus Maximus or Flavian. Here again is the golden-roofed Pantheon and a great number of other temples to such ill-assorted gods as the Egyptian Serapis and Isis, Neptune, Minerva of the Campus, and the old Latin goddess Juturna. Notable, too, are the triumphal arches raised across several of the broad avenues.

You can in fact wander on across this region from one marvelous structure to another until the eye and brain become weary trying to enumerate, much more to comprehend the succession of buildings every one of which is a triumph of marble and of sculpture. Pressing on to the marge of the Tiber itself, the river above the commercial bridges is seen covered with gay pleasure skiffs plying about under bright flags. The shores are lined with handsome little houses, usually decorated in the doors with potted shrubs or boughs of foliage. Innocent they look in the day time but at night when their windows blaze with lamps they will be veritable traps of iniquity for the enjoyment and then the ruin of the unwary.

316. The Tombs of Hadrian and Augustus. — Across the river near its main bend, can be noticed the green slopes of the hill of the Vatican uncrowned as yet by any temple of fame, but with the suburban Circus of Nero stretching along its slopes. Directly across the current, also, is rising the enormous circular mass of the Mausoleum of Hadrian, with the derricks and staging still above it swinging to place the last of that galaxy of statues which will look down upon the Tiber.[1]

We do not cross over to the new structure, but proceeding along the bank to the point where the Via Flaminia

---

[1] The Tomb of Hadrian was not actually completed until 139 A.D. — after his death.

CASTLE OF ST. ANGELO: Tomb of Hadrian in its present state.

continuing " Broadway " bears down beside the river, we
see before us the older but very majestic Mausoleum of
Augustus.   It lifts itself fully 220 feet in the air, its base
composed of a vast cylinder coated with sculptured marbles,
above which there is heaped a conical mound of earth, planted
with evergreen trees, while on the summit stands a colossal

TOMB OF HADRIAN.   *Restored after Von Falke.*

statue of its mighty builder himself.   Within repose the urns
not merely of Augustus, but of nearly all the worthier members of the imperial families.

These are only some of the features of the Campus Martius
which foreign visitors such as Strabo acclaim as the most
remarkable section of Rome, if not the one most charged with
her past history.   Time fails to visit the other great public
pleasure-grounds upon the slopes of the Pincian — the
" Gardens of Lucullus " and the " Gardens of Sallust," or
that other wide park northeast of the Esquiline, the " Gar-

dens of Mæcenas," presenting yet other vistas of shrubbery, groves, promenades, and green lawns, interspersed with pleasure pavilions. It behooves us now to return to Rome and to visit some of the most important centers of its life — the theater, the amphitheater, and the circus.

CHAPTER XIX

THE PUBLIC GAMES: THE THEATER, THE CIRCUS, AND THE AMPHITHEATER

317. Roman Festivals: Their Great Number. — One thing only, besides a long session of the Senate, ordinarily will keep men of the class of Publius Calvus away from the great thermæ — the celebration of one of the greater Public Games.

The *Ludi Publici*, around which so large a part of Roman life revolves, like the Pan-Hellenic games and similar Greek festivals, always have religious origin; they are in honor of some god or group of deities. But the secular has long intruded into their routine. Nobody worries greatly about the fact that the *Ludi Apollinares* are for the glory of Apollo, save perhaps as one adds an extra fervent invocation of the Delphian god during the placing of wagers. The time consumed by the Public Games represents a period of recreation and festival, which other ages will find in Sundays and Saints' Days.

Altogether there are some 76 days per year normally set aside for these great *Ludi Sollemnes*, including such prolonged periods as those of the *Ludi Romani* or *Magni* which extend from September 4th to 18th, on a stretch, with several others for six days and more. When to these periods are added various extra or very special holidays, during which the ordinary life of the city is broken up, the courts are closed, and only the most necessary labors of commerce and industry are conducted, it is plain that the plebeians and even the slaves get pretty ample respite in their year of toil. Without attempting a close study of the official lists of holidays it is safe to say that the average Roman gains many more periods of lawful vacation than the laboring classes can enjoy in other ages, — another factor which tends to make the metropolis abound with idlers and parasites.

318. Passion for Public Spectacles: Mania for Gambling. — Besides the great public theaters, amphitheaters, and race courses (circuses) there are many smaller private establishments. Good money can be made from gladiator fights and chariot races, and they are often given by speculators, although more frequently in a provincial town than in Rome.

The passion for such spectacles and contests is incredible; — no " baseball " or " football " of another era can so monopolize the popular mind. The wagering on all kinds of contests is incessant in every insula, shop, or mansion, and, of course, ordinarily it is entirely lawful. Only the few select spirits cry out vainly against the passion, although Juvenal's famous protest will echo across the centuries, " The Roman people who once gave commands, consulships, legions, and all else now yearn simply for two things — *free bread and the Public Games!"*

The government doubtless encourages this tendency. If the multitude is engrossed with the merits of two charioteers, so much less is the scrutiny upon strange doings at the Palatine; yet even excellent emperors give very elaborate spectacles as a kind of lawful tribute to the multitudes of that city which affords them their right to the purple. After the conquest of Dacia, Trajan celebrated his victory by giving contests which lasted 123 days, during which 10,000 wild and domestic animals were said to have been killed and 10,000 gladiators fought, although probably most of the latter were allowed to survive. So incessant in fact are the contests of some variety, that rare is the day when a thunderous roar

does not reverberate over the city telling that the " Blue "
or " Green " jockeys have won, or a favorite gladiator has
plunged home his trident.

319. Expenses of Public Spectacles to Great Officials. —
Naturally the cost of these contests is enormous.   The presidency and supervision of them is distributed around among

AT THE THEATER ENTRANCE.   *After Von Falke.*

the magistrates, with the chief glories and burdens falling
usually upon the consuls and prætors.[1]   The State gives
each official a respectable sum to pay for the spectacles, but
this falls far short of the actual cost.   The glory of presiding
in the central box at the Flavian Amphitheater or Circus
Maximus is so great that a magistrate is bound to sacrifice a

---

[1] Under the Republic the ædiles had to preside over very expensive
games.   Augustus, however, turned the *Cura Ludorum* ("supervision of
the games") over to the prætors, and the ædiles only gave spectacles
voluntarily.

good share of his entire patrimony in order to make a fine display, to win the " Ave ! " of the populace, and to hold up his head among his noble rivals. When Hadrian was prætor, his kinsman, Trajan the Emperor, gave him personally 4,000,000 sesterces ($160,000) towards the cost of those games which the prætorship demanded.

Our Publius Calvus, with no imperial connection, deliberately saved and economized for years prior to his elevation to the prætorship, and during his term of office he spent almost as much energy in corresponding with a friend who was legatus of Numidia to get African leopards, and negotiating with certain racing interests to secure a very desirable jockey, as he did in settling a certain great lawsuit before his tribunal. One good set of chariot races can cost 400,000 sesterces ($16,000), and some of Calvus's richer colleagues have found the prætors' games coming to a dozen times as much. He congratulated himself, therefore, on getting out of office for about half their outlay; as it was he had to live very sparingly for the next two years, and sell off a villa.[1]

320. Indescribable Popularity of the Games. — Everybody in Rome attends the games. Once slaves were forbidden to be present, but that law had broken down several generations ago. Few are the masters that risk the unpopularity of refusing to let their familia frequent at least the more famous contests. The waiting litter bearers, the idling footboys, all the parasitical menials about the great mansions discuss every coming event most frantically and wager all the coppers which their masters give them upon the outcome, and their zeal is matched by the ragged plebeians who infest the fetid insulæ, or sleep under the porticoes.

Seemingly half of Rome exists only from one chariot or gladiator exhibition to another. Every contest is a display

---

[1] In the later Empire we hear of the case of Symmachus, an office-holder whose games cost him 2000 pounds of gold, about $400,000.

of social importance. The front seats are assigned to the magistrates, who occupy curule chairs in the order of their rank; there are other seats of honor for the senators, others directly behind them for the equites. If the Emperor is present, he sits in a special box (*cubiculum*), which Trajan with democratic condescension caused to be thrown wide open that all the spectators might see him.

These seats of honor are free, but the great multitude of well-to-do spectators are expected to purchase tickets for all the better ranges behind the tiers of the equites.[1] The prices ordinarily are low, but concerning these tickets there is a complaint not unknown in another age: that the box-officers (*locarii*) in charge buy up many reserved seats for the more popular games, then sell them over again at an outrageous advance. However, behind these reserved seats there are still a certain number of others thrown open free to the first comers, and behind these is a wide space where plebeians and slaves can stand as a gesticulating, shouting, steaming mass, gazing down on the spectacles below.

321. The Theater Less Popular than the Circus or Amphitheater. — The public exhibitions are three general kinds, — the theatrical performances, the circus races, and the gladiatorial combats.

For the great masses, the theater can never have the same vulgar appeal possessed by its two rivals; on the other hand some men of intelligence and rank do not hesitate to dismiss the latter as " for the mob " and affect a great contempt for charioteers and " Thracians." Even the most sophisticated Romans, however, never are true Athenians. Tragedies dealing with profound human problems, such as won trophies for Æschylus and Sophocles, would fall absolutely

---

[1] Italian audiences stowed very close. According to the marking upon the stone seats in the theater at Pompeii, only 16 inches were allowed for each spectator.

flat beside the Tiber.[1] There is even a growing distaste for
the better kind of comedies. What delights the Roman
audience in the theater most is some kind of elaborate horseplay.

The stage as a rule is long and narrow, some 120 by 24 feet,
and is raised only about three feet above the orchestra where

THEATER AT POMPEII.

a chorus can dance and parade.[2] The rear of the stage has a
fixed background painted to represent the front of a palace;
it is pierced by three doors, and is adorned with columns and
niches for the inevitable statues of the Muses, of Apollo, and
of like deities. A large curtain, not dropped from above

---

[1] High-flying tragedies were indeed ground out by Seneca and by many
inferior literary dabblers, but these "dramas" were hardly intended to
be genuine acting plays, but only to be read aloud.

[2] The ancient orchestra was of course for the dances of the chorus
never for seating the spectators.

but rolled up from the bottom, can uncover the most amazing spectacles upon this stage. Long ago Horace complained of how a Roman audience would depart discontented if the play did not require in its middle " either a bear or a boxing match." For four hours and more the curtain is " kept down " while " squadrons of horse and bodies of foot are seen flying, while luckless kings with hands tied behind their backs and chariots of all kinds and even ships go hurrying along, and while spoils of ivory and Corinthian brass are borne by in state."

There are, however, two kinds of performances more certain to crowd the theater than these very cheap spectacular plays — they are the mimes and pantomimes.

322. The Mimes: Character Plays. — The mimes are a native Latin product, although they have a certain kinship with the Greek " New Comedy." They are character plays of everyday life without the actors' masks and buskins; and they are always coarse, vulgar, and in the nature of roaring farces. The language is often exceedingly gross and the situations frequently match the language. The actors wear a kind of harlequin costume, extremely grotesque, and along with the chief *mimus*, who takes the leading part, there is usually a second actor who draws thunderous applause from the upper benches. He is the *strepidus* or *parasitus*, a kind of pantaloon, a clown with puffed cheeks and shaven head, who has to stand a great amount of boisterous slapping from the chief actor.

Other parts can be taken by women, who are forbidden to appear on the stage in " legitimate " tragedy and comedy. Often the dances and postures of these actresses are indescribably vulgar, and their reputation for easy conduct is too well established. For all that, their presence brings unsteady youths to the theaters like flies, and affairs with actresses are quite normal things with a type of young bloods. Once

Cicero was defending a free and easy client, a certain Plancus. "He's accused of having run off with an actress?" declared the advocate. "Why *that's* just an amusement excellently sanctioned by custom!"

The stories portrayed by the mimes correspond with their general character:—a robber chief befooling the clumsy constables sent to take him, a lover surprised by the return of a jealous husband and forced to hide in a large box, a beggar who suddenly stumbles into a fortune, a descent into the world of ghosts, episodes revolving around the introduction of a very clever trained dog, etc. Some of the acting is of high order, but there are few mimes which do not abound in lines and situations extremely gross,—for all that the open-air theaters are packed from morn until sunset.

323. The Pantomimes: Their Real Art.—All considered, the pantomimes represent a higher degree of art. Here we have only one actor, who, with the aid of a chorus and a great orchestra of lutes and lyres, undertakes to tell a whole story merely by his dancing and rhythmic motions. A really great *pantomimus* wins and deserves the favor of highly cultivated aristocrats. Pylades and Bathyllus in Augustus's day had the fashionable world practically at their feet, and Paris was one of the prime intimates of Nero.

The greater the skill the fewer the words that need to be spoken; the chanting of the chorus while the pantomimus is changing his costumes giving hint enough of the characters he is portraying. The music, florid and descriptive, keeps the audience in mood for the dancing. All sorts of subjects can thus be portrayed, including those of old Greek tragedies, the actor slipping from one character to another with consummate art:—now he is Agamemnon, now Clytemnestra, now Orestes. He can take male or female parts alternately, delineate the deepest passions, and tell a whole story with what his admirers call his " speaking hands," and his " eloquence of dancing."

To see a great pantomimus, clad perhaps in fleshings of soft light red Canunian wool, setting off perfectly his graceful figure, dance through the story of how Achilles disguised as a maiden was discovered by Ulysses and summoned away to the Trojan War, is a joy to the most sophisticated and intellectual. The dancer can take many parts — the fair youth concealed in the palace of Lycomedes, the embassy of Ulysses and Diomedes, the young warrior betraying himself by his interest in the helmet and cuirass concealed in the mass of gifts intended for women; — the whole impersonation in short may be wonderful.

Not all the dances, however, are so innocent. Many of the coarsest stories in Græco-Roman mythology are acted out on the stage, and the grosser they are often the louder the applause of the groundlings. Nevertheless, the leading pantomimi rightly have the entrée to lordly houses, enjoy great incomes, and are among the most admired personages in Rome. They are outdistanced, however, by two sets of more vulgar rivals — the charioteers and the gladiators.

324. Extreme Popularity of the Circus. — When a series of superior contests is announced for the Circus all Rome seems to become racing mad. Words fail to describe the excitement, the tense discussion of the charioteers and their fours, the wave of betting from the inner Palatine to the most sordid insula, and then the exuberant joy or immoderate grief over the results.

Superior folk try in vain to appear disdainful of these contests. Thus Pliny the Younger has recorded his deep disgust that " so many thousands of men should be eager, like a pack of children, to see horses running time after time with the charioteers bending over their cars." " The multitude," he asserted, " were not interested in the speed of the teams or the skill of the drivers, but solely in the ' *racing colors.* ' " " If in the middle of the race (he added) the colors were changed, the enthusiasm of the spectators would change with them, and they would suddenly desert the drivers and horses whom they now recognized afar and whose names they shouted aloud. Such is the influence and authority vested in one cheap tunic ! "

325. Popular Charioteers (*Aurigæ*): the Great Racing Factions. — It is all very well to write this, but neither Pliny nor anybody else can prevent the greatest charioteers from enjoying temporary incomes surpassing those of a majority of the senators. Many of these lucky *aurigæ* are Moors, dark-skinned, hawk-eyed rascals, with sharp white teeth and sinews of iron; but a considerable sprinkling of them are Spaniards, as was that Diocles, whose heirs proudly recorded on his tombstone that in a professional career of twenty-four years he drove in 4257 races, and conquered 1462 times, with total winnings of nearly 36 million sesterces (say $1,440,000). He, however, was not the most fortunate — there are drivers on record who boast of at least 3500 victories, though, of course, many of these were probably won in the provinces.

No sport will ever be more thoroughly standardized and professionalized than that of the chariot races in Rome. When a magistrate or other seeker for applause decides to give a series of contests he appeals to the great circus syndicates (" factions "). There were originally only the Red and the White; then the Blue and the Green have been added, and finally the Purple and the Gold. Each faction maintains huge racing stables with expert drivers, grooms, trainers, and veterinaries, as well as many superb " fours " of horses.

The donor of the games has to arrange with these organizations how many contests he will require, each " faction " entering a chariot in each race. Ten races a day is the minimum; twenty-four the ordinary maximum. After the contracts have been signed and the programs posted all over the city, anxious days follow for all concerned to insure an honest race. The wagering is always so general and so reckless, that infinite precautions are needful to keep the horses from being drugged, the drivers from being bribed to throw the contests, or (if they prove incorruptible) the charioteers from being poisoned enough to make them lose. The tricks of the race-track will simply endure across the ages.

326. The Circus Maximus. — After such preparations and excitement no wonder that people complain that the Circus Maximus is sometimes too small. This long narrow depression between the Palatine and Aventine has provided an excellent natural race course since the days of the Tarquins. At first the slopes of the hills were simply lined with crude wooden benches. By Julius Cæsar's time many of these benches were made of stone, and in all could seat at least 150,000 spectators. After a great fire in 36 A.D. Claudius presently rebuilt the whole structure so there are now seats, partly of marble and partly of wood; and Trajan added still more tiers and more marble ornaments. At present the Circus Maximus covers the enormous area of 600 by 2000 feet, and it is declared that there is at least standing room, if not seats, for 385,000 spectators — a good fraction of the entire adult population of Rome.[1]

327. The Race-Track: Procession before the Races. — Inasmuch as horse races are not peculiar to the Imperial Age let a brief description of the Great Circus and its contests suffice. The long reaches of seats are, of course, portioned off to give the senators and equites the coigns of vantage. There is a lofty imperial box (*pulvinar*) on the northern side

---

[1] This figure seems decidedly too high; but the present ruinous state of the Circus Maximus makes it very difficult to determine the number more exactly.

leading directly down from the Palatine. Here the Emperor
and his suite can refresh themselves, and from a wide terrace
command a marvelous view over the long area of the immense
hippodrome.

Down the center of this area runs its central " backbone "
(*spina*), forming a long low wall separating the outward and
inward tracks, adorned with an unusually elaborate set of
statues, columns upholding trophies, and even with one or

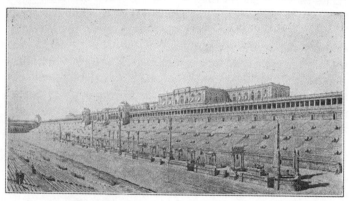

CIRCUS MAXIMUS. *Restoration by Spandoni.*

two tapering obelisks imported from Egypt. In a kind of
open pavilion at either end of the spina can be seen seven
huge marble eggs and as many marble dolphins. One of
each of these will be removed as each lap is finished, there
being seven laps normally in every race.

The great yellow race-track on gala occasions can be
sprinkled with some powerful perfumes, and with glittering
particles of mica or with red lead. When at last the multitudes have gathered, the contestants enter in solemn procession by the Triumphal Gate at the extreme eastern end of the
Circus, and ahead of the array of chariots first of all there
goes the magistrate giving the games, himself in a magnificent

car and surrounded by a brilliant hedge of attendants on horse and foot. Very likely he is then followed by certain priestly colleges in pontifical vestments, by statues of deities piously borne on gilded litters, by bands of trumpeters and harpists raising their clangor, and then last, but not least, come the racing cars themselves.

328. Beginning a Race in the Circus. — The master of the games takes his seat in the *podium,* the center of the reserved benches near the end of the track. The chariots disappear in the great line of *carceres,* "prison houses," the carefully closed stalls at the western end of the Circus. After due waiting, fidgeting, chattering, wagering along the mountainous slopes of the benches, all the trumpets blow together. Silence for an instant grips the tens of thousands, while the president rises in his lodge and waves out a broad *mappa,* a white cloth visible far up and down the entire circus.

Instantly the doors of the carceres fly open; the six chariots[1] dash forth at full bound. The aurigæ, in tight-fitting tunics of the colors of their factions, stand erect in the light cars, the reins looped around their waists, snapping the loose ends over the flying horses. Instantly they have dashed to the three tall pillars of the nearer goal (*meta*), and only by miraculous chance is a disastrous collision avoided at the outset. Then the whole circus rises and shouts together. The familiar figure of Scorpus the Moor, a brown giant in the tunic of the Greens, shoots ahead. His magnificent *quadriga* of bays have taken the wall at one leap. The flying dust cloud, as the other five cars dash after him, almost dims the sight of the race. The noise from the benches is deafening. The backers of the trailing cars are in an agony.

329. Perils of the Races; Proclaiming the Victors. — Scorpus's chariot whirls around the lower goal like lightning

---

[1] As many as ten cars could contend at once in the greatest games.

and comes tearing back on the opposite track, while each one of the balls and dolphins is removed to indicate the progress of the race. The other cars press hard; and as the teams gather speed it is a marvel how the drivers keep their stand with the cars leaping hither and thither under them, their wheels barely touching the flying track.[1]

Five times around they go, with Scorpus gallantly maintaining his lead. Then at the sixth turn the " Gold " driver reins too sharply. His chariot crashes over in a complete somersault, but, by a desperate maneuver just as he is thrown, he whips out the knife held ready in his belt and cuts the reins about his waist. By a miracle he is flung out sprawling upon the yielding sands, yet escapes death under the car racing just behind. The spectators, therefore, escape the brutal and familiar sight of an auriga trampled or crushed to death by the rushing chariots and horses. Meantime Scorpus losing not an instant has hurried again past the upper goal; a frantic attempt by Cresconius, the " Red " driver just behind, fails to head his steeds, and amid a deafening tumult he sweeps past the president of the games to victory.

The official *jubilatores* immediately stride out into the track crying with loud voice the name of the winner, and the news is soon flying all over the city. Nay, some of the outlying towns are speedily informed of the general results, for a certain sports-loving senator has come with a cage of homing pigeons, each colored to match one of the factions. The instant Scorpus is acclaimed, green pigeons are released to tell all the gamblers in Ostia and Præneste that the " Green " cars have won the first round.

---

[1] The description of the Roman-style chariot race in Lew Wallace's famous novel " Ben Hur " is technically as well as rhetorically admirable and accurate. However, no high-rank Roman, such as Messala is represented to have been, would have driven a quadriga in the public circus. The drivers were nearly always low-born men of provincial if not of servile origin.

RACE IN THE CIRCUS MAXIMUS.

After the noise has subsided, the trumpets blow again, another set of chariots is ready and the whole excitement is repeated. So the contests keep up through the day. If there is a long interval between the races, rope-dancers, acrobats, and trick-riders are ready to amuse the populace. Probably at the end there will be the crowning and decisive race between the winners of the preceding contests. If Scorpus can triumph in this also, he will carouse with his companions, doubtless more praised and fêted for one glad night than even the Emperor.

330. Gladiatorial Contests Even More Popular than the Circus. — Yet Scorpus with all his adulation and ephemeral wealth turns green with jealousy toward a rival for fame — the victorious gladiator in the last combats in the Flavian. The sports of the arena perhaps excite greater favor with the mob, betting more reckless, passions more frantic than do even the contests of the Circus.

The gladiatorial games are peculiar to Roman civilization; nothing exactly like them will follow in later ages.[1] They illustrate completely the pitiless spirit and carelessness of human life lurking behind the pomp, glitter, and cultural pretensions of the great imperial age. True it is that persons of intellectual tastes sometimes affect greater contempt for these contests than they do for the Circus. " No doubt the gladiators," such men as Seneca write to one another, " are criminals deserving their fate, but what have *you* done to deserve being compelled to witness their last agonies ? " No matter ; nothing will gain " popularity " for a ruler or for a magnate sooner than announcing a fight in the arena.

The very best Emperors arrange elaborate series of combats — perhaps with a sigh in their hearts, as colossal and bloody bribes which must be thrown constantly to the mob ; and

---

[1] The Spanish bull fights at their very worst were a relatively harmless imitation.

Imperator, great officials, senators, priests, nay, the Vestal Virgins themselves, will all be on hand in the reserved front benches. There is even given out a philosophical justification for the butcheries, namely, that the spectators become hardened to the sight of death and are, therefore, the more courageous when their own hour comes. The reigning Hadrian considers the arena combats to be useful also for keeping up the military spirit; in short the whole Latin half of the Empire delights in them, although they never have become very popular in the Greek portion.[1]

331. Gladiator Fights at Funerals. — Gladiatorial fights claim an Etruscan origin, and in Rome they were first exhibited at funerals of the great, possibly with the idea that the spirits of the slain would serve the dead lord in the underworld. It is still very fashionable to give a sizable gladiator fight as the aftermath of any pretentious funeral, but this is perhaps more common in the provincial towns than in Rome, where the government likes to control such martial spectacles.

We actually hear of the populace of one small city that would not let the funeral procession of a distinguished lady proceed through the gates until her husband had promised them some public combats. Pliny the Younger's friend Maximus presented a gladiator fight to the citizens of Verona " in honor of his most estimable wife," a native of the place, but the exhibition was not quite a success because " on account of bad weather the numerous African panthers he had bought failed to arrive on the expected day."

332. Gladiator " Schools " (*Ludi*): Inmates Usually Criminals. — There are four great imperial " schools " (*ludi*) of gladiators in Rome maintained as public institutions. These

---

[1] The gladiatorial games were never introduced in Athens. Once when, in the local council, it was proposed to imitate Rome and build an amphitheater, a prominent philosopher quashed the whole project by moving "first to abolish the altar of Pity."

can be drawn upon for the regular public games; but there are plenty of private " schools " maintained by speculators who can often supply quite as good fighters.

If, as a magistrate, or as a bereaved kinsman or widower, you decide to give some combats, and if your purse is full, the rest is easy. You merely contract with the *lanista* (keeper and trainer of a school) for so many contests upon specified terms; although, in really pretentious affairs, gladiators from several rival schools can be pitted together — this adds to the excitement. When the fight is over the free gladiators are paid off, the slave fighters are returned to their owners and indemnification is given the owners of the slain — all on set business terms. There is great expense in training good gladiators and slain champions cannot fight again; and this solid fact often prevents combats from being *too* destructive, while wounded survivors may be carefully nursed just as a sick race horse may be cared for.

Anybody will tell us that no pity need be wasted on gladiators. Many a low-born criminal is dragged from the præfect's court with a relieved grin on his felonious countenance; the magistrate has not ordered " To the cross with him ! " but merely " Train him for the amphitheater." Many an incorrigible slave has been sold to a lanista by his master instead of being promptly whipped to death.

Not a few unfortunate prisoners of war and kidnapped persons, however, if they have stout physiques, find their way also to the lanistæ instead of to the ordinary slave markets, and brutal masters will sometimes sell perfectly innocent slaves if the latter appear likely to make good swordsmen. On the other hand many plebeians of the baser sort are caught by the glitter and glory of the arena, and submit voluntarily to the discipline of the " schools," while under the tyrannous emperors even men claiming noble rank have fought upon the sands to truckle to the whims of an evil Cæsar.

333. Severe Training of Gladiators; Their Ephemeral Glory. — The lanistæ's discipline is terribly severe, as is perhaps needful considering the wretches placed under it. The gladiators are kept in prison-like barracks. Nothing is omitted to brutalize them and to make their whole life center around mere skill with their weapons. They are fed upon great quantities of meat. Cruel floggings follow the least breach of discipline, and in every *ludus* is a lock-up, with a long line of stocks and shackles, which never wants its many occupants.

On the other hand many a stupid wretch is made to forget the doom probably awaiting him in the next combats, by dreaming of the glories promised a truly successful gladiator. If he can emerge victorious from a series of combats, he is more talked of than even the most daring charioteer; great nobles will visit his quarters to watch his training and feel of his muscles; his owners will do everything to pamper such a valuable piece of property; innumerable women, even among the silken-robed *clarissimæ*, will dote upon him; and perhaps he can actually elope with a senator's wife.

Not merely the youths but all the girls in Rome will sing the champion's praises and dream of his valor. He will be named in countless wall-scribblings as " The Maiden's Sigh," " The Glory of the Girls," " The Lord of the Lasses," or " The Doctor (*medicus*) of the Little Darlings."[1] If he has lost an ear, if his face is one mass of disfiguring scars, the women run after him all the more. " Never mind *that*," scolds Juvenal, " he is a gladiator."

The end of this glory ordinarily comes speedily and tragically, but sometimes the very fortunate and skilful fighter will win such favor that, at the popular demand, the giver of the games will present him with a wooden sword — the token

---

[1] Actual epithets bestowed on gladiators in the Pompeiian wall inscriptions.

of honorable discharge. If he is not a slave-criminal, he can now quit the *ludus* with plenty of money and a merry life before him, but the taint of his " profession " will always stick to him. He can never become a Roman citizen, much less can he be enrolled as an eques whatever the extent of his wealth.

334. Normal Arrangements for an Arena Contest. — Strictly speaking the amphitheater is used for two kinds of entertainments — wild beast hunts (*venationes*) and direct combats between men. Each form is extremely popular, although human gore appears a little cheap and ordinary compared with that of an expensive tiger, panther, or lion. It always makes a hit with the crowd to turn, for example, a tigress and a fierce bull-elephant loose on the sands and watch the two brutes rend one another.

It is true nevertheless that nothing can really take the place of a sustained combat between two thoroughly trained pupils of the " schools." Ordinarily the management will have the hunts in the morning at the amphitheater and the human contests in the afternoon. That will send the myriads away happily satiated after a day spent amid the perpetual sniff of gore.

No scene visited in our prolonged " day " in Rome can be more repellent to non-Roman tastes than that of the amphitheater, but to complete the picture it must not be omitted, although horrid deeds will be dismissed with few words and still less of moralizing. Publius Calvus's friend, Decimus Cluentius, this year is Prætor. He is a wealthy senator and has been saving money carefully for " his games." He has already made a good public impression by his program of races in the Circus; now he will " add to the luster of his fame " by a day of contests in the Flavian. Already the notice writers have distributed the list of the gladiators that he has engaged, in every eating-house and wine-room in the city.

The impression thus made has been excellent : " Cluentius is living up to his riches. Many of his gladiators are freemen — the finest blades, no running away, the kind of fellows that will stand right up and be butchered in mid-arena. Besides, he's been lucky enough to get from the præfect a farm steward who was caught insulting his master's wife — a good dinner for the lions. These fights won't be as when that miserly Norbanus exhibited — his gladiators were such a cowardly, feeble lot they'd have fallen flat if you breathed on 'em." [1]

335. The Flavian Amphitheater (Later " Colosseum "). — Such an exhibition can only be held in the Flavian Amphitheater, the vast structure known to later ages as the " Colosseum." In Republican days gladiator fights were held in the open Forum or in the Circus, but these were ill-adapted for the purpose. To see the fine points of the combats the audience must be concentrated around the contestants as closely as possible ; hence the " amphitheater " — an immense oval of seats looking down upon a central arena.

The building of such a quantity of seats out of permanent materials is very expensive and wooden structures were largely used until about 70 A.D., when Vespasian and Titus began their vast " Flavian " (dedicated in 80 A.D. by an enormous beast hunt), now among the chief wonders of Rome. Common report has it that thousands of Titus's Jewish captives had to toil first on the masonry and then for the most part to lose their lives fighting one another in the opening games.

To avoid prolixity any description of this vast structure must be very brief : it stands an oval cylinder, its outer major diameter 620 feet ; and the greatest diameter of its inner arena 287. Its innumerable blocks of travertin are bound together by metal clamps ; the exterior is faced with

---

[1] Taken from the "Gladiator Gossip" at Trimalchio's Dinner in Petronius's "Satyricon."

marble and adorned with hundreds more of those statues
which populate Rome.   The structure rises 157 feet in four
stories.   The lower three of these tiers are composed each of
a series of eighty arches backed by piers.   In the first story
the flanking columns are Doric, the second Ionic, the third
Corinthian.   The fourth story has no arches but merely

FLAVIAN AMPHITHEATER (COLOSSEUM): exterior, present state.

windows and pilasters of the " composite " order.   Between
these upper pilasters project stone brackets which hold
lofty wooden masts for the great awnings that stretch over the
arena.   These masts and awnings (red, blue, and yellow)
when spread out under a brilliant sky, make the Flavian look
somewhat like an enormous galley under a cloud of sail —
the effect, of course, being heightened by the sheen of the
marbles of the exterior and the garish paint and gilding covering the statues.

336. Exterior and Ticket Entrances to the Flavian Amphitheater. — Outside of the Amphitheater is a wide circular area whereon converge many thoroughfares.   This open space is scattered with huckster's booths and with small ticket stands much like those around many amusement places in another age.[1]   Here one can place wagers, purchase programs for the day, obtain food to consume between the events, and very probably buy or hire cushions in case the stone benches prove too hard.

Also on the outside and close to the foot of the main structure runs a high wooden palisade.   This is to aid in controlling the crowds.   You go in at one or two entrances, showing your tickets, then circle the masonry until you reach one of the staircases, located under every fourth arch, and next you can promptly mount to your reserved seat in one of the seventy-six sub-sections (*cunei*).

337. Interior Arrangements of the Flavian. — Once inside, the admirable arrangements of the structure impress the visitor no less than its enormous mass.   Everything converges upon the central arena; even from the topmost seats one can see all the details of the contests below.   The seats are divided into three great terraces, so easily accessible by the stairways and corridors that the fifty thousand spectators can pass in and out with the minimum of confusion. The lowest tiers, made of marble and comfortably cushioned, are reserved here as elsewhere for the senators; and for the *editor* (the giver of the contests), his fellow magistrates, the chief priests, and the Vestal Virgins, there are seats of peculiar honor directly upon the *podium*, the crest of the twelve-foot wall girding the arena; — seats which are protected alike from chance missiles and from the leap of desperate beasts by a heavy trellis-work of gilded metal.

---

[1] As we know from paintings showing the surroundings of the Amphitheater at Pompeii.

Above this podium like the billows of a frozen ocean rise the enormous tiers of masonry seats; first those for the equites, then the great mass for the paying spectators, then the space crowded with wooden benches for the slaves and least select plebeians. An open gallery runs around the entire summit of the benches and here alone, by a restriction doubtless often lamented, women are allowed to watch the contests from afar, unless they are Vestal Virgins or ladies of the Imperial family, with the special privilege of the podium.

All the arches, stairways, sections, and tiers are numbered. If you have a ticket, it may read "VIth section (*cuneus*), lowest row, seat No. 18," marked upon a round or flat piece of bone. The attendants are lynx-eyed for impostors, but legitimate visitors are quickly seated. A detachment of sailors from the fleet of Misenum shifts the enormous awnings so that the thousands [1] can sit comfortably in the shade while a full blaze of sunlight falls on the arena.

By the middle of the morning the multitudes are in place; Cluentius the Prætor, with full official magnificence, is in the central box of the podium; and strong detachments of Prætorians have been quietly distributed in certain half-concealed guard inclosures near the lower railing — for gladiators *have* been known to mutiny and desperate lions can leap very high.

338. Procession of Gladiators. — Presently now trumpets and cymbals announce the procession which files through one of the four gates leading directly into the arena. The gladiators, some forty in number, march two and two, nearly naked save for their glistening armor; knitted foreheads, white teeth, wolfish scowls, magnificent physiques are displayed by all of them. From far up the applauding benches they can

---

[1] Ordinarily it is stated that there was room for about 87,000 persons in the Flavian Amphitheater. There were seats, however, for only some 50,000, although possibly 20,000 more could find standing room in the great upper sections.

be recognized, and many favorite *retiarii* and *Thraces* are met with a storm of cheering.

The company marches solemnly down the arena led by an enormous lanista, one of their trainers, the scarred hero of all the youth of Rome. Before Cluentius on the podium they halt and flourish their weapons defiantly. Everybody knows that they have just taken their fearful oath " to be bound, to be burned, to be scourged, to be slain, and to endure all else required of them as proper gladiators, giving up alike their souls and their bodies." [1]

339. Throwing a Criminal to the Beasts. The Animal Hunt. — However, the contests do not begin immediately; there is a preliminary spectacle in store. The Prætor's friend, the City Præfect, most luckily has handed over to him a vicious freedman caught maltreating his patron's lady. The wretch, of course, deserves death : — how proper, therefore, that he can be made to amuse more honest folk by his very exit ! Into the middle of the arena they lead him, a pitiful gibbering object, half-dead already with fright. The guards strike off his fetters, thrust a cheap sword into his hands, and themselves hastily retire into one of the numerous caged chambers lining the arena. A tense stillness for an instant holds the Flavian.

Suddenly the rattle of chains is heard. In the very center of the sands (part of which are over wooden substructures) the arena opens ; a cage appears lifted by pulleys, and then is opened by some mechanism. Forth bounds a tawny lion, lashing his tail and growling with hunger and rage. The unskilled victim has been given a sword with the vain promise that if he can actually kill the lion his own life will be spared. His chances are infinitesimal, but a few desperadoes have thus actually saved themselves.

---

[1] The regular gladiatorial oath.

Will the prisoner fight? To the infinite disgust of the thousands he collapses upon the sands in sheer terror before the lion can so much as strike him. The beast finishes his life almost instantly. The multitude hoot and curse — they have been cheated of their passionate desire to see a human victim struggling in desperate combat with the great beast. Fortunately, they remind themselves, this is only the beginning of the performance.

If one need not moralize, one need not linger. After the sacrifice of the criminal there are more beasts turned loose in the arena. Of course, no Prætor can be expected to show the hundreds of animals which an Emperor will exhibit in his greater games, but Cluentius has done the thing very respectably. He has in all ten bears, eighteen panthers, five lions, and six tigers.

First the animals are goaded on to fight one with another. A bear is torn to death by a lion, but kills the lion in a last mortal hug. Then the trumpet sounds — some of the gladiators rush into the arena. The arena is now covered with frightened, snarling, reckless beasts. Even with keen weapons and skill, it is desperate work to slay them. One fine young German slips as a tiger bounds on him. His life is crushed out at the very foot of the editor's stand. One panther, driven frantic, with a terrific leap almost clears the trellis directly before a Vestal Virgin; there is a general scream and recoil from the podium as the luckless beast drops back upon the spear of a hunter.

340. Interval in the Contests: Scattering of Lottery Tickets. — At last the *venatio* is over. All the beasts have been killed with reasonable skill, and barring only the German, with no accidents. It is now noon and a comfortable intermission follows. Food has been brought by many, or is passed about by hawkers. Cluentius, with great condescension, remains in the editor's seat, and dines in public so that everybody present can go home boasting merrily, " We have been to prandium with the Prætor ! " [1]

After hunger has been appeased the spectators begin to grow restive. It is the immemorial privilege of the crowds to shout out whatever they wish in the Circus or Amphitheater. An unpopular Commissioner of the Grain Supply is seen rising in the podium ; instantly the great awning quakes with the hootings. There is even a volley of date and olive stones ; when, luckily for the Commissioner, the Prætor

BOXERS.

orders the attendants to begin scattering lottery tickets along the benches.

Instantly all else is forgotten ; dignified men scramble over one another. In the free benches there are several genuine fights and many a torn toga or lacerna. The winning tickets to-morrow will draw jars of wine, packages of edibles, or even quite a few denarii in cash ; but if the editor had been the Emperor the prizes could well have been fine jewelry, pictures,

[1] Augustus once protested against the custom of eating in the amphitheater as being undignified and said he would prefer to go away and return. "That is all right for *you*," answered his hearer, "but *your* seat is sure to be kept for you !"

beasts of burden, tidy sums of money, or even — as the grand
prize — a small villa.

This distribution silences all the discordant howlings; and
the people are further amused by a kind of theatrical pageant,
some popular pantomimes giving the Judgment of Paris in a
clever and not inelegant manner, without scenery in the
broad arena. After that two ostriches are unloosed and the
crowd is put in an excellent humor while four Moorish riders
on shining desert steeds chase down the speeding, doubling
birds and finally lasso them. All is at last ready for the
real business of the day -- the gladiators.

341. Beginning the Regular Gladiatorial Combats. —
The hunters of the beasts, duly reënforced by many others,
reënter the arena again in grim procession. Approaching
the editor's seat on the podium they can be seen passing up
their weapons for Cluentius, to let him satisfy himself that
every edge is sharpened beyond the possibility of shamming.
He hands back each spear or sword with a nod, then the long
file straightens and every combatant lifts his right arm:
" *Ave, prætor!* " sounds the deep chant, " *morituri te saluta-*
mus! " " *Ave!* " answers Cluentius gesturing haughtily.
" Low-browed scoundrels," mutters Calvus to a fellow senator; " Most of them are lucky to end up this way and to
escape the cross. — Ah! they begin."

First, however, to get well limbered, wooden swords are
handed about, and the troop fence with one another skilfully
yet harmlessly; but the people are waxing impatient —
" Steel! Steel! " rings the shout from the whole amphitheater, and the dense array of women in the upper gallery
is calling it as fiercely as the men on the ocean of benches.
A terrific blast of trumpets sounds from mid-arena, and a
gigantic lanista acting as a kind of umpire motions with his
spear. Soon every heart in the myriads is thrilled by the
clash of weapons.

Cluentius (an unoriginal though free-spending magistrate) has arranged a very conventional series of combats. First two Britons dash about in chariots pelting each other with javelins. Their armor turns the darts for long, then one of the horses is wounded and while his driver is struggling to control him another missile strikes through a joint in the warrior's armor. He totters in the car while all the amphi-

GLADIATORS SALUTING THE EDITOR BEFORE JOINING IN MORTAL COMBAT.

theater rises and yells together " *Habet!* "   " He's got it ! " — and then as the poor wight tumbles back into the sands, " *Peractum est!* "   " He's done for ! "

Immediately there appears a grotesque figure, arrayed as Charon, the dead man's ferryman. He bears a hammer wherewith he strikes the body of the victim to see if he is counterfeiting death. The fallen chariot warrior stirs not — and " Charon " with a long hook drags away the corpse into one of the dens under the podium. The benches are now leaping, gesticulating, and yelling — the noise is indescribable, and Cluentius's friends hasten to tell him that the combats have started admirably.

342. Mounted Combats: the Signals for Ruthlessness and Mercy. — The surviving charioteer disappears amid plaudits. In his place ride out four horsemen; and two mounted duels can thus take place at either side of the arena.

DEFEATED GLADIATOR APPEALING FOR MERCY: spectators, with Vestal Virgins in front seats, turning "thumbs down."

One pair contend evenly and stoutly, but the other contest soon ends — the less skilful rider is dashed from his seat by his opponent's sword, and is so hurt he can barely lift himself upon the sands. The victor leaps down and stands over him waving his reddened blade, while his disarmed victim in sheer helplessness raises the right hand, the fist clinched except for one upraised finger — the demand for "Mercy!"

The conqueror obsequiously looks toward his employer Cluentius upon the podium, and the Prætor, bound to be gracious to the populace, motions somewhat inquiringly toward the spectators — let them decide! If the defeated gladiator had fought more gamely and had striven to rise and renew the fight, possibly enough white handkerchiefs — the token of mercy — would have been waved to warrant the editor in flourishing his own also; — but the fellow had collapsed too easily and the mood of the crowd demanded blood. "*Occide! Occide!*" "Kill! Kill!" is the yell; and thousands of thumbs are ruthlessly pointed downward. Cluentius's own thumb is pointed down likewise. The victor raises his weapon and without scruple plunges it in the breast of the vanquished, who sustains the honor of his profession by receiving the mortal blow without flinching.

Again the Charon enters with his hook and clears the arena. In the interval the other mounted duelists, cool and experienced warriors, have partly suspended their combat and now they profit through their comrade's death by the umpiring lanista's declaration of a draw. The people are sated for an instant and Cluentius nods approval as the two ride out; he is inwardly glad to spare them, because the owners of dead gladiators have to be indemnified.

343. Combats between Netters (*Retiarii*) and Heavy-Armed Warriors (Thracians). — So combat follows combat, while the sands grow red and one warrior falls simply by slipping upon the gore. The suffocating fumes of blood rise through the bars of sunlight under the great awning. The people grow more and more excited. There will be hundreds of beggars to-night in Rome on account of the reckless wagering.

At last the trumpets sound for what is always the crowning feature of the exhibition — the chief thing which the multitudes have really waited all day to see — ten *retiarii* are to fight ten "Thracians." The retiarii ("netters") wear not the least armor. They carry nothing but three-pronged

lances and thick nets, which last they endeavor to fling over
their adversaries, entangle them, and then stab with their
tridents ere they can cut loose. The " Thracians " have
heavy suits of armor and formidable swords.[1] If a netter
misses his cast, there is nothing for him to do but to fly for
dear life. The sight of a powerful, armed Thracian toiling
after the leaping, dodging retiarius is a source of universal
joy to the amphitheaters. The people rise on the benches
and join in a kind of intoxication and blood orgy. *"Verbera!
Verbera! Occide! Occide!"* " Lay on! Kill ! " — rises as a
thunder to heaven.

344. End of the Combats: Rewarding the Victors. — It
profits not to dwell on the half hour which follows. Plenty
of skill, valor, and swiftness are shown alike by netters and
by heavy-armed warriors. One by one part of the twenty
drop, and for a while the passions of the people permit no
mercy. The Charon appears several times; but there is a
young Spanish netter whose nimbleness and reckless courage
win great favor, and many are muttering, " We want to see
him again." There is also a very experienced Thracian whose
owner will demand from Cluentius a round indemnity, if
the fight is pushed to a finish and his precious chattel is
slain.

As a result when four wounded men together drop their
weapons and signal for mercy, white handkerchiefs begin
waving all over the amphitheater and Cluentius is glad to
shake out his also. The combats are over. The victorious
gladiators, if they are unhurt enough to stand, are led before
the podium and to each are handed palms of victory.

There is furthermore a crowning ceremony. One Certus,

---

[1] There were at least two other types of heavy-armed gladiators who
are often mentioned — the "Samnites" and the "Myrmillones"; but
it hardly seems profitable to examine the small particulars in which their
arms differed from those of the "Thracians."

a very famous netter, has by previous understanding taken only a formal part in the combats. Now, while the whole multitude leaps up to acclaim him, Cluentius himself rises and gives him the wooden sword — the sign that he need fight and risk his life no more. Henceforth Certus will become himself no doubt a *lanista*, and train hundreds of other brawny youths to yield up their lives for the amusement of Rome.

The amphitheater empties from all its numerous *vomitoria*. The crowd goes home well contented, praising Cluentius and hoping he will be assigned a fine province to govern. True it has not been as if the Emperor were present — then there might have been two hundred or more gladiators, an enormous slaughter of beasts; fountains could have played in the arena to refresh the air, and perfumes could have been scattered from the awnings; or the arena might easily have been flooded for a sea fight between two squadrons of small galleys.

Nevertheless, Cluentius has done very well for a mere Prætor; and he will have to pay indemnity for about fourteen of his forty gladiators, a very fair average to get butchered. "It has been a pleasant enough holiday (say many) in a toiling and busy world, and the rumor goes that for the next Ides at the Consul's games they have rounded up a whole gang of robbers who will all be fed to the lions!"

CHAPTER XX

THE ROMAN RELIGION: THE PRIESTHOODS, THE VESTAL VIRGINS

345. Religious Symbols Everywhere in Rome. — The circus races and the amphitheater butcheries are nominally in honor of some god. It is perhaps Vulcan in whose name Cluentius has hired the gladiators to slaughter one another. Everywhere about Rome are imposing temples and lesser shrines, and there are almost more statues of gods and demigods than there are people in the swarming streets. The symbolic snakes for the Lares of the locality or of the household, are painted upon thousands of walls. All this would indicate that the Romans of the Empire are extraordinarily religious. How far does this outward seeming correspond to the actual facts?

346. Epicureanism and Agnosticism among the Upper Classes. — If we penetrate the life of men like Publius Calvus and others of the upper circle, apparently we are dealing with persons who are almost, if not complete, agnostics. Some are cheerful Epicureans who formally deny that there are any deities that concern themselves with mortal affairs, and who for their own part look upon the world as a chance aggregation of atoms, and upon life as one physical sensation after another with nothing later awaiting a man but eternal slumber in the grave. Moral " laws " merely exist to adjust human relationships, so that you can win the maximum enjoyment from day to day.

Theories like this can be justified in sonorous, noble language, as in the great poems of Lucretius, but the underlying philosophy remains the same. Cluentius, the Prætor, whose library is crammed with Epicurean writings, has, in fact, just been ordering chiseled on his ostentatious funeral monument, " *Eat, drink, enjoy yourself — the rest is nothing.*" [1]

347. Stoicism: Revival of Religion under the Empire. — Calvus himself, a decidedly practical man not too fond of

MAISON CARRÉE, NÎMES, FRANCE: the best preserved temple of the Roman type in existence.

nice speculations, takes greater pleasure in the theories of the Stoics. The stern teaching that " duty " is the be-all

---

[1] An actual Roman epitaph. The Epicurean theory was capable of statement in much more pleasing language than is given above, but the effect of such a philosophy upon the ordinary human viewpoint and conduct was inevitable.

At the Roman colony of Thamugade in Africa, a checkerboard was found scratched in the pavement of the Forum, and beside it this plebeian version of the Prætor's inscription: "*To hunt, to bathe, to gamble, to laugh — that's living !*"

and end-all of life, and that true freedom and happiness come only by a scrupulous discharge of every obligation, appeals strongly to many hard-headed Romans. It fits in well with their old native religion, and they accept it without much abstract philosophizing. But the " God " discussed by Zeno, Cleanthes, and the later Stoics is only a hard, impersonal, resistless force, — " Eternal Law " under another name. He is in nowise a merciful Heavenly Father, any more than he is a youthful, beauteous, and very human Apollo. Calvus, in short, is hardly more convinced than his friend Cluentius, the Epicurean, that there really exists any personal deity.[1]

However, religion as an outward institution, has been steadily gaining under the Roman Empire. Probably never were there ever more unabashed atheists than such personages as Sulla and Julius Cæsar in the last decades of the Republic, — men not without pet superstitions perhaps and a belief in their " stars," but who were almost cynical in their expressions of disbelief in any ruling Providence, and to whom temples and worship were only convenient political engines for befooling the mob.

Augustus nevertheless was probably somewhat more of a believing man himself, and he grasped the enormous value of reinvigorating the old cults, rebuilding the crumbling shrines, and finally of rekindling the conviction that there existed a stabilizing and avenging host of deities as a means for getting moral sanction and support for his new imperial régime. Since the battle of Actium, temples have multiplied, priesthoods have been carefully maintained, and solemn religious ceremonies and sacrifices have been promoted by the gov-

---

[1] In all the extensive correspondence of Pliny the Younger there is hardly a single reference indicating that he had any religious beliefs, or took the least interest in religious matters save as they involved outward ceremonies or official policies.

ernment; in short, a great and partially successful effort has
been put forth to galvanize into a kind of life that early
" Religion of Numa," which once molded the ideals of the
little city by the Tiber.

348. Foreign Cults Intruded upon the "Religion of Numa."
— Religious beliefs and institutions at Rome, however, are
only in part derived from the cults and forms of old Italy,
whether Etruscan or Latin. The Greek mythology has
been so taken over by the poets that often it is hard to
sift out the indigenous Italian stories from the great mass of
imported legends in which Jupiter and Juno manifestly are
merely the Latin names for Hellenic Zeus and Hera. Furthermore, there has come a perfect influx of oriental gods:
Egyptian Isis, Syrian Baal, Phrygian Cybele, Persian Mithras — these are merely some of the more important.

The Roman attitude toward foreign deities is tolerant;
provided one keeps up the outward forms of reverence for
the old native deities, it does no serious harm if people feel
happier because they burn incense to the dog-headed Anubis,
or to the uncouth gods of Phœnicia. Of course these alien
rites must not be too gross; such as were the outrageous old
Bacchanals who were broken up in 186 B.C., or the Gallic
Druids who permitted human sacrifice. Otherwise a "foreign superstition" is a matter merely for a contemptuous
shrug or sneer.

The result is that the cults seen in Rome under the Empire
often appear as a vast jumble of things Greek, Levantine,
Oriental, and even Celtic. The Emperor and Senate seldom
bother themselves about matters of inward belief; Rome has
its gladiators but it has no Inquisition.

Nevertheless, the old Italian religion is still the official
cultus of the state. Its forms are carefully cherished; it is
insensibly modified but it is never repudiated. There are
almost the same priesthoods, the same sacred formulas and

machinery of religion as in the days of the Punic Wars.[1] They are kept up partly out of patriotic pride in all survivals of the heroic past, partly because they help the government to control the " mob " and the highly superstitious soldiery, partly (it must in fairness be added) because very intelligent persons believe that the ancient Italian religion somehow contributes to the safety and stability of the Empire, — that when Jupiter Capitolinus falls the dominion of Rome will actually fall with him.

349. Superstitious Piety of the City Plebeians. — As for the multitude, the enormous population in the insulæ, if it has little intelligent faith, it has abundant ignorant credulity. The outward service of the gods brings good luck.

If the public rites fail and if blasphemers (like the execrable Christians) arise, the corn ships will not get through from Alexandria, the Tiber will overflow, the pestilence will sweep off thousands and — almost equal calamity — the favorite aurigæ and gladiators on the gamblers' tablets will lose in the games. If a private man neglects the gods, his shop or business ventures can go bankrupt, his children die, his wife decamps with a freedman, disease can rack him, premature death smite him, and his tomb be demolished to the complete obliteration of his memory. Possibly even his ghost will drift about unhappily in desert places. Every possible motive, therefore, requires governors and governed to stand in well with the gods.

Let us, therefore, examine this " Religion of Numa " which is living yet, as the official cultus of Rome; then a few words can be said about its alien competitors.

350. Roman Religion Originally Developed by Italian Farmers. — The old Italian farmers who shaped this religion

---

[1] This apparently continued true until well into the fourth century, when the whole pagan system was swept away by Christianity.

were singularly lacking in imagination. Very few are the myths for which the poets can claim a non-Greek origin. The world is conceived of as being full of deities which often are so little personified that one cannot be sure of their actual sex: " Be propitious, O Divine One (*numen*), be thou male or be thou female ! " is the proper formula for beginning many ancient prayers.

Some of these divinities, to be sure, are well-defined and powerful gods such as Jupiter the Sky-God, Mars the War-God, and Juno the potent and matronly spouse of Jupiter. Such deities came with the ancestors of the Italians when they wandered down from the North into that southern peninsula which they occupied many centuries ago.

Other divinities are ancient adoptions from the Etruscans or from the Greeks. Minerva, the protectress of such female arts as weaving and spinning and later of the more masculine arts, sciences, and learning, is pretty clearly the Minerva of the Etruscans, and has caught many attributes from the Pallas Athena of the Greeks. Apollo came, perhaps, via Etruria, where they called him Aplu, and not directly from Hellas, but no temple was built to him until after Greek as well as Etruscan influence in Rome had become very strong. Diana or Luna (" Madame Moon ") was an old moon goddess, possibly the same as the Etruscan Losna, and only by a late and very unfortunate identification has she become confounded with Apollo's Greek sister Artemis, the virgin huntress on the Arcadian hills.

One great goddess, however, Venus, is probably a good old Italian deity of substantial homely virtues: she is still invoked as Venus Cloacina (" Venus the Purifier "), when it is necessary to cleanse the great sewers; a function seldom remembered when giddy youths confound her with the Greek Aphrodite, and beg her to help their illicit love affairs !

351. Native Italian Gods: Janus, Saturn, Flora. The Lares and Penates. — All these gods and certain other familiar deities such as Mercury patron of trade and gain, Neptune lord of the sea, Vulcan the clever smith, and finally, but in nowise least, Vesta the hearth goddess, and Ceres the Mistress of the Corn, make up the official " Great Gods " in

whose honor the public games are held, and to whom Emperors and Consuls proffer vows and sacrifice.

Highly important also is the strictly native Italian Janus, the two-faced lord of beginnings and endings, probably an ancient Sun-God; whom one should invoke at the opening of every fresh day, and in whose honor (quite appropriately) the month of

FARMER'S CALENDAR: showing festivals each month.

January is named with New Year's Day especially designated to his festival.[1] There is furthermore Saturn, a rural deity, who has been identified with the Greek Cronos ("Father Time "); there is Orchus who rules the underworld; there is Liber the masculine field god, consort of Ceres and sometimes confounded with the Greek Bacchus; there is Bona Dea (" Good Goddess ") a mistress of agriculture, possibly only another aspect of Ceres; there is Flora,

---

[1] Janus had no Greek counterpart. It was one of the absurdities of the late Græco-Latin mythology that his wife Diana (*Dia Jana* = "Madame Goddess Jana") should have been confounded with Artemis.

the kindly patroness not merely of the flowers but of all the prosaic vegetable gardens; and there also is Robigus, a malevolent garden deity who must be propitiated with frequent offerings or he will mildew the crops.

All these gods (except the evil Robigus) are near and dear to the average plebeian, and especially to the farmers. In addition there are the Lares and Penates. We have seen how they are guardian spirits of the households — never forgotten in any mansion or upon any social occasion.

The state has its own " Public Lares and Penates " as well as private households; the former are the spirits of the gallant patriots of old like the first Brutus, Cincinnatus, Camillus, and Scipio Major. The second are the immortal " Twin Brethren " — Castor and Pollux, who have ridden to rescue Roman armies on many a hard-fought field. No public sacrifice can avail unless at least formal reference is made to the public Lares and Penates along with the special god receiving honor.

Reënforcing these divinities is a whole host of special rural deities, who, in a country still very dependent on agriculture, receive special honor in all the profitable villas and farms crowding up to the gates of Rome; Faunus and Lupercus are herdsmen's gods well matching the Hellenic Pan; Silvanus presides over the woodlands and timber-lots, Pales is a much beloved shepherd's god, Pomona cares for the orchards, Vertumnus for the normal change of the seasons; Anna Perena is the goddess of the circling year; and Terminus takes care that the boundary stones (so important to farmers) are not disturbed.

352. Personified Virtues as Gods: Cold and Legalistic Character of the Roman Religion. — However, these deities are increased by a great host of personified moral and civic qualities. Nothing is easier in Rome than to assume that every desirable virtue must have some kind of a numen (divine potence) behind it. Around the city one can find temples, *e.g.* to Honor, Hope, Good Faith, Modesty, Concord, Peace, Victory, Liberty, Public Safety, Youth, and Fame. This is only a minor part of the list.

CIRCULAR TEMPLE, PROBABLY OF OLD ITALIAN GODDESS MATUTA: now Church of Sancta Maria del Sole, Rome.

It is assumed in fact that every act or process of human life has its special numen who can be invoked to make that act successful. Thus after young Sextus, Calvus's son, was born, his very pious nurses first invoked Vaticanus who opened his

mouth for his first cry, then Cucina who guarded his cradle,
then Edulia and Potina who taught him to eat and drink,
Stabilius who aided him first to stand up, and Abeona and
Adeona who watched over his first footsteps " going " and
" returning." His sophisticated parents doubtless smiled at
this scrupulous piety, but they did nothing to discourage it.

These cold impersonal divinities stand to man in a legal
rather than a theological relationship. Men and the numina
have made a kind of contract — so much prayer and ceremonial sacrifice must be offered in return for so much good favor,
prosperity, and protection. *Do ut des* (" I give that you may
give ") sums up the whole spirit of the Roman religion.

Numa the alleged founder of so many cults was not a
prophet or an inspired poet but a king and lawgiver. A wise
man is always pious ; that is, he always gives to the gods their
precise due according to carefully set forms, otherwise the
divinities may evade their part of the contract, just as a merchant is not bound to execute a bargain in which the other
party has failed to do precisely as was stipulated.

If prayers and sacrifice fail in their purpose, it is reasonable
to suppose that the fault lies in the formula and the victims
employed. The pig, sheep, or other victim must then be
sacrificed over again with greater scrupulosity. On the other
hand, willful neglect of worship is as surely punished by the
gods as willful neglect of paying one's debts is punished
by the Prætor. The fate of the impious will be somewhat
like that of the absconding debtor, only much more dreadful.

Needless to say this " Religion of Numa " contains no
more spirituality than the hard stones which pave the Forum.
It does, however, put a genuine premium upon the rigid
performance of duty, and thereby sometimes reacts favorably
upon human conduct.

353. Priestly Offices : Little Sacrosanct about Them. —
For these necessary ceremonies mankind requires priests,

but they are not revered interpreters of the divine will, nor are they mysterious mediators between Providence and men; they are rather attorneys employed by men to represent them competently in their dealings with the divinities.

Small religious matters, the minor private sacrifices, etc., can be attended to without a priest, just as you do not need a jurisconsult to assist in petty purchases. Greater religious matters, private and still more if public, however, require experts to see that the right formulæ are spoken and sacrifices proffered. Any Roman of flawless birth and of good character is eligible for most of the priesthoods, although there are a few reserved for the narrow circle of the old patrician families. Holding these religious offices does not ordinarily imply dropping one's secular interests or having the least philosophical belief in the ceremonies so carefully performed. Julius Cæsar was Pontifex Maximus while he was Proconsul of the Gauls, and while he was a firm disbeliever in the existence of any gods at all.

Of course every small temple has to have its proper custodians whom we may call " priests," to attend to the private sacrifices; and there are besides plenty of unofficial diviners and soothsayers who can answer your question, " Is this a lucky day for the wedding of my daughter? " or " Do the omens warn against buying this farm? " The great public ministers of religion, however, are really officers of state, appointed by the Emperor,[1] and usually they are grouped in famous " Sacred Colleges " wherein the members hold office for life. Ordinarily the persons thus honored are distinguished senators selected after an honorable civil and military career.

354. The *Pontifices*. — On the whole the greatest official glory comes to the fifteen *pontifices*. Not merely do they

[1] Under the later Republic these sacred colleges were filled according to the majority vote of 17 tribes of the people, selected by lot from the entire 35 tribes into which the Comitia Tributa was divided.

possess the general oversight of everything concerning cultus, but they have as their chief colleague the Emperor himself, who always holds the post of *Pontifex Maximus* — head of the Roman religion.

Before Julius Cæsar reformed the calendar the pontifices had the important task of settling each year what days were to be *dies fasti*, whereon alone legal business could be lawfully conducted, and they have still the power to interfere in almost any doings concerning sacrifice, ritual, temple properties, etc. Their head, the Pontifex Maximus, has particularly to watch over and control the Vestal Virgins; and the college at large still has the custody of the famous *Libri Pontificales*, the " Pontifical Books," famous and ancient volumes containing instructions for all kinds of unfamiliar religious rites and procedure in strange religious emergencies.[1]

355. The Augurs. — The pontiffs, however, are really " Commissioners for Religious Affairs " rather than actual priests, and along with them goes another important group of " sacred " personages who seem almost equally unpriestly. These are the *augurs*, the official interpreters of the will of heaven; and almost every senator cherishes the hope of being appointed to this college, notwithstanding the fact that long ago Cicero remarked that " two augurs ought never to meet without winking! " There are sixteen augurs, who are entitled to wear the embroidered toga prætexta and to carry the sacred crooked staff, the lituus. The science of augury, whereof they are supposedly the supreme custodians, is something whereon the men of old, especially the Etruscans, expended an enormous amount of energy.

The Italians in general put relatively little trust in astrology and not much more in dreams as revealing the divine

---

[1] In early times the Pontifex Maximus also kept a kind of dry annals of sacred and profane events (*Annales Maximi*), valuable for the preservation of many facts in early Roman history.

intentions. What greatly matters is the flight of birds, the strange actions of animals, monstrous births, thunder, meteors, and like prodigies. Even in Hadrian's day plenty of intelligent men will shudder with dread if they behold a crow cawing on their funeral monument; or will give up a journey if a black viper shoots across the road just as their carriage is starting.

Sneezing or stumbling furthermore can mean much, and before many an atrium the janitor is constantly shouting " *Dextro pede !* " " Right foot first ! " to every guest entering the vestibule. Certain signs are very dreadful; *e.g.* any gathering at which somebody is seized with epilepsy (a manifest token of divine anger) must be instantly dissolved.

If, however, the gods do not speak thus openly, no public act should be performed without at least asking the formal question, " Is heaven favorable? " This may be done by watching the consecrated chickens while they devour the grain as at the opening of the Senate (see p. 340),[1] but more elaborate and reliable is a careful watching of the heavens for signs. If an augur sees ravens on the right-hand side of the sky, the sign is lucky; but a crow in order not to forbode evil must appear on the left. The actions of eagles, owls, woodpeckers, and certain other birds are more complicated. Their cries, the manner of their flight, as well as the direction whence they come all have to be considered.

Time fails to describe the careful ritual necessary for the augurs, when, at the request of some high magistrate, they interrogate the gods to see if heaven is pleased at some pro-

---

[1] A general in the field had to "take the auspices" to get good omens for his army, but of course he could not always have an augur present. Once in the first Punic War, Publius Claudius, a consul about to engage in a naval battle, was disgusted to be told, "The chickens will not eat." "Very well then," he retorted, "let them drink !" and flung them into the sea. To his own ruin and to the vindication of the official religion he was thereupon completely defeated by the Carthaginians !

posed official action. It is not necessary, however, to get
a positively favorable sign; often it is enough that during
a suitable interval the augur should *fail* to observe any unhappy bird, any meteor, thunder claps, or the like. This
propitious interval constitutes a formal " silence " (*silen-
tium*); and many an augur has shown himself conveniently
deaf or blind to noises or sights that might prohibit some
desired deed. Nevertheless the solemn farce is always maintained, for when do Romans ever discard any time-honored
custom?

356. The *Flamines*. — The augurs rank with the pontiffs
high in public honors, but the most important actual priests
in Rome are the *flamines*. There are fifteen flamines distributed among the services of the various gods, but three
rank above all others — the flamens of Jupiter, Mars, and
of Quirinus (deified Romulus), with the first named, called
more particularly the *Flamen Dialis*, at their head.

It is an extraordinary honor to be named Flamen Dialis,
and Gratia reckons it among the chief of her family glories
that she has an uncle now enjoying for life this high priesthood. The Flamen of Jupiter is entitled to a curule chair as
if he were a magistrate, and takes social precedence above
nearly everybody save the Emperor and the consuls; he
also wears the toga prætexta like other exalted personages,
although it must be of thick wool woven by the hands of his
wife. In addition he has to appear always crowned with a
special high pointed cap, not unlike the " fool's-cap " of
other times, and tipped with the *apex*, a pointed spike of olive
wood wound with a lock of wool.

Old Papirius is among the most envied men in Rome, yet
he complains bitterly of the price he has to pay for his glory.
He cannot mount a horse, or even look upon an army in
battle array. He cannot swear an oath, or spend a single
night away from the city, however comfortable may be his

family villas in the hot season. The cuttings of his hair and nails must be carefully preserved and buried beneath an *arbor felix* (lucky tree). He must never eat of or even mention a goat, beans, or several other forbidden objects.

Above all Papirius's wife, the *flaminica*, whom he had to marry with special ceremonies, is indispensable to him in many acts of religion and he is forbidden to divorce her, although his life with the noble Claudia is none too happy. Worse still if she should die, he must immediately resign his office. The other fourteen flamines enjoy somewhat lesser glories, offset by slightly lesser taboos. They are, however, the fifteen most sacred male individuals in all Rome.

357. The *Salii* (" Holy Leapers "). — Of less glory than the flamines, but nevertheless of venerable sanctity are the twelve other priests of Mars, the college of the *Salii* (" Holy Leapers"). To them are committed the twelve holy shields, the *Anciliæ*, one whereof is affirmed to have fallen from heaven.

Calvus has an elderly cousin, Donatus, who lately was appointed by Hadrian to the Salii. During the last Kalends of March nobody cracked a smile when these twelve sedate and aristocratic gentlemen, wearing their apex-crowned caps, long embroidered tunics, and brazen cuirasses, with spear in one hand and the holy shields on the other, went through the city stopping in many of the squares and before the larger temples and executing violent dances, leaping, cavorting, and chanting with loud voice " Salian Hymns " — verses in such ancient Latin that they hardly understood their own shrill jargon. When the round of the city was ended and they had danced and sung for the last time, the holy men were quite exhausted.

The consolation for these holy men followed quickly, however. That evening they held a grand corporation dinner. The augurs are famous for their elaborate banquets

worthy of an Apicius, but the Salii on the whole surpass the
augurs.   A *Saliares daps* — " Holy Leaper's dinner " — has
become the synonym for the triumph of good eating.

**358. The *Fetiales* (" Sacred Heralds ") :   Ceremony of
Declaring War.** — Calvus himself belongs to a religious
college of rather waning consequence, but of great antiquity.
He is a fetial.

Anciently at least no treaty was binding unless it had been
ratified with most solemn religious ceremonies.   To deal
with the gods in international affairs Numa is said, therefore,
to have established a college of twenty *fetiales* — the holy
heralds.   Their president, the *Pater Patratus*, represented
the whole Roman people when it came to swearing the oaths
and offering the sacrifices for concluding a treaty, and even
in Hadrian's day some of the ancient usages are maintained.
A peace has lately been made with the King of Parthia, and
in the presence of his envoy at Rome the venerable ex-consul,
the Pater Patratus, took his sacred flints, laid a special wreath
of the holy " verbena " plant on the altar, and kindled the
fire for the sacrifice that confirmed the peace.[1]

More important once was the chief herald's duty in declaring a war ; for it seemed useless to hope for victory unless
first by legalistic formula the enemy was put in the wrong
before the gods.   The Pater Patratus with at least three of
his colleagues was expected to march solemnly to the hostile
frontier, next with due ceremony to recite the wrongs of
Rome and demand redress and to hurl a spear dipped in blood
across the boundary ; then and not till then could the legions
march forth in any offensive war.

It is a great distance now, however, to the frontier of the
Empire and the white-headed Pater Patratus keenly dis-

---

[1] These plants (*verbenæ*) seem to have been grown within one special
inclosure on the Capitol hill.   They were carried by one of the fetiales
known as the *verbenarius*.

likes to quit for months his luxurious residence on the Quirinal; but legal ingenuity has long since enabled him to preserve at once his bodily comfort and the good old custom. Before the Temple of Bellona in the Campus Martius is a bit of ground whereon stands a certain column. When recently it seemed desirable to declare war on an unneighborly German tribe, a captive from these barbarians was duly hunted up in the slave market at Rome, and a legal deed was solemnly made out transferring this land to the prisoner. The spot was now technically "hostile ground," and the Pater Patratus and his fellow fetials all ordered their litters and were peacefully taken out to the Temple of Bellona. The Germans were carefully summoned to "do the Romans right," and no answer coming, the head fetial with all the ancient formulas and curses flung the spear into the column.

The war could now proceed with the gods' full blessing — a thoroughly Roman proceeding, and very typical of many other survivals, religious or secular.

359. The Arval Brethren (*Fratres Arvales*). — There is another "ancient and honorable" religious brotherhood — the *Fratres Arvales*. There are twelve Arval brethren, always including the Emperor. In May they hold a three-day festival to the *Dea Dia*.[1] Besides regaling themselves then with an extraordinarily luxurious feast, they assemble in the grove of the Dea Dia and offer to her two pigs, a white heifer, and a lamb. Next they clear her temple of all but the necessary priests and attendants, and dividing themselves into two bodies of six, tuck up their long tunics and execute a solemn dance around the holy house, singing meantime a kind of hymn for the blessing of the fields, a hymn preserved in such an uncouth antique Latin that the meaning of many words is doubtful.[2]

---

[1] A rustic goddess sometimes also called Ops.

[2] For a translation of this "Song of the Arval Brethren" see the author's "Readings in Ancient History," vol. II, p. 6.

It is a most desirable thing to be one of these " Brothers of the Fields." The records of the college are kept with the greatest care and their dinners compete with those of the Salii.

These are *some* only of the holy colleges, membership wherein carries marked social prestige. The fifteen " Keepers of the Sibylline Books," the *Epulones* who arrange many of the banquets in honor of the gods, and the *Haruspices* who assist the augurs particularly in interpreting the omens from the entrails of slaughtered victims, are all distinguished personages. How many of them have one scintilla of belief in the deities they address and the rites they execute it were most unbecoming to inquire closely!

360. Rustic Ceremonies; Soothsaying, Astrologers, and Witches. — This religion, then, is one purely of outward ritual coupled with not a little superstition. In the country the farmers at the festival to the Lemures (malevolent ghosts of the dead) still may rise at midnight, walk barefoot through the house, fill their mouths with black beans which they spit forth nine times without looking around, saying each time, " With these beans I redeem me and mine." Then they clank two brazen vessels together and nine times shout out, " Manes depart!" This is a sample of many similar ceremonies.

Soothsayers, who are often sheer charlatans, are very naturally in constant demand among the unlearned to resolve such queries as, " Will my mother-in-law recover from jaundice?" or " How long will my husband live and keep me from my lover?" Such rascals usually tell the future by examining the lungs of a dove. The entrails of a dog, however, are better although much more expensive.

Among the rich, however, " Chaldæan astrologers " are somewhat fashionable, slippery Orientals who know how to wheedle the gold out of credulous parvenus, even if the official religion sets no great store upon star-gazing.[1] The women are inevitably the best patrons of these pretenders, but their husbands and brothers often refuse to start on a journey or to begin anything else important until assured " the horoscope is favorable." Time fails us to tell of the employment of Etruscan witches, or of the belief in ghosts and goblins. The latter are dreaded by many hard-headed epicureans who will argue convincingly that there can be no such thing as a god or immortality.

361. A Private Sacrifice. — Nevertheless, with all its faults this Roman religion has few truly *debasing* superstitions. There are practically no human sacrifices, no constant and outrageous use of sordid ceremonies, no acts or beliefs which actually degrade one's manhood or womanhood.[2] All is deliberate, ordered, and, within certain pagan limitations, tolerably reasonable.

ROMAN ALTAR.

A typical Roman sacrifice is a dignified and well standardized procedure. Only recently Publius Calvus enjoyed

[1] As is well known Tiberius in his ignoble retirement on the Isle of Capri surrounded himself with "Chaldæans" and other types of star-gazers and magicians.

[2] There were a few isolated survivals in Italy of the practices of ancient savagery. For example at Aricia, in Latium about 16 miles from Rome, there was a holy grove of Diana wherein the priest was always a runaway slave who obtained his position by killing his predecessor. He was then safe from pursuit as long as he remained in the grove, until another fugitive slave in turn killed him — and so on through a succession of tragedies!

a birthday, and custom required that all his kinsmen should
come to congratulate him while he offered to the gods a
snow-white lamb, in gratitude for another year of life and
prosperity. The ceremony took place at a small temple of
Juno near the senator's mansion on the Esquiline, Juno being
accounted the special patron deity of the Junii Calvi. The
victim was carefully selected by Calvus himself, who paid an
extra price for a creature newly weaned and with horns just
sprouting. Ostentatious freedmen sometimes offered a fat
bull on their birthdays, and poorer folk merely a small pig,[1]
but a white lamb was a very fitting private sacrifice, not too
mean, not too pretentious, and fell in perfectly with the Roman idea of dealing with the gods on honorable business
principles.

362. Ceremony at the Temple. — On the day of the ceremony Calvus presented himself at the temple, with his toga
girded tightly around his body in the special " Gabinian
Cincture " required in sacrifices. The groups of kinsmen,
friends, freedmen, etc., all followed decorously. The special
Flamen of Juno, a friendly senator, appeared with his vestments and apex, to direct Calvus in the technical details of
the ceremony, but, be it noticed, the actual priest was Calvus
himself.

After all the company had gathered near the altar and put
on chaplets of ivy, a public crier (*præco*) commanded in
loud voice, " Let there be silence ! " and a tense interval
followed, every person holding his breath lest an unlucky
cough or sneeze should vitiate the whole proceeding. Nothing ill-omened following, the elder of Calvus's small sons
acting as camillus (acolyte) extended to his father a silver
basin of purifying water wherein the latter carefully washed
his hands, dried them upon a towel borne by his younger

---

[1] Pigs were very common Roman offerings and were the regular victims in most of the rustic sacrifices.

boy, then drew the great folds of his toga over his head, almost but not quite concealing his face.

At this juncture a flute player standing near promptly struck up with a piercing blast, which he continued much of the time until the ceremony was nearly over, not to supply music but simply to prevent any ill-omened sound from being

A MILITARY SACRIFICE; TRAJAN'S ARMY ON THE DANUBE: from Trajan's Column.

heard. Thereupon other youths led up the lamb. Its little horns had been gilded and a heavy garland of flowers twined about its neck. It was needful for the creature to *seem* to approach willingly, therefore the halter had to be quite slack, but a little fodder spread under the altar made the brute only too ready for its fate.

Calvus approached the victim, and with the flamen at his elbow to dictate every detail, took wine, incense, and a mixture of meal and salt, and sprinkled a trifle of each upon the hungry creature's forehead. A professional attendant cut a few hairs from between the horns and cast them on the burning altar. Then again prompted by the flamen, Calvus prayed aloud:

363. A Formal Prayer; the Actual Sacrifice. — " O Mother Juno, I pray and beseech thee that thou mayest be

ROMAN ALTAR WITH DESIGN SHOW-ING A SACRIFICE.

gracious and favorable to me and my home and my household, for which course I have ordained that the offering of this lamb should be made in accordance with my vows; that thou mayest avert, ward off, and keep afar all disease visible and invisible, all barrenness, waste, misfortune and ill-weather; that thou mayest cause my family, affairs, and business to come to prosperity; and that thou grant health and strength to me, my home and my household ! " [1]

It was all very like the formulas used by the lawyers before the Prætor. No waste of fine words, but very comprehensive and no contingency unprovided for.

When Calvus finished, the temple attendant (*popa*) standing near by asked in set form, " Shall I strike ? " " Strike him ! " ordered Calvus. Instantly the attendant smote the lamb a single merciful blow on the skull with a heavy mallet. The creature dropped dead, and his slayer immediately

---

[1] Slightly adapted from the form of prayer given in Cato the Elder's "Handbook on Agriculture."

knelt and stabbed him with a knife. As the blood ran out, it was caught in a basin and sprinkled upon the altar, along with some wine, incense, and a consecrated cake.

The lamb was now promptly cut up, and a crafty-looking haruspex inspected the color and form of the still palpitating entrails. If these had been declared " unfavorable " in form, color, or otherwise, a second lamb must have been procured and the whole ceremony perforce repeated until the results were fortunate, but the haruspex, certain of his fee, after a decent studying of the gall, intestines, and liver, lifted his head and said solemnly, " *Exta bona!* " " The entrails are good ! " Thereupon the flamen, hitherto passive or muttering formulas, stepped forward, threw wine, meal, and incense upon the entrails ; then cast the whole mass of them upon the brightly kindled altar-fire. Meantime the actual flesh of the lamb was being gathered up by Calvus's servants to take home for private consumption.

Calvus himself now drew the toga up over his head the second time, and then called on Juno with loud voice, " since thou hast accepted this lamb, duly proffered," to continue her favor on him and his house during the coming year, " in which case I vow unto thee another lamb, white and without blemish even as is this." He was again, it would seem, the lawyer reminding the other party to the contract that by the acceptance of the payment proffered, he or she was strictly obligated to continue friendly for the next twelve months.

The ceremony was therewith ended. The flamen raised his hand and spoke the solemn word of dismissal, " *Ilicet*," " It is permitted to go." Sacrificer, flamen, spectators, and attendants all now hurried away with shout and laughter to Calvus's residence, there to join in a fine feast wherein everybody received a portion of the slaughtered lamb.

364. The Vestal Virgins : Their Sanctity and Importance. — Great are the pontiffs, the augurs, the flamens, and the mem-

bers of the other sacred colleges. But they are all too pragmatic and secular to be taken quite seriously when they
demand religious veneration. There is one Roman college,
however, which is beyond words holy, at whose claims the
most godless never scoff, and whose members will keep alive
the best traditions of the religion of Numa until old Rome
is tottering to its fall — the
Sisterhood of the Vestal Virgins.

VESTAL VIRGIN.

Numa himself, hoary tra-
dition affirms, instituted this
body of six holy maidens,
although no doubt similar
companies could have been
discovered in many other
primitive Italian communities. Their origin is clear
enough. To early man, fire
was a thing very mysterious
and very necessary. Before
the discovery of flint and
steel it was no trifling matter
to kindle a new blaze by
rubbing together a hard stick
and a soft; every village, therefore, maintained a central
hearth (*focus*) where some brands were ever smoldering and
whither a boy could be sent running for a spark to replenish
the kitchen fires.

But beyond all other peoples the old Latins made of this
homely need a sacrosanct institution and a ritual. The
Temple of the Fire Goddess was perhaps at first only the
hearth of the king, and her priestesses were the king's own
daughters. Then the king disappeared: the Pontifex Maximus took his place; and quite naturally just as the high

pontiff's official residence, the Regia, stood on the verge of the Forum, the Shrine of Vesta and the home of her maiden ministers stood close beside it.

All across the ages this fire of Vesta has burned, tended with inconceivable care; and for this humble shrine of Vesta and the six Vestal Virgins all Romans from Emperor to lowest plebeian still retain more genuine reverence than for anything else in the world, not excluding the gilded Temple of Jupiter Optimus Maximus crowning the Capitol and its pompous Flamen Dialis.

365. The Temple of Vesta and the House of the Vestals. — The Temple of Vesta, directly on the verge of the roaring Forum and under the shadow of the Imperial Palatine, is an ostentatiously small, simple building, with a circular portico of pillars and surmounted with a low cupola covered with sheets of metal. Often repaired, great pains have been taken (so Ovid tells us) to preserve the original " style of Numa." Directly behind it, as you go east from the Forum, is the *Atrium Vestæ*, the House of the Vestals, noticed when we traversed the Heart of Rome.

Very simple externally, once inside those privileged to enter the House discover not merely a fine comfortable dwelling, suitable for ladies of rank and their numerous female attendants, but a very beautiful garden some 200 feet long by 65 wide. There are spreading trees, winding paths, marble seats, fountains and even a tiny grove — all within easy stone's throw of the very center of the metropolis.

The need for this garden, however, is obvious. The Vestals are women of the very highest rank, yet they cannot leave Rome in the hot season when nearly all other noble ladies flee to their cool villas. The garden is their breathing spot and their recompense. Around the garden runs a line of statues of the *Maximæ* (Senior Vestals), an imposing array of dignified elderly women of the grave Roman type. Here too in the Atrium Vestæ, in a little room, is a small hand-mill where the sacred virgins themselves can be seen each day laboriously grinding the consecrated meal required in the cult of the Hearth Goddess.

Within this house also the six Sisters spend their lives in a routine of holy duties, and although the building is not an officially consecrated " temple " it is really the most revered and sacrosanct spot in Rome.   In the Atrium Vestæ, there-fore, are deposited the wills and other precious documents of half the nobility, and the gods pity the wretch who may do the place violence, — his fate at human hands will be awful !

366. Appointment of Vestals. — This little sisterhood is divided always into three categories — the novices, the active members, the senior Vestals, of two members each. When there is a vacancy the Pontifex Maximus makes choice among the girls of between six and ten years in the patrician families,[1] who have both of their parents living and happily married.   A girl has to be physically perfect and intellectually acute, certain, in short, to do honor to the greatest position open to women in Rome.

The present Maxima is Salvia, a distant kinswoman of the late Emperor Nerva.   She was appointed many years ago in the reign of Titus.   There was such competition for the vacancy then that several noble families offered their daugh-ters, but Salvia was chosen because her parents were on the best of terms, whereas her nearest rival's father and mother were known to have quarreled.   The high pontiff (Titus) solemnly took her by the hand repeating the ritualistic words, " I take you to be ' Amata,' that as Vestal Virgin you may perform the sacred rites lawful for vestal virgins."   The

---

[1] This qualification of patrician birth was sometimes waived under the Empire, when genuine old-line patricians had become extremely few, but great pains were taken as to all the other requirements.

title of *Amata* was simply honorary. It implied the gentle and loving character of the service of Vesta.

Salvia was immediately led over to the house of Vesta, her hair was cut off, and hung upon the sacred lotus-tree in the garden ; she was clothed in long white garments with a special white band around her head, the holy *infula;* and next she took oath to abide in her office and to maintain her virginity not less than thirty years. She was now a lawful vestal, withdrawn from the power of her father, and subject only to the jurisdiction of the Pontifex Maximus.

367. Duties of the Vestals: the Maxima. — The six vestals enjoy no sinecure. From the fountain of Egeria by the Cœlian Hill they must bear all the water required for kneading their sacred cakes.[1] Daily they must carefully cleanse the actual Temple in front of their mansion with a mop, and deck it around with laurel. There are various great festivals in which they have to play an important part, especially in the very important Vestalia held June 9th, when all Rome unites to honor the beloved Hearth Mother ; and on June 15th when there is the official cleansing of the Temple, and all the refuse of the year is collected and removed with scrupulous ceremonies just as a good farmer should cleanse his barns before the harvest.

The chief duty is, however, the simple and gracious task of tending the sacred fire. For the first ten years of her sisterhood Salvia was learning her responsibilities in this all-important particular ; for the next ten, she, or her associated second-class Vestal, had the actual watch-care of the holy flame on the maintenance whereof seemed to rest the prosperity of Rome ; after that as one of the two senior Vestals she could turn over to her juniors the active duties, confining

[1] Alone of all the important buildings in Rome, the Atrium Vestæ had no piped water-supply ; everything had to be borne in by the vestals or (for non-religious purposes) by their numerous attendants.

herself to the general oversight of the sisterhood. When the older senior Vestal died she herself became Maxima — the most important woman in Rome, enjoying a reverence and a certainty of tenure by no means shared by every Empress.

368. Punishments of Erring Vestals. — To allow the sacred fire to go out, by some fearful mischance, is an almost unheard-of calamity. The ancient books ordain that the responsible Vestal on duty shall first be stripped and scourged by the Pontifex Maximus, administering his blows in the dark, then two pieces of wood must be taken from a " lucky tree " and he must laboriously rekindle the fire with elaborate ceremonies. After that other prolonged rites are needful to save the state from the results of such a fearful " prodigy."

Such lapses in the service of Vesta almost never occur. Slightly more frequent have been charges of breaking the vow of chastity. In the few recorded cases the guilty sister after trial before the college of pontiffs has been buried alive with a kind of funeral ceremony in the " Accursed Field " (*Campus Sceleratus*) just within the Colline Gate. It is " bad luck " actually to put to death a consecrated Vestal, but a deep pit is dug and in it are placed a couch, a lamp, and a table bearing a little food. Then the guilty woman is lowered into the pit and earth heaped upon it. She has simply been dismissed from the presence of men : — what occurs out of all human sight is strictly the affair of gods ! Meantime her paramour has been publicly scourged to death in the Forum with every form of ignominy.

The vow of virginity, nevertheless, is not perpetual. After thirty years in the service, at an age still far below old womanhood, a Vestal can quit the Atrium, and marry ; but Salvia and her sisters seldom dream of such a thing. Public opinion, though not the law, frowns upon the act, and it means resigning a position of incomparable importance, honor, and dignity.

369. Remarkable Honors Granted the Vestals. — If Salvia, for twenty years at least, has thus taken her duties very seriously, she has her great compensation. The Vestal Sisterhood is rich with a great corporate income. The members alone of all Romans give their testimony in court without the least oath. They have the seats of honor at all public games and festivals. A lictor precedes each of them everywhere, securing for his mistress the same public honors granted a magistrate, and a magistrate's lictors lower their fasces in respectful homage when in a Vestal's superior presence.

The slightest molestation of these priestesses' persons is of course punished capitally. They have the right to intercede even with the Emperor in matter of pardons, and they nominate to sundry public offices — *e.g.* the librarianship of the Imperial library, and certain military tribuneships. Finally if they chance accidentally to meet a criminal bound for execution, upon their demand he must be spared and released — not out of motives of mercy, but because it is a bad omen for the State for any holy Vestal to meet a person formally condemned to die.[1]

One crowning honor also Salvia can anticipate: even Emperors must ordinarily be buried outside the consecrated city limits (*pomerium*), but the law specifically admits Vestals not merely to the glories of a public funeral, but to burial inside the Heart of Rome itself. What wonder that Salvia is loath to quit a post of such glory and power for the uncertain prospects of matrimony!

Despite all the ceremonies, irrational and vain though they

---

[1] This did not prevent Vestals from attending the arena spectacles. The gladiators and persons thrown to the beasts had in theory a chance for life.

may seem to a later standpoint, the worship of Vesta, the goddess of the honest home, and the corporate life of her six maiden ministers remain among the fairest things of the Roman Empire. Matters cannot be hopelessly bad, when thus, in the center of the great, luxurious, sensual Imperial city, womanly purity and orderly virtue are preëminently honored.

CHAPTER XXI

THE FOREIGN CULTS: CYBELE, ISIS, MITHRAS. THE CHRISTIANS IN PAGAN EYES

370. Saturnalia : the Exchange of Presents on New Year's Day. — Could our visit to Rome be prolonged across the year we should dwell on such so-called religious festivals as the Saturnalia which lasts seven days, beginning the 17th of December, when the whole city abandons itself to carnival mirth, when slaves for a brief and happy interval put on the tall pileus, the liberty cap, are allowed to be very pert to their masters, and indulge in all kinds of pranks and liberties ; and when people exchange with all their friends semi-comic gifts of wax tapers and amusing little terra-cotta images, or other gifts of real value such as napkins, writing tablets, and dishes of preserved sweetmeats.[1]

More decorous is the ensuing holiday on the Kalends of January (New Year's Day) when ceremonious official calls are paid on every magnate from the Emperor downward, and more gifts are exchanged, often of the highest value.[2] In these festivities and distributions of presents can perhaps be found the prototypes for the winter holidays of another religion and later age.

371. Multiplication of Oriental Cults. — One dare not quit the Rome of Hadrian, however, without a cursory inspection of something extremely evident since we began our

---

[1] It was quite proper to play "April Fool" jokes at the Saturnalia : e.g. to present what seemed a platter of delicious food when all the viands were actually of clay.

[2] Substantially on the scale of "Christmas presents."

explorations on plebeian Mercury Street — the foreign religions and their temples.

Very reluctantly did the grave fathers of the old Republic admit Anatolian, Syrian, and Egyptian cults into their beloved city. Even unlicensed Greek ceremonies were frowned upon and the disorderly orgiastic rites of the Eastern gods for long were extremely repulsive to the dignified builders of the Commonwealth. But as the Republic declined the foreign cults thrust themselves in and with the coming of the Empire all attempts to prohibit them practically disappeared. The most the authorities can now do is to see that these strange private worships are conducted with a certain degree of decency. Rome has never countenanced the vile revelings of the groves of Syrian Astarte, much less the horrid child-burnings of the Phœnician Moloch.

The votaries of these Eastern gods are not merely Orientals who have drifted to Rome. The new religions have a great appeal to many persons of good old Latin stock and especially to the women. The reason for this is fairly obvious: the Roman official religion is a legalistic religion devoid of the slightest spirituality. " Sin " except in the sense of reckless contract breaking, " communion with God," " reconciliation with God," " The Hereafter," " Life Eternal," and like phrases are utterly unknown to pontiff, augur, or flamen.

For intelligent persons to whom neither the Stoic nor the Epicurean guesses at the riddle of existence prove satisfying, who are torn in conscience, bowed with bereavement, or crushed by disaster, there must be some outlet better than that of scrupulously offering a black pig to Mars. Atheism can never satisfy for long, — and the Oriental religions, appealing at once to the love for the mysterious, and to the passionate desire for some supernatural explanation of the problems of humanity, as a result draw in their votaries by thousands. Some of these worshipers are utterly ignorant and credulous. Others are men and women of wealth and deep learning, who can turn the Syrian or Egyptian jargon into elegant Platonic myths, and see, behind the coarse Levantine ritual, spiritual allegories which would have astonished old Memphis or Tyre.

372. The Cult of the Deified Emperors. — The Imperial Government itself has added to this tendency to multiply cults — it created a new and a very important one, that of the " Deified Emperors." Augustus Cæsar was far too shrewd and matter-of-fact an Italian to permit himself to be worshiped as an actual deity within his native land; but he did not discourage Orientals (accustomed to adore almost any successful monarch as a " god ") from setting up altars to him, and he took a great satisfaction in having his adoptive father Julius Cæsar officially deified at Rome, and then in accepting for himself the glories coming to the *son* of the " Divine Julius."

Furthermore, even a living Emperor has his *genius* — his special guardian spirit, often to be half-confounded with his own personality. The worship of Augustus's genius was soon an important part of the state religion. Oaths were taken by it; an insult to it became the vilest blasphemy. If Augustus did not become a god in his lifetime, the aura and effluence of divinity assuredly played all around him.

373. The " Divine Augustus " and His Successors. — The instant Augustus died a solemn decree of the Senate forthwith made him " Divus Augustus," with temples, priests, and ritual — all the paraphernalia in short of a prominent member of the Pantheon. Since then in the provincial towns the priests of Augustus, *Augustales*, are ordinarily appointed from among the rich freedmen — men of short lineage but of great economic influence, who are delighted at the trappings and pompous honors awarded this holy office, and who become, therefore, the ardent supporters of the imperial régime.

Since 14 A.D. there have been still other gods thus enrolled by vote of the Senate — notably the " Divine Claudius " (" dragged to heaven by a hook," people sarcastically remark, remembering Agrippina's poisoned mushrooms), and the equally " divine " Vespasian, Titus, Nerva, and Trajan. Their temples and cults are among the most splendid and prominent in Rome. In the basilicas and in the government houses (*prætoria*) and magistrates' halls all over the Empire stand the arrays of statues of these Deified Augusti along with that of the " genius " of the reigning Hadrian himself. Every litigant and every witness must cast his pinch of incense into the brazier before them and swear by their godhead.

Intelligent men, of course, understand that these Imperial " gods " somehow differ in nature from Jupiter, but the homage offered to them seems really an affirmation of loyalty to the great principles of law and order which bind the vast Empire together. Every good Emperor is entitled to expect this honor, after a worthy reign. " I think I'm becoming a god ! " muttered the pragmatic Vespasian while on his death-bed. On the other hand the refusal of deification is a form of branding a tyrant's memory ; and Tiberius, Caligula, Nero, and Domitian receive no incense.[1]

The state thus teaches all its subjects how easily new deities can be introduced — apparently by very human agencies. Of the host of Oriental gods that have thrust themselves into Rome there are three or four which have won peculiar prominence ; notably the cults of Cybele, Isis and Serapis, and

---

[1] Owing to rough dealings with the Senate, Hadrian himself came near missing deification, but Antoninus won his title of "Pius" by his zeal for vindicating his adoptive father's memory. Antoninus Pius himself and Marcus Aurelius after him were, of course, promptly deified.

Mithras. There is also the extremely despised sect of the Christians.

374. The Cult of Cybele, the " Great Mother." — The cult of Cybele is the oldest and best recognized of this foreign group. Cybele is an Asiatic goddess with her most famous temple at Pessinus in Galatia. In the crisis of the Hannibalic War when public opinion was on edge, the Romans fetched an image of this " Great Mother of Pessinus " to Rome and set up a temple to her on the Palatine. The Roman matrons, henceforth, honored her with the festival of the Megalesia.

The worship of Cybele, the Great Mother, despite this naturalization, retains something about it that is grossly orgiastic and un-Italian. Everywhere over the city can be met groups of her priestesses, the Corybantes, and especially of her smooth-cheeked, squeaky-voiced eunuch priests, the *Galli*, executing their wild, noisy dances with drums, cymbals, and trumpets, and leaping about in suits of armor which they clash violently, while uttering screams alleged to be inspired.

ARCHI-GALLUS, PRIEST OF CYBELE.

In the country districts bands of these Galli are reported to drift frequently from village to village, exciting the rustics by displays of " mysteries " which are simply a gross hocus-pocus, and which often wind up in scenes of sheer depravity. Nevertheless, the cult has great attractions for the superstitious. The processions of these effeminate figures with redolent locks, painted faces, and soft womanish bearing are always able to wheedle the sesterces out of the crowd.

The coarse legends of the Great Mother are furthermore caught up by the philosophers and given a refined, metaphysical meaning, and among the priests at her temples about the city are enrolled many senators and equites, and among the priestesses a good many more of these noblemen's wives. To be a chanter, drummer, or cymbal player at her great spectacular " orgies " has a morbid fascination — all the

SHRINE OF CYBELE.

more because much of the cult of Cybele worship is so gross that words may not describe it. The Great Mother is, therefore, one of the most undesirable of all the gifts offered to Rome by the conquered East.

375. Cult of Isis and Associated Egyptian Gods. — Worthier and more popular with the better classes is the worship of Isis.

The Egyptian story of Isis and Osiris, of the temporary death of the latter and the sufferings of the former, a story that connected itself with the Greek myths about Demeter and Dionysus, and also those about Adonis, had become very old a thousand years before the founding of Rome. The cult was a late invader of Italy; not until the time of Sulla did it figure even as an important private superstition, and on account of the marked Oriental tendencies of the Isis worship the Senate for long discouraged it; nevertheless the stately ritual and the appeal of the mysterious made the cult extremely popular with the multitude.

In vain in 50 B.C. the consul Lucius Æmilius himself (his superstitious lictors hesitating) struck the first blow with the ax to demolish a prohibited Isis temple. Augustus had to content himself merely with forbidding the erection of such buildings within the official pomerium of Rome, but these could multiply in the suburbs, and by the time of Vespasian practically all restraints disappeared.

Everybody now frequents the shrines of Isis, and many of the noblest citizens and matrons are among her initiates. Her great temple in the Campius Martius is among the stateliest in Rome and every morning before its doors are arrayed a perfect host of votaries.

376. Ceremonies at an Isis Temple. — If we desire, it is easy to witness a large part of the ritual, although the meaning of the allegories is refused the unelect.[1] Before daybreak the shaven-skulled priests, clothed in trailing robes of snow-white linen, enter the temple by a side entrance and throw back the great central doors, although a long white curtain still hangs across the interior. The multitude of the devout now stream into the temple. The curtains whisk aside, and a statue of the goddess, a majestic female sculptured somewhat in the Egyptian style, with her head crowned

---

[1] Much of what we know of these cults of the pagan Orient comes from early Christian writers who have no hesitation in betraying the "Mysteries," but whose statements naturally are often biased and very incomplete.

with a lotus flower and in her right hand a holy rattle (*sistrum*), is exposed to view. At her side stands her son Horus, a naked boy, holding his forefinger in his mouth, a lotus flower also upon his head, and a horn of plenty in his left hand.

The worshipers now stand or sit on the stones for a long time in silent prayer and contemplation; while the new light of the rising sun streams athwart the silent columns and draperies of the great temple. Presently a priest appears bearing a golden vessel of holy water from the Nile, and he pours it over a sacrifice of fruits and flowers upon the altar standing before the images. The worshipers all prostrate themselves in awe, then rise. The ceremony is over.

This is the ordinary side of the Isis worship but at times there lack not violent dances; processions of all manner of harlequin participants, men robed as soldiers, hunters, or gladiators, women leaping in white gauzy garments, and shaven priests bearing holy vessels — usually wrought with Egyptian hieroglyphics, and carrying especially as center of all the tumult a sacred snake, lifting its wrinkled and venomous head upon an ark of burnished gold.

The Isis worship appeals often to men of high intelligence who grow weary and disgusted at the failure of secular philosophy to solve the great problems of existence. An elaborate explanation exists for all these symbols; one might even add a spiritual meaning. It is even claimed that Isis is simply " Nature," and that her cult is merely the worthiest expression of " the One Sole Divinity whom the whole earth venerates under a manifold form."

To the initiates (into whose esoteric lore we cannot penetrate) is promised in this world a very fortunate life and that then " having accomplished the span of this existence, they shall descend to the realms below, and even there, dwelling as they shall in the Elysian fields, they shall frequently adore me — the goddess." [1]

377. Cult of Serapis and of Other Oriental Gods. — The Isis worship thus has its nobler side. Not unworthy too is that of her Græco-Egyptian associate Serapis, the patron deity of Alexandria, who has a considerable following in Rome, acclaiming him as " lord of all the elements, dispenser of all good and master of human life." Unfortunately, however, along with these deities there goes a whole swarm of lesser Oriental divinities who do nothing but provide fine chances for the scoffers and the charlatans.

The priests of the dog-headed Nile-god Anubis are denounced by Juvenal as a " linen-clad and cheating crew," who levy on silly women, and who will declare any infamy to be morally " pardoned " for the bribe of a fat goose or some thick slices of cake. Korybus, Sabazius, the bull Apis, and the Syrian Baal cannot pretend to be better. Many a decent Roman beholding their worship will reëcho Plutarch's recent words, " Better not to believe in a god at all, than to cringe before a god who is worse than the worst of men." Nevertheless there is *one* Oriental cult now penetrating Rome which seems to lay stress on moral purity and on noble living — the religion of Mithras.

378. The Cult of Mithras : Its Relative Nobility. — Mithras is by origin the Sun God of the Zoroastrian Persians. [2] He is the " fiend smiter " ; the beneficent light which disperses mental as well as material darkness. *Sol Invictus* — " The All-Conquering Sun " — his votaries call him, but in

---

[1] The quotations are from Apuleius, "The Golden Ass" (book XI, *passim*), and are given at greater length in the author's "Readings from Ancient History," vol. II (Rome), pp. 282–284.

[2] Technically he was the highest archangel under the one actual god Ahura-Mazda, but the Persian "magi" soon attributed to him practical divinity.

statues and pictures he is commonly represented as a handsome youth, wearing the Phrygian cap and mantle, and kneeling upon a bull which has been thrown upon the ground, and
whose throat the god is cutting.   In the Mithras pictures
there often appear also the mysterious figures of a dog, a
serpent, and a scorpion, all somehow connected with the ritual
of the god.

This cultus first passed from the East to the hardy pirates
of Cilicia, whom Pompey the Great subdued in the last years
of the old Republic.
Then gradually the
Western world began to
learn about the Mithras
" chapels," about the
seven grades of initiates,
about solemn purifica-
tions from sin, and
about an esoteric teach-
ing which laid great
stress on personal right-
eousness, condemned
vicious pretenses and
claimed to reconcile man
with god in a manner
promising the former a joyous and noble hereafter.

MITHRAS THE BULL-SLAYER.

The Mithras cult is now making its way very rapidly,
especially in the imperial army.   All up and down the great
garrison towns and standing camps along the frontiers
" Mithras chapels " are being erected, small chambers suitable
for only a few dozen of initiates.   The rites and teachings
are very secret, and it is impossible to penetrate them as we
can part of the worship of Isis.

Mithras worship furthermore makes no pretense of being
a cult for the masses — it is a blessing reserved strictly for

the proved and purified. All we know about it, however, convinces us that its ethics are noble, that it repudiates all coarse sensuality, and that it leaves its votaries genuinely better men and women, summoning them to be coadjutors of the " Unconquerable Sun " in his glorious war against spiritual darkness.

As yet the Mithras worship in the West is relatively young, but the time will approach when great Emperors, Aurelian and Diocletian, will proudly number themselves among its initiates, and in Mithraism ancient paganism will make its last real proffer for the allegiance of high-minded men.[1]

379. The *Taurobolium* (" Bath in Bull's Blood "). — Connected with these Oriental cults, worthy and unworthy, there has come in a ceremony utterly strange to the religion of Numa, which, nevertheless, is gaining increasing vogue, — the *Taurobolium*. Originally it belonged to the votaries of Cybele, but the Mithras worshipers have adopted it likewise.

MITHRAIC EMBLEMS.

The rite is supposed to give one a peculiar cleansing from sin, and being decidedly expensive appeals not a little to

---

[1] Nearly all our evidence for Mithraism is archæological; we know little of either its doctrines or its ritual. Apparently it had a system of priests not unlike the Christian clergy and a ceremony resembling the Christian sacrament. It owed its success largely to the real nobility of its doctrines, but could not in the end maintain itself by appealing simply to a remote myth, while Christianity was able to appeal to a personal Founder.

wealthy personages who do not mind showing how their riches can put them on better terms with heaven than is possible for the run of mortals. With increasing frequency can be seen tombstones of magnates inscribed " Reborn to Eternity through the Taurobolium," and it is held by many that persons submitting to this ordeal are assured of a happy immortality — at least, if they should die within twenty years of the ceremony; after which it can be repeated.

Old line Romans ordinarily have not as yet felt a great need for the Taurobolium,[1] but one of Calvus's acquaintances, the senator Faventinus, has followed his initiation into Mithraism by celebrating the rite. It is indeed something which only deep religious convictions can induce persons of sensitive and luxurious tastes to undergo, although the special priests who conduct the proceeding know how to render it an impressive ceremony.

Faventinus appeared at the appointed place before a concourse of Mithraic initiates, wearing a golden crown and with his toga tightly girded about him; then he descended into a deep pit over which was placed a platform of stout boards. With mystical words and songs a consecrated bull was led upon the platform and there directly slaughtered in a manner causing its blood to flow freely through the chinks in the timbers upon the worshiper below. As the blood descended Faventinus extended his arms and uplifted his face that as much might cover him as possible.

When the initiate was taken out — his whole person and garments blood-soaked — other mysterious liturgies were recited over him. He was now a " Father " in the Mithraic order — of the highest class of initiates, purged of all human

---

[1] Mithras worship was only beginning to be important in the Age of Hadrian, and the Taurobolium was then still comparatively rare; by 200 A.D. it had become decidedly common; by 300 A.D. it was very frequent indeed.

dross, and entitled to close communion with the deity. After all, the price of a fine bull and round fees to the priests seem little enough to pay for such an exalted privilege.

380. The Christians: Pagan Account of Their Origin. — There is still another cult in Rome, although cultivated men and women no less than the run of plebeians speak of it with utter aversion. Since the reign of Claudius there has existed a sect of degraded creatures, at first Jews[1] and Levantines, but later comprising also Greeks and Italians, known as *Christians*.

Excluding the vulgar tattle of the mob, as good an authority as Tacitus writes thus: "Christus from whom the name of the sect is derived was put to death in the reign of Tiberius, by the procurator Pontius Pilatus. The deadly superstition having been checked for a while, began to break out again not only throughout Judea, where this mischief first arose but also at Rome, where from all sides all things scandalous and shameful meet and become fashionable."[2]

By Nero's time the Christians were in such disfavor with the populace, being "misanthropes" and "enemies of the human race," as well as blasphemers of the gods, that the evil Emperor tried to make them scapegoats for the burning

---

[1] From the age of Augustus to that of Nero Judaism had a considerable popularity in Rome. Its austere monotheism coupled with the mysterious Mosaic law and ceremonies made a considerable appeal to public opinion, and many fashionable persons — including apparently Nero's Empress, the notorious Poppæa Sabina — gave "Jewish doctrines" a superficial patronage. It was also somewhat the fad to treat the Hebrew Sabbath as a kind of "holy day." All this favor collapsed after the destruction of Jerusalem by Titus. The Jews became a scattered and persecuted sect, without influence. As for Christianity, after 70 A.D. it lost nearly all its Jewish element and became pretty strictly a Gentile religion.

[2] Tacitus undoubtedly obtained his statement about Christ and Pilate from the official government reports in the Roman Record Office. There is no reason to suppose that he, any more than his friend Pliny, investigated Christian sources.

of Rome — although the pretense was too thin. People said the Christians were wicked enough, but that they were not guilty at least of *that!*

381. The Persecution of Christians: Their " Insane Obstinacy." — Nowhere, in those respectable quarters in which our visit has moved, can we get any detailed information as to what these Christians really do and believe. Very few important persons have so far adhered to them, although there is a story that Flavius Clemens, a consul and a kinsman of Domitian (who put him to death along with so many other nobles), was actually caught by their supposedly crazy doctrines.

The sect has been declared unlawful ever since Nero's day, and from time to time its members have been arrested and their conventicles (usually held in half-concealed burial places or in sand pits in the suburbs) have been broken up. The magistrates, however, are slack; the vigiles are busy chasing down ordinary thieves and murderers; and the Christians most of the time are left alone. Hadrian, in fact, with his general tolerance, is said somewhat to have discouraged active persecution. The Christians, nevertheless, are still under the ban of the law; and being mostly slaves, freedmen, and resident foreigners, get very short shrift if actually brought before the Præfect.

It is extremely easy to convict them: there is no need of elaborate testimony, you merely summon the defendants to burn incense to the image of the Genius of the Emperor and to curse the name of Christus. No Christian will ever do this. The trials therefore are usually very brief, and soon after they occur the crowd at the Flavian is ordinarily gratified by the sight of one of the Christians' " overseers " (bishops) or " assistants " (deacons) instead of an ordinary bandit, awaiting the spring of the lion.

These sectaries are said to be very bold, professing not to

fear death which will only give them a surer and a better immortality than that secured by the Taurobolium. Beyond a doubt (any cultivated man will tell us) such defiant persons ought to be executed, if merely for their " insane obstinacy," although the edicts are only enforced spasmodically and the Christians are often allowed several years of peace.[1]

382. Current Charges against the Christians. — If popular gossip, however, means anything, these people should deserve the worst possible fate. At their nocturnal gatherings, where men and women assemble, it is alleged, for a wild orgy, the central rite is said to consist of killing a babe and drinking its blood, while celebrants pledge themselves to commit every kind of wickedness. Finally they tie a dog to the lamp standards and incite the brute to upset the lights; then in the ensuing darkness follow deeds of violence indescribable.

It is also rumored that their Christus (who, of course, died the basest of possible deaths on the cross) actually had the

[1] The following are *some* only of the reasons why the Roman government insisted on persecuting the Christians, despite its usual policy of religious tolerance :

1. The Christians persistently refused to sacrifice to the deified Emperors and to the Genius of the reigning Emperor, an act practically amounting in common opinion to a denial of loyalty to the government, or at least capable of that construction.

2. The Christians demanded the repudiation of the old gods, including, of course, the official gods of Rome ; they were not content with simply worshiping "Christus" along with Jupiter, Apollo, etc. as were for example the devotees of Isis.

3. The Christians maintained a tight interior organization, separate socially from the pagans, under the control of its bishops, presbyters, and deacons, and so far as possible judging the disputes of its members. This seemed meddling with political matters, a ticklish business with any Emperor.

4. The private meetings of the Christians, and the misconstructions laid upon their ceremonies, gave rise to the vilest possible stories.

5. The great proportion of slaves and of the lowest grade of plebeians in the early Church seemed to justify the belief that here was a subversive, degraded, and illicit movement.

head of an ass. You can see crude wall drawings deriding his votaries, as for example, one showing a youth kneeling before an ass-headed figure on a cross, with the scribbled legend, " Alexander is adoring *his* god." [1]

How far are these gross charges true? Such aristocrats as Calvus merely shrug their shoulders; they are not interested. However, about 112 A.D. Pliny the Younger, while governor of Bithynia, being compelled to enforce the Anti-Christian laws, seized two Christian women known as " deaconesses " and put them to torture in order to find out what *really* happened at their gatherings. He reported that he had discovered that nothing criminal went on but only " a perverse and excessive superstition." Probably, senatorial circles will assure us, there is not much to be dreaded from such a movement which cannot possibly appeal to educated men well grounded in philosophy. Of course, Mithraism is very much more respectable, and according to all fashionable judgment has a far greater future before it!

---

[1] An actual wall-picture. For the charges here given against Christian assemblies and for many gross details, see Minucius Felix ("Octavius" VIII, 9.), who quotes the stories in order to refute them.

It seems needless in a book concerned strictly with pagan Rome, to discuss the actual tenets and liturgies of the Early Christians. The only point to be understood here is the vile character of the charges brought against them by the ignorant heathen.

CHAPTER XXII

A ROMAN VILLA. THE LOVE OF THE COUNTRY

383. Appreciation of Country Life by the Romans. — No study of Rome can be complete without recognition of one cardinal fact — the intense desire of all Romans to get away from their turbulent city for a large part of the year. The wealthier the citizen the longer is likely to be his absence, although no doubt many a senator or eques growing weary of his luxurious retreat begins to sigh again for the Curia or the counting room long ere the formal " season " has ended.

During the parching summer months the city is really deserted by a great part of its inhabitants. Only the most needful business goes on; the public games are attended merely by the humblest type of plebeians; the rhetoric schools cease their floods of oratory; the great baths really seem empty; and the Forum crowd becomes thinned and spiritless. Every person blessed with a moderate income and leisure has sought the seashore or the mountains.

384. Praises of the Country Towns and Villas. — Never in after ages will the blessings of country as against city life be better appreciated than under the Roman Empire. The congestion, the noise, the hurly-burly of the world metropolis probably exceeds that of any future competitor.

The poets all sing the praises of existence amid rural charms. Martial for example waxes enthusiastic over the chance to " get away " from the porticoes of cold, variegated marbles and from the need of running on morning greetings, so that he can empty his hunting nets before his own fire, lift the quivering fish from the line and draw the yellow honey

from the " red-stained cask," while his plump stewardess
cooks his own eggs for him. Juvenal extols the cheapness
and satisfaction of living in the country towns where for the
rent of a dark garret in Rome you can afford to buy a small
house with a neat little garden and a shallow well whence you
can draw the water for your own plants. Wealthier folk
share the same passion, and Pliny the Younger writes that
he longs for the pleasures of his villas " as ardently as an
invalid longs for wine, the baths, and the fountains."

Traveling Carriage (*Reda*).

The sentiment, indeed, is so common that no further
instances need be cited, save that of Similis, Trajan's veteran
prætorian præfect, who, having retired under Hadrian, has
just died after seven years of honorable self-banishment in a
quiet country retreat. On his tombstone he has ordered to
be graven: "*Here lies Similis, an old man, who has LIVED
just seven years.*"

**385. Comfortable Modes of Travel : Luxurious Litters and
Carriages.** — So then at least by the time of the " tyrannous
reign of the Dog Star or the Lion " (mid-summer and September) all the roads leading from Rome are covered with the

great cortèges, if indeed, the magnates have not quitted the city much earlier.

This is no place to speak of the admirable Roman road system which spreads as a vast network all over the Empire, and which is, of course, at its best in Italy. Travel for the rich in Hadrian's day is extremely luxurious if not correspondingly rapid. If you are in no hurry, you can ride in a comfortable litter borne by six or eight even-paced bearers and so outfitted that you can read, write, sleep, and even play

ROMAN BRIDGE: typical of thousands which covered the Empire.

at dice, while your retinue is winding its slow way over the Campagna, or up into the mountains. If you are in greater haste, there are speedy if somewhat less steady gigs and other open carriages which energetic people drive themselves, although great folk, of course, demand plenty of postilions and "well-girt running footmen." In any case the journey from Rome is a matter of great display for anybody with claims to fortune. Fifty slaves and twenty baggage wagons are hardly enough to become a senator; and four times as many of each is not an excessive retinue.

However, less distinguished people can drive about in their own light, open two-wheeled carriages (*cisia*), or can hire them at the posting stations just outside the gates, and time would fail to tell of all the kinds of *carpenta* (two-wheeled covered vehicles) or *redæ* (four-wheeled traveling carriages) which one can meet on the Via Appia or the Via Latina.

Since Rome is a city without railroads and without first-class shipping facilities, necessity has developed this carriage service to a fine point. Some people indeed still bestride mules, like that of Horace, " short of tail and heavy of gait," and government carriers ride horseback — but the wheeled vehicles are excellent. It will be a long time before they can be surpassed in comfort.[1]

386. Multiplication of Villas: Seashore Estates at Baiæ, etc. — Distant journeys we cannot consider, nor the service of imperial and private messengers to the provinces. Our concern is with the fact that over the whole of west-central Italy, well up into the Apennines, and all along the Etruscan, Latin, and Campanian coasts one luxurious estate follows upon another.

Many of these vast establishments indeed combine profit with pleasure. Landed property is the most genteel form of wealth and close beside the sumptuous *villa urbana* which imitates the glories of the city mansion, there often spreads the humbler and more utilitarian *villa rustica* which houses the great gangs of slaves or hireling laborers who keep the broad acres under cultivation.

One cannot turn aside to examine Italian agriculture, but the residence villas are so essential to every Roman of breeding and property that to ignore them is impossible. Persons of means seem always purchasing more villa property, indeed there are not a few magnates who can take a long journey up

---

[1] Probably the Roman carriages were more convenient than anything known later in Europe prior to 1800 ; and travel facilities in general were as good, the inns possibly averaging worse but the roads decidedly better, than at the dawn of the Nineteenth Century.

and down Italy, spending each night upon one of their own estates. If Publius Calvus contents himself with only *four* country residences, he shows that he is poorer and less pretentious than many fellow senators of prætorian rank.

Inevitably certain places are preferred beyond others. Upon the Bay of Naples people of leisure, who do not mind a hundred and fifty mile journey from Rome, find a famous and delightful center at Baiæ; and indeed in the entire region of this bay, recovering now from the ravages of the outbreak of Mt. Vesuvius. Outward along the more southerly Bay of Pæstum [Bay of Salerno] the shore is lined with one lofty marble-crowned villa after another, often erected upon elaborate jetties thrusting far out into the sapphire sea.

There is, however, a whole series of handsome seaboard villas all the way southward from Ostia — and Antium, Circei, Tarracina (where the Via Appia strikes the coastline), and Formiæ are only a few of those luxurious colonies to which the wealth and fashion of Rome scatter during several months of the year. Many is the senator, eques, or great freedman who can boast also of his magnificent yacht, painted in gay colors, with purple sails, purple awnings on the poop, with rigging entwined on gala days with leaves and flowers, and with liveried rowers who are trained to swing together like automata.

387. Villas in the Mountains; Small Farms near Rome. — A great many Romans, however, disperse towards the hills; indeed there are many rich persons whose business will not permit them to go many miles from the city, and others who keep a suburban villa for casual visits from the town, reserving the seashore or the Apennines for the months when the law courts are closed and the Senate forgets to assemble. Calvus, we have seen, possesses a remote estate in the North by one of the Italian lakes which he can visit only

on set occasions, another at Bauli close to Baiæ, also somewhat rarely visited, a third in the Etruscan hills which is his
regular retreat in hot weather, and a fourth, a simpler affair,
located a few miles up the Anio toward Tibur.

This last near Rome, so the senator likes to boast, is of real
Spartan simplicity.   He affects to take great pleasure there
in his hennery maintained so near to the metropolis, the great
flocks of geese, Numidian (guinea) fowl, and Rhodian cocks
and hens and the fields of vegetables very grateful when sent
down by the *villicus* (farm steward) to the city mansion.
One suspects, however, that there is greater satisfaction
taken in the hot houses where, under the expensive but well-
known luxury of glass, rare fruits are ripened in cold weather,
and whence roses, violets,
narcissus, hyacinths, and
lilies are dispatched to Rome
for the *clarissimus's* banquets.

ROMAN SPADES.

This establishment near the
capital is, in fact, hardly the
kind of retreat Calvus likes
best, although a good many
literary gentlemen, like Sue-
tonius the biographer of the Cæsars, retire to modest suburban estates " large enough to engage their minds but not
large enough to give them worry."   In such retreats they
can pursue their learned labors, " get rid of their headaches
and walk lazily around their boundary paths," and yet keep
in touch with their city friends.

388.   Great Estates in the Hills : Pliny's Tuscan Villa. —
It is the great villa in the hills which is the normal retreat
and joy of Calvus, his noble Gratia, and their equally noble
children.   Such places, be it noticed, the true Roman does
not care to locate very near to grandiose mountain scenery.
He is not fond of overpowering sublime views ; what he pre-

fers is a gentle aspect over smiling plains, lush meadows, and fertile corn-fields.

Lucretius rejoiced in the happy intervals when he could " recline by a brook of running water beneath the leafage of a lofty tree," and Virgil desired " that he might always love tilled fields and streams that flow among the valleys." Ha-

RUINS OF HADRIAN'S VILLA AT TIVOLI (*Tibur*): partial view.

drian is somewhat exceptional, among other ways, in that he enjoys toiling up high mountains like Ætna for the sake of the magnificent view. The average senator desires to ascend no further than he can comfortably drive in his cisium, or be swung along in his litter.

The Tuscan villa of Calvus is easily visited. It constitutes, in fact, an estate which the senator purchased some years ago from the heirs of the younger Pliny. Few changes beyond needful repairs have been made since its completion, and no

words of ours can surpass those of its former owner in explaining why life seems very pleasant to those whom Jupiter or
Destiny have made rich and fortunate in the imperial age.[1]

389. Charming Location of Pliny's Villa. — " This property (wrote Pliny) lies just under the Apennines, which are
the healthiest of our mountain ranges.   In winter the air is
cold and frosty ; myrtles, olives, and all other trees which

RUINS OF HADRIAN'S VILLA AT TIVOLI (*Tibur*): partial view.

require a constant warmth the climate spurns, although the
laurel usually prospers.   But in summer the heat is marvel-
ously tempered ; there is always a breath of air stirring, and
mild breezes are more common than high winds.   The con-
tour of the district is most beautiful.

" Picture an immense amphitheater, wrought by Nature,

---

[1] The following is an abridgment of Pliny the Younger's well-known
description of his Tuscan villa.

with a wide-spreading plain ringed with hills and the summits thereof covered with the tall and ancient forests. Here there is plenty of hunting, while down the mountain slopes there are stretches of underwoods, and among these are rich deep-soiled hillocks which bear excellent crops. Below these hillocks in turn, along the whole hillsides, stretch the vineyards which present an unbroken line far and wide, bordered with a fringe of trees. Then you can come down to the mead-

VILLA OF PLINY THE YOUNGER: restored.

ows and fields where the soil is so thick that only the most powerful oxen can tug the plows; but the meadows are jeweled with flowers, and produce trefoil, and other herbs, always tender and soft.

" Through the middle of this plain flows the Tiber. Here it is navigable for boats which carry down grain to the city in winter and spring, although in summer the channel is only a dried-up bed. Gazing over the district from the heights you think you are not looking so much upon earth and fields but at a landscape picture of wonderful loveliness.

" My villa, though, lies at the foot of the hill enjoying as

fine a prospect as though it stood on the summit, the ascent
is so gentle, easy and unnoticeable.   Behind lie the Apennines, but at a considerable distance, yet even on a cloudless
day the spot gets a gentle breeze duly tempered from the
hills."

**390.   Terraces of the Villa : the Porticoes : Summer-Houses
and Bedrooms.** -– " Most of the house faces southward inviting the sun as it were into the portico which is broad and long
to correspond, and contains a number of apartments and an
old-fashioned hall.   In front there is a terrace bounded with
an edging of box, then comes a sloping ridge of turf with
figures of animals on both sides cut out of the box trees,
while on the level ground stands an acanthus tree, with leaves
so soft that I might almost call them liquid.   Around about
there is a walk bordered by evergreens pressed and trimmed
into various shapes;   then comes an exercise ground, round
like a circus, which surrounds the box trees which are cut
into different forms, and the dwarf shrubs that are kept well
clipped.[1]   Beyond these there stretches a meadow delightful
for its natural charm as the things just described are for their
artificial beauty.

" At the head of the portico juts out the triclinium from the
doors whereof can be seen this terrace, meadow, and the
expanse of country beyond.   Almost opposite the middle of
the portico is a summer-house with a small open space in the
middle shaded by four plane trees.   Among them stands a
marble fountain, from which the water plays upon and
sprinkles slightly the roots of the plane trees and the grass
plot around the four.

" In this pavilion there is located a bed chamber which
excludes all light, noise and sound, and adjoining it is another
dining room especially for my friends, which commands also

---

[1] The Romans delighted in formal and highly artificial gardens such
as were in vogue in the Italian Renaissance and the France of Louis XIV.

a delightful view. There is still another bed chamber, however, which is embowered and shaded by the nearest plane
tree and built of marble up to the balcony; above [in the
ceiling] is a picture of a tree with birds perched in the branches,
equally as beautiful as the marble. Here, too, there is a
small fountain with a basin around the latter, and into it the

ROMAN GARDEN SCENE.

water flows from a number of little pipes which produce a
most agreeable liquid sound.

" In the corner of the portico there is yet a third bed chamber leading out of the dining-room, some of its windows
looking forth upon the terrace, others upon the meadow, while
the windows in front face the fish-pond which lies just beneath
them: right pleasant it is both to eye and to ear, as the water
falls from a considerable height and glistens like snow as it
is caught in the marble basin. This bed room is agreeably

warm even in winter, for it is flooded with an abundance of sunshine."

391. The Baths: the Rear Apartments: the Riding Course. — " To the last named room adjoins the calidarium

MARBLE URN OR GARDEN ORNA-
MENT.

of the baths, and on a cloudy day we can turn in the steam heat to take the place of the warm sun. Next comes an ample and cheerful undressing room for the bath, from which you pass into the cool frigidarium containing a large and shady swimming pool. Adjoining this cold bath is the mild tepidarium, for the sun shines upon it lavishly, although not so much as upon the hot bath which is built further out. Above the adjacent dressing room is a ball court where various kinds of exercise can be taken and several games can go on at once; and close to this are more bed-chambers all commanding enchanting views over the gardens, meadows, vineyards and mountains.

" Such is the front part of the villa. In the rear and to the sides are still other dining rooms and bedrooms; especially there are certain that are so far underground as to be perfectly cool even in the hottest weather. There is also an elaborate set of quarters for the servants.

" However, the most delightful part of the entire establishment is perhaps the riding course. Around its borders are plane trees covered with ivy, which creeps along the trunks and branches and spreading across to the neighboring trees joins the whole line together. Between the plane trees are set box-shrubs, and on the further side of the shrubs is a ring of laurels which mingle their shade with that of the plane.

" At the farther end, the straight boundary of the riding course is curved into a semi-circular form which quite changes its appearance. It is inclosed with cypress-trees, casting in places a dark and gloomy shade, though spots are left quite open to the sunshine; in these last bloom roses, and the warmth of the sun gives a delightful change from the cool of the shadows. All around these avenues run paths lined with other box-shrubs; and here and there are more of the box trimmed into a great variety of patterns, some being cut into letters forming my name, as being the owner, or that of the gardener."

392. The Fountains and Luxurious Pavilions in the Gardens. — " At the upper end of this hippodrome is a couch of white marble covered with a vine. Jets of water gush from under the couch through small pipes, and look as if they were forced out by the weight of the persons reclining on the pillows, while the water rushes down into a graceful marble basin with an underground outlet so it fills but never overflows. When I dine at this spot the heavier dishes and plates are set by the side of the basin, but the lighter ones, made in the shape of little boats and birds, float on the surface and turn round and round.

" Directly opposite this couch is a sleeping pavilion. It is formed of glistening marble, and through the projecting folding doors you can pass at once among the foliage, while from the windows you look upon the same green picture. Within is a bed, and the shade is so dense that little light can enter, while a wonderfully luxuriant vine has climbed upon the roof and covers the whole building. You can fancy you are in a grove as you lie here, only you do not feel the rain as you do amid the trees. Here, too, a fountain rises, then immediately loses itself underground. There are a number of marble chairs placed up and down, very restful if you do not wish the bed. Near these chairs, yet again, there are little fountains, and throughout the whole riding course you can hear the murmur of tiny streams carried through pipes which run wherever you please to direct them."

393. Life of Sensuous Luxury at Such a Villa. Contrast in Human Conditions under the Roman Régime. — " Besides the beauties herein describ̄d one has perfect comfort, repose, and freedom from anxiety at such a villa. I need not don the heavy toga; no neighbor ever calls to drag me out; everything is placid and quiet; and this peace adds to the healthfulness of the place, giving it, so to speak, a purer sky and a more limpid air. Here I enjoy better health both in mind and body than anywhere else, for I exercise the former by study, and the latter by hunting. May the gods preserve to me this place in all its beauty ! "

If life can consist of nothing more than a series of delightful sensations, the eye to be pleased by entrancing vistas of marble, greenery, or wooded hills, the ear by the soft murmur of musical fountains, and every creature want ministered unto by scores of highly trained menials, whose sole object in life seems to be to anticipate their masters' needs, — what greater fortune, one may ask, can any age provide than to be possessor of such a villa, with the wealth and rank such possession must imply? Happy its former, happy its present owner! Is it forbidden to regret that one's lot is not cast for a lifetime in Italy in these prosperous days of the Empire?

Yet tarry — even while as Calvus's guests we take our seats upon his marble benches beside the musical fountain under the whispering cypresses, and before we can converse amiably with the senator, perhaps upon the Stoic theory of " The Highest Good " there are sounds discordant — the clink of fetters, the snap of whips, the curses of drivers, the groans of human cattle.

Along the road concealed by the shrubbery, is passing the slave coffle, the gang of " speaking tools " on its way from the underground dungeon (ergastulum) upon the great farm attached to the villa, to the daily toil in the fields beneath a broiling sun.   The refined luxury of the fortunate few is purchased by the squalor, the ignorance, and often by the life-long misery of the brutalized many.

CHAPTER XXIII

THE RETURN OF THE EMPEROR

394. Character of Hadrian: Prosperity and Good Government of His Reign. — Purposely we had visited Rome in the absence of Hadrian; our interest had been in the city and its people, not in the versatile, ever-wandering Cæsar and the administration of the Empire. But before Publius Calvus could set forth for his Tuscan villa he and all other Senators had to attend a great state ceremony — the reception of the Emperor returning from his travels.

More than any other Roman ruler Hadrian had been an insatiable traveler. The frontiers of Britain, Syria, and Africa, the garrison towns on the Rhine, and the Danube — he knew them all. The peaceful cities of Gaul, Spain, and Egypt reaped the benefits of his intelligent benevolence when he visited them. Twice he had sojourned in Athens, the city which perhaps he loved the best in all the world, finishing the great Temple of Olympian Zeus left uncompleted since the days of the Peisistratidæ and otherwise beautifying the now sleepy old university town, so that its grateful dwellers acclaimed him as a second founder like unto the original Theseus.

Hadrian's personal life had been indeed marred with certain acts of arbitrary caprice and even of cruelty; many senators grumbled at his long absences from Rome and they somewhat dreaded his sudden judgments, but the Empire at large had been incalculably happy under his sway. The legions were under firm discipline, wars there were not save petty rumblings on the frontiers and the embers of the last struggle of the unhappy Jews, while peaceful commerce whitened the Mediterranean, and merchants' caravans wound confidently over the great road system with little fear of bandits.

Under such an Emperor laws were scientifically administered without fear or favor. The provincial governors were, despite an occasional plunderer such as we saw haled before the Senate, men of genuine intelligence, probity, and zeal. If the Senate was becoming a venerable debating club, if the other forms of political liberty were either dead or dying, under Hadrian despotism was showing its fairest face — with a highly capable monarch earnestly devoting himself to his subjects' good. What man, surveying the august fabric and social and governmental machinery of the Empire, could have failed to

HADRIAN.

echo the current notion — that the dominion of Rome was divinely ordained and find that her departed Cæsars were worthily ranked among the gods? [1]

395. Return of Hadrian to Italy. — But Hadrian had been growing old and a little weary of his philanthropic wander-

---

[1] Well known, of course, is the famous dictum of Gibbon ("Decline and Fall of Roman Empire": vol. i, chap. 2. Bury edition, p. 78): "If a man were called to fix the period during which the condition of the human race was most happy and prosperous he would, without hesitation, name that which elapsed from the death of Domitian to the accession of Commodus." From the standpoint of a believer in aristocracy or monarchy this opinion is largely justifiable.

ings. And now at length a peaceful armada had borne him back from Greece to Puteoli. Hence with an enormous cortège he had traveled by easy stages along the " Queen of Roads," the Via Appia, to the outskirts of the capital. And now to welcome him back to the Palatine the obsequious magistrates arranged the inevitable public spectacle.

The Emperor is not returning as a conquering *triumphator*. No formal triumph can therefore be ordained in his honor. He cannot wear laurel as he rides in a gilded chariot, preceded by the long files of fettered captives and, followed by the cohorts of his acclaiming army, drive his car through the Porta Triumphalis near the Circus Flaminius, next take a long circuit through the Circus Maximus and then down the Via Sacra and across the Forum and finally mount upward to pay his vows to Jupiter Best and Greatest on the Capitol. A magnificent procession, nevertheless, is possible. At the third milestone from the city along the Via Appia all the senators and equites in gala robes meet the advancing Imperator. His Empress Sabina is greeted with equal ceremony by the wives of the entire aristocracy.

In the city all the vast colonnades are hung with garlands of spring flowers, all business is suspended ; all the fora and streets along the line of march are packed with throngs in brilliant costumes and equally brilliant chaplets. One grows weary counting the magnificent litters everywhere passing, followed by the gorgeously liveried retinues of the wealthy.

396. Imperial Procession Entering Rome. — At last after duly impressive delays the imperial procession starts from the spot known as the Three Fountains.[1] The Prætorians are there in full force, the City Cohorts, and heavy drafts of the vigiles, all the tribunes, centurions, and privates parading

---

[1] Where according to firm Christian tradition St. Paul was beheaded in the days of Nero, having been rearrested after having once been set at liberty.

in silvered or gilded armor with scarlet plumes and mantles. The magistrates and ex-magistrates all wear the colorful toga prætexta.

The ruler himself, " Holder of the Tribunician and Proconsular Power, Pontifex Maximus, Cæsar Augustus, Father of his Country, First Citizen and Imperator "; that is to say Hadrian in person rides in the glittering chariot wherein Augustus rode in his triumph after the battle of Actium. Four snow-white horses draw the car, and beside the slim Greek charioteer stands the object of universal envy, the man who is all but a god even in Italy, who is the " Son of the Divinity," Trajan, and who is actually worshiped as a deity before a thousand altars throughout the subjected East.

Hadrian is a handsome bearded man of stature above the average. The gray of advancing age is streaking his hair, but he retains that graceful presence and piercing glance which would make him a notable figure had he never donned the purple. Before him, bound to the end of staves, are carried placards in large letters reciting the benefits he has conferred on hundreds of communities; there is also a large roll of papyrus symbolic of the " Perpetual Edict " which he has inspired the learned jurist Salvus Julianus to compile preparatory to the codification of the vast Civil Law.

Directly before the Emperor there is borne upon an open car a gilded image of the beautiful youth Antinöos, Hadrian's favorite companion, whose mysterious death in Egypt the monarch has never ceased to mourn; while behind the imperial chariot rides the marveling envoy of Chosröes the Parthian King who has received peace at the hands of the Cæsar. The hundreds of senators and thousands of equites marching in the procession, now and again, perhaps at some signal, raise shouts of applause to the master and sun of that glorious human universe wherein they rejoice as the fortunate stars.

397. Hailing the Emperor. — So the procession enters Rome. At sight of the tall, majestic Imperator, whose purple mantle gleams with gold, all the streets and plazas burst into tumults of cheering. " *Io Triumphe! Io Triumphe! Ave Cæsar! Ave Hadriane!* " while not a few in ecstatic loyalty make haste even to salute him as " *Dominus et Deus!* "

As the imperial car passes each crossing of the streets, victims are sacrificed, while loud prayers are raised for the monarch's safety. The air grows heavy with the perfumes of the incense burning on hundreds of improvised altars. From the balconies matrons rain down masses of roses; and at many a turn great volumes of saffron are sprinkled over the marchers.

Onward Hadrian rides, his handsome features curling perchance with pleasure but looking not to the right hand nor the left. Perhaps he recalls that were this a formal triumph, a slave would have been required to stand behind him whispering at intervals, " Remember, you are but a man! "

398. The Donatives, Fêtes, and Games. — The procession thus sweeps along the Sacred Way, pauses for a moment that the Emperor may survey the latest touches upon his new Temple of Venus and Rome, passes the holy House of Vesta and then turning away from the Forum and the Capitol ascends into the Palatine. Here the gorgeously arrayed companies of the official bureaucracy swell again the " *Io Triumphe!* " and Hadrian dismounts from the car to offer his own special thanksgiving for safe return, and to burn his own incense within the Temple of Apollo of the Palatine.

All that afternoon the fête continues. The great public baths stand open, absolutely free, not even the petty quadrans being exacted from the plebeian visitors. The grain and bread doles are doubled; the ticket holders receiving to

boot measures of oil and wine. The Prætorians drink deeply
the imperial health — for a special donative of 1000 sesterces
($40) per man has been ordered for the entire corps.

In the Flavian Amphitheater Hadrian himself presides in
the podium while a lioness contends with an elephant, the
most famous and skilful netters and Thracians slaughter
one another, and a
desperate robber is
done to death by three
panthers. Late into
the evening the streets
are illuminated; there
is feasting, dancing, re-
veling all through the
wide parks and the
bosky groves stretch-
ing across the Campus
Martius to the Tiber.
Everybody is praising
the greatness and glory
alike of Emperor and
Empire; and as for
Rome, Imperial Rome,
the center of all the
earth, who doubts that
her power is ordained
to stand forever?

VIEW IN THE CHRISTIAN CATACOMBS:
present state.

**399. A Christian
Gathering.** — Not all Rome this night is given over to roses,
wine, and reveling under the torchlight. In one of those
subterranean burial galleries near the Via Appia, which a
later age will call " Catacombs," in a spot where a chamber
of some dimensions has been excavated, a group of soberly
clad folk have gathered. They have met stealthily, — post-

ing sentries to give the alarm, for the vigiles may not have become too drunk that night to be active.

The leader of their service is the Bishop Higinius whose name will stand as the eighth Pope following the Apostle Peter. During their simple liturgies some strains of boisterous music from the luxurious, sensual, pitiless metropolis outside interrupt their hymns, and the good bishop signs to one of the deacons. The latter opens the scroll of the Book of Apocalypse where under the cryptic name of " Babylon " is forewarned the fate even of imperial Rome; and thus he reads :

" For her sins have reached unto heaven, and God hath remembered her iniquities; therefore shall her plagues come upon her in one day, death and mourning and famine; and the kings of the earth who have committed wickedness and lived deliciously with her shall bewail and lament her when they see the smoke of her burning.

" And the merchants of the earth shall weep and mourn over her, for no man buyeth their merchandise any more; — the merchandise of gold and silver, and precious stones, and of pearls, and fine linen and purple and silk and scarlet and all rare woods and all manner of vessels of ivory, and all manner of vessels of most precious wood, and of brass, and iron, and marble, and cinnamon, and odors and ointments, and frankincense, and wine, and oil, and fine flour, and wheat, and beasts, and sheep, and horses, and chariots, and slaves, *and souls of men.*"

INDEX

[References are to pages.]

Index

479

Latrunculi (game), 205.

Lawyers (*see* Advocates).

Legacies, 170; hunting for, 171; public bequests, 172.

Legal procedure, highly scientific, 353; great tribunals for, 354; forms of verdicts, 355; importance of advocates, 355; cheap pettifoggers, 356; character and slave witnesses, 357; use of written evidence, 357–358.

Legate of the legion, 329.

Legionaries, enlistment of, 314; organization of, 315; training of, 316; weapons of, 317–318; armor of, 318; rewards and punishment of, 319–320; retiring bonuses for, 329; pay and rations of, 320; training of, 321; nonmilitary labors of, 322; petty officers of, 322–323; centurions of, 323–324; *primipilus* of, 325; eagle of, 325.

Legions, number of, 309; organization of, 315 ff.; location and names of, 326; commanders of, 328; (*see also* Legionaries).

Letters, 207, 208.

Libraries, size of, 217; private, 218; public, 219; of Trajan, 280.

Literary fame, passion for, 214 ff.

Luncheon (*prandium*), 111.

Magistrates, public honors paid to, 24.

Mansions (see *Domus*).

Manumission, 139, 140.

Marble trade, 241.

Marriage, men often reluctant to marry, 61; usually arranged by girls' parents, 63; marriage treaties, 64; betrothal before, 65; dowries, 66; dressing bride, 66, 67; actual ceremonies of, 67 ff.; contract of, 68; wedding procession, 69; ceremonies at bridegroom's house, 70; often unhappy, 72; divorce, easy and frequent, 74; happy marriages, 75.

Masks, death (*imagines*), 54.

Matrons, honors paid to, 71, 72; (*see* Women).

Meals and meal times, 110 ff.

Meat and poultry, 105.

Medicine (*see* Physicians).

Mimes, 380.

Mithras, worship of, 445–446.

Morning, how spent by gentlemen, 110.

Morra, game of, 205.

Mosaics, in Roman mansion, 43.

Names, intricacy of, 186; irregular, 187; of slaves, 188; of women, 188; confusion of, 189.

Nero, colossal statue of, 262.

Notices, public, 29.

Old Forum, 265 ff.; noble traditions of, 266; impression created by, 267; crowds in, 268, 269; area of, 268, 269; western end of, 269; Rostra, 269; Golden Milestone, 269, 270; Tullianum, 270, 271; Basilica Æmilia, 271; Temple of Janus, 271; Senate House, 272; Basilica Julia, 272; Lacus Curtius, 274.

Olive oil, 107.

Omens, belief in, 419–420.

Oratory, passion for, 200; training in, 201 ff.; in Senate, 343 ff.

Ostia, trade through, 239; shipping at, 247; naval shipping at, 248; harbor town at, 249.

Pænula, 85.

Palace, imperial, 288 ff.; magnificent aspect of, 289; famous buildings in, 290; triclinium and throne-room of Domitian, 291–292; enormous luxury of, 292, swarm of officials present in, 293.

Palatine, view from, 260; history of, 286; fine residences upon, 287; Augustus settles upon, 287–288; commanding view from, 288; imperial palace upon, 288 ff.

Palla, 88.

Pantheon, 280–282.

Pantomimes, 381; high art in, 382.